A Companion to
Catholic Education

A Companion to
Catholic Education

edited by

Leonardo Franchi
and
Stephen McKinney

GRACEWING

First published in 2011

Gracewing
2 Southern Avenue, Leominster
Herefordshire HR6 0QF

UK ISBN 978 085244 757 4

Typeset by
Action Publishing Technology Ltd, Gloucester GL1 5SR

Contents

Preface

During his Apostolic Visit to the United Kingdom, Pope Benedict XVI was keen to meet as many teachers and students from our Catholic schools and colleges as possible. The *Big Assembly*, held in the sports arena of St Mary's University College in Twickenham, on Friday 17 September 2010, was a real highlight of a visit which challenged and inspired the Catholics of our country, enabling the Pope to address those who had gathered from Catholic schools and colleges across the country, and those who were watching on television and via the internet. He reminded them, and us, that there is a distinctive Catholic *attitude* to education:

> In your Catholic schools, there is always a bigger picture over and above the individual subjects you study, the different skills you learn. All the work you do is placed in the context of growing in friendship with God, and all that flows from that friendship. So you learn not just to be good students, but good citizens, good people. As you move higher up the school, you have to make choices about the subjects you study, you begin to specialise with a view to what you are going to do later on in life. That is right and proper. But always remember that you are part of a bigger picture.
>
> A good school provides a rounded education for the whole person. A Catholic school, over and above this, should help students to become saints.[1]

At the very heart of this Catholic attitude is our understanding that the pupil or student 'may have life, and have it to the full' (John 10:10); this is because we believe that true fulfilment of the human

---

[1] Benedict XVI, Address of the Holy Father to Pupils, 17 September 2010, http://www.vatican.va/holy_father/benedict_xvi/speeches/2010/september/documents/hf_ben-xvi_spe_20100917_mondo-educ_en.html [accessed 1 March 2011].

person can only be realized in a close friendship with Jesus Christ – as Pope Benedict put it, by becoming saints.

This attitude has led the Church to be intimately involved in the education of young people; many centuries ago, the Church gave birth to seats of learning for children and adults in the establishment of monastic schools and universities, and that work continues today in Catholic schools and colleges around the world.

Here in Great Britain, our Catholic schools hold a very special place in the heart of our parish communities. Our forefathers worked hard to build our schools; in London, Cardinal Manning, Archbishop of Westminster between 1865 and 1892, worked hard to establish schools in some of the poorest areas, to rescue children from the workhouses and to resist over-intervention by the State. Many parishes built schools before they built churches, celebrating Mass in the classroom each morning before educating the young people of that community. Many parish priests and members of religious orders gave their lives to this project, which was paid for by the huge sacrifices made by the Catholics of this country. Our Catholic schools and colleges are the result of that vision, and we can be immensely proud of them and all their hard work.

However, our schools and colleges have to be different from others, and the key to this is in the word 'Catholic'. It identifies them, and marks them as sharing in the evangelizing mission of the one, holy, catholic and apostolic Church. By word, deed and example, they help our young people, Catholic and non-Catholic, grow in faith, and preach the Gospel to those who have not yet heard it; they enable our teachers and students to journey into truth, moving into our goal in life, which is none other than sharing in the very life of God himself, in whose image and likeness we have been made, and who has revealed himself to us as Father, Son and Holy Spirit:

> In His goodness and wisdom, God chose to reveal Himself and to make known to us the hidden purpose of His will by which, through Christ the Word made flesh, we might in the Holy Spirit have access to the Father and come to share in the divine nature [...] By this revelation then, the deepest truth about God and human salvation shines out for our sake in Christ, who is both the Mediator and Fullness of all Revelation.[2]

---

[2] Second Vatican Ecumenical Council, Dogmatic Constitution on Divine Revelation *Dei Verbum*, 18 November 1965, n. 2.

The Christian life is a call to a deeper communion with God and with one another, and this finds particular expression in our schools, which are rightly recognized as being families themselves, where no one is a stranger and where everyone, whatever his or her background or academic ability, is welcomed, treasured, supported and helped to become the person whom God calls them to be. All of this flows from our Catholic faith, and since it forms and informs our schools and colleges with this distinctive vision, it is important for all who are concerned with Catholic education to have a good working knowledge and understanding of the faith.

This timely publication, which explores key areas of Catholic thought that are relevant for Catholic teachers before looking in closer detail at matters pertaining to religious education and the broader Catholic life and identity of our schools, will enable all who read it to grow in this understanding. Catholic schools not only teach the Catholic faith, but must live the Catholic faith as an authentic witness to God's never-failing love, and all who are involved in schools as governors, leaders and teachers must primarily be 'examples to the flock' which has been entrusted to them (1 Pet. 5:3).

In England and Wales we are celebrating the Year of Catholic Education, in response to Pope Benedict's visit in 2010, which will recognize past achievements and look forward with confidence to a future in which we will ensure that our young people continue to receive a Catholic education of the highest standard in schools which truly are the light of the world and the salt of the earth; all who read this book will be well equipped to help our schools in that task.

Rt Rev Malcolm McMahon, OP
Bishop of Nottingham
Chairman of the Catholic Education Service in England & Wales

An Introduction to Catholic Theological Thinking

Leonardo Franchi and Stephen McKinney

This series of informative essays introduces the key theological themes of Catholic Religious Education today. This volume will be an appropriate core text for those who are being educated to become Catholic teachers and preparing to work in Catholic schools. We envisage this book as being a useful resource for managers and classroom teachers in Catholic schools as well as being a very useful aid for catechists and parents of children in Catholic schools.

This book is a resource for Catholic educators designed for use in conjunction with other dedicated textbooks and good curricular material. It does not claim to be a stand-alone reference guide for educators but will orientate those new to the study of theology and Religious Education towards the key theological themes which they will encounter in their teaching and act as a catalyst for further and deeper study of the range of themes covered. Teachers and student teachers can use this text to chart their way through the many curricular packages with which they are faced today.

A student new to the field of Catholic theology is entering a world of words, images and concepts which have been part of university courses since their beginning early in the Second Millennium. The foundation of these ancient European universities was an attempt by the Catholic Church to prepare young men for service in the Church and the study of theology was at the heart of this process.

The study of theology is not an esoteric discipline but, to the Christian, represents the highest ideals of academic life. In today's world it is not hard to imagine why some might see the study of theology as a luxury, no more than a highbrow activity for priests and others involved in religious proclamation. Others would take a different view and see the study of religious ideals and thoughts as a broad field which helps explain the evolution of contemporary society. In his Letter to Seminarians, Pope Benedict exhorted the students to deepen their love of theology:

> What we call dogmatic theology is the understanding of the individual contents of the faith in their unity, indeed, in their ultimate simplicity: each single element is, in the end, only an unfolding of our faith in the one God who has revealed himself to us and continues to do so.[1]

It is not claimed that every Catholic teacher should have a specialized knowledge of theology. However, we do claim that all Catholic educators should have a knowledge and understanding of Catholic theology which is commensurate with their general educational level and a teacher of Religious Studies or Religious Education in a Catholic school ought to have knowledge at first degree level.

In the light of this, Catholic educators are encouraged to develop their knowledge of theological issues so as to understand better their vocation as both educator (in the secular sense) and faith-former (unique to Catholic education and other forms of faith education). This requires some form of systematic study of Catholic teaching at an appropriate level.

By introducing the term 'systematic study' we run the risk of focusing too much on the cognitive processes involved in learning. Blessed John Henry Newman was an advocate of the partnership in Higher Education of intellectual and moral formation. The study of Catholic theology includes and cannot deny the work of the mind and intellect but finds its greatest expression in the response to the invitation to live a life of faith which is demonstrated by active participation in the liturgy and a life of love. Bishop Tartaglia reminds us of this when he states that 'You do theology on your knees or you do a pale reflection of theology.'

This study of the deposit of faith is a lifelong process. What is necessary is to move beyond a simple knowledge of doctrine and its expression in formulae and standard textbooks towards a broader understanding of the roots and sources of this body of doctrine. The study of Catholic theology, therefore, is not a 'neutral' search for enlightenment but a serious attempt to use human faculties, or reason, to understand what is believed to be revealed truth.

[1] http://www.vatican.va/holy_father/benedict_xvi/letters/2010/documents /hf_ben-xvi_let_20101018_seminaristi_en.html

In the Catholic tradition the terms *faith* and *reason* are often linked. By faith, we mean the belief which gives full assent to the idea of a creator God. It is a supernatural gift received by the human person who is open to the grace of God. Reason, on the other hand, is the use of the natural powers of thought inherent in the human person which allows us to come to a knowledge of God.

In Catholic thought, there is a partnership between these concepts but we must be wary of avoiding extreme positions. A person who emphasizes the primacy of faith to the exclusion of reason is adopting a position known as fideism; those who emphasize reason to the exclusion of faith are exhibiting rationalism. Neither position is in keeping with Catholic tradition and a more balanced relationship is necessary.

We will deal first with reason. The Church claims that the use of reason can allow the human person to discover the attributes of God. It argues that God has implanted in the human mind the natural powers of reason and thought which, with the aid of divine grace, allow us to discover his existence and his attributes: goodness, beauty and truth. There are arguments designed to 'prove' the existence of God through reason which are dealt with in the chapter by Victoria Harrison.

There are some aspects of the mystery of God which are beyond the powers of reason to understand fully. The Christian doctrine of the Trinity is one such area. This is the ultimate mystery of Christianity and all Catholic theology is centred on developing an understanding of this. In claiming that God is both one God and Three Persons, Christianity distinguishes itself from the other monotheistic religious traditions of Islam and Judaism for whom the notion of God becoming a human person is problematic. This is deemed, therefore, a matter of revealed faith as human reason cannot grasp its complexity.

It is perfectly fair to ask how this 'Revelation' comes about. How do we know what is claimed to be revealed is true? In Catholic Christianity, there are three sources of Revelation: Scripture, Tradition and Magisterium.

In Catholic Christianity, Scripture is the root and foundation of all belief. It is in Scripture that theology finds its key sources and the fruit of theological study is a better understanding of the riches and mysteries contained in these texts. God is ultimately the author of all Scripture and he inspired the human authors of these texts to communicate his words. This inspiration is crucial and allows the reader to have confidence in the truth of the text. This truth is not to be understood simply as a literal truth as, according to the tradition of the Church, there are two senses of Scripture. The first is this literal understanding of the texts and is complemented by the spiritual sense which has a tri-partite expression: the *allegorical*, which looks at Old Testament events as signs of future New Testament events; the *moral*, which considers the texts as prompts to improve our actions; the *anagogical*, which looks at events in the context of their eternal significance.[2]

The written word of Scripture does not mean that Catholic Christianity can be reduced to a 'religion of the book'. Allied to the importance of Scripture is the equal consideration afforded to Tradition as a source of Revelation. Tradition in this context does not refer to traditions and patterns of belief which have evolved in different countries. Nor does it have connotations of being 'old-fashioned' which often accompany its use in modern society. The theological understanding of Tradition, better called Sacred Tradition, refers to a living transmission of the doctrines of the faith through the ages by the Church. This is distinct from, but complementary to, Sacred Scripture as both originate in the mystery of Christ.[3]

The third source of Revelation, the Magisterium of the Church, refers to the living teaching office of the Catholic Church. This teaching office is integrated within Sacred Tradition and Sacred Scripture and ensures that, with the help of the Holy Spirit, it guards the deposit of faith.[4] The fullest expression of the Magisterium is the action of the Bishops of the Church in communion with the Bishop of Rome (the Pope). It is important to distinguish between the Solemn Magisterium and the Ordinary Magisterium. The Solemn, or Extraordinary Magisterium refers to formal definitions of the Church in Councils or 'ex cathedra' teachings of the Pope. The Ordinary Magisterium applies the teachings of the Church to developments in society and offers a Catholic perspective on how to understand them. Examples of this would be the Magisterium's pronouncements on abortion, in vitro fertilization and the world banking crisis in 2010.

Catholic theology cannot be fully understood without an explanation of the role of grace.[5] Divine grace is the undeserved help we receive from God which allows us participate in the divine nature. It is grace which moves the human person to love God and to love

---

[2] *Catechism of the Catholic Church* (henceforth CCC) 115–18.
[3] CCC 80.
[4] CCC 85.
[5] CCC 1996–2004.

his or her neighbour. It is not an infringement on human freedom but allows us to use that freedom for the most worthy cause of all: the adventure of love.

This series of essays is a map on the territory marked out by grace and is framed within the borders offered by Scripture, Tradition and Magisterium. It is offered to Catholic educators as a work of service and, hopefully, as an incentive to further study.

The book is divided into two parts. The first part explores key areas of Catholic thought that are relevant for Catholic educators. The second section focuses on pedagogical matters pertaining to Religious Education and the broader Catholic life and identity of the Catholic school.

Part One commences with a contemporary discussion of the question of God and philosophy. In Chapter One, Victoria Harrison explores some of the key concepts and the major arguments for the existence of God. This is an important grounding for the subsequent chapters that will be focused on aspects of Catholic Christianity, a revealed religion. Chapter Two provides an overview of the place of Scripture within the teaching and life of the Catholic Church. Karen Wenell examines both the Old and New Testaments, their interrelationship, and some of the key ideas such as covenant. Chapter Three is focused on the crucial issue of Christology. Bishop Philip Tartaglia introduces this conceptually challenging topic and outlines the christological heresies in a lucid manner. He makes it clear that it is important that the Catholic educator understand these heresies as they often re-emerge in different guises. In Chapter Four, Fr Tom Kilbride examines the doctrine of the Church by drawing heavily on images from scripture and the 'four marks of the Church'. The theme of Chapter Five is active participation in liturgy. Leonardo Franchi explores the history of the development of liturgy and emphasises authentic participation in liturgical celebrations. In Chapter Six, Fr John Bollan provides a useful and necessary introduction to the seven sacraments as instruments of divine grace in the life of the Church. In Chapter Seven, Fr John Keenan uses the theology of the body as a lens for understanding the fundamental principles of Catholic moral theology and teaching. John Deighan uses Catholic social teaching to stress the role of the Church is promoting social justice and the centrality of marriage in Chapter Eight.

Part Two begins with a rationale for Catholic schools. In Chapter Nine, Stephen McKinney, drawing heavily from the Vatican documentation, sets out the main precepts that underpin the rationale for Catholic schooling for the twenty-first century. This broad overview sets the scene for the following three chapters which deal with approaches and methodology in Religious Education. In Chapter Ten, Leon Robinson argues that Catholic educators should have a knowledge and understanding of the wider conceptual frameworks prevalent in contemporary debates about Religious Education. This provocative chapter challenges the Catholic teacher to look beyond his or her own tradition for insight and breadth of vision. In Chapter Eleven Mary Lappin reminds the Catholic educator of the importance of story at the heart of scripture, Religious Education and the life of the Catholic school. Catherine O'Hare demonstrates the place of sacred art in the life of the Church and in the teaching of Religious Education in Chapter Twelve. An important aspect of this chapter is that it explores the images of Mary, the Mother of God, as a case study, and this is where Catholic teaching about Mary can be found in this book. Finally in Chapter Thirteen, Roisín Coll explores aspects of the vocation of the Catholic and the role of the Catholic teacher in the pastoral and spiritual life of the Catholic school.

In conclusion, we would like to thank the many contributors to this book for their willingness to participate in this project. We would also like to thank the publishers, Gracewing, for their diligence and patience and for the excellent advice that was promptly delivered. A special thank you is offered to our diligent proofreader, Ronnie Convery, the Director of Communications of the Archdiocese of Glasgow. We are indebted to him. We offer a special thanks to Bishop McMahon OP for agreeing to write the Preface and to Vanessa Rasoamampianina for the production of the Index.

It was our aim to produce a book that would be useful for a wide readership. We hope that we have achieved this.

All Magisterial documents cited in these essays are available at www.vatican.va

Abbreviations

CCC   *Catechism of the Catholic Church*
CCE   Congregation for Catholic Education
RE   Religious Education

Part One
Theological Knowledge

Chapter 1

God and Philosophy

Victoria S. Harrison

Introduction

People have always asked questions about God. Philosophy is a discipline that deals with questions, and many philosophers have been interested in the questions which ordinary people ask about God. This chapter begins by looking at some of the ways in which philosophers have approached the idea of God. It then explains the conception of God at the core of traditional forms of Abrahamic theism. Consideration of some philosophical questions generated by this conception leads to an examination of three ways of arguing for the existence of a God conceived in this way. Discussion of this conception of God raises a number of topics of vital current concern. We consider the challenge that science seems to present to belief in God as well as the difficulties for belief raised by religious diversity. These two topics are especially interesting because thinking about them has caused some philosophers to reject the traditional conception of God in favour of radically different alternatives. They claim that such alternatives are required if any conception of God is to survive in an age when most people take for granted both a scientific worldview and religious diversity. The claim that the traditional conception of God has no place with a Worldview appropriate for the twenty-first century will be considered in the concluding section.

Philosophical Thinking about God

'Philosophy' literally means 'love of wisdom' and its origins in the West can be traced back to antiquity. Ancient Greek philosophers, such as Socrates (*c.*469–399 BC), shaped philosophy into an intellectual tradition structured around asking questions. Do not be surprised, then, if this chapter raises more questions than it answers! Many of the questions that philosophers through the ages have asked concern the existence and nature of God. Until relatively recently such questions were a central part of all philosophical inquiry, but nowadays they are dealt with in a special branch of philosophy called philosophy of religion. Philosophers of religion are concerned with certain kinds of questions about God. Typically these are questions that have no easy answer. The seeming intractability of philosophical questions about God explains why many of the same questions have preoccupied philosophers from very different eras for well over 2000 years. It also explains the potentially bewildering variety of answers to such questions that different philosophers have proposed.

So what kinds of questions do philosophers ask about God? How do they attempt to answer them? Philosophers interested in God typically ask questions that cannot be answered by means of conducting experiments on the world. We cannot answer philosophical questions by employing the methods of the natural sciences. Nor can we answer these questions by resorting to the methods of the social sciences. Philosophers are not interested in questions such as: what percentage of the UK adult population believes in the existence of God? Such questions are the preserve of the social sciences, and can be answered by means of a survey or questionnaire. Philosophical questions cannot be resolved by polling people to find out what they believe.

Here is a genuinely philosophical question concerning God, and it is one which philosophers of religion are keen to answer: Does God exist? Given that philosophers attempt to answer this question neither by devising experiments, as a natural scientist might, nor by passing around a questionnaire, as a social scientist might, you may well wonder how they do go about answering this question. Philosophers seek to answer questions like this by developing arguments.[1] Ideally, these arguments should be based on claims (what philosophers call 'premises') with which all rational people can agree. The conclusion of a philosophical argument should follow from these premises in such a way that if the premises are true the conclusion must also be true. Later in this chapter we will consider some arguments that have been used in the attempt to establish

---

[1] It is customary to distinguish between two forms of Western philosophy: analytic (or Anglo-Saxon) philosophy and Continental philosophy; both rely on argument although each presents their work in a distinctive style.

the conclusion that God exists.

But before we can look at arguments about the existence of God, we need to define 'God'. Philosophers of religion have devoted considerable attention to this issue. In fact, twentieth-century philosophy of religion was dominated by inquiry into the meaning of the term 'God'.[2] One difficulty with defining 'God' is that God is not present in our experience in the same way as the everyday furniture of the world, such as houses, tables and chairs. The difference between God and anything else which might be thought to exist is made clear when one considers some of the attributes that have been assigned to God by philosophical theists. These attributes are included in the traditional conception of God, and philosophers of religion use them to explain what the term 'God' means. To do this philosophers use a method called conceptual analysis.

Try this method for yourself by thinking about the concept 'God' and asking yourself what other ideas come into your mind. You might find yourself thinking about certain other concepts that are often associated with God: omnipotence (the property of being all-powerful), omniscience (the property of being all-knowing), and omnibenevolence (the property of being perfectly good), for example. Concepts such as these are part of what, in the Western tradition, make up our understanding of the meaning of the term 'God'. It might be helpful to think of 'God' as what philosophers call a 'cluster-concept'. In other words, the concept 'God' is made up of a cluster of related concepts (centrally including those listed above). When ordinary people, as well as philosophers, ask whether or not God exists, they usually have in mind a being that is characterized by possessing the attributes of omnipotence, omniscience, and omnibenevolence.

Now it often happens that when a philosopher thinks about God, and carefully analyzes the attributes traditionally assigned to God, certain problems come to light. For example, how can we reconcile the claim that God is all-powerful, all-knowing, and totally good, with the presence of evil in the world? This problem has been a major focus of philosophical thought about God, particularly since the eighteenth century, and it is known as the problem of evil.[3] Problems such as this one have led some philosophers and theolo-

---

[2] See Victoria S. Harrison, *Religion and Modern Thought* (London: SCM, 2007), Chapters 4 and 5.

[3] For a good collection of essays on this problem, see Marilyn McCord Adams and R. Merrihew Adams (eds), *The Problem of Evil* (Oxford: Oxford University Press, 1990).

gians to suggest that the traditional understanding of God must be mistaken. Some have argued for alternative conceptions of God that would explain why God appears not to act to stop bad things happening. We shall consider some alternative conceptions of God later in this chapter, but first we need to say more about the traditional account of God.

The God of Traditional Theism

Theism is the view that God exists and has the attributes mentioned above. Commitment to theism is shared by Jews, Christians, and Muslims.[4] Some Hindus also believe in the existence of one ultimate God, but most worship many gods (they are polytheists). Many forms of Buddhism also teach that a number of gods exist. In this chapter we are only concerned with theism as it is found in the three Abrahamic religions. Let us now explore in more detail the philosophical elaboration of the traditional conception of God held by theists of this type.[5] Its basic components are as follows. God is regarded as personal. This is taken to mean that God is conscious, has beliefs and intentions, and is capable of acting. Despite these features, God is taken to be incorporeal – in other words, God is thought to be a person without a body. Because God does not have a body, God cannot act on the world in the same way that an embodied person like you or I can. Instead God is thought to act merely by willing that something be the case. When God wills that something be the case, that thing necessarily comes about. This is what philosophers and theologians mean by the claim that God is omnipotent. If whatever God wills come to be, God can do anything that God can will. Most philosophers of religion agree that this really means that God can bring anything about that is logically possible. So, for example, they would claim that God could not bring it about that a round square came into existence. Why? Because it is logically impossible that there be a round square, therefore even God cannot will that there should be one.

The idea that God is omniscient follows from the claim that God is omnipotent. To see this, consider the limitations that would be

---

[4] See Harrison, *Religion and Modern Thought*, Chapter 2.
[5] For an excellent introduction to the concept of God at the root of the Abrahamic faiths, see Charles Taliaferro, *Philosophy of Religion: A Beginner's Guide* (Oxford: Oneworld, 2009), Chapter 2.

imposed on God's power to act if God lacked complete knowledge of the world. To claim that God is omniscient is to claim that God knows whatever can be known. Philosophers of religion, however, differ about what falls into the category of what can be known. Some, for example, argue that God cannot know the future, particularly the future free acts that people will perform. The philosophical concern is that if God's knowledge includes knowledge of free future actions, then those actions will be determined in advance and therefore cannot be genuinely free. So, just as the concept of omnipotence is qualified by many philosophers, the concept of omniscience is also limited to a certain range.[6]

As mentioned above, theists also hold that God is perfectly good – omnibenevolent – which is usually taken to imply that everything created by God is also good. Moreover, God is regarded as the creator of everything that exists. (Notice that these two ideas taken together seem to entail that everything that exists is good, and this gives rise to the need to explain why not everything within the world seems good to us: mosquitoes, for example.) Theists not only believe that God created the cosmos; they also typically believe that God is its sustainer and governor. Without the continuous sustaining activity of God, many theists claim, the cosmos would cease to exist. This idea highlights a contrast at the heart of theism between the contingency of the cosmos and the necessity of God.[7] The cosmos is said to be contingent because it depends on something else for its existence. God, on the other hand, does not depend on anything else for his existence, and in this sense his existence is necessary.[8]

Having defined God, in the following section we turn to the question of whether such a being exists.

Arguments for the Existence of God

Before considering some specific arguments for the existence of God, it is worth thinking about the different routes by which people have claimed to have reached knowledge of God's existence. The first route is through revelation or faith. People who believe that knowledge of the existence of God is possible

[6] For a more detailed account of the classical theistic view of God and a discussion of some of the philosophical and theological problems it raises, see Thomas V. Morris, *Our Idea of God: An Introduction to Philosophical Theology* (Vancouver: Regent College Publishing, 2002).

[7] See Morris, *Our Idea of God*, chapters 6 and 8.

[8] The God of traditional theism is almost invariably referred to as 'he'.

through these means will either judge philosophical arguments to
be redundant or at most to be a preparation for faith and revelation. The second route is through the use of abstract reason.
Ontological arguments for the existence of God are an example of
this because they aim to prove that God exists just by thinking
about the meaning of the term 'God'. The third route is through
reflection on the natural world. Design arguments for the existence of God are the prime example of this approach. We will look
at the structure of both ontological and design arguments below.
We will also consider cosmological arguments, which are less
abstract than ontological arguments but also less concrete than
design arguments.[9] What these arguments have in common is that
they try to prove that God exists on the basis of premises which
every rational person can accept. How far they succeed is a matter
which you will have to judge for yourself.

Ontological, cosmological and design arguments have each
enjoyed a long history. Cosmological arguments, for example,
trace their pedigree back to the ancient Greek philosophy that
flourished before the birth of Christianity. Given the extended
period of time over which these arguments have developed, it is
not surprising that each argument comes in a number of different
forms. It is helpful, therefore, to regard each 'argument' for the
existence of God as a family of arguments sharing a similar structure rather than as a single argument. The accounts of the
arguments provided below are by no means exhaustive; they simply
explain the structure of the main ways of arguing for theism's
central claim: God exists.[10] Along the way we will also look at a few
questions raised by these arguments.

The Ontological Argument Family

Ontological arguments are the most abstract of all the arguments
for the existence of God.[11] Philosophers who use these arguments
hope to reach their conclusion just by thinking about what the

---

[9] We cannot consider all the available arguments for the existence of God
here: other arguments include moral arguments and arguments from religious
experience.

[10] For more information and a wide range of resources on ontological and design
arguments, see the Philosophy of Religion Mind Mapping Project:
http://www.gla.ac.uk/Acad/Philosophy/mindmapping/

[11] For a detailed study of different forms of ontological argument, see Graham
Oppy, *Ontological Arguments and Belief in God* (Cambridge: Cambridge
University Press, 1996).

term 'God' means, without appealing to any experience or empirical evidence. Here is an example of an ontological argument that illustrates the typical structure shared by arguments of this type:

Premise 1:   God is the most perfect being imaginable.
Premise 2:   The most perfect being imaginable must exist,
              otherwise it would not be the most perfect being
              imaginable.
Conclusion: God exists.

The eleventh-century Christian monk, St Anselm, developed an ontological argument. He began by defining God as 'that being than which nothing greater can be conceived'.[12] In other words, according to Anselm's definition, God is the most perfect being imaginable. Anselm argued that the most perfect being imaginable must exist, because otherwise we could imagine a more perfect being – one which was more perfect because it existed. So from the definition of God it is supposed to follow that God must exist; philosophers say that God must exist *necessarily*. If this argument is successful it will support the conclusion of the cosmological argument, which we consider below.

However, Anselm's argument raises a number of questions. Some of which were noticed by Gaunilo, who was a contemporary of Anselm.[13] Gaunilo argued that Anselm's argument led to absurd consequences when it was applied to things other than God. To show this Gaunilo deployed the idea of a perfect island. Using Anselm's argument it seems that we are forced to conclude that the most perfect island must exist, because if it didn't it would not be the most perfect island. If that is correct then Anselm's argument does indeed seem to generate absurd conclusions; it can appear to demonstrate the existence of all sorts of perfect things.

Questions have also been raised about the assumption ontological arguments seem to make that existence is a property in the same way that being omnibenevolent, omnipotent or omniscient are properties. Ontological arguments, like Anselm's, seem to assume that God possesses the property of existence in much the same way as God possesses the property of omnipotence. But critics, such as Immanuel Kant (1724–1804), point out that existence is not a property like the other things listed.[14] The differ-

---

[12] See the extract from Anselm's work in Brian Davies (ed.), *Philosophy of Religion: A Guide and Anthology* (Oxford: Oxford University Press, 2000), Chapter 29.
[13] See Gaunilo in Davies, *Philosophy of Religion*, Chapter 30.

ence is that a being couldn't have any of the other properties unless it already existed. So existence is not a property but is rather the precondition of having any properties at all. By defining God as having certain properties like 'being perfect' then ontological arguments already presuppose that God exists.

The difficulty of proving that God exists merely by thinking about the meaning of 'God' has led many theists to explore another type of argument, one which still employs abstract conceptual reasoning but focuses that reasoning not on 'God' but on the existence of the universe.

The Cosmological Argument Family

Cosmological arguments start with a fundamental question about our universe that any reflective person might ask, irrespective of whether or not they are religious. The question is: What explains the existence of the universe? The simplest form of cosmological argument attempts to provide an answer to this question. Here is its basic structure:[15]

> Premise 1:   Everything that exists has a cause outside itself.
> Premise 2:   The universe exists.
> Conclusion: The universe has a cause outside itself.

Theists argue that God is the best candidate for the role of the cause of the universe, because only God exists independently of the universe.

Lying behind this argument is a widely accepted philosophical principle called the Principle of Sufficient Reason. According to this principle, everything that exists has a reason for its existence. If you identify the reason for the existence of something, you will have explained the existence of that thing. The principle seems to apply to everything within the universe (me, you, my dog, your house, etc), and is taken for granted in the natural sciences. It seems only natural then to apply it to the universe as a whole, and to look for a sufficient reason for its existence.

What sort of thing might be a sufficient reason for the existence of the universe? This is just another way of asking what sort of thing might explain the existence of the universe. In answering this ques-

[14] See Kant in Davies, *Philosophy of Religion*, Chapter 34.
[15] For a comprehensive account of different forms of cosmological argument, see William Lane Craig, *The Cosmological Argument from Plato to Leibniz* (New York: Barnes & Noble Books, 1980).

tion theistic philosophers have claimed that whatever explains the existence of the universe must have a very special characteristic: it must exist necessarily. If the cause of the universe did not exist necessarily (that is, if it could have not existed), then it could not be a sufficient reason for the existence of the universe. We would have to look for a further reason that would explain the existence of the cause of the universe. An adequate explanation for the existence of the universe must then be something that does not require an explanation for its own existence. As we have seen, the God of traditional theism is thought to be a necessarily existing uncaused being (that is, a being that does not require a cause for its existence), so it fits the bill here.

The key philosophical question this argument raises is how to avoid the difficulty that the argument begins with the premise 'Everything that exists has a cause outside itself' and ends with a claim that seems to contradict this: that the cause of the existence of the universe does not have a cause. As we have seen, theists argue both that a satisfactory explanation of the existence of the universe must appeal to an uncaused cause, and that a necessary being provides the only satisfying explanation for the universe's existence. But others argue that this is not so and that postulating the existence of a necessary being raises as many questions as it answers.

The numerous questions raised by arguments relying on abstract reasoning, such as ontological and cosmological arguments, have encouraged many theists to explore another style of argument, one which pays more attention to the details of our actual experience of the world.

The Design Argument Family

Design arguments are sometimes known as 'Teleological Arguments' (from the Greek word '*telos*' which means purpose or goal). Many design arguments start from the claim that when we look at the natural world we can observe that many things in it are designed for a specific purpose. The human eye is often used as an example of an extraordinarily complex natural object that seems to have been designed for a special purpose, namely, to enable us to see.

But doesn't design presuppose the existence of a designer – an intelligence or mind which puts the design into the world? The basic idea behind design arguments is that design can only be explained by positing the existence of an intelligence or mind.

Here is the basic structure of this style of argument:

Premise 1:   The world shows evidence of design.
Premise 2:   Design is the product of intelligence.
Conclusion: An intelligent designer of the world exists.

Most of the controversy surrounding this form of design argument concerns premise 1. Unfortunately, like many philosophical claims, there is no obvious way of either proving or refuting the claim that the world shows evidence of design. Some people claim to observe design; others respond that what looks like design is the product of evolution by natural selection. There are two main types of reply which a theist might make to the suggestion that evolution explains why so many things seem purposeful. First, she might say that the natural world exhibits too much complexity to be the result of natural processes and blind chance. Second, she might claim that evolution is the mechanism through which God acts.[16]

Design arguments are the focus of lively contemporary discussion. Because of the recent interest in this topic many philosophers of religion have turned to the task of trying to explain the relationship between science and religion. As part of this task many pondered what conception of God, if any, would be compatible with a Worldview shaped more by science than by religion. We turn to this question below.

Contemporary Issues

Here we consider two issues of vital current concern: first, the challenge that modern scientific worldviews seem to pose to the traditional conception of God. Second, the problem that religious diversity raises for belief in the existence of God as traditionally conceived.

Theism and Science

Given the importance accorded to science within contemporary culture, theistic philosophers have been concerned to show that belief in God is compatible with a scientific Worldview. In the mid-

---

[16] For a more detailed discussion of design arguments, see Thomas H. McPherson, *Argument from Design* (Basingstoke: Macmillan, 1972). For a good selection of more recent work on this topic, see Neil A. Manson (ed.), *God and Design: The Teleological Argument and Modern Science* (London: Routledge, 2003).

twentieth century, many people believed that science and religion were fundamentally opposed and that a rational person could not accept both belief in God and science.[17] This view was shored up by the conviction, popular at the time, that science could – at least potentially – explain everything. Science, like philosophy, is concerned with questions and uses arguments to try to answer them. The answers that scientists give to questions change as their knowledge about the world increases. Nowadays people are more accustomed than they were in the past to the idea that scientific theories are provisional, and this inclines them to caution about the claim that the natural sciences can explain everything that there is to explain about our world.[18]

If science does not explain absolutely everything, there may not be a direct conflict between the claims of science and belief in God. Nevertheless, certain aspects of the theistic Worldview do seem to have implications for scientific inquiry. For example, the claim made by proponents of the design argument that God is responsible for the design exhibited in the natural world, as we have seen, raises the question of whether or not design is evident in the natural world. Surely this is a question which natural scientists might be expected to have something to say about. To take another example, the claim made by many proponents of cosmological arguments that God is the cause of the universe seems to be relevant to cosmology, which is that branch of natural science that investigates the origin of the universe. One might, then, expect some convergence between the inquiries of cosmologists and philosophers working on cosmological arguments. But this does not seem to be the case, philosophers of religion make little contribution to the scientific understanding of such matters, and natural scientists seem to have an equally negligible impact on philosophy of religion.

One possible explanation for this is that philosophers, on the one hand, and natural scientists, on the other, are concerned with fundamentally different subject matter. According to this suggestion, philosophers of religion and theologians are concerned with questions of value, whereas natural scientists are concerned with matters of empirical fact. Despite the advantage of making a clear distinction between science and religion, this view does not take adequately into account the overlapping concerns of scientists and

[17] Bertrand Russell, for example, held this view.
[18] There are of course notable exceptions. See the work of Richard Dawkins and Edward O. Wilson.

philosophers of religion. It also has the consequence that claims about God could only really be about values and not about fact. On this view, 'God exists' does not make a factual claim, but just a claim about what the person saying it values. Given these difficulties, theistic philosophers have set out to show how science and theism can be compatible without resorting to the view that the former concerns facts and the latter values. In research that deals with the interface between science and religion, philosophers such as Keith Ward and Holmes Rolston III have come up with some very creative ways of combining scientific theories and theological claims.[19]

However, in their attempt to reconcile belief in God with science, they have had to stretch almost beyond recognition the traditional conception of God as omnipotent, omniscient and omnibenevolent. Thus, Ward has described God as 'the sustainer of a network of dynamic interrelated energies'.[20] Rolston, in a similar vein, regards God as 'a Ground of Information, or an Ambience of Information'.[21] He also describes God as 'a counter-current to entropy, a sort of biogravity that lures life upwards'.[22] Views like this have evolved a long way from the traditional conception of God. However, their proponents believe that if the concept of God is to continue to be meaningful in a world that is understood primarily through a scientific lens, the traditional conception must give way to a view that can fit more readily with other aspects of our understanding.

Perhaps what has given rise to this problem is that the natural sciences have explained so much about the origin and functioning of the universe that there is little left for God to do. God seems to play no explanatory role in an understanding of the world that is shaped by science. Many people find the notion of an omnipotent, omniscient, omnibenevolent God redundant in a world that is understood by means of sciences that appeal only to natural (as compared to supernatural) causes.[23] A world in which everything that happens is believed to be completely explainable by means of natural causes seems to leave no scope for God to act (except

---

[19] See Harrison, *Religion and Modern Thought*, Chapter 6.

[20] Keith Ward, *God, Chance & Necessity* (Oxford: Oneworld, 1996), p. 57.

[21] Holmes Rolston III, *Genes, Genesis and God: Values and Their Origins in Natural and Human History* (Cambridge: Cambridge University Press, 1999), p. 359.

[22] Rolston, *Genes, Genesis and God*, p. 364.

[23] For a critical examination of naturalism, see Stewart Goetz and Charles Taliaferro, *Naturalism* (Michigan: William B. Eerdmans Publishing Company, 2008).

through natural causes): in not allowing for divine intervention the scientific worldview calls into question the point of religious activities such as asking God for help. Given such difficulties it is not surprising that many philosophers have joined Rolston and Ward in arguing that the traditional view of God is no longer tenable. Alternative conceptions of God are thought to be required: these alternatives conceptions are typically so indefinite – 'God' is 'cosmic serendipitous creativity',[24] for example – that there is no difficulty holding them within an understanding of the world shaped by modern science. A further advantage of definitions of 'God' like the ones considered above is that they avoid the problem of evil. We don't need a special theory to explain why 'cosmic serendipitous creativity' does not act to prevent bad things happening, because it doesn't make any sense to think of it as acting at all. Clearly, according to these definitions, 'God' is not a person and hence does not have a plan for the world and the people in it. Such definitions of God may appear to solve the problem of reconciling theism and science, but in requiring that the concept of God be entirely stripped of its traditional content they come at a high price. Given this cost, many might wonder if it is worth continuing to use the word 'God'.

Theism and Religious Diversity

Religious diversity is another fact of everyday experience that has challenged the way that many people think about God. Traditional Jews, Christians and Muslims hold that there is only one, unique God.[25] On the face of it this seems to entail that people who are not responding appropriately to this God are making a serious mistake. In the past this belief probably came naturally to people who had little direct contact, if any, with those of other religious traditions. But nowadays proximity to people of other faiths, and of none, has forced many theists to ask the following questions: Why doesn't everyone believe in God? What sort of mistake is being made by atheists and sincere followers of non-Western religious traditions?

The puzzle of religious diversity and atheism is intensified by the

---

[24] Gordon Kaufman, 'Mystery, God and Constructivism' in A. Moore and M. Scott (eds), *Realism and Religion: Philosophical and Theological Perspectives* (Aldershot: Ashgate, 2007), p. 26.

[25] The Christian understanding of this is modified by a commitment to Trinitarianism.

way that God is traditionally conceived: an omnipotent God could make everyone believe in him just by willing it to be so. An omnibenevolent God would surely want everyone to believe in him given the further premise that it is a great good to believe in God and thereby to enjoy the relationship to God that is made possible by faith. Given this understanding of the nature of God it seems incomprehensible that there should be so many people lacking belief in him. This difficulty raised by the traditional conception of God is known as the problem of divine hiddenness, and some philosophers argue that it constitutes a decisive objection to belief in the existence of that God.[26]

Despite the intuitive power of this objection to belief in God, its force will be weakened if there is a way to reconcile a traditional conception of God with the facts of religious diversity.[27] One well-known attempt to do this has been proposed by the philosopher of religion John Hick.[28] Hick argues that each of the world's religious traditions is a culturally shaped response to an ultimate reality, which he calls the 'Real'. Roman Catholicism has developed as a response to the Real, so has Sunni Islam, and so has Reformed Judaism, to take just a few examples. Despite the fact that all of these traditions have culturally specific ways of conceiving God, Hick argues that all of these different conceptions point to a more ultimate reality that cannot be described.[29] The Real can be characterized negatively to some extent, so we might say for example that it is incorporeal. The important thing, according to Hick, is that each religious tradition is directed towards this reality and therefore all are on a par with respect to what they can tell us about ultimate divine reality. The traditional theistic conception of God is that image of God which has proved particularly effective in the West at directing people towards the ultimate, unknown reality.

Hick's pluralist theory of religions is an attempt to explain why there are so many different conceptions of the divine available. Given that many of the world's religious traditions claim very different things about the divine, this diversity might be taken to suggest that at most one of these traditions could be making true

[26] See John Schellenberg, *God and the Reasonableness of Non-Belief* (Oxford: OUP, 1990).

[27] Different answers to this question are surveyed in Harrison, *Religion and Modern Thought*, Chapter 7.

[28] See John Hick, *An Interpretation of Religion: Human Responses to the Transcendent* (London: Macmillan, 1989).

[29] For an excellent survey of conceptions of God from different religious traditions, see Keith Ward, *Concepts of God* (Oxford: Oneworld, 1987).

claims. Hick's theory provides a way to avoid this conclusion. The central claims of all religious traditions can be true, according to him. That they say different things is not an obstacle to this because each is correctly describing their own conception of the divine. The Abrahamic religions describe the divine by means of the traditional conception of God, other traditions do not. There is no contradiction here. Hick argues that a religious believer can recognize the value of a range of religious traditions without feeling that their own conception of the divine is somehow thereby invalidated.

According to Hick, one can be a religious pluralist without abandoning belief in the God of traditional theism. But Hick's view raises the question as to what extent one can actually remain committed to a traditional conception of God once one acknowledges that this conception is only one possible way of pointing to a more ultimate religious reality. Typically, traditional theists have regarded their conception of God as representing the ultimate religious reality more accurately than any other available conception. On Hick's view, it is just as correct as any other, but is it also just as far off the mark. To adopt Hick's form of religious pluralism, the price a theist must pay is in fact to accept a dramatic alteration to the traditional conception of God. This is because the concept of God can no longer be regarded as absolute; instead it is thought to be relative both to culture (which partly shaped it) and to something else which exists independently of human thought and culture, namely, the Real. Interestingly, Hick does not regard the Real as an alternative conception of the divine; instead he claims that it is a theoretical postulate whose job is to explain why there are so many different conceptions of the divine available. Because of this, Hick asserts that we would be mistaken to regard the Real as God and to attempt to relate to it directly through worship or prayer. As we can know nothing definite about it at all, our religious activities must remain focused on the conceptions of the divine that we do have. Despite the radical nature of Hick's view then, the traditional theistic conception of God remains an essential part of religious thought and life within those traditions that recognize it as the principal way of responding to the Real. But why should people continue to use this conception of God, given all the questions that it raises?

Conclusion: Is God out of date?

Given the various challenges faced by the traditional conception of God, only some of which have been considered here,[30] one might wonder whether or not this conception of God has a future. Much in the contemporary intellectual climate seems hostile to religion in general, and to the traditional idea of God in particular. Despite this there are signs that interest in theism is waxing rather than waning. Ironically, this interest has been partly aroused by the work of prominent atheists such as Richard Dawkins, in the United Kingdom, and Sam Harris, in the United States. God has suddenly once again become a hot topic both in the academic and in the public domains. This shows that questions about the existence and nature of God still attract the attention of people in a world in which both the sciences and religious diversity are taken for granted. Indeed, in a multicultural, globally aware environment in which religion still enjoys a significant social and political impact, it is surely more important than ever to encourage people to think seriously about the traditional conception of God. As I hope I have shown in this chapter, there is much in the Western philosophical tradition that can help people to think clearly and deeply about the idea of God.

---

[30] Another important challenge comes from feminist philosophy of religion. See, for example, Pamela Sue Anderson, *A Feminist Philosophy of Religion: The Rationality and Myths of Religious Belief* (Oxford: Blackwell, 1997).

Chapter 2

Scripture

Karen Wenell

The 'What' and 'Where' of Scripture

What is Scripture? Where is Scripture located? These are important questions to grapple with, and the second has particular
significance for teaching Scripture in the twenty-first century world
in which we live. First, let us consider the question of what
Scripture is. The answer may not be as straightforward as you
expect, and there are several ways in which the question 'What is
Scripture?' could be answered. From the point of view of terminology, the term 'scripture' comes from the Latin *scriptura*, meaning
'writings' (in Greek *hai graphia*). So, we could understand scripture
as a collection of writings, or even a whole library within one
volume, containing different genres and forms, but all concerned
with God's relationship to humanity. The term 'scripture' might
also be considered synonymous with 'the Bible', meaning 'book'
(Greek *biblion*), or with the Old and New Testaments. In the
context of academic study, you may come across the use of the
term 'Bible' or 'biblical text' in a rather detached, objective way to
talk about scripture as a collection of writings with a particular
history and comparable to other literature. The term 'scripture' or
'Scripture', however, has the immediate connotation of being
sacred writings, not just important historical texts, but important
writings for living faith.

Another, more theological, way to answer the question, 'what is
Scripture?' is to say that it is an account of the relationship between
God and human beings, the story of faith and salvation. Angus
Paddison, in a recent book engaging with Scripture from a strongly
theological standpoint, says this:

> To attest the texts of the Old and New Testaments as 'Scripture' is
> to make specific claims about this text: that it is drawn into the

activity of the triune God of Israel, that its ultimate destination is the worshipping church and that it has a ministry in shaping Christian thinking and acting. Scripture is not first a source for historical inquiry, nor a text that delights our literary sensitivities; calling these collected texts 'Scripture' points to its commissioned role in the saving purposes of God.[1]

Of all the different terms we might come across, the term Scripture perhaps most clearly draws our attention to the location of these texts. Our 'where' question becomes centrally important when we recognize that Scripture is located in believing communities. Or, to put it another way, within believing communities, a collection of writings of different genres becomes a living text which shapes theology and ethical action. Clearly, a Catholic school, with its Christian ethos, is a community of faith. Thus, the *Congregation for Catholic Education* states: 'The Catholic school, far more than any other, must be a community whose aim is the transmission of values for living ... Christian faith, in fact, is born and grows inside a community.'[2] Furthermore, the document states that the Catholic school 'must continually be fed and stimulated by its Source of life, the Saving Word of Christ as it is expressed in Sacred Scripture, in Tradition, especially liturgical and sacramental tradition, and in the lives of people, past and present, who bear witness to that Word.'[3] The connections between the school community, Scripture and faith are clear. Yet, even in a non-denominational school where these connections are not made in relationship to the overall ethos, the Bible may still be understood as Scripture, and explored in the classroom, not just for its content, but for its significance to living faith communities.

One of the challenges for teaching Scripture from our twenty-first century location in the Western world, where Judeo-Christian traditions have had such a major influence on history and culture, is that the texts may be too familiar and can be seen more as part of the moral fibre of society than as formative texts for living faith. The Bible is important to history and culture but it also belongs in communities of faith. It is important to recognize the place of the Bible in society, but also to pay attention to its theological and religious significance. If we focused on translations of the Bible's original Hebrew, Aramaic (OT) and Greek (NT) into English

---

[1] Angus Paddison, *Scripture: A Very Theological Proposal* (London: Continuum, 2009), p. 1.
[2] Congregation for Catholic Education, *The Catholic School* (1977) 53.
[3] Congregation for Catholic Education, *The Catholic School* (1977) 54.

alone (an entire book could not cover every aspect of this, let alone begin to cover translation into other languages), we could also ask questions about which versions of the English Bible are significant for which communities. For example, the King James Version, commissioned by King James IV and celebrating its 400th anniversary in 2011, is associated with the Protestant Church, and is less familiar to Catholic Christians.

Not just familiar translations, but even the content of Catholic and Protestant Scriptures is slightly different, and this brings us to a final question about the location of Scripture – *whose* Scripture are we speaking of, *whose* sacred writings? Here, another term becomes important, that of 'canon' (Greek *kanon*), or 'measuring rod'; for Jewish, Catholic, Protestant and Orthodox traditions each accept as authoritative and sacred a different collection of books. As a 'measuring rod', a canon defines and guides a community in belief and action. The Jewish Scriptures contain twenty-four books. These same twenty-four books are counted as thirty-nine books in the Christian Old Testament because the Book of the Twelve from the Jewish Bible is counted as individual books in the Christian Bible. The Protestant canon includes only these thirty-nine books, but the Catholic and Orthodox Churches also regard books of the Apocrypha as part of their canon (though with slightly different inclusions). For the Catholic Church, the apocryphal books are designated deuterocanonical, or 'canonized secondarily' because they were not originally part of St Jerome's Latin Vulgate translation of the fifth century CE.[4] With only a few minor exceptions, all Christian canons of Scripture include twenty-seven books of the New Testament.

Throughout this chapter, we will pay careful attention to issues of terminology, but perhaps more importantly, we will also open up a discussion about the meaning of Scripture and its importance to religious communities, to faith and living interaction with the texts.

The Covenant, the Old Testament and the New Testament

The term 'covenant' – *berit* in Hebrew – is a formal agreement in which two parties show commitment and mutual obligations are

---

[4] BCE = Before the Common Era = BC or before Christ; CE = Common Era = AD or *anno domini* 'in the year of Our Lord'. BCE and CE are more common today although BC and AD are still used, especially in Christian scholarship.

established. The Hebrew term is translated in Greek as *diatheke*, and the Greek term was translated into English as 'testament'. Therefore, this is where the terminology for the Old and New Testaments, or covenants, originates. In the New Testament Letter to the Hebrews, the author interprets the concept of covenant from Jewish Scripture and places it in relationship to faith in Christ. The Letter to the Hebrews can be described as an extended sermon, and the author outlines the inadequacy of the old covenant and shows how God establishes a new covenant through Christ who is the minister of the new covenant. The new does what the old cannot, as in Hebrews 8:13: 'In speaking of "a new covenant", he has made the first one obsolete. And what is obsolete and growing old will soon disappear.' This language of 'old' and 'new' covenants in Hebrews draws our attention back to the question of community and calls for careful avoidance of any suggestion based on Scripture that living Jewish faith is somehow obsolete from a Christian point of view. The danger here is that the 'Old' covenant is considered subordinate or inferior to the 'New' covenant, and this then becomes translated, or put onto the two communities of faith we associate with these covenants – the Jewish community and the Christian community. We should remember that in New Testament times, the law was not considered to be a burden to God's people Israel, but rather a gift that allowed them to maintain the relationship of the covenant. Though anti-Semitism is a very strong term, more subtle forms of negative views toward Judaism in Christianity, often based on the involvement of Jewish authorities in the death of Jesus, have plagued the Christian Church. Following the horrific events of the Holocaust, the Catholic Church made very clear statements to reinforce the point that 'Although the Church is the new people of God, the Jews should not be presented as rejected or accursed by God, as if this followed from the Holy Scriptures.'[5] If we value both living faith communities and their relationship to Scripture, we will take active care to avoid super-sessionism, which is the idea that the Christian community is superior to, or supersedes, the Jewish community.

If we look to the beginnings of the notion of covenant in the Hebrew Bible, there are three major priestly covenants: the primeval covenant (between God and all creation), the ancestral covenant (between God and Israel), and the Sinai covenant (between God and Israel). Sometimes these are named after the

---

[5] Second Vatican Council (1965), *Nostra Aetate* 4.

figures through whom the covenant was established: the Noahic, Abrahamic and Mosaic covenants.

Each covenant also had an accompanying sign. The primeval, or Noahic, covenant had the sign of the rainbow to show that God would not destroy the earth with a flood again.[6] The Abrahamic covenant included the sign of circumcision, which was required from Abraham and all of his descendants.[7] In the New Testament book of Acts, Stephen's speech mentions the 'covenant of circumcision' referring to the Abrahamic covenant.[8] The sign of the Mosaic covenant was that of the Sabbath dictating that the Sabbath would be kept separate and holy to God.[9] Apart from these covenants, the Old Testament also contains the Covenant Code, which is found in Exodus 20:22–3:33. This was a collection of Israelite laws, including the idea that God (or Yahweh) should be worshiped in just one place, or central sanctuary. The regulations of the Covenant Code may consist of some of the most ancient material of the Jewish Scriptures. Other books of the Old Testament also mention and reinterpret the notion of covenant. The prophetic book of Jeremiah, for instance, has the most frequent use of the term of any book of the Hebrew Bible. Most famously, in Jeremiah 31:31–4, the author speaks of a new covenant. This poetic description describes an internalized covenant, with God's laws written on the hearts of his people and the author of the Letter to the Hebrews explicitly quotes the text of Jeremiah 31:33–4 in Hebrews 10:16–17. Covenant is a way of understanding and articulating the relationship between God and his people, and it is to be expected that communities of believers (both Jewish and Christian) will reinterpret this relationship and find 'new' ways of expressing what is required from each party in the agreement.

Old Testament

We have already introduced the idea of the canon of the Jewish Scriptures, and also discussed why, from a Christian point of view, these texts are referred to as the Old Testament. The Hebrew Bible is made up of the Law, the Prophets and the Writings and was

[6] Gen. 9:12.
[7] Gen. 17:11.
[8] Acts 7:8.
[9] Exod. 31:13, 17.

written by different authors over a period of about 900 to 1000 years. In Hebrew, the first letters of the Law (Torah), Prophets (Nevi'im) and Writings (Ketuvim) are joined by vowels to give the name of the TaNaK. Each of these terms refers to the same Jewish canon of books (see terminology box below).

Notes on Terminology:

Old Testament = Hebrew Bible = Jewish Scriptures = Tanak (Torah, Nevi'im, Ketuvim)

Torah = Law = Pentateuch = Five Books of Moses
JEDP sources = **J**/Yahwist, **E**lohist, **D**euteronomist, **P**riestly
Nevi'im = Prophets = Former + Latter Prophets [= Major + Minor Prophets]
Ketuvim = Writings

Beginning with the books of the Law, it should be noted that these five books – Genesis, Exodus, Leviticus, Numbers and Deuteronomy – are also referred to as the Torah or the Pentateuch (because of an association between the five books and five scroll jars). We should also mention that Torah can have a broader meaning than just that which defines it as the first part of the Old Testament. It can refer more generally to the teaching and revelation of God. The books of the law were canonized around 400 BCE.[10] They contain instruction and teaching, though their authorship and the exact dating of their composition are unknown. Traditionally, Moses is considered to be the author of the Pentateuch (see, for example, Joshua 8:31–2), though a practical barrier remains in that Moses' death is described in Deuteronomy 34:5–12: thus it is hardly possible for Moses to have written it himself! Moses is also sometimes spoken about in the third person. It is perhaps more helpful to speak of compilers and sources than individual authors when it comes to the material found in the Torah. Scholars have detected four main sources of the Pentateuch: the Yahwist (named 'J' for the spelling Jahwist in German) where God is referred to as Yahweh; the Elohist source where God is referred to as Elohim; the Deuteronomist source, dating to the seventh century BCE, which is concerned with historical matters and reform; and the Priestly source, dating to the sixth century BCE and concerned with legislation.

---

[10] Canonize here means 'to include in a literary canon'.

For Religious Education at school level, some of the stories with
which pupils will be made familiar are found in the first eleven
chapters of Genesis: from creation to Noah and the covenant of
the rainbow; from Adam and Eve to the spread of humanity over
the face of the earth and to Shem, the ancestor of Abraham. The
stories of Genesis 1–11 are called the Primeval Story, or accounts
of the origins of life and humanity. Originally, the Primeval Story
would have developed through oral and written traditions as separate stories and genealogies. Famously, there are two accounts, or
versions of the creation story in Genesis 1–3. The Priestly (P)
source in Genesis 1:1–2:4a and the Yahwist (J) source in Genesis
2:4b–3:24 each give an account of creation which establishes how
the world began and the creation of the first human couple.
Interestingly, the Yahwist creation story is older than the Priestly
one, but it appears after it. The Yahwist story is concerned with the
problem of sin and temptation, and the Priestly source emphasized
divine blessing in creation, as in the repeated refrain, 'God saw
that it was good'. In the story of the flood, God's work of creation
was undone in watery chaos, though Noah and his family represent
a new start for humanity (and for animal life too!). There are
ancient Near Eastern parallels with the creation and flood stories
of Genesis, and the Deluge Tablet and the Gilgamesh Epic in
particular show close similarities with the flood in the Primeval
Story.

The Prophetic books, or Nevi'im, were finalized around 200
BCE and include books of the Former (Joshua, Judges, 1 and 2
Samuel, 1 and 2 Kings) and Latter (Isaiah, Jeremiah, Ezekiel and
the Book of the Twelve) Prophets. The Latter Prophets are further
divided into Major and Minor Prophets. The books of the Former
Prophets have a more historical focus and relate to the period of
the conquest and settlement of Canaan, the rise of kingship, and
the establishment of the two kingdoms of Judah and Israel. They
end with the destruction of Judah by the Babylonians and the
beginning of the period of captivity for the survivors of the devas-
tation in exile in Babylon. They are concerned throughout with
the relationship between God and Israel in the different stages of
the nation's history. The Latter Prophets focus on specific
prophetic figures, individuals with a special role in society who
provided a divine perspective on the events of their time(s). The
Major Prophets – Isaiah, Jeremiah and Ezekiel – are the most
developed prophetic narratives. We should not think of the
prophetic books as written by the individual prophet for whom the
book was named; rather, it is likely that some materials – oracles

and pronouncements – from the original prophet or his 'school' were retained, written down, compiled and edited. It is interesting that the book of Isaiah can actually be divided into three parts (chapters 1–39, 40–55, and 56–66), each constituting a sub-collection of material relating to different historical periods. The first section, or First Isaiah, contains the material which is attributable to the 'original' prophet, Isaiah of Jerusalem of the Assyrian period (eighth century BCE). The Minor Prophets (Hosea to Malachi) are unfortunately named, as the designation of 'minor' relates to their length rather than their importance. In the Hebrew Bible, these books are grouped together under the Book of the Twelve. The Minor Prophets are concerned with wisdom and righteousness in their messages, and they reveal the nature of prophecy in ancient Israel. Although the Oxford English Dictionary defines prophecy as 'the action of foretelling or predicting the future' (in fairness, they also include a definition based on biblical prophecy), we should understand prophecy in the Bible less in terms of predicting the future, and more in terms of reflection on the future in light of the present. Perhaps we can all relate in one way or another to the kind of concerned 'prediction' which says 'if you keep going like this, this will happen ...'. The prophets were figures who knew intimately Yahweh's requirements and demands – a recurrent phrase in prophetic literature is 'thus says the Lord' – and analysed the situations they saw and experienced in light of them, looking toward the future. They also reminded the leaders and community about the demands as well as the promises of the covenantal relationship.

It is much more difficult to say when the Writings, or Ketuvim, were finalized, though they are the last of the Old Testament books to come together into their canonical form. They are grouped together at the end of the Jewish canon, but separated and integrated into the Christian canon based on chronological relationship to other books. In general, we can say that the Writings relate to the postexilic period, when the exiles returned from Babylon after the Persian king Cyrus' degree in 539 BCE, and Jerusalem was rebuilt.[11] The Writings include the Psalms, Wisdom literature (Proverbs, Job, Sirach), the Five Scrolls (Song of Songs, Ruth, Lamentations, Ecclesiastes, Esther), Historical books (1–2 Chronicles, Ezra-Nehemiah, 1 and 2 Maccabees) and an apocalyptic writing, the Book of Daniel.

---

[11] Ezra 5–6.

The Psalms as poetry are characterized by parallelism (though this also occurs in Proverbs and elsewhere), where two lines of a couplet are related. In synonymous parallelism, the two lines say the same thing, so in Psalm 51 we read: 'Wash me thoroughly from my iniquity, and cleanse me from my sin. For I know my transgressions, and my sin is ever before me.' In antithetic parallelism, the two lines say the same thing in opposite ways, so in Psalm 1 we read: For the Lord watches over the way of the righteous, but the way of the wicked will perish.'

Wisdom literature can be described as theological in nature, and connected to the tradition of Solomon. One particularly tricky theological issue dealt with in this literature is *theodicy*, or 'the justice of God'; here we are talking about the ancient problem of how a good God can allow evil, suffering and injustice to take place. The collection of Five Scrolls (cf. above – and not to be confused with the Pentateuch!), or Megilloth, each have an association with a particular Jewish festival: Ruth with the Festival of Weeks; Song of Songs with the Passover; Ecclesiastes with the Festival of Tabernacles; Lamentations with the Ninth of Ab; Esther with Purim. Finally, the Book of Daniel can be described as an apocalypse, or a writing which 'discloses' or 'reveals' events to be enacted by God to a human subject or messenger. The Book of Daniel in particular is concerned with giving hope to Judeans who were persecuted under the Seleucid ruler Antiochus Epiphanes. There are four visions in the later part of the Book of Daniel (7–12), and there are also several chapters of Daniel which are in Aramaic (2–7).

New Testament

There are some obvious and striking differences we could point out between the Old and New Testaments. Whereas the Jewish Scriptures were written over a period of 900–1000 years, the New Testament was written in a brief space of time, only about 50–100 years. Also, the Old Testament was written in Hebrew, with a small amount of Aramaic and the New Testament was written entirely in Greek, the *lingua franca* of the Roman Empire at the turn of the era. Although the Jewish Scriptures contain twenty-four books and the New Testament twenty-seven, the length of the books of the New Testament is significantly shorter, so much so that the New Testament can jokingly be referred to as an appendix to the Old in terms of the amount of space it takes in a one-volume edition!

There are four main genres found in the New Testament: Gospels (Matthew, Mark, Luke and John); history (Acts); Epistles, or letters (thirteen written by Paul (and known as 'Pauline Epistles') and eight General Epistles); and an apocalypse (Revelation). It may surprise you to learn that 1 Thessalonians, one of Paul's letters, is thought to be the first book of the New Testament to be written, at about 50 CE. Many people – even devout Christians – might find it difficult to recall the contents of 1 Thessalonians, neither the most famous nor the most well-read of New Testament books. It is natural to think of the gospels as the beginning of the story of the New Testament because of their content and placement in the canon. Although Paul's letters were the first to be written (in the 50s CE), there were oral traditions about Jesus circulating in his lifetime and after his crucifixion (in c.30–33 CE) before they were incorporated into the written gospels with which we are familiar, in the second half of the first century (c.70–90 CE). Indeed, Paul himself writes about handing down tradition: 'For I handed on to you as of first importance what I in turn had received: that Christ died for our sins in accordance with the scriptures.'[12]

We will look at the Gospels in more detail in the next section, though with regard to the book of Acts, it is worth noting that Luke and Acts together is the only two-volume narrative found in the New Testament. The canonical order separates Luke from Acts with the Gospel of John, but rightfully they belong together – the same author tells the story of Jesus' life, death and resurrection in Luke, and then relates the continuing story of Paul and the Early Church in Acts. Sometimes, such as in the description of Paul's conversion in Acts 22 and 26 and in Paul's own letters such as Philippians 3:3–17 and Galatians 1:11–17, there are some points of difference between the information we get from the author of Luke-Acts and from Paul himself. There may be various explanations for this, but it also suggests the great value in Paul's letters that they are direct testimony of his own experiences and developing theology at a very early stage in the development of Christianity. And yet, there are further complicating issues when it comes to the study of Paul's letters. There are disagreements among New Testament scholars as to how many of the letters attributed to him, Paul actually wrote. The seven undisputed Pauline Epistles are Romans 1 and 2, Corinthians, Galatians, Philippians, 1 Thessalonians and Philemon. The other six Pauline epistles which are disputed by scholars are Ephesians, Colossians,

---

[12] 1 Cor. 15:3.

2 Thessalonians, 1 and 2 Timothy, and Titus. For some of these, it is possible that a disciple or close follower of Paul authored the letters. For all of them, disputed and undisputed, we can say that they are 'occasional' letters, that is, they were written for particular congregations facing particular issues and circumstances. The General Epistles – Hebrews, James, 1 and 2 Peter, 1, 2 and 3 John and Jude – are sometimes called catholic epistles because, unlike Paul's letters, they were written to all the churches, not to particular congregations. The Second Letter of Peter is likely to be the last New Testament book to be written, between 95–150 CE. The Apocalyptic book of Revelation has as its subject matter the culmination of Christianity and responds to the pressures of alienation and persecution by Rome. Like the apocalyptic book of Daniel, it was intended to bring hope to its hearers and readers in difficult times.

The writings which form the canon of the New Testament were in existence by the middle of the second century CE, and were emerging as a collection of authoritative writings for Christian faith and practice. Athanasius, Bishop of Alexandria in Egypt, confirmed in a letter in 367 CE our list of twenty-seven books, an important step in the process of canonization amidst various controversies and councils which contributed to this process. It was important to the Early Church to preserve these writings and to affirm traditions going back to Jesus himself, to Paul and the other apostles. However, we might also keep in mind that many, if not most, of the writings we find in the New Testament were not originally written to be sacred Scripture. For the New Testament authors, their Scripture was the Hebrew Bible, or more correctly the Septuagint, the Greek translation of the Hebrew Bible, written around 250 BCE (sometimes referred to as the LXX, the Roman numerals for 70, which is the traditional number of Jewish scholars working independently on the translation). If you take the time to read the book of Philemon, you can easily understand why this letter, written by Paul about a particular situation concerning the freedom of the slave Onesimus, was not originally intended to form part of a new canon of Scripture. From another perspective, we can understand why some of the *non-canonical* gospels were excluded when we stop to read them and consider some of their content. In the non-canonical *Gospel of Peter*, a cross speaks; more startlingly, in the *Infancy Gospel of Thomas*, the boy Jesus kills a child and brings him back to life. Even if it may seem reasonable to us that gospels such as these were eventually excluded from the canon which established the acceptable doctrine of Christianity, they do

tell us something important about the ways that religious imagination had developed up to the time of canonization, particularly
around the figure of Jesus himself.

Four Gospels

There are four canonical gospels: Matthew, Mark, Luke and John.
All of the four canonical gospels were originally anonymous but
various Early Church writings associate them with particular
authors. The Gospels of Matthew, Mark and Luke are called the
Synoptic Gospels. For the Synoptic Gospels, the first obvious point
to make about them is that they do not include John's Gospel. Why
is John not a synoptic gospel? It is because John's Gospel is written
in quite a different way to the other three Gospels. 'Synoptic'
means literally 'same eye', or 'seeing together'. The Synoptic
Gospels, Mark, Matthew and Luke, have a great deal of material in
common. It is not just that they tell the same stories; they actually
use the same Greek words, often in the same order with the same
forms and tenses, or close to it. Sometimes it can be difficult to
appreciate this when reading the Gospels in English, but even in
English, it is worth looking at a side-by-side comparison (or synop-
sis) of the Gospels to get a sense of the close similarities and the
shared traditions between them. Although students today would be
accused of plagiarism for following another author so closely, this
would have been a completely foreign concept to the gospel
authors.

Scholars can't be absolutely certain about the order in which the
Gospels were written, but the dominant theory is that Mark was
written first, around AD 70 or soon after, and then Matthew and
Luke wrote some time after this, each using Mark's Gospel as a
source and also another source that they both knew, called 'Q' (for
the German Quelle, or 'source'). Another possibility is that
Matthew had a copy of Luke or vice versa. This would also explain,
perhaps more simply, the reason that Matthew and Luke have
material in common which is not shared by Mark. To illustrate the
theory, we could imagine Luke at his 'desk' writing. As he begins
to put pen to parchment to write his opening words, he has on his
writing table several sources. One is a copy of the Gospel of Mark;
another is a copy of 'Q'. As he writes, he also brings other material. Some comes from the Septuagint, the Hebrew Scriptures
translated into Greek, and some material is that only he himself
has knowledge of (special 'L' material). Perhaps this special

material comes from oral tradition that he has heard and believes to be important. He weaves all of these into his story of the life and death of Jesus as he uses up more and more parchment in his writing.

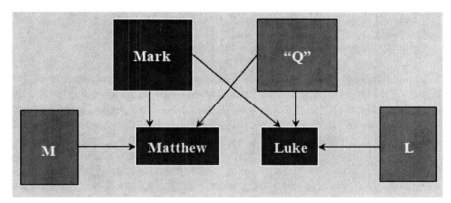

This story of Luke at his imaginary 'desk' draws our attention to another way that scholars can look at the synoptic gospels, and that is for the distinctive mark that each author makes in telling the story of Jesus, and the way they understand Jesus as Christ, or the Christological titles they use. Luke, for example, has a particular concern with bringing 'good news to the poor'[13] and is interested in the history of salvation between God and his people. Only Luke includes the Magnificat (Mary's great hymn of praise),[14] the Benedictus, Zechariah's song of praise at the circumcision of the Baptist[15] and the Nunc Dimittis, Simeon's song at the circumcision of Jesus.[16] Mark's Gospel refers to Jesus (and has Jesus refer to himself) as the Son of Man and his identity as the Son of God is also important to Mark's portrayal. A key moment in Mark's Gospel is Peter's declaration in chapter 8: 'You are the Christ'. Five sections can be identified in Matthew's Gospel which display a 'Torah structure' in which Jesus is understood as a new Moses, delivering a new Law. Matthew is also concerned with mission and the Church, or *ekklesia*.

As mentioned, John's Gospel is not similar enough to Matthew,

---

[13] Luke 4:18.
[14] Luke 1:46–55.
[15] Luke 1:68–79.
[16] Luke 2:29–32.

Mark and Luke to be considered 'synoptic'. A basic outline of John shows some of the way he has structured the life of Jesus differently:

Prologue (1:1–18)   Philosophical Introduction
Part 1 (1:19–12:50)   Public Life and Signs
Part 2 (13:1–20:30)   Passion and Glorification
Epilogue (21:1–25)   Another Conclusion

The prologue to John's Gospel does not include any account of the birth or childhood of Jesus, but sets his life in relationship to the cosmos and constitutes a philosophical reflection on Christ's place in creation as 'the Word made flesh'. John places the Temple scene at the beginning of his Gospel in Chapter 2 and has Jesus' ministry taking place over two to three years with three Passovers mentioned. The synoptic gospels only describe Jesus going to the Temple once, at the end of his ministry, before his crucifixion. John does not focus on Jesus proclaiming the Kingdom of God, and does not relate accounts of exorcisms or the telling of parables like the synoptics. However, there are numerous famous accounts which appear in John but not in the Synoptics: The wedding at Cana, The raising of Lazarus, and the washing of the disciples' feet. Notably, baptism and the institution of the Eucharist are missing, causing some to call John anti-sacramental. John does include a striking set of 'I am' sayings, showing Jesus' confidence in his role and mission: 'I am the bread of life';[17] 'I am the light of the world';[18] 'I am the gate for the sheep';[19] 'I am the good shepherd';[20] 'I am the resurrection and the life';[21] I am the way, the truth and the life';[22] 'I am the true vine'.[23]

Parables

As we conclude this chapter on Scripture, it is useful to take the example of parables to illustrate a final point. In the recent School Inspectors' Report on the teaching of Religious Education in

[17] John 6:35.
[18] John 8:12.
[19] John 10:7.
[20] John 10:11, 14.
[21] John 11:25.
[22] John 14:6.
[23] John 15:1.

England and Wales, this is said about the parables and their teaching in schools:

> In the majority of the schools visited, weaknesses in the provision for teaching Christianity were reflected in several ways. The primary schools in particular were often uncertain about whether Christian material should be investigated in its own right, as part of understanding the religion, or whether it should be used to consider moral or social themes out of the context of the religion. For example, it was common for teachers to use Jesus's parables to explore personal feelings or to decide how people should behave and not to make any reference to their religious significance. As a result, they lost the opportunity to extend pupils' understanding of Christian beliefs.[24]

What is the religious significance of the parables? This may seem obvious in the context of our discussion of the gospels. They are significant as part of the story of the life and ministry of Jesus. However, there is more to explore when it comes to parables. The parable of the Good Samaritan is perhaps the most used and (misused!) text in all of Religious Education in the United Kingdom. It (and other parables too) is often reduced to the message that we should 'be nice' to each other. One of the most interesting things about parables is that they were never meant to give us clear answers or even clear moral messages. Although the gospels do contain aphorisms which are wisdom sayings, or pithy truths, such as 'a tree is known by its fruit'[25] or 'the labourer is worthy of his hire',[26] the parables are different, and are not meant to be read like Aesop's fables, where everything is neatly summed up in one sentence at the end of the story. Instead, they are open stories, inviting us to interpretation, to finding ourselves and our moral decisions in their images and situations. Because of this open quality of parables, they have a rich history of interpretation in Christian tradition which is well worth exploring in the context of teaching. For example, the parables have been depicted in art through the centuries and in countless Christian contexts across the world. In these interpretations, there are connections to Christian communities, to their beliefs, and their practices as believers. This takes us back to our discussion in the beginning of this chapter, of the way that the biblical text can be transformed

---

[24] Ofsted (6 June 2010), *Transforming Religious Education.*
[25] Matt. 12:33.
[26] Matt. 10:10.

and become a living text in community. Clearly, a textbook cannot provide the contextual reading that is found in the Catholic school (or perhaps the non-denominational school would wish to explore with a local Christian community), but it can encourage teachers and students to make these connections to Christian faith and practice, to a deeper understanding of Scripture.

Conclusion

The Bible is a familiar book to many in our contemporary society. You would probably catch the reference (or insult!) if someone said that something (or someone) was as old as Methuselah[27] and you would likely also understand that someone had been betrayed by another who was supposed to be their friend if thirty pieces of silver were mentioned in conversation.[28] Yet, despite this familiarity, it is important as teachers to obtain knowledge of the complexities of Scripture, and to have an attitude of willingness to explore the significance of Scripture in community. In this chapter, we have attempted to introduce Scripture in terms of an overview of its content and the rich material contained within it. It remains the open invitation and task of teaching Scripture to engage meaningfully with this rich material, keeping in mind its significance in shaping communities of believers throughout history and in our own locations today.

Further Reading

Bandstra, Barry L., *Reading the Old Testament: An Introduction to the Hebrew Bible* (2nd edn; Belmont, CA: Wadsworth Publishing Company, 1999).

Brown, Raymond E., *An Introduction to the New Testament* (New York: Doubleday, 1997).

Carr, David M., *An Introduction to the Old Testament: Sacred Texts and Imperial Contexts of the Hebrew Bible* (Oxford: Blackwell, 2010).

Carr, David M. and Conway, Colleen M., *An Introduction to the Bible: Sacred Texts and Imperial Contexts* (Oxford: Blackwell, 2010).

Ehrman, Bart D., *The New Testament: A Historical Introduction to the*

---

[27] Gen. 5.
[28] Matt. 26:15–16.

Early Christian Writings (2nd edn; Oxford: Oxford University Press, 2000).

Gorman, Michael J., *Apostle of the Crucified Lord: A Theological Introduction to Paul and His Letters* (Grand Rapids, MI: Eerdmans, 2004).

—— (ed.), *Scripture: An Ecumenical Introduction to the Bible and Its Interpretation* (Peabody, MA: Hendrickson, 2005).

Riches, John, *The Bible: A Very Short Introduction* (Oxford: Oxford University Press, 2000).

Wenham, David, and Walton, Steve, *Exploring the New Testament, Volume 1: The Gospels and Acts* (London: SPCK, 2001).

Chapter 3

Christology

Philip Tartaglia

Where do we start? What is the question?

Jesus Christ is the centre of the Christian faith. Christology is the
area of systematic or dogmatic theology which considers the
person, activity and significance of Jesus Christ. This chapter will
limit itself to a consideration of the mystery of the personal identity of Jesus of Nazareth, where the term 'mystery' is to be
understood in its Pauline meaning of God's inscrutable design
revealed in the history of salvation which centres on the person we
call Jesus Christ.

In Christian theology, theology is classically understood as 'faith
seeking understanding'. Theology is a rigorous and demanding
intellectual exercise into the faith of the Church. 'Credo ut intel-
ligam', said the great St Augustine of Hippo, 'I believe that I may
understand.'

Students should note that this great saint and theologian took
faith as the starting point of understanding. Far too often nowadays, people make their own understanding the measure of faith,
with rather negative consequences for faith of the Church and
especially for the faith of young people and children.

When I was studying theology, a renowned professor of mine at
the Gregorian University in Rome, Father Maurizio Flick SJ, introduced his course on the Dogma of Original Sin with the following
statement: 'This course is called the Dogma of Original Sin. It is
not the denial of the dogma or the challenging of the dogma or
the doubting of the dogma. It is called the Dogma of Original Sin.'
And then he proceeded to teach a course of the most learned and
meticulous investigation into the theology of Original Sin which
was a model of theological method, namely faith seeking understanding.

So, Christian theology, especially in the Catholic tradition, presupposes a deposit of faith which is rigorously investigated as to its basis in positive theology: Scripture, Tradition, and the Magisterial teaching of the Church. The mystery of faith uncovered in this way is clarified, elucidated and understood anew in speculative theology by analogy with natural realities (the analogy of reason), and by the interconnection of the mysteries of faith themselves (the analogy of faith). Once known for certain, the deposit of faith is not an open question. Everything else is.

Where do we start with Christology? Christology is the systematic study of the Church's faith in Jesus Christ. So a good place to start is with the question, 'Who is Jesus Christ?' In fact Jesus himself asked this very question of Peter the Apostle: 'Who do you say that I am?'[1] And that is the fundamental question of Christology. The student will not get away with giving a detached answer!

A true theology, which is faith seeking understanding, does not allow that. Another kind of enquiry may allow you that luxury, but not theology. In the view of many eminent theologians, such as Hans Urs Von Balthasar, theology involves your mind and your heart, your knowledge and your love. If you try to do theology without faith and prayer, you may well be doing some kind of intellectual investigation into Christianity, but it is not theology in its classic sense. You do theology on your knees or you do a pale reflection of theology.

The answer that Peter is said to have given to Jesus' question was astonishing: 'You are the Christ the Son of the living God.'[2] This answer shaped the faith of the Christian Church. There is a direct line between Peter's profession of faith in Matthew chapter 16 and the doctrine of the Council of Chalcedon (AD 451) which taught that Jesus Christ is true God and true man. And so the fundamental question which Christology investigates and answers is this: How did Jesus of Nazareth come to be recognized and believed in as the Christ, the Son of God, true God and true man?

The Resurrection of Jesus

The resurrection of Jesus is central to Christology. It is central first of all in terms of method. Christology is based mostly on the canonical Gospels and on the other New Testament writings. These are the primary sources of Christology and these are all 'paschal' or

---

[1] Matt. 16:13.
[2] Matt. 16:16.

resurrection documents: they were written after the resurrection and are written not simply as historical sources but as a profession of faith in the crucified and risen Jesus.

There are other sources, both Jewish (the Apocryphal Gospels, Flavius Josephus) and Roman (Tacitus, Suetonius, Pliny the Younger) which attest to the existence of Jesus of Nazareth, to his impact on the events of the day and to his influence on his followers who called him Christ and spoke of him as if he were divine.

Undoubtedly the earliest sources for Christology are the four canonical Gospels and the other writings of the New Testament. These documents are all influenced by the resurrection in that they are written above all to show that Jesus is the Christ, the Son of God, and that salvation comes through faith in him and through following his message. This does not mean that these writings are non-historical. Indeed there is huge historical material in these writings and most of it has been shown to be quite reliable. But what it does mean is that these writings are not a historical biography of Jesus in the modern sense. Their focus was on something else: his identity and meaning for human kind. In that sense, these documents are confessional. They advocate what they believe, and they do so confidently because of the resurrection of Jesus.

This makes the historicity (historical reliability) of the resurrection a key theme in Christology. 'If Christ is not risen from the dead, our faith is in vain', St Paul said memorably.[3] Paraphrasing those words, you might equally say that if Christ is not risen from the dead, Christology would be presenting a totally different picture of Jesus of Nazareth from the one it has traditionally presented and which it still presents in orthodox Christian theology.

If there were no resurrection, there would be no real Christology. At best it would perhaps be a 'Jesus-ology', talking more of a special, enlightened and loving man who was unjustly persecuted by his enemies and who left a legacy of wisdom and good example for his followers. We would almost certainly not be talking about the Jesus Christ, the Son of God and Saviour who was worshipped by the early Christians, in whom they believed as true God and true man, and for whom many of them were prepared to be martyred.

In fact there is good basis for the historicity of the resurrection in the accounts of the resurrection in the four canonical Gospels.[4] Critical study shows that they all speak of the same event but with elements of continuity and discontinuity which would be expected

---

[3]   1 Cor. 15:14.
[4]   Cf. Matt. 28:1–15; Mark 16:1–8; Luke 24:1–12; John 20:1–10.

in the recording of eye-witness accounts. That same event was this: that Jesus who was crucified on Good Friday and who was buried in a tomb had risen from the dead on the third day. When his followers went to complete the burial process after the Sabbath day, they found that the tomb was empty. Despite accusations, they knew that they had not stolen the body and that they were not lying. They remembered that he had spoken about being put to death and rising again on the third day. They reckoned they now knew what he meant. In the days and possibly weeks after the resurrection, some of the apostles and disciples actually declared that they had seen the risen Jesus in his own body: he both looked like himself and yet was a bit different, the same but also transformed. They spoke with him, touched him, and ate with him in scenes reminiscent of normal human and inter-personal activity.[5] They knew they were not creating some kind of ancient literary myth about a god dying and coming back to life. They knew what they witnessed in Jesus was not the same as Lazarus,[6] the son of the widow of Nain[7] or the daughter of Jairus[8] who all came back to this life from the dead, but there was no element of glorification or metamorphosis as there was in Jesus. They concluded that Jesus was risen from the dead in his true body. If they could not say that he was risen in his body, or if his body should have turned up, or ever turns up, claims that Jesus is risen from the dead would have been and would be severely compromised.

An apologetic for the historicity of the resurrection might also point to the amazing growth in a short time of the number of disciples, of the early Christian community and as the phenomenon which Christians understand as the Church. In this development, in a time when communication was primitive, it is scarcely credible that the followers of Jesus of Nazareth could have divinized this man within a short span of time of some twenty years. It is much more credible that they came to the realization that Jesus, risen from the dead, was the Son of God.

In the end, the resurrection, even with so many elements which point to its historical reliability and its reasonableness, is a matter of faith. That the disciples of Jesus believed that Jesus did rise from the dead goes some way to answering the central question of

[5] Cf. Matt. 28:9–20; Luke 24:13–43; John 20:11–29; John 21:1–23; 1 Cor. 15:3–8.
[6] John 11:43–4.
[7] Luke 7:11–17.
[8] Mark 5:21–43.

Christology: how did Jesus of Nazareth come to be acknowledged by his followers as the Christ, the Son of God, true God and true man.

The Virginal Conception of Jesus

The virginal conception of Jesus is a major theme in the teaching of the Church on the personal identity of Jesus of Nazareth, born of Mary. In discussing this subject, an important distinction has traditionally been made. Theology since at least the fourth century has spoken about Mary's virginity before birth (*ante partum*), in birth (*in partu*), and after birth (*post partum*).

Using these categories, the Catholic and Orthodox Churches especially have articulated the doctrine of the perpetual virginity of Mary (*aeiparthenos* = ever virgin) as a matter of faith: Mary was a virgin **before** the birth of Jesus; her virginal integrity was preserved **in** the birth of Jesus; and she remained a virgin **after** the birth of Jesus.

The following observations refer only to the first part of this doctrine, Mary's virginity **before** the birth of Jesus (*ante partum*), the doctrine of the virginal conception of Jesus, summarized in the Nicene Creed as follows:

> We believe in one Lord, Jesus Christ, the only Son of God ... by the power of the Holy Spirit he became incarnate from the Virgin Mary, and was made man.

We might notice in passing that the virginal conception of Jesus is not the same as the 'Immaculate Conception' (of Mary). It is surprising how many seemingly knowledgeable people speak of an 'immaculate conception' of Jesus when they really mean the virginal conception of Jesus. And of course, in the teaching of the Catholic Church, Mary was immaculately conceived but not virginally conceived.

It is important to realize that for the Early Church, this affirmation of the virginal conception of Jesus was not primarily about exalting Mary. In the first place it was about exalting her child, underlining his identity as the Son of God. So this central Christian teaching that Jesus was born of the Virgin Mary was in the first place a Christological doctrine and by implication a teaching about Mary.

In approaching this question of the virginal conception of Jesus, we also need to realise that cultural assumptions bear on this doctrine to a considerable degree. In the past, Christians especially were disposed to accept the idea of a virginal conception: if Jesus worked miracles, then it is hardly surprising that a miracle might accompany his birth. But in the modern era, there is more of an assumption in educated circles and among opinion-formers that God does not intervene in the world. This assumption tends to militate against acceptance of the idea of virginal conception. It is important not to be swayed unduly by either assumption. It is especially important not to be swayed by the default position of the contemporary world that God does not exist or is not active: no one has ever proved that God cannot or does not exist.

Turning to the scriptural sources of Christology, it is clear that the evangelists Matthew and Luke, who composed their Gospels towards the end of the first century of the Christian era, were convinced that Mary, in conceiving Jesus, did not have sexual relations with Joseph, her betrothed. Both these evangelists write as if they are describing facts.[9] Neither knew of the other's account of the matter. A researcher would have to conclude that neither of them was the originator of the story. They were both repeating in different ways a pre-existent tradition. Thus, as far as the evangelists were concerned, they were dealing with non-fiction.

However, the accounts in Matthew and Luke also present some difficulties. The fact that the details of the accounts are unable to be reconciled suggests that their historical reliability is limited. Exegetes also speak of elements of folklore and family memories in the accounts. However, it is unmistakable that both accounts agree on the essential fact of the virginal conception of Jesus, and this points to a pre-existent tradition around which have been built some stories with lesser historical foundation.

There are also some other problems in assessing the accounts which have been handed down in the Gospels according to Matthew and Luke. For instance, St Paul does not say anything about the virginal conception, although it is not known what to make of this silence. He does speak of Jesus as 'born of a woman' (without mentioning Joseph and using a Greek word for 'born' which he does not use of other progenitors) although he also calls Jesus 'seed of David' and 'seed of Abraham'. It may be that Paul thought the doctrine of virginal conception conflicted with his teaching about the pre-existence of Jesus, and it was only in the development of the apostolic tradition in and from the redaction

---

[9] Matt. 1:18–25; Luke 1:26–38.

of the Gospels according to Matthew and Luke's and then of the
Gospel according to John that the two doctrines were seen not to
be mutually exclusive: the pre-existent Son of God took flesh
(human nature) in the womb of the Virgin Mary. The eternal
Word was made flesh in Jesus of Nazareth, child of Mary.

Uniquely, the Gospel according to Mark, the earliest of the four
Gospels, does not introduce Jesus of Nazareth as the son of Joseph
or as the son of the carpenter, but as son of Mary.[10] Does this mean
that Mark knew something of the virginal conception, even if he
does not use this term or language? Again, from a theological
point of view, even if the Gospel according to John does not use
the language of virginal conception, the emphasis with which the
evangelist presents Jesus as the eternal Son and Word of God made
flesh is at least consistent with some knowledge of the virginal
conception.

From the evidence, it does seem possible to conclude that the
fact of the virginal conception may have been known within a
limited circle of the first generation of Christians and that it was
only later, as the apostolic tradition developed, that it became
more widely known in different communities such as the ones for
whom Matthew and Luke were writing.

It has been objected too that the virginal conception is simply a
variant of a common ancient theme: that great figures of antiquity
are honoured by attributing to their birth some marvellous quality,
as a sign that God had chosen them from the beginning. The Bible
itself has examples of this: in the Old Testament God seems to
intervene in the births of Isaac and of Samuel. In the New
Testament, the most famous example is the birth of John the
Baptist. However, these examples are all to do with births subsequent to the normal sexual process of human generation. It is
striking that the virginal conception of Jesus has nothing in
common with these births. The conception of Jesus represents an
absolute novelty is respect of the biblical tradition of special births.

Similarly, the objection has been raised that stories and legends
from outwith Christianity present some parallels with the birth of
Jesus, such as the births of the Emperor Augustus or of the Hindu
deity Vishnu. However, these presumed parallels are based on the
idea of a 'sacred husband' (Gk *ieros gamos*): a divine god in disguise
comes down to earth and impregnates a human woman with his
semen or through penetration. Once again, it has to be emphasized that the virginal conception of Jesus through the Holy Spirit

---

[10] Cf. Mark 6:3; Matt. 13:53; Luke 4:23.

(non-sexual, non-seminal, non-penetrative) in the Gospels of Matthew and Luke is not paralleled satisfactorily by these other examples. In fact, no search for parallels gives a satisfactory answer to the question why Christians came to believe that Jesus had been virginally conceived.

Finally, there is always the accusation that Mary's pregnancy was the result of an unlawful sexual encounter and that Jesus was an illegitimate child. It is clear even from Matthew's account of the conception of Jesus that this accusation was around from the earliest times and he tried to counter it in the way he wrote the story.[11] Over the centuries, this accusation has routinely been made that Jesus was not virginally conceived but illegitimately conceived. There is of course no evidence for this. The evidence all points towards a unique birth rather than an illegitimate one, and one cannot rule out the possibility that a certain disdain and mockery accompanies this allegation.[12] Sometimes a Christian just has to shrug his shoulders!

The *Catechism of the Catholic Church* acknowledges the difficulties that people may have in respect of the virginal conception of Jesus and makes this insightful observation:

> People are sometimes troubled by the silence of St. Mark's Gospel and the New Testament Epistles about Jesus' virginal conception. Some might wonder if we were merely dealing with legends or theological constructs not claiming to be history. To this we must respond: Faith in the virginal conception of Jesus met with the lively opposition, mockery or incomprehension of non-believers, Jews and pagans alike; so it could hardly have been motivated by pagan mythology or by some adaptation to the ideas of the age. The meaning of this event is accessible only to faith, which understands in it the 'connection of these mysteries with one another' in the totality of Christ's mysteries, from his Incarnation to his Passover. St Ignatius of Antioch already bears witness to this connection: 'Mary's virginity and giving birth, and even the Lord's death escaped the notice of the prince of this world: these three mysteries worthy of proclamation were accomplished in God's silence.[13]

Very soon after the writing of the Gospels, the doctrine of the virginal conception of Jesus was widespread in the early Christian Church. At the beginning of the third century around the year AD 215, this doctrine entered the creedal faith of the Church in the

[11] Matt. 1:19–20.
[12] John 8:41.
[13] CCC 498.

Roman Baptismal Symbol which professed faith in Christ Jesus the Son of God who was born 'of the Virgin Mary by the Holy Spirit.'[14]

The massive fact of history is that since the beginning Christians have accepted the virginal conception of Jesus as a mystery of faith. Only since 1800 has there been any doubt or uncertainty. Even these doubts, however, are not sufficiently well-founded to disturb the sense of faith preserved by the Church that Jesus was conceived of the Virgin Mary. This doctrine of the virginal conception, based on the faith of the Scriptures, professed in the creeds, homologated by authentic Christian teaching and professed week in week out by millions of Christians down through the centuries to the present day, provides another dimension of the central enquiry of Christology which investigates why Jesus of Nazareth came to be acknowledged as the Christ, the only Son of God, true God and true man.

The Titles of Jesus

Another important piece of the Christological jigsaw is the way in which Jesus' identity was designated in titles. Joseph Ratzinger as Pope Benedict XVI gives a masterly account of the relevant biblical evidence and scholarship in his monograph *Jesus of Nazareth*. Increasingly three fundamental titles began to emerge: Christ (Messiah); Kyrios (Lord); and Son of God.

The title 'Messiah' (translated into Greek as Christos = the anointed One, or 'the Christ') made little sense outside of Semitic culture. This designation quickly ceased to function as a title and was joined by the name of Jesus: Jesus Christ. What began as an interpretation ended up as a name. What this teaches us is that it was evident to his followers that Jesus' mission and his person were inseparable. It was therefore perfectly natural for his mission to become part of his name.[15]

The title 'Kyrios' (Lord) was a paraphrase of the divine name (YWHW). Its application in the New Testament to Jesus claimed for him a communion of being with God himself and identified him as the living God present among men.

---

[14] 'The Apostolic Tradition of Hippolytus' in J. Neuner and J. Depuis (eds), *The Christian Faith* (Bangalore: Collins, 1983) no. 2, p. 3. Latin original – 'de Spiritu Sancto ex Maria virgine' Denzinger-Schönmetzer (eds), *Enchiridion Symbolorum Definitionum Declarationum* (Herder, 1965), p. 20, 10.

[15] Joseph Ratzinger (Pope Benedict XVI), *Jesus of Nazareth* (New York: Bloomsbury 2007), p. 319.

Similarly the title 'Son of God' connected Jesus with the being of God himself. However, what sort of connection with the being of God this indicated cannot be concluded simply from the title itself. Is Jesus 'son' in some kind of derivative sense, implying a special closeness to God, or does the term 'imply that within God himself there is Father and Son, that the Son is truly equal to God, true God from true God?'[16] After fierce controversy, this question will eventually be answered definitively in the latter sense of full onto-logical divine sonship by the First Council of Nicea (AD 325). But there is further biblical evidence to ponder.

Jesus' own self-designation

(i) Son of Man

What does Jesus call himself? Jesus' title of preference for himself was 'Son of Man'. In Mark's Gospel, for instance, he uses it to speak of himself fully fourteen times. With the exception of the martyrdom of Stephen,[17] which is really a quote from Jesus himself,[18] the title is found only on the lips of Jesus. In later New Testament, the content of the title 'Son of Man' is transferred to the other titles (Christ, Lord, Son of God). According to Pope Benedict XVI, this is a clear finding. Yet, he warns, the debate on this title in modern exegetical study is immense and is a 'graveyard of contradictory hypotheses.'[19]

In the scope of this chapter, we cannot enter into the intricacies of the scholarly debate on the title Son of Man. Suffice it to say that the dominant trend among exegetes is to attribute total historical authenticity only to those uses of the term Son of Man in which Jesus seems to suggest that the Son of Man who will come in glory is someone other than him[20] while attributing to the later traditions those texts which identify Jesus with the mysterious figure of the Son of Man who forgives sins[21] who claims authority over the Sabbath[22] who will come on the clouds of heaven[23] at the right hand of God, and who will suffer and die and rise again.[24]

---

[16] Ibid., p. 320.
[17] Acts 7:56.
[18] Mark 14:62.
[19] Ratzinger, *Jesus of Nazareth*, p. 320.
[20] Luke 12:8; 17:24.
[21] Mark 2:10–1.
[22] Mark 2:27.
[23] Mark 14:62.
[24] Mark 10:32–4.

Pope Benedict XVI's concern about the debate is that in concentrating on which uses of the title can be safely attributed to the historical Jesus, the debate does not begin to explain the radical novelty and powerful impact of the Jesus-event. If the dramatic newness of the person of Jesus does not originate in Jesus himself, the anonymous community has to be credited with 'an astonishing level of theological genius'. To limit Jesus' own understanding of himself in the title Son of Man to a kind of toned-down eschatological expectation of an unidentified future 'Son of Man' (which just means 'man') just does not seem to cut it. The title Son of Man deserves to be interpreted in its totality as coming from Jesus himself: the Son of Man is one person alone and that person is Jesus.[25] Pope Benedict XVI concludes his argument in this way:

> The enigmatic term 'Son of Man' presents us in concentrated form with all that is most original and distinctive about the figure of Jesus, his mission and his being. He comes from God and he is God. But that is what makes him – having assumed human nature – the bringer of true humanity.[26]

(ii) The Son

Son of God

In the language of the Christian faith, the titles 'Son of God' and 'Son' overlap. But they were originally quite distinct. The title 'Son of God' derives from the political theology of the ancient Near East. In Egypt and in Babylon the king was known as the son of God. His ritual accession to the throne was seen as his begetting from God: this was interpreted sometimes as a mysterious origination from God and sometimes as a more reserved juridical relationship.

Israel adopted this concept of Son of God for the king of Israel, but modified it significantly. In the Old Testament, Israel – in the sense of the whole people – was called the Son of God, as also was the king personally who personified the privileged status of Israel. However the idea of begetting is replaced by election: the king is begotten by God in the sense of being chosen. And the king's dominion is not so much a present reality (since Israel was never a great and powerful nation, and was always liable to attack and subjugation) but a promise and a hope for the future.

---

[25] Ratzinger, *Jesus of Nazareth*, p. 320.
[26] Ibid., pp. 333–4.

Christians then were quick to realize that the resurrection of Jesus fulfilled the promise of Psalm 2 in which God addresses King David: 'You are my son, today I have become your father.' Jesus' resurrection is recognized by faith as the long-awaited fulfilment of the 'today' of that psalm: 'God has now appointed his king and has truly given him possession of the peoples of the earth as a heritage.' However, it should be noted that the Christian under-standing of 'Son of God' has now uncoupled itself from the political pre-history of the term, becoming an expression of 'a special oneness with God that is displayed in the cross and resur-rection'.

At the time of Jesus, the great earthly power was the Roman Empire. In that context the political theology of the title Son of God was transferred from the ancient Near East to Rome. At first cautiously adopted by Caesar Augustus, under whose dominion Jesus was born, the title son of God was soon part of a full cult of the Roman Caesars who were regarded as possessing divine sonship. This claim to divine sonship by the Caesars was met in that particular historical moment by the claim that 'The risen Jesus was the true Son of God, the Lord of all the peoples of the earth, to whom alone belongs worship in the unity of the Father, Son and Spirit.'

The insight of Pope Benedict XVI on this is exquisite and deserves to be fully quoted:

> Because of the title 'Son of God' then, the fundamentally a-political Christian faith, which does not demand political power but acknowl-edges the legitimate political authorities (cf. Rom 13:1–7), inevitably collides with the total claim made by the imperial political power. Indeed, it will always come into conflict with totalitarian political regimes and will be driven into the situation of martyrdom – into communion with the Crucified, who reigns solely from the wood of the cross.[27]

Son

The title 'Son' is predominantly found on the lips of Jesus in the Gospels. The decisive testimony is in the Gospel according to John where it is found eighteen times. We must also add the amazing 'Johannine' passages at Matthew 11:25–7 and Luke 10:21–2 which are known as the messianic Hymn of Jubilation. In these texts, this

[27] Ibid., p. 339.

simple title 'Son' finally gives the originally political title 'Son of
God' its definitive Christian significance.

We do not have the space here adequately to analyse all these
texts. Pope Benedict XVI summarizes the scholarly findings of his
own study and of other supremely qualified authors such as
Joachim Jeremias, C. K. Barrett, Rudolf Schnackenburg and others
in the following way:

> The term 'Son' ... gives us a true glimpse into the inner being of
> Jesus – indeed, into the inner being of God himself. Jesus' prayer is
> the true origin of the term 'the Son'. It has no prehistory, just as the
> Son himself is 'new', even though Moses and the Prophets prefigure
> him ... We have to reckon with the originality of Jesus. Only he is
> 'the Son'.[28]

(iii) The 'I am' Sayings

As Pope Benedict explains in his recent book, the 'I am' sayings of
Jesus also tend to support the unique dignity of Jesus as Son of the
Father. These sayings are of two kinds and are to be found predominantly in the Gospel according to John. Jesus sometimes says
abruptly 'I am' or 'I am he'. In seven other usages, Jesus says: I am
the bread of life; the light of the world; the good shepherd; the
door; the resurrection and the life; the way, the truth and the life;
and I am the true vine. The apparent intelligibility of the second
group of sayings makes the first all the more fascinating.

It is now recognized by scripture scholars that the background
for these sayings is to be found in the Old Testament and in
Judaism. The 'I am' sayings of Jesus recall God's self-identification
in Exodus 3:14 and in Isaiah 43:10 where God reveals his name as
I am who I am (YHWH): God without qualification, the one who is
in his utter oneness.

In applying this saying to himself, Jesus is claiming that in him
the mystery of the one God is present: 'The Father and I are one'.[29]
The 'I am' sayings are to be situated completely in the relatedness
of the Father and the Son. 'Before Abraham ever was, I am.'[30]
These sayings denote a fundamental distinction of nature, a totally
unique mode of being which transcends human categories. A
flavour of this is found also in the Synoptic tradition in Mark 6:50:

[28] Ibid., pp. 344–5.
[29] John 10:31.
[30] John 8:58.

'Take heart, it is I ['I am he'].' These are Jesus' words to the disciples after he has calmed the storm. This bears all the hallmarks of
a theophany, a revelation of God, in the encounter with the
mystery of Jesus' divinity.

When the longer sayings are added, 'I am the bread of life' etc.,
the interpretation is unmistakable. All these sayings speak of the
life that Jesus brings to those who believe in him. 'Jesus gives us life
because he gives us God. He can give us God because he himself is
one with God, because he is the Son. He himself is the gift – he is
life.'[31]

The question we first asked was this: how did Jesus of Nazareth
come to be acknowledged as the Son of God, true God and true
man? The titles given to him by others – Christ, Lord, and Son of
God – in part answer that question. But in his own testimony to his
identity three terms have emerged – 'Son of Man', 'Son' (Son of
God) and 'I am He' which both conceal and reveal the mystery of
the person of Jesus of Nazareth as the Son who is one in being with
God the Father. The amazing originality and newness of Jesus'
identity in the New Testament was made fully explicit in the theological and doctrinal tradition of the Church of the early centuries,
not without passing through stages of development and some
fierce debate.

True God and True Man: Teaching of the Early Ecumenical Councils

In our times, people struggle to believe in God and so it has been
the divinity of Jesus which has caused the most difficulty in modern
theological thinking. However, in ancient times people had no
problem believing that Jesus was God. The earliest problems were
with believing that Jesus was human. One such set of ideas, known
as Gnostic Docetism, asserted that Jesus was a divine being but
simply clothed as a man, such that Jesus was only apparently
human. Against this, the apostolic tradition, the Christian faith
insisted on the true incarnation of God's son 'come in the flesh'. It
can be a temptation of very pious people even today to treat Jesus
as if he were God simply clothed with humanity, instead of truly
human.

However, the opposite tendency also appeared at an early stage.
In the third century, a church council at Antioch had to affirm the

---

[31] Ratzinger, *Jesus of Nazareth*, pp. 352–4.

true divinity of Jesus against Paul of Samosata who suggested that Jesus was not Son of God by nature but by adoption. Forms of adoptionism are also very common in contemporary Christology and in the way people commonly think about Jesus. They often think of him as simply a great prophet or a very special man to whom we accord the honorific title of Son of God, but who is not truly God in his being.

A biblical aphorism says that there is nothing new under the sun. This is so true when it comes to distortions of the Christian doctrine about God and about Jesus! Nearly all the so-called heresies of the early centuries return in another form from time to time and most of them can be found today in both academic and popular theology.

The most archetypal early heresy is probably Arianism. Arius, a priest of Alexandria in Egypt, did not deny that Jesus, the Son of God, was divine but presented the identity of the Son of God as a lesser god, a god who was brought into being from things that were not, in something like the same way as the world was brought into being out of nothing, but from a different substance from God. In this understanding of the mystery of the Trinity, Jesus, as Incarnate Son of God, could not be truly God. In the year AD 325, the Council of Nicea confessed that the Son of God is 'begotten, not made, of the same substance [Greek: *homoosious*] (one in being) with the Father'. This word *homoousios* was the only philosophical term incorporated into the Nicene Creed. Its purpose is to safeguard the meaning of the biblical term 'Son'.

As Pope Benedict XVI puts it, the use of this term tells us that when Jesus' witnesses call him 'the Son', this statement is not made in a political or mythological sense – those being the two most obvious interpretations, given the context of the time. Rather it is meant to be understood quite literally: Yes in God himself there is an eternal dialogue between Father and Son, who are both truly one and the same God in the Holy Spirit.[32]

Once again, it is not uncommon nowadays to hear people speak about the Holy Trinity as if the Son and the Holy Spirit are not as truly divine as the Father, so that the Trinity can appear as a hierarchy of divinities. This, of course, leads to tri-theistic and subordinationist understandings of God, so that the whole notion of one God in three divine persons is seriously undermined and is easy to dismiss as a version of historic mythology.

The most famous, or infamous, Christological heresy of the

[32] Ibid., p. 320.

ancient Christian centuries was probably the one which bears the name of Nestorius, the Archbishop of Constantinople. To put at its simplest, Nestorius proposed the idea that there were two persons in Christ, a human person joined to the divine person of the Son of God. This dual identity of Jesus Christ suggests that there were two centres of thinking and acting in Jesus. In response to this rather schizophrenic view of the personal identity of Jesus, the Council of Ephesus of the year AD 431 taught that the eternal Word, 'uniting to himself in his person the flesh animated by a rational soul, became man'.

As the *Catechism of the Catholic Church* explains succinctly, 'Christ's humanity has no other subject than the divine person of the Son of God, who assumed it and made it his own, from his conception.'[33] An important corollary to this teaching was that Mary could be called not just mother of Christ, as Nestorius claimed, but also mother of God (hence her Greek title Theotokos or God-bearer) because the identity of the child to whom she gave birth was that of the Son of God made man. In this respect the following passage from the Council of Ephesus is worth pondering:

> Mary is to be honoured as 'Mother of God', not that the nature of the Word or his divinity received the beginning of its existence from the holy Virgin, but that, since the holy body, animated by a rational soul, which the word of God united to himself according to the hypostasis, was born from her, the Word is said to be born according to the flesh.[34]

The importance of the Nestorian controversy is that the Council of Ephesus established the doctrinal principle that Jesus Christ, both divine and human, is one person with one personal identity, which was that of the Son of God made man. This teaching prepared the way for the culminating moment in the development of the traditional doctrine regarding the identity of Jesus Christ.

The Monophysite (literally, 'one nature') heresy presented the orthodox Christian tradition with the opportunity to compose the classic formulation of Christological doctrine. The Monophysites contended that the human nature of Jesus ceased to exist when it was assumed by the Word of God in the Incarnation. In response, the Council of Chalcedon in the year AD 451 confessed that Jesus was the Incarnate Son of God, true God and true man.

[33] CCC 466.
[34] Ibid.

The shorthand is to say that Jesus is one person (the Incarnate Son) with two natures (human and divine). Because of its monumental importance to Christian faith, it really is worth quoting the appropriate text *in extenso*:

> Following the holy Fathers, we unanimously teach and confess one and the same Son, our Lord Jesus Christ: the same perfect in divinity and perfect in humanity, the same truly God and truly man, composed of rational soul and body; consubstantial with the Father as to his divinity and consubstantial with us as to his humanity; 'like us in all things but sin'. He was begotten from the Father before all ages as to his divinity and in these last days, for us and for our salvation, was born as to his humanity of the virgin Mary, the Mother of God. We confess that one and the same Christ, Lord, and only-begotten Son, is to be acknowledged in two natures without confusion, change, division or separation. The distinction between the natures was never abolished by their union, but rather the character proper to each of the two natures was preserved as they came together in one person (*prosopon*) and one hypostasis.[35]

Following the Council of Chalcedon, later ecumenical Councils worked out the doctrinal logic of the declaration of Chalcedon that Jesus Christ was one person of the Incarnate Son of God with two natures, a human nature and a divine nature.

The Council of Constantinople in AD 553 stressed that Our Lord Jesus Christ is one personal subject so that the divine Son of God made man is the subject of the activities and experiences of the human nature of Jesus.[36] This is important, for it means that when Jesus says, does and feels things as a man in his human nature, the ultimate subject of action is the Son of God. Thus when Jesus suffers and dies, the Son of God truly undergoes the human experiences of suffering and death. This is far from the docetic Christ or monophysite Christ in whom his divinity would protect him against the reality of the human experience.[37] This would not be an incarnation as such. Instead the true doctrine of Christ's identity means that the Son of God truly assumes and experiences the human condition. For that reason, he can be our Saviour. The early Fathers of the Church used to say, 'What is not assumed is not saved.'

---

[35] CCC 467.
[36] CCC 468.
[37] Docetism and Monophysitism were early Christian heresies. Docetism claimed that Jesus only seemed to be human. Monophysitism claimed that Jesus had only one nature – the divine nature.

In fact, interestingly enough, even before the Council of Chalcedon (AD 451) had made its definitive doctrinal determination that Jesus Christ the Lord was one divine person with two natures, that very doctrinal principle had been invoked by Pope Damasus I in his response to Apollonarius of Laodicea. Apollonarius, with his own brand of psychological monophysitism, had sparked off an interesting controversy when he asserted that in Christ the divine Word substituted for the human soul (mind/spirit). In response, Damasus I made it clear in his letter of the year AD 378 to Eastern Church bishops that the eternal Son had also assumed a human rational soul.[38]

The importance of this teaching is that the presence of a human soul in Jesus allows his human knowledge to grow and develop. The fact that the historical Jesus learns things, seems in some things to have no more knowledge than anyone else and is able to grow in wisdom and knowledge, shows that the Incarnation is a true assumption of human nature in which the Son of God has an authentic experience of what it is to know humanly.[39]

At the same time, the union of a human nature with the divine person of the Son of God also means that in his humanity, Jesus knows the mystery of God and intimate communion with his Father.[40] In his human knowledge he also demonstrates a divine insight into the hearts of others. *The Catechism of the Catholic Church* puts it this way:

> By its union to the divine wisdom in the person of the Word Incarnate, Christ enjoyed in his human knowledge the fullness of understanding of the eternal plans he had come to reveal. What he admitted to not knowing in this area, he elsewhere declared himself not sent to reveal.[41]

Again, following the principle of one person and two natures, in AD 681 Constantinople III, the Sixth Ecumenical Council, taught that since Jesus had a human and a divine nature, he also possesses a human and a divine will. In his human will, Jesus humanly assents to what must be done according to what he had willed in his divinity with the Father and the Holy Spirit in the design of salvation.[42]

---

[38] CCC 471–472.
[39] Cf. Mark 13:32; Luke 2:52.
[40] Matt. 11:27.
[41] CCC 474.
[42] CCC 475.

If we were to summarize the doctrinal tradition of the ecumenical councils of the early Christian centuries, we might say that this tradition articulated in universal categories of being the insight of the New Testament that the personal identity of Jesus of Nazareth could not be expressed without giving voice to his uniqueness as Lord, Christ and son of the Father.

In so doing, the early tradition agreed that explanations or formulations of the mystery of the identity of Jesus of Nazareth which short-changed either his oneness of nature with God (divinity) or oneness of nature with us (humanity) had to be rejected. Equally to be rejected was any interpretation which, proposing some kind of unwieldy personal dualism, compromised the oneness of the personal identity of Jesus.

With those parameters, the early ecumenical councils converged towards the Chalcedonian formulation which declared in essence that Jesus was one divine person possessed of an integral human nature and an integral divine nature. This formulation especially protected both the unity of the person of Jesus, the Incarnate Son, and the integrity of his human nature through which Jesus was able to reveal humanly the truth about God and through which he was able to carry out his work of redeeming the human condition from sin and death. In a word, this formulation favours the best account which has been offered to date of holding together the component elements of the mystery of the God-man.

For the Roman Catholic Church, the Orthodox Churches and mainline Protestant Churches, although perhaps with some different emphases, the teaching of early ecumenical councils on the person of Jesus Christ faithfully reflects the teaching of the Sacred Scriptures and remain the touchstone of faith and the measure of the truth of every other attempt to put together a theological understanding of Jesus. There is in truth a direct line from Peter's profession of faith in Jesus as the Son of the living God to the teaching of the early ecumenical councils that Jesus is true God and true man, the one person of the Incarnate Son possessed of a human nature and of a divine nature.

Further Reading

Kasper, Walter, *Jesus the Christ* (New York / London: Burns & Oates/ Paulist, 1977).

Kelly, J. N. D., *Early Christian Doctrines* (London: A&C Black, 1960).

O'Collins, Gerald, *Christology: A biblical, historical and systematic study of Jesus Christ* (Oxford: Oxford University Press, 1995).
Ratzinger, Joseph, *Introduction to Christianity* (San Francisco: Ignatius Press, 1990).

For a good general bibliography for Christology, use the following link: http://camellia.shc.edu/theology/Christology.htm

Chapter 4

Understanding the Church Today

Thomas Kilbride

Introduction

What do you think of when you hear the word 'church'? A land-mark piece of architecture, with spire and stained-glass windows, perhaps? A familiar place in a local area? What do you think of when you hear the phrase 'the Church', or 'the Catholic Church'? Perhaps this phrase conjures up ideas of institutions, hierarchies and mitred clerics. Perhaps an image of St Peter's Basilica in Rome with its famous dome, or a well-known cathedral, comes to mind. Each of these responses would certainly be understandable, and capture something of church, but is there not more? Would you think instinctively about the people you might find inside the church building, or of your own local community or parish, when you hear these terms? This chapter is intended to help us understand what Catholics mean when they think about the Church, and where these ideas come from.

Some Helpful Starting Points

During the 1960s, Bishops from all over the world gathered at the Vatican to reflect on the Church, its mission, and its relationship with the world around it. This gathering, known as the Second Vatican Council (or Vatican II) after much prayer, reflection and debate, came to some important conclusions about how the Church should see itself.[1] Three points are worth mentioning in this respect.

---

[1] One important text, well worth keeping in mind while reading this chapter, is found in the document on the Church, *Lumen Gentium*, 9: 'God wills to save us not as individuals but as a People.'

First, the Church is a religious body consisting of people expressing a relationship with God. While this might be obvious, it is nonetheless worth stating, since it highlights that the Church is not simply a social organization, a political ideology, nor a philanthropic society (no matter how generous its members nor laudable its activities). Rather, at its core is a sense of the sacred and belief in a personal God who wishes to interact with creation and with humanity.

Second, the Church is not a loose association of like-minded individuals who band together for support or to pool resources. Rather, it is first and foremost a group whose bonds make of this group something greater than the sum of its parts. Its members become something new by reason of their togetherness.

Finally, the Church is a group of people who understand themselves to be united by more than simply shared ideas, aspirations or activity. Rather, in light of the first point above, those bonds are forged and strengthened as bonds of common belief, common worship, mutual support and shared hope. In other words, it is a community whose sense of itself transcends national, cultural and linguistic barriers across the world. Moreover, its members also see themselves as bearers of a tradition which extends in history too. Just as any 'People', in an ethnic or political sense, see themselves as bearers of history and tradition, of shared memory and reflection, so the Church understands itself as a community which is shaped by its past, its collective memory, its tradition.

Origins of 'Church'

Before beginning, it is worthwhile pausing to think about language. In English, like other Germanic languages, we use the word 'church' to describe the reality under discussion. This word (like *Kirche* in German, *kirk* in Scots, *kyrkan* in Swedish) derives from the Greek word *kyriakê*, meaning 'of the Lord' (the *Kyrios*), usually from the phrase *kyriakê oikia* or 'House of the Lord'. In languages drawing on Latin, however, the term used comes from the Latin 'ecclesia' (French *église*, Spanish *iglesia*, or Portuguese *igreja*). This too is a word whose origins are Greek: this time *ekklêsia*, from the word meaning 'to call out', 'to summon' or 'to call aside'. This, in fact, draws us into the origins not only of the words, but of the idea of Church, since this Greek word is used even before the time of Jesus, to refer to the assembly of the Jewish People, 'called apart' or 'summoned' to hear God's word and offer worship, as we shall see.

When we use the phrase 'the Church', we know we are using a 'Christian' term. Were we speaking of a different religious tradition, we might speak of 'synagogue', 'mosque' or 'temple'. Nonetheless, it is important to realize that the origins of the term, and the concept it implies, go back long before the time of Jesus and his first followers.

The books referred to by Christians as the Old Testament record the history, reflections, experiences and promptings of a unique, ancient People: the Hebrews or Israelites. Theirs was a religion which worshipped only one God at a time when monotheism was, at best, rare. Moreover, they believed that they had been chosen by this Creator God – whose name was never to be pronounced, but who could be addressed as *Adonai* ('Lord') – to be a people who would reveal and mediate divine power and presence to the rest of the world. God had chosen to enter into a close relationship with them, a covenant, and they in turn were to honour and worship God, and live according to what was revealed to them. These ideas are expressed most fully when the people are freed from slavery in Egypt and are given a revelation through Moses at Mount Sinai:

> You yourselves have seen what I did with the Egyptians, how I carried you on eagles' wings and brought you to myself. From this you know that now, if you obey my voice and hold fast to my covenant, you of all the nations shall be my very own for all the earth is mine. I will count you a kingdom of priests, a consecrated nation.[2]

In later texts, this idea would be summed up in what is often known as the Covenant Formula: 'I will be your God and you will be my people.'[3] In other words, God's plan 'to make ... a people who might acknowledge him and serve him in holiness', as *Lumen Gentium* 9 expresses it, does not begin with the gathering of a community of believers around Jesus, but in the history of the People of the Old Covenant.

In time, the Greek word *ekklêsia* was being used to refer to the People of Israel in ancient texts, particularly among Greek-speaking Jews, who used a version of the Scriptures (commonly known as the 'Septuagint') translated into Greek from Hebrew. There, *ekklêsia* was used to translate the Hebrew word *qahal*, which identifies the people, especially when they gather in assembly for

---

[2] Exod. 19:4–6.
[3] See Lev. 26:12; Jer. 11:4; Ezek. 37:27; Zech. 8:8. Deut. 7:6 (echoed at 14:2) contains a slightly fuller phrase expressing the same idea.

particular reasons. For example, at Nehemiah 8:2, we hear Ezra the Priest reading the Torah to the *qahal*, or assembly of men, women and older children. On occasions it is used of the worshipping assembly, as opposed to the 'people' in general. This is suggested, for instance, in some of the laws regarding those to be excluded from the *qahal*.[4] The *ekklêsia* or *qahal*, then, refers to the people, called out for worship or to express their covenant relationship with God in some way.[5] Thus, it can be seen that the origins of the notion of *ekklêsia* are found in the notion of the covenant people formed by God from the Israelites. But can we justifiably draw the conclusion that the Christian Church has its origins there?

First, it is necessary to note that Jesus in his ministry actively forms a community around himself, a community made up not of blood relatives, but of those who accept his message. Moreover, this group is constituted around a core group of twelve individuals referred to as the 'apostles' who, it is said, are given a share in his own ministry.[6] That there is an echo of the covenant *qahal* here is suggested by the number twelve: Jesus has chosen a number which would represent the twelve patriarchs or twelve tribes of Israel of old. This connection is made explicit in some of the later New Testament texts.[7] In addition, phrases used to describe Israel in the Hebrew Scriptures are soon applied to the community of those who believe in Christ.[8]

That this community will take on the character of the Covenant People is suggested by the use of the Greek word *ekklêsia* at Matthew 16:18. In this passage, Matthew's Gospel expands on the tradition of Peter's profession of faith in Christ in Mark 8:29 by including the famous commission: 'You are Peter, and on this Rock I will build my Church (*ekklêsia*).' That this is the only place in the Gospels where this term is found might suggest the influence of later Christian thought, but the nuance is clear: the community

---

[4] Deut. 23:2–8.

[5] The context of worship can be seen when we remember that the Hebrew name of the biblical book of *Ecclesiastes* is *Qoheleth*, a noun related to the word *qahal*, and a name which is often rendered as 'Preacher' in English. *Qahal, ekklêsia* and their cognates seem to have a notion of a worshipping community intimately involved in their meaning.

[6] Mark 3:13–19.

[7] See Rev. 21:12–14, where the heavenly Jerusalem is presented as having twelve gates, engraved with the names of the twelve tribes of Israel – a vision echoing that of Ezek. 48:31–5 – and twelve foundation stones, engraved with the names of the twelve Apostles.

[8] See 1 Pet. 2:9: 'a chosen race, a royal priesthood, a consecrated nation, a people set apart ...' echoing such texts as Exod. 19:5–6 above, or Isa. 43:21.

formed around adherence to Jesus the Christ takes on the character of the Covenant People of Israel.

Finally, one important aspect of the shift from Israelite covenant
assembly to Christian community can be traced in the early development of the Church as witnessed in the New Testament. Paul,
who took great pride in his Jewish ancestry and tradition, eventually rejected its importance in favour of faith in Jesus the Christ.[9]
Moreover, Paul saw it as his duty to bring that faith to the world,
including the pagan, non-Jewish world. What was given in the first
instance to the Hebrew people, has now been opened to the whole
world through Christ. For Paul, God's promises to the People of
Israel are not revoked. However, the promises were first made to
Abraham – and therefore predate the giving of the Law through
Moses – and foresaw blessing for everyone. Through Jesus, Paul
says, this blessing has now come, and the doors to the Chosen
People have, as it were, been opened, allowing whoever has faith to
enter the Covenant – the new covenant, that is, established
through the cross of Jesus Christ. Using his imagery, the pagans
have been 'grafted on' as new shoots to the old olive tree.Thus, the
Church is, for Paul, the product of reconciliation brought about by
Christ's death, in which all are now part of the covenant, Jew and
Gentile alike.

The Church in the New Testament

If, as has been seen, the New Testament writers establish the continuity of the Old Testament People of Israel and the New
Testament followers of Christ, they also furnish us with some of the
foundational imagery by which the Church understands itself.

People of God

Like the People of Israel, the Church is called to be a 'priestly
people': by virtue of the grace of God given in Baptism, and
through the sacraments, the Church, in its members and as a
whole, mediates grace to the world, intercedes for it before God,
and offers sacrifice in union with Christ, above all in the Eucharist,
but also in the sacrifices offered in daily life.[10]

---

[9] Phil. 3:5–13.
[10] Rom. 12:1.

Secondly, Scripture gives ample witness to the prophetic voice, calling for justice and truth, challenging wrong-doing and offering hope to the afflicted. Christ himself was often thought of as a prophet, since he spoke God's word with authority.[11] The Church is called to be a People taking up this prophetic role in the world, to speak with authority, speaking for justice and offering hope, and give witness to the message of Christ.

Finally, the Church has a role as bearer and herald of the Kingdom of God (Reign of God), understood not as a place or a state of being, but rather as a dynamic action on God's part, present and guiding the Church, the world, and, indeed, the whole of Creation, towards its fulfilment. Although a far greater reality, only fully realized at the end of time, the Church is its herald and sign.[12] Christians may at times take kingdom imagery all too literally, by investing themselves with the trappings of worldly power. The challenge is to recognize – and embody – the kingship of Christ crucified, the one crowned not with gold but with thorns, and demonstrate how true authority is exercised in service.

Body of Christ

Paul, when writing to his communities, returns often to the image of the human body when exploring the nature of the Christian community.[13] In this way, he underlines both the underlying unity of the Christian community, and at the same time acknowledges the differences that exist within it: differences of origin (Jew and Gentile), of role (preachers, teachers, prophets) and of gifts (tongues, interpretation, miracles). Secondly, the image of the Body hints at a necessary ordering of the community and its life, and allows him to say that, while some roles or charisms may be more 'important', all are necessary. Finally, it offers him the possibility of underlining that the Church is no mere public association or political organ: its head is Christ, and all are dependent on and connected to him, looking to him for life. All share equally in the same life-giving force, the Spirit of God, given to each in Baptism.

Christ together with his Church is sometimes referred to as *totus*

---

[11] Mark 1:27; 6:15.

[12] See *Lumen Gentium*, 5: 'She is the seed and the beginning of that kingdom. While she slowly grows to maturity, the Church longs for the completed kingdom.'

[13] In order of complexity of argument, 1 Cor. 12:12–30; Rom. 12:8; Eph. 4:3–13; Col. 1:24. Paul seems to have hit on an image he finds helpful, and returns to it time and time again.

Christus, the whole Christ, Head and Members. Such is the unity between believers and Christ that the two become one new reality.[14] This expresses the profound unity of Christ and the Church: as in a marriage, each party retains its own uniqueness as the one is not dissolved into the other. Such imagery of the Bride of Christ culminates in the Book of Revelation, where the climax of the end-time drama is the marriage of the Lamb (Christ) to his bride, the Church.[15]

Temple of the Spirit

If the Church is the Body of Christ, in union with Christ as its Head, then the life force which flows through its veins is the Holy Spirit. The Spirit distributes those gifts which are necessary for the growth of the Church community. Moreover, the Spirit is the source of unity among believers and enlivens the Church to fulfil its mission in the world. For the New Testament writers, the Church, then, fulfils the role which the Temple in Jerusalem held for the Old Covenant: there God lived among his people; there only those who were truly members of the covenant people could approach the sanctuary, and there they could offer worship and sacrifice. To the New Testament writers, the Church itself, even in its individual members, now fulfils that role:

> By God's grace I succeeded as an architect and laid the foundation on which someone else is doing the building ... Didn't you realise that you were God's temple, and that the Spirit of God was living among you?[16]

By use of the word *naos* in Greek, which refers above all to the inner part of the Temple, the Sanctuary, Paul suggests that the Christian community, because it is imbued with the Spirit of God, shines forth God's glory to the world and guarantees God's presence in the midst of Creation. Through the Church, all people can approach and worship the one, true God. The Church is a building – but not a merely brick-and-mortar building. It is a building constructed of living stones, the believers, all aligned on the one corner-stone, Christ, and bearing the presence of the Spirit of God to the world.

[14] See Eph. 5: 21–33.
[15] Rev. 21:2, 9–10; 22:17.
[16] 1 Cor. 3:10, 16.

Other New Testament Images

The Church is often described as 'the flock', its ministers are often termed 'pastors', and its work 'pastoral'. This is familiar language, even in a post-modern, post-industrial society, but it draws us into the earliest phase of the Church's existence and its agricultural roots. However, there is also a more ancient derivation in Old Testament imagery concerning Israel. For instance, the famous Psalm 22(23) speaks of God as shepherd, while the prophet Ezekiel speaks of Israel as a 'flock', and its rulers as its 'shepherds' in a text in which God announces that he will be a shepherd to his people in substitution for those who have failed to lead and care for them.[17] Like all imagery, there can be shortcomings. Surely no one wants to be thought of as a sheep, which in contemporary imagery might connote stupidity, unreflective obedience, or anonymity within an identikit community? However, at its root lies the image of a God who cares for each one intimately and individually, a God who has entered the world, to offer consolation, direction and life. That the Church might be seen as a 'flock', says more about the 'Shepherd' than the 'sheep'. Other imagery derived from agriculture include the vine-branches in John 15 which mirrors the image of the Body, as Head and Members; the field in 1 Corinthians 3:6–9 in which the Gospel is sown as a seed, and in which the first signs of the growth of the Kingdom can be seen; the olive tree in Romans 11:17–24 which, as we have seen, suggests the union of Gentile and Jew in the one new community, heirs to the promises of old, and bearers of the Spirit of the end-times.

The Church Beyond the New Testament

The imagery and language of the New Testament lays the foundations for the Church's self-understanding, and gives us some clues as to the tensions and dynamics at work in those formative decades. The influx of Gentile converts following the first missionary endeavours provoked much soul-searching, and not a little debate – sometimes heated – about what it meant to follow Jesus of Nazareth, and the status of the Law of Moses, so cherished by many of the Jewish adherents to the new faith. Paul's letter to the Galatians (especially chapter 2) leaves us in no doubt about the tensions and about what was at stake, even if the Acts of the

---

[17] Ezek. 34.

Apostles seems to paint a more harmonious picture (see for example Acts 15, which addresses the same issues). In Paul's mind, the Law's role is now fulfilled, and Gentiles converting to faith in Christ are not bound by its demands. There is a new covenant, sealed in the blood of Christ, which demands love and service; the old covenant in Moses, with its demands in ritual and purity, has been surpassed.

As noted above, tensions with the parent faith seem to have come to something of a head in the aftermath of the destruction of Jerusalem and its Temple system after AD 70, such that, by the turn of the first century, 'Christianity' was a reality more or less clearly delineated from Rabbinic Judaism.[18] Indeed, in keeping with the missionary impetus of the Christian community, the Gospel had reached far into the Roman Empire, as missionaries plied the trade and sailing routes in all directions, into Syria, Egypt, Asia Minor, and Rome itself. It is this last, the Imperial capital, which, claiming to have been visited by the great leader-apostle, Peter, and the missionary-thinker, Paul, becomes a focus for the new *ekklêsia*. Traditions concerning the martyrdom of the two apostles in Rome are ancient, attested already in the second century,[19] and Ignatius of Antioch, as well as naming both Apostles in his letter to the Church at Rome, seems to suggest it has a degree of precedence over other churches.[20] Whatever he intended, it remains clear that, by the early second century, the Church was overwhelmingly an urban reality, found in the major cities and centres of activity, trade and learning of the Roman world (and, traditions claim, beyond). Over the next two centuries, its life would be marked both by growth and conflict, missionary endeavour and persecution.

As the Christian message spread in a Hellenistic (Greek) culture,

[18] As late as AD 50, the distinction between Jews and Christians seems not to be clear, at least in the minds of pagan authorities. Acts 18:2 speaks of an edict of the emperor, Claudius, by which Jews were expelled from Rome. This edict, mentioned by the historian, Suetonius, was decreed around AD 49 or 50. Priscilla and Aquila, who are clearly Christian by this time, have fallen foul of it and end up in Corinth.

[19] Clement of Rome, writing to the Corinthians in the late first century, seems to infer that Peter and Paul were both martyred in Rome (1 Clem. 5). Likewise, Ignatius of Antioch writing to the Roman church cites them together as examples of authority and courage (Ign. Rom. 4).

[20] Ignatius of Antioch addressed his letter to the Roman church to 'the church holding chief place in the territories of the district of Rome'. Debate, however, continues as to whether by 'territories' of Rome he means the whole Empire or simply some of the area and local churches around the city itself.

it encountered religious and philosophical schools which sought to make it their own. Such schools of thought were, for example, docetism (which maintained that Christ only 'seemed' to be human – *dokein* is the Greek word for 'to seem') and various forms of gnosticism (which maintained that the soul ought to transcend the material and the bodily, in search of ever higher realms of knowledge, or *gnôsis*). Such intellectual challenges were met by Christian thinkers and pastors keen to ensure that believers understood and remained faithful to the apostolic witness. Such individuals as Irenaeus, bishop in Lyons, Justin, Origen, Tertullian and Cyprian of Carthage emerge among many others as significant writers and thinkers, eloquently explaining the faith to their contemporaries, while challenging the 'heresies' (meaning the 'groups' or 'sects') which were promoting their own interpretations of the Gospel.

Meanwhile, Churches benefited from the general Roman tolerance of 'foreign' religious beliefs and practices. However, such tolerance really extended only to those who were prepared to maintain the Imperial Cult. Christians were not so inclined. Moreover, their practices often met with hostility: rejecting the imperial gods, they were considered 'godless'; speaking about eating Christ's flesh and drinking his blood, they were accused of cannibalism; refusing to attend local temples – places of social as well as religious interaction – they were considered anti-social and subversive.

Through these centuries, as the Church sought to consolidate its self-understanding and its understanding of the Gospel, it faced periods of often violent persecution by a society which did not understand it, and which found it a threat to the system of the Empire itself. Tertullian would note, however, in his timeless aphorism: 'The blood of martyrs is the seed of Christians.' Christianity may not yet have achieved a majority status in population terms, but its presence would prevail, despite even the bloody persecution of Diocletian in the first decade of the fourth century.

Diocletian's successor, Galerius, issued a decree favouring tolerance for Christians (in AD 311), but events the following year were to prove decisive not only for the Church of that time, but for the subsequent history of the Church as such. In AD 312, Constantine, already ruler of parts of the Western Roman Empire, defeated his great rival, Maxentius, at the battle of the Milvian Bridge on the outskirts of Rome, was said to have been inspired by a vision of the Cross. Constantine granted Christianity equal status with the official state religion, seeing its potential as a unifying force for his empire. Although this idealism would be undermined by divisions within the Church, first caused by the Donatist schism and later by the Arian debates – the first concerning the source of sacramental authority, the latter the nature of Christ himself – nonetheless, Constantine sought to promote the Church as a powerful source of unity. In AD 325 he summoned Church leaders to a gathering at Nicea in Asia Minor to discuss – and resolve – the conflict surrounding understanding of the person of Christ at the heart of the Arian controversy. This gathering in council – the first to be called 'ecumenical', that is, 'world-wide' – would give the Church the Nicene Creed, the core of the Creed still professed by Christians of many denominations today. However, it was a Council summoned and presided over by the secular Emperor. The relationship between Church and State, between Pope and Emperor, between bishop and king, would occupy the energies – and cost the lives – of many over the ensuing millennium and beyond.

What was the internal life of the Church like in these early centuries? From New Testament times, the Church had sought structures of leadership and service. Acts of the Apostles gives a glimpse into the appointment of *diakonoi* ('deacons') who were to assist in the practical, even social, service of the community,[21] while at Ephesus, *presbyteroi* ('presbyters' or 'elders') seem to exercise leadership.[22] Moreover, in the later Pauline letters, we hear of *episkopoi* ('overseers' or 'presiders'), *diakonoi* and *presbyteroi*, all of whom seem to exercise discrete functions in the Church.[23] By the early second century, Ignatius of Antioch writes that these are three kinds of official without which 'no church has any right to the name'.[24]

Can we infer from this that the three-fold structure of 'bishop-priest-deacon' of the Sacrament of Holy Orders already shaped leadership or ministry in the Early Church? Perhaps not, and for two reasons. Firstly, the terms *episkopos* and *presbyteros* often seem to overlap, referring to the same role. In fact, Philippians 1:1 refers to the *episkopoi* and *diakonoi* at Philippi, but makes no mention of the *presbyteroi*. The distinctions between the 'orders' and the precise meaning of the terms seems to have developed only gradually.

---

[21] Acts 6:1–6.
[22] Acts 20:17.
[23] 1 Tim. 3:1–7, 8–13; 5:17–22.
[24] Ignatius of Antioch, *Letter to the Trallians*, 3. In the *Letter to the Ephesians* (4), he writes: 'your justly respected clergy ... are attuned to their *episkopos* like the strings of a harp' while the *Letter to the Magnesians* refers to their *episkopos*, Dama, his two clergy, Bassus and Apollonius and his *diakonos*, Zotion.

Secondly, it is clear from reading the New Testament, at least, that there were other roles and ministries which seem to have been equally important and authoritative: for example, apostles, prophets and teachers are given an order of precedence. Moreover in 1 Timothy, which outlines the requirements and responsibilities of the *episkopoi*, *presbyteroi* and *diakonoi*, we find also the requirements and responsibilities of widows – including instructions on when and how to accept them into this 'office'. In short, it would seem that the Church's earliest period was characterized by variation in what constituted the structures of authority and service, what was considered of most value, and what terminology was to be used.

The Four Marks (Notes) of the Church: One, Holy Catholic and Apostolic

How can the Church be 'one' when there are so many divisions within the Christian family? How can it be 'holy' when its members are sinners, and sometimes far from holy? Are Christians who are not 'Catholic', that is, Roman Catholic, excluded? Such questions vex, but provoke reflection on what each of these 'notes', as they are commonly termed, actually imply, and why they would be contained in the Creed, part of the faith tradition, rather than mere adjectives or ideals.

The Church is 'One'

Acts describes a community 'faithful to the fellowship.'[25] It speaks of a community who pray and act 'united in heart and soul.'[26] As we have seen, however, the Early Church knew factionalism and even among the apostles there were disagreements.[27] What, then, is this 'unity', which is expressed as a statement of faith, yet seems so elusive in practice?

As was seen above, the Church finds an understanding of unity in the image of the 'Body of Christ'. That is, the differences among believers do not contradict the underlying unity in Christ. He is the principle of that unity, while the Spirit guarantees the bonds between believers. In that sense, we believe in one 'Church', even

[25] Acts 2:42.
[26] Acts 4:32.
[27] 1 Cor. 1:11; 3:3.

though there may be many 'churches' because there is one Christ. There cannot be more than one Church, that is, more than one 'People of God', any more than there can be 'two bodies' of Christ. Going further, as God is worshipped in faith as a communion of persons (the Trinity of Father, Son and Holy Spirit), so the Church is formed to be a communion of love. As was noted in our opening principles, the Church is more than simply a human community, but draws its self-understanding from its relationship with and unity in God.

This, in turn, brings us to the profound theological notion of 'communion'. The Church is one as a communion of communities: the many local churches form one Church, greater than the sum of its parts. Indeed, Pope John Paul II has said that the concept of an 'ecclesiology of communion' was the central and fundamental idea of the documents of the Second Vatican Council.'[28] This communion – echoing the term *koinonia* in Greek, translated as 'fellowship' in Acts 2:42 – is real and visible, expressed in activity fostering the common good, in the shared profession of faith and in worship in common prayer. It is seen in the unity of the local church with the See of Rome as its 'mother church', and with the Pope as its chief pastor. Communion is also invisible, however, expressed supremely in the Eucharist which, by no accident, is referred to as the Sacrament of Holy Communion. The believer enters a profound communion with Christ who is received, but also with the whole Church, through the symbolic action of breaking bread and the sharing of the sacramental meal. The Eucharist is the expression, source and impetus to communion, and so is the source, symbol and expression of the Church itself. 'The Church draws her life from the Eucharist,' wrote John Paul II in an encyclical which took that sentiment as its title.[29] 'This truth does not simply express a daily experience of faith, but recapitulates the heart of the mystery of the Church.'

However, the Church is also called to be an instrument and sign of unity in the world.[30] As such, the theology of reconciliation by Christ's Cross becomes fundamental to an understanding of where

[28] Pope John Paul II, *Ecclesia De Eucharistia: Encyclical Letter on the Eucharist and Its Necessity Within the Church* (2003), 34.

[29] Pope John Paul II, *Ecclesia De Eucharistia*, 1. See also Pope Benedict XVI, *Images of Hope: Meditations on Major Feasts* (San Francisco: Ignatius Press, 2006), 33: 'Eucharist is the basic form of the Church. The Church is formed in the Eucharistic assembly .. The Church can remain "one" only from communion with the crucified Christ.'

[30] *Lumen Gentium*, 1.

the Church comes from and why it exists at all: to draw all people into a unity of life and love with God.[31]

How, then do we deal with the reality of division in the Christian body? The *Catechism* suggests: 'Christ always gives his Church the gift of unity, but the Church must always pray and work to maintain, reinforce and perfect the unity that Christ wills for her.'[32] That is, unity, as well as being gifted to the Church by Christ in the Spirit – to make it a community of life and love, a people of shared belief and tradition, a communion of grace with the Trinity, and sign of unity for the world – is also a responsibility and a task for the Church, a precious reality that cannot be taken for granted in the face of human weakness and historical realities. At the Last Supper, Christ prayed for the unity of his followers. This in turn motivates what has sometimes been called the 'ecumenical imperative'. The search for visible unity is as fundamental to the Church's self-understanding as its communion with Christ.[33]

The Church is 'Holy'

As a theologian, Joseph Ratzinger, later Pope Benedict XVI, wrote these challenging words:

> We are tempted to say, if we are honest with ourselves, that the Church is neither holy nor catholic ... and so for many people today the Church has become the main obstacle to belief. They can no longer see in her anything but the human struggle for power, the petty spectacle of those who, with their claim to administer official Christianity, seem to stand most in the way of the true spirit of Christianity ...[34]

This succinctly cuts to the heart of the problem: how can the Church be 'holy' when its members are sinners, and is, at times, tainted by very public and scandalous sin?

As above, however, the first principle in this is the holiness of God and of Christ, who imbues his Church with the Spirit. Holiness is not, in the first instance, a merit of Christians or of the Church, but is a gift of grace, and a statement of belief in Christ.

---

[31] CCC 850.
[32] CCC 820.
[33] Pope John Paul II, *Ut Unum Sint: On Commitment to Ecumenism* (1995), 9.
[34] Joseph Ratzinger, *Introduction to Christianity* (San Francisco: Ignatius Press, 1990) pp. 262–3.

By dint of union with Christ through baptism, the Christian community can be called a 'holy people', and its members 'saints' (see Romans 1:7). However, the *Catechism*, quoting *Lumen Gentium* 48, reminds us that, like its unity, the Church's sanctity is 'real though imperfect' and 'perfect holiness is something yet to be acquired.'[35] The Church has been given all the means necessary to journey towards this holiness (prayer, the sacramental system, Scripture, and the bonds of communion among believers) and its members are invited to use these to grow in holiness. One of the Council's great gifts to the Church was its recognition that the call to holiness is for everyone.[36]

As well as being an instrument through which God's grace sanctifies, the Church is itself a sign, a sacrament of communion with God and of unity among all people. The Church, therefore, sanctifies and points to a sacred reality beyond itself: profound communion with God. Here we meet again the key notion that the Church, like the People of Israel before, must be a sign to the world of the covenant God has made, only now a covenant into which all people are invited. That the Church is 'holy' expresses, then, not the moral character of its members (which would quickly be exposed as a fallacy!) but rather its purpose and the nature of its fundamental relationship with God.[37]

The Church is Catholic

The word 'catholic' often means something narrower than originally intended. Whereas its Greek etymology suggests it refers to the Church as a 'universal' or 'global' community, for all people in all places,[38] it is used most often now to contrast one Church with others ('Catholic' as opposed to 'Orthodox' or 'Reformed'). Indeed, the period of consolidation of doctrine and structure in the early centuries of the Church is sometimes called 'early catholicism', as a time when the Church shifts from being a fluid

---

[35] CCC 825.

[36] See *Lumen Gentium*, 5. Here, as before, we might recall the ideal community of Acts in which believers are faithful to the prayers and the breaking of bread (Acts 2:42).

[37] See again the notion of the 'holy nation' in Exod. 19:5, holy because God is holy (Lev. 20:26).

[38] The term *katholikos* is a compound word formed from the Greek word *holos* meaning 'whole' or 'entire'. It thus suggests a literal meaning such as 'all-encompassing' or 'wholly inclusive' – in other words, 'universal'.

association of missionary communities towards more stable structures of authority, teaching and discipline.[39]

What then does 'catholic' mean, if it is to be more than a statement about one particular Church? First, the Church is 'catholic' because it has been given all the means of salvation and holiness by Christ through the Holy Spirit: sacraments, profession of a complete faith, and an ordered ministry and structure at the service of its mission. Secondly, it is 'catholic' because it has a universal mission, commissioned to make disciples of all the nations as commanded in Matthew 28:19. It is catholic, therefore, since it is international and intergenerational, transcends particular cultures and historical periods, and offers a vision of life and community which can speak to all people in all places. The Pentecost story in Acts 2 offers an exemplar of this: that people from all over the known world could hear the disciples preaching about the marvels of God in their own language.

It is important to note, however, that such 'universality' does not override local experience or culture. The Church exists in historical forms, in a diversity of cultures, and speaks a multitude of languages. Indeed, it could be argued that such diversity actually makes the universality all the more obvious: Catholicity is not uniformity, but a recognition of a common vocation, mission and message, which is the possession of no one group or culture, but which is realized in a diversity of cultures and localities, bound by the communion of holiness and life described above. In fact, the 'multiplicity of local Churches, unified in a common effort, shows all the more resplendently the catholicity of the undivided Church'.[40] That is, the whole is enriched and supported by the unique gifts of each part, as befits the Body of Christ. Perhaps here the imagery of the Church as God's family is illustrative, for as a family comprises different individuals, with unique qualities, roles and relationships, yet living in a common bond which goes beyond mere social convenience, so the Church mirrors this unity-in-diversity.

---

[39] See in this regard Nobert Brox, *History of the Early Church* (London: SCM Press, 1994) p. 77 'Historical theology talks of the rise of early catholicism. The term is a most apt description of the new period which marked the transition from earliest Christianity to the catholic church of the following centuries. However, "early Catholicism" is often meant as a criticism of this development ... The charismatic community, as earliest Christianity understood it, living by the spirit of the gospel and immediately responsible to Christ, is said to have been replaced by an organized church with legal structures of authority and subordination.' Caution must, therefore, be exercised when using this terminology.

[40] *Lumen Gentium*, 23.

Such universality, respectful of local diversity, raises the question of the relationship between Christians and those of other faiths, just as the note on 'unity' raised the question of ecumenical relations among Christians. The Church has a mission to draw all people into unity, but not a mandate to coerce others or to reject everything it finds in other religious traditions. Rather, the Church 'rejects nothing of what is true and holy' in other religions.[41] Hence, the Church has to keep two seeming opposites together: universal mission and respect for the religious experience of others. Catholicity becomes the key to balancing these, however, since it acknowledges that a legitimate diversity can go hand-in-hand with a universal mission. Hospitality, openness and service emerge as key to the Church's catholic identity.

The Church is Apostolic

To some extent, 'apostolicity' resumes what has just been said. That is, since the word 'apostle' comes from the Greek word meaning 'to send out', the terminology itself is rooted in mission: an 'apostle' is an 'emissary', one 'sent out' by another. 'Apostolic' and 'missionary' seem almost synonymous and, as has been seen, mission is fundamental to the Church's self-understanding.

However, use of the term 'apostolic' also connotes a real relationship with those who were first given that title, the group of twelve whom Jesus gathered around himself. Acts records that in choosing a replacement for Judas, the first group were careful to select one who had been 'with [them] the whole time' and who could 'act as a witness to the resurrection' of Jesus.'[42] This seems to have moved Paul to claim apostolic status. True, he may not have been an eye-witness to Jesus' ministry, but 'have I not seen the Lord?'[43] It is because of his unique encounter with the Risen Jesus that Paul claims to be an apostle, sent out to bring the pagan nations to the obedience of faith: no one beyond that first generation could claim that experience.[44] Hence, the Church is 'apostolic' in that it takes as its foundation the preaching of that first group, and both accepts and hands on as reliable their

---

[41] Vatican II, *Declaration on the Relation of the Church to Non-Christian Religions* (*Nostra Aetate*), 2.

[42] Acts 1:21–2.

[43] See also 1 Cor. 15:8–10, where Paul places his vision of the Risen Christ among those of the other Apostles, and then, having humbly suggested he barely deserves the title 'apostle', confidently asserts 'but that is what I am.'

[44] See CCC 860.

testimony. The Church remains faithful to the teaching of the Apostles.

However, the Church and its mission did not end with the death of the last eye-witness. Rather, as can be seen from both the New Testament (for example, the letters of Peter or Paul's letters to Timothy) and from the early post-apostolic writers (such as Clement of Rome, Irenaeus and Ignatius of Antioch), the apostles handed on their authority to others appointed to look after communities they had founded or to which they had preached.[45] This appointment of successors to the apostles affords the Church a sense of continuity with its origins. Hence 'apostolicity' becomes something not only characteristic of the Church in its first phase, but a guarantee of its fidelity to a message handed on from generation to generation. Indeed, the Church 'continues to be taught, sanctified and guided by the apostles until Christ's return, through their successors in pastoral office: the college of bishops, "assisted by priests, in union with the successor of Peter, the Church's supreme pastor"'.[46] In Catholic thought, real communion is possible only where the Christian holds to a unity with this apostolic succession, gathered round the Pope as successor of Peter, appointed by Christ to 'strengthen the brothers'.[47] Just as the ideal community in Acts was formed around Eucharist, prayer, community living and the teaching of the Apostles, so today, the Church only fully exists where there is Eucharist, shared prayer, communion of life and profession of an apostolic faith, in fellowship with the successors of the Apostles.

Nonetheless, 'apostolicity' cannot simply be reduced to the hierarchical arrangement of Church ministry and authority. Rather, the Church is apostolic because, as well as adhering to the deposit of faith handed on from the Apostles, its members take up that deposit and participate in the ongoing mission of spreading the Good News of the in-breaking of the Reign of God to contemporary men and women. This is the 'apostolate' to which the Church is called. In a particular way, the baptized lay faithful are called to carry out this evangelization of culture through witness to faith in the home, the workplace and the public arena. The Church is

---

[45] See Clement's *Letter to the Corinthians*, 42: 'Christ received his commission from God, and the Apostles theirs from Christ ... And as they went through the territories and townships preaching they appointed their first converts – after testing them by the Spirit – to be bishops and deacons for the believers of the future.'.

[46] CCC 857.

[47] Luke 22:33.

apostolic because it continues to do what the apostles did on the
first Pentecost day: it stands up before the world, tells it of God's
saving action in Jesus Christ, and calls it to a new and better way of
living, according to the values of the Kingdom inaugurated by
Jesus. The Church was born on that first Pentecost: it is called to be
a community faithful to its spirit.

Some Concluding Thoughts

The Church is a multi-faceted reality which holds together a variety
of sometimes contrasting characteristics. It is universal, but incarnate in the local. It is holy in its nature, yet made up of sinners. It
is one, in perfect union with Christ as its Head, yet often divided
through human weakness. It transcends history, yet is situated in
history, with all its conditions, careful to pass on from generation
to generation its precious faith. It is a servant to the world, in principle renouncing worldly power, yet it leads and teaches with a
claim to an authority which speaks to all people.

Such a reality transcends social or human associations, even the
most worthy, since it claims that its origins lie in something sacred,
and its ultimate end in that which is not yet fully known. In that lie
its hope and its confidence that, whatever ravages of history, persecution or rejection, the Church will endure because it is united
with its Head, and sustained by the Spirit of God. This not as a
boast or assertion of power, but confident trust in the One who has
formed it to be herald of God's reign and servant of humanity, a
sign and sacrament of the unity which is the Father's will for his
beloved Creation.

Chapter 5

Active Participation in the Liturgy

Leonardo Franchi

Introduction

This chapter begins by looking at the definition of liturgy and identifies the link between the Christian understanding of God as Trinity and the principles underpinning the Church's liturgical worship. Following this, and in order to set the debate in context, the chapter traces in broad strokes the development of the Roman Rite over the centuries with particular emphasis on the active participation of the laity in the Mass. Next there is a potted explanation of the Roman Rite where it is suggested that an appreciation of the structure of the Mass and the Liturgical Year is essential for sound doctrinal formation. Finally, there is a consideration of the wider understanding of liturgy as a catechetical instrument with an explanation of the meaning of selected liturgical symbols.

What is Liturgy?

Liturgy is defined as the public worship of the Church which is separate from, but related to, individual prayer and personal piety.[1] At the heart of Catholic worship is the active participation of the people in the liturgy. Liturgy is the centre and source of all Christian life and a proper understanding of its place in the Christian educational vision is fundamental to the effectiveness of all teaching. This definition is better understood when placed in the wider context of the core doctrines of Christianity.

The story of Christianity is that of a God who acts in human

---

[1] CCC 1069.

history. These acts, or interventions, of God reveal him as an invisible actor who uses signs and symbols to reveal his glory to the human race. All Christians make the extraordinary claim that the divine Person of Jesus Christ is the Son of God and the manifestation of God to the human race. In the divine Person of Jesus Christ, God has revealed himself fully to his people. Despite this intervention in history, our flawed humanity still requires further use of signs and symbols to allow deeper growth in awareness and understanding of the Christian mystery.

Christians read the Old Testament as a gradual unfolding of the love of God for his chosen people, the Jews.[2] The events of Salvation History, beginning with the creation stories, the covenant with Noah and continuing throughout the Old Testament, reveal a God who offers divine blessings to his people who, in return, offer praise and thanksgiving to him in acts of worship. Some examples of this are: the creation poem in Genesis 1 which is described as a liturgical response to the wonders of creation;[3] the references in Genesis 12 to Abraham's building of an altar after his people arrive in the land of Canaan; in Exodus 12 the liberation of Israel from slavery is remembered and celebrated during a ritual meal. These historical events form a patchwork of symbols and signs through which God's saving love is made alive in the present. Similarly, the Passover celebrated by Jewish people today is not understood as solely an historical re-enactment of a past event but as the one Passover of the Lord made present in time.

The same principle of historical remembrance applies to Christian liturgy as Christ's Paschal Mystery – the passion, death, resurrection and ascension of Jesus – is made present for all time through the liturgy. This is a key liturgical principle as the liturgy, the public worship of the Church, is where the Paschal Mystery is proclaimed, celebrated and re-presented for Christians living today.[4]

As the doctrine of the Trinity is the central mystery of Christianity it follows that Christian liturgy is a Trinitarian act of worship in which Catholics pray to the Father, with the Son, in the Spirit.[5] Within this framework, all worship is offered to the Father, the first person of the Trinity and the source of all blessing and faith. The liturgy is where God acts to reveal himself through its

[2]   CCC 54–64.
[3]   CCC 1079.
[4]   CCC 1067.
[5]   CCC 243.

rituals and symbolic language and the fruits of this worship are reflected in the active charity of the baptized. In praying to God the Father, Catholics do so with Jesus, the second person of the Trinity. In the Catholic tradition it is Jesus who celebrates the liturgy through his Body, the Church.[6] This is where the work of salvation is accomplished and the Christian people are strengthened in faith, hope and charity.[7] In understanding the Church as the fruit of the Holy Spirit (see, for example, John 20:19–23) the liturgical rites allow the members of the Church to pray with the assistance of the Holy Spirit. This openness to the Spirit enables the 'pray-er' (person who prays) to participate in the saving work of the Church. Although Catholic Christianity encourages devotion to Mary and the saints, this devotion is always secondary to the worship and adoration which is offered only to God.

However, liturgy is much more than a solemn thanksgiving act which recalls God's saving action in historical events as recorded in the Scriptures. In the liturgy, Catholics believe that they are looking forward to the time when Christ will come again in glory. This eschatological dimension enables the believer to anticipate the heavenly banquet at the end of time, the time when God will reveal his glory to all. Liturgical texts are often helpful aids to study and the Memorial Acclamation 'Christ has died, Christ is risen, Christ will come again' brings together in a neat formula an important aspect of the theology underpinning the Mass.

In summary, a correct understanding of the liturgy is fundamental to Christian life as it allows the believer to encounter the mystery of God as Trinity in its rites. To appreciate how the topic of liturgy can enhance teaching and learning in catechesis and Religious Education it is necessary first to trace some key moments in the historical development of liturgical thinking.

The Development of the Roman Rite

It is not intended in this section to offer a detailed history of liturgical developments through the ages, but a brief historical perspective can shed light on the contemporary issues. The public worship of the Church is intended to sanctify time and remind the believer of his eternal destiny and, furthermore, provides the

---

[6] CCC 1070.
[7] Second Vatican Council, *Sacrosanctum Concilium* (1963).

believer with a succession of celebrations which concretize religious concepts in contemporary culture. This public worship is
centred on the celebration of the Mass and the daily prayer of the
Church, sometimes called the 'Divine Office'. The focus in this
chapter is on the celebration of the Mass.

Jesus Christ was born into a Jewish community and the Gospels
record his full participation in the Jewish liturgical life of the time.[8]
The Last Supper was celebrated as a Passover meal (a principal
feast of Judaism) and the format and prayers of this celebration
would have been familiar to Jesus from his early years. However,
Jesus did something quite remarkable during the Last Supper: he
instituted a new sacrifice which became the heart of the Apostles'
life of faith.[9] He took the existing form of the Jewish Passover
meal and added words which made him – and his impending death
– the centre of the celebration.[10] This was a radical departure from
the accepted meaning at the time of the Passover meal which
focused on the reliving of the Jewish people's liberation from
slavery.[11]

Along with this focus on the centrality of Jesus in the 'new'
Christian celebration, the first Christians initially, and unsurprisingly, maintained continuity with the Jewish liturgical tradition in
which they had grown up and knew well:

> And day by day, attending the temple together and breaking bread
> in their homes they partook of food with glad and generous hearts,
> praising God and having favour with all the people.[12]

In this important passage we see a Christian community which was
rooted liturgically in the Jewish tradition of Psalms recited in the
Temple yet was also participating fully in the new Christian ritual of
'the breaking of the bread', what Catholics today call the Mass. This
historical picture is the core of all future worship patterns and this
celebratory structure has remained remarkably similar throughout
the ages. St Justin Martyr (c.100–165) has bequeathed us a portrait
of the early worship patterns which resembles closely the modern
form of Mass:

---

[8] Mark 14:12–25.
[9] Ibid.
[10] Luke 22:19.
[11] CCC 1341.
[12] Acts 2:46–7.

On the day we call the day of the sun, all who dwell in the city or country gather in the same place. The memoirs of the apostles and the writings of the prophets are read, as much as time permits. When the reader has finished, he who presides over those gathered admonishes and challenges them to imitate these beautiful things. Then we all rise together and offer prayers for ourselves and for all others, wherever they may be, so that we may be found righteous by our life and actions, and faithful to the commandments, so as to obtain eternal salvation. When the prayers are concluded we exchange the kiss. Then someone brings bread and a cup of water and wine mixed together to him who presides over the brethren. He takes them and offers praise and glory to the Father of the universe, through the name of the Son and of the Holy Spirit and for a considerable time he gives thanks (in Greek: *eucharistian*) that we have been judged worthy of these gifts. When he has concluded the prayers and thanksgivings, all present give voice to an acclamation by saying: 'Amen.' When he who presides has given thanks and the people have responded, those whom we call deacons give to those present the 'eucharisted' bread, wine and water and take them to those who are absent.[13]

In reading this passage we can draw parallels with the contemporary form and structure of the Mass. In the fifth century Pope St Gregory the Great (*c.*546–604) consolidated and reformed the liturgy as practised in the city of Rome to ensure that the people of Europe shared in the one Roman Rite. Later, in the aftermath of the Council of Trent (1545–1563), Pope St Pius V (1504–1572) facilitated a renewal of all liturgical texts, including the Roman Missal. By the dawn of the twentieth century, there was renewed theological interest in the trends and movements of early Christianity which revitalized many areas of Church life, including Scripture scholarship, liturgical thinking and catechesis. What is known today as the Liturgical Movement grew from this new scholarship and one of the aims of this Movement was to refocus the Church's worship in the light of the worship patters of early Christianity. Included in this liturgical renewal was the concept of the liturgy as the meeting-point between prayer and dogma where the people both participate in and learn from the liturgy without the distractions of private devotions.[14] Furthermore, it was argued at this time (rightly or wrongly) that the celebration of Mass had

---

[13] This is cited in CCC 1345.
[14] Romano Guardini, *The Spirit of the Liturgy* (New York: Crossroads Publishing Company, 1997), p. 21.

become too 'clerical' and that the full participation of the people in the liturgy was hindered by a perceived over-emphasis on a dry ritualism where the congregation had become passive spectators at an event performed by others on their behalf.[15]

Alongside this new scholarship, the Church's Magisterium sought to revitalize the liturgy in a number of ways and two Popes contributed much to liturgical reform in the early twentieth century. St Pius X (1835–1914) fostered the 'active participation' of the congregation in the context of sacred music in the liturgy.[16] Pius X later reduced the age when children received their First Communion to the 'age of reason' (around seven years of age).[17] Following this, Pope Pius XII (1876–1958) integrated further the principles of the Liturgical Movement into mainstream Catholic worship by advocating that Christian people should 'take part more easily and more fruitfully in the Mass'.[18] By this statement, it is important to note, Pius XII referred especially to praying the responses and singing hymns and liturgical chant.

However, it was the publication of the 1962 Roman Missal which confirmed the next stage of the integration of some of the principles of the Liturgical Movement into the heart of the Church's life. This Missal retained the use of the 'Tridentine' rite – so called as its form was codified by the sixteenth-century Council of Trent – but this Missal was soon placed under further scrutiny with the publication in 1963 of the Second Vatican Council's document on the Liturgy, *Sacrosanctum Concilium* (henceforth SC).

The Second Vatican Council (1962–65) was a major event in the history of the Church in the twentieth century. It produced sixteen major documents on all aspects of Catholic life. SC placed liturgical reform at the heart of the work of the Council. Much of the contemporary debate around liturgy centres on how this document's recommendations are interpreted. SC reiterated the fundamental liturgical principles of the Catholic tradition and followed in the footsteps of Popes Pius X and Pius XII in recommending that the congregation should participate fully and actively in the celebration of the liturgy. SC also engaged with other issues which the early twentieth century Liturgical Movement had fostered: it recommended, for example, that a more flexible approach to the use of the vernacular languages

[15] It is important to stress that this is a very concise picture of what remains a highly nuanced debate.

[16] Pope Pius X, *Tra le Sollecitudini* (1903).

[17] Pope Pius X, *Quam Singulari* (1910).

[18] Pope Pius XII, *Mediator Dei* (1947), 105.

should complement the continued use of Latin in the texts of Mass, especially the readings from Scripture.[19]

In general, SC was a modest reform document which recognized the value of the insights offered by the Liturgical Movement and was hopeful about the prospects for liturgical and Church renewal which it promoted. Reflecting on these issues more broadly, it is not difficult to discern a gradual movement in the twentieth century towards encouraging external participation of the people in the liturgy while reaffirming the value and primacy of internal participation. The assessment of the success, or otherwise, of the Council's intention to revive Catholic liturgical life is for another time. However, the events of the Council set in motion moves towards a revised Roman Missal which appeared in 1969 and is sometimes known today as the Missal of Pope Paul VI.

This Missal did appear more radical in practice than the written intention of the Council. The most obvious changes to the congregation were the increased use of the vernacular languages and the requirement of the priest to say Mass while facing the people, where the existing practice was for priest and people to face East during the Eucharistic Prayer which meant that the priest had his back to the congregation. While some welcomed these changes as the fruit of the Holy Spirit and as signs of a new openness to other Christian traditions, others viewed these developments as a radical break in the Catholic liturgical tradition. This debate continues today.

The publication of the Missal engendered some deeper consideration of key liturgical principles. The ensuing debate centred on whether the revised Missal of Paul VI represented a genuine organic continuity in liturgical tradition or whether they were rooted in a more radical understanding of liturgy based on particular interpretations of the Council. This latter view came increasingly under scrutiny by theologians, among whom was Joseph Ratzinger (1927–), who was elected as Pope Benedict XVI in 2005.

In a number of his theological writings, the then Cardinal Ratzinger had expressed some unease at the evolution of modern liturgical trends. He was concerned about a gradual loss of a sense of the sacred in the liturgical life and what he perceived to be the false understanding of 'active participation' that focused on

---

[19] Second Vatican Council, *Sacrosanctum Consilium* (1963).

specific external liturgical roles for lay people.[20] It was to be expected, therefore, that his Pontificate would usher in some rethinking of liturgical practice.

In 2007, as Pope Benedict XVI, he issued an important document which brought liturgical reform to the heart of his pontificate. *Sacramentum Caritas* encouraged the Christian people to see the Eucharist as the fount of charity towards others and encouraged all to rediscover the beauty and transcendental nature of the Eucharist. This document is worth reading in its entirety as it is a scholarly and pastoral treatise which serves as a contemporary commentary on the Second Vatican Council's liturgical recommendations.

In the same year Pope Benedict XVI issued a letter *Summorum Pontificum* which, in many respects, was more radical than any other liturgical document issued in recent times. Here, the Pope gave all priests the right to celebrate Mass using the 1962 Missal without seeking prior permission from their bishop. In this short document Pope Benedict proposed that the Mass of Paul VI (from the Missal of 1970) be called the 'Ordinary Form of the Roman Rite' and that the older rite be given the title of 'Extraordinary Form of the Roman Rite'. Although the Roman Rite now has two forms of celebration, it is intended that they remain distinct celebrations of the one Eucharistic mystery with the possibility of mutual enrichment. Catholic educators should at least be aware of this important liturgical development and consider ways in which their teaching of liturgy reflects this complementarity.

In summary, liturgical history offers a rich panorama set within the doctrinal framework of the Church. There is no golden age of liturgy to which we must return but each generation receives, conserves and develops this liturgical heritage. While recognising that the Mass is primarily an act of worship of God as Trinity, the Mass also offers possibilities for Christian education and formation through a careful study of its structure, organization and theological underpinning. We will now consider how the structure of the Mass and the Liturgical Year can shape programmes of liturgical catechesis in parishes and schools.

---

[20] See Pope Benedict XVI's Preface in Alcuin Reid, *The Organic Development of the Liturgy* (San Francisco: Ignatius Press, 2005) and Joseph Ratzinger, *The Spirit of the Liturgy* (San Francisco: Ignatius Press, 2000).

The Mass Explained

The Mass is one liturgical act with two connected principal parts: the Liturgy of the Word and the Liturgy of the Eucharist, flanked by the Introductory and Concluding Rites.[21] The reading of Scripture develops and nourishes the faith of the believers leading to the reception of the Eucharist – the highest form of participation in the Mass.[22] This structure of Word-Eucharist reflects the influence of the liturgy of the Old Covenant.[23] The Old Testament readings and Psalms remind contemporary believers of the saving action of God as recorded in the Old Testament. As the first Christians worshipped in the Temple before retiring to private homes for the 'breaking of bread' contemporary Christians listen to the Word of God before participating in the Liturgy of the Eucharist. This unity is rooted in Scripture, both the Old and New Testament, which provides the words and images for the various prayers which make up the Liturgy of the Eucharist.[24]

The fostering of the congregation's 'active participation' in the liturgy remains a key task today as it did in the early 20th century for Popes Pius X and XII. There is a contemporary tendency to define participation in the Mass as solely that which is visible: reading, serving, taking part in the music ministry, to name a few examples. In Catholic schools teachers are often encouraged to prepare liturgies for children and parents often expect, quite understandably, that their child will have a visible part to play in these events. However, recent liturgical thinking has encouraged a more spiritually nuanced definition of participation.[25]

In the liturgy, the active participation of the laity in the Mass is internal, rooted in prayer and achieved principally by belief in the significance of the liturgical signs and symbols leading to active charity in daily life. While reception of Holy Communion at Mass by the majority of the congregation today is the normal practice, this stands in contrast to the early days of the Liturgical Movement when the reception of Holy Communion had to be encouraged as

---

[21] A careful study of CCC 1348–1355 is indispensable for a sound grasp of the theology underpinning the liturgical celebration of the key movements of the Mass. This section is based on, and is an adaptation of, these paragraphs.

[22] Pope Benedict XVI (2007) *Sacramentum Caritatis*, 44.

[23] Acts 2:46–7; CCC 1093.

[24] See CCC 1096 which summarizes the key points of the link between the Jewish and Christian liturgy.

[25] Second Vatican Council, *Sacrosanctum Consilium* (1963).

the most fruitful and intimate way of participating in the sacrifice of the Mass.[26]

In this light of this, the Catholic Church teaches that the liturgy is not enhanced in its nature by the external involvement of any member of the congregation. This, of course, is a cultural challenge to those who understand active pupil participation in education as a leitmotif of the post-modern age. In response to those who would say that the silent and prayerful participation of the laity in the Eucharist is insufficient today, Catholic tradition responds by saying that the liturgy is not the work of the congregation but is the act of God's saving power. At Mass, the grace of the sacrament is not offered in proportion to the take-up of various lay ministries. Hence it is more fitting to focus on the transcendence of the Mass and eschew any 'activist' constructions of liturgical roles.[27]

Faith in the value of the liturgical symbols flows into the practice of the related virtues of hope and charity. Active participation in the Mass, properly understood, demands a life of charity in keeping with the demands of the Gospel. Catholic Christianity stresses the importance of grace in the life of the ordinary believer and this grace fosters a response which is reflected in the good works and holy life of the members of the Church community.[28] In his First Encyclical – *Deus caritas est* Pope Benedict XVI draws out the communal dimension of the Eucharist and remarks, tellingly, that 'Love can be commanded because it has first been given.'[29] He develops this at length in Part II of the Encyclical where he demonstrates how charity is the fruit of liturgical love. Liturgical catechesis is one way of highlighting the connection between prayer and active charity and its importance is highlighted in the *General Directory for Catechesis* (1997) where it is called a fundamental task of catechesis alongside the other classical pillars of catechesis: doctrine, moral life and prayer.[30]

The term 'Liturgical catechesis' is broad enough to include a range of different meanings. Here it refers to the wider understanding of liturgy as a means of formation and to active participation in the liturgy, as defined above, as the ultimate goal

---

[26] Joseph Jungmann, *The Good News Yesterday and Today* (New York: Sadlier Inc, 1962), p. 120.

[27] CCC 1066–1073.

[28] The question of grace is fundamental to Catholic theology. See CCC 1996–2005.

[29] Pope Benedict XVI *Deus Caritas Est*, (2005), no. 14.

[30] Congregation for the Clergy *General Directory for Catechesis* (1997) 85.

of all catechesis. In order to do this, the Church sets out its key beliefs in a chronological time frame know as the Liturgical Year.

We all work in and are familiar with various time frames: the calendar year from January to December; the academic year; the sporting year; the tax year. As God created order from chaos in the creation stories, so the Church orders its worship in this calendar. The Liturgical Year is the Church's way of sanctifying time and of re-presenting the mysteries of God afresh to its people.[31] Indeed it is no less than a classic course on Christian education centred around the twin poles of Christmas and Easter.[32]

The Liturgical Year begins on the First Sunday of Advent and is followed by the season of Christmas which ends on the feast of the Baptism of Jesus. A spell of 'ordinary time' follows before we enter the six weeks of Lent on Ash Wednesday followed immediately by the fifty days of Easter which end on Pentecost Sunday. Ordinary Time is then resumed until Advent comes round again.[33] One way of understanding this interchange of seasons is to regard it as a connected series of feasts and fasts centred on the Risen Jesus.[34]

Feasts

The celebration of Easter is the reference point for all liturgical celebrations. The Easter Triduum – Mass of the Lord's Supper on Holy Thursday Evening, Good Friday's Celebration of the Passion of the Lord and the Mass of the Easter Vigil – is the pinnacle of the Liturgical Year. This ushers in the Octave (period of eight days) of Easter which are then followed by the Easter Season ending with the feast of Pentecost, fifty days after Easter Sunday.

The Feast of Christmas is second in importance to Easter although in the popular mind it seems to be the most important. At Christmas, Christians recall the love of God who 'came down' from heaven and became one of us. This 'incarnation' – the taking of human flesh – distinguishes Christianity from other monotheistic faiths. The time between Christmas Day and 1 January, known as the

---

[31] 'Thus, the liturgical year should be considered as a splendid hymn of praise offered to the heavenly Father by the Christian family through Jesus, their perpetual Mediator' (Pope Pius XII, 1956, 161).

[32] Jungmann, 1962, p. 83.

[33] CCC no. 1168.

[34] 'Hence, the liturgical year, devotedly fostered and accompanied by the Church, is not a cold and lifeless representation of the events of the past, or a simple and bare record of a former age. It is rather Christ Himself who is ever living in His Church' (Pope Pius XII, 1956, 165).

Octave of Christmas, is followed by the Christmas season which ends on the Feast of the Baptism of Jesus, the date of which varies but is usually in early January.

All Sundays are feast days. The Christian Sunday is distinct from the Jewish Sabbath in that Sunday is the day of Resurrection, the weekly commemoration of Easter and the celebration of the new creation (eighth day).[35] The value of Sunday as a day of rest, recreation and prayer shapes the rest of the working week and is integral to a Christian understanding of the relationship between work and family/community life. The word 'holiday' in English comes from 'holy day', feasts days of the Church on which little, or no, work was done.

Fasts

Lent is the major penitential season in the liturgical year. The period of forty days (excluding Sundays) prepares the faithful for the celebration of Easter. This is the period when those who are preparing for Baptism at the Easter Vigil – known as Catechumens – receive their most intense teaching and the whole Church joins with them in prayer. For others, it is a time to practise prayer, fasting and almsgiving, the Church's traditional formula for Lenten practice. Both Ash Wednesday, the first day of Lent, and Good Friday, are days of fasting and abstinence: these are days when Catholics are asked to pray with the body by abstaining from meat and eating only one full meal.

Advent is less penitential that Easter but is still a preparation for a feast. There are two key themes: in the first weeks of Advent the focus is on the Second Coming of Jesus as the end of time. The final week of Advent (from 18 December) changes the focus to preparing to commemorate the first coming of Jesus as recounted in the Gospels of Matthew and Luke.

Every Friday is considered a day of penance in memory of the passion and death of Jesus. This is the day when the Church reminds its people that sadness and pain are not punishments from God but reflect the incompleteness of this life and can be used as a means of sanctification. Some form of voluntary mortification is recommended and indeed, encouraged on this day but it is not mandated what is to be done specifically. (In the recent past, Catholics abstained from meat on a Friday. Perhaps modern Catholics could abstain from alcohol or social networking sites?)

---

[35] CCC 2174.

In addition to the use of the Liturgical Year as a living 'curriculum' for catechesis and Religious Education, liturgical symbols and
Church artefacts have a pedagogical purpose and inform this liturgical curriculum in creative ways. An explanation of some of these
symbols now follows.

Liturgical Symbols and Catechesis

Catholic tradition recognizes the value of all signs and symbols in
the life of the Church. The chapter on Christology emphasized the
centrality to Christian thought of Jesus as God-Man, as opposed to
the Arian notion of Jesus as someone who is less that fully God. In
saying that Jesus is the sacrament (or sign) of God, the Christian
does not lessen His divinity but allows for further reflection on
what is understood by the term 'God Incarnate'.

This reflection on the Incarnation emphasizes the value of the
physical world. Christianity emphasizes and takes delight in the
beauty of the created world and freely endorses the importance
placed by the ancient philosophers on Truth, Beauty and
Goodness. This second element, beauty, is often expressed
through matters liturgical and thus music, architecture and art are
ways in which the Church believes people can absorb the mystery
of faith. In the medieval Church, much emphasis was placed on the
visual as a catechetical tool and, more recently, the Church has
reminded us of how visual elements are integral to the catechesis
of children:

> The liturgy of the Mass contains many visual elements and these
> should be given great prominence with children. This is especially
> true of the particular visual elements in the course of the liturgical
> year, for example, the veneration of the cross, the Easter candle, the
> lights on the feast of the Presentation of the Lord, and the variety of
> colours and liturgical appointments.
>
> In addition to the visual elements that belong to the celebration
> and to the place of celebration, it is appropriate to introduce other
> elements that will permit children to perceive visually the wonderful
> works of God in creation and redemption and thus support their
> prayer. The liturgy should never appear as something dry and
> merely intellectual.[36]

---

[36] Congregation for Catholic Education, *Directory of Children's Masses*, 1973, 35–6.

The church building as the 'House of God' is a sign to the wider community of the divine presence in the world. It is far more than a gathering-place for the assembled community. In its architecture and design, both external and internal, it reveals the greatness and beauty of God and it is important to teach young people how to 'read' a church building and, in so doing, develop an appreciation of the relationship between physical structure and ornamentation and the divine.[37] To illustrate how this can be done, we will take the related examples of the sanctuary and the altar.

- The Sanctuary (from the Latin *sanctus,* meaning holy) is the place where acts of worship are carried out. At the heart of the sanctuary stands the altar. This is where the sacrifice of the Mass takes place and is much more than a common meal table. The sanctuary should, ideally, be visibly elevated from the rest of the church and in some churches is marked out by an altar rail – although this is less common today. This necessary setting apart is not designed to exclude the congregation but to emphasize the need for people to see the liturgy as something elevated, indeed as heaven on earth.

- The Tabernacle is normally, but not always, on the sanctuary and is where the Blessed Sacrament is reserved for the sick and as a focus for prayer. In Catholic teaching, Jesus remains sacramentally present in the Host after the Mass and this *Real Presence* of Jesus is signified by a red sanctuary lamp. Catholics acknowledge this by genuflecting on one knee whenever they pass a tabernacle.

The function and purpose of sacred music in the liturgy provides another context for liturgical catechesis and we have already seen how music was regarded as one of the vehicles for the full participation of the laity in the Mass. Today there is much emphasis placed on hymn singing at Mass but the function of liturgical music goes beyond the traditional use of hymns at certain points in the Mass. The Church has never ceased to renew its emphasis on the necessity of recognizing the value of sacred music, especially Gregorian chant. It often surprises people to find out that the Second Vatican Council recommended that Latin should be retained in the ongoing renewal of the liturgy.[38] Bearing this in mind, we need to consider the relationship between singing hymns

---

[37] Stratford Caldecott, *The Seven Sacraments* (New York: Crossroads Publishing Company, 2009).
[38] SC 114–116.

at particular points of the Mass and the singing of liturgical texts integrated within the Mass. Examples of this latter group are the *Kyrie* and the *Sanctus*. In learning the Greek/Latin versions of these, where appropriate, pupils are encouraged to step beyond the comfort zone of their own experiences and allow themselves to be embraced by Sacred Tradition and begin to glimpse therein the catholicity of the Church.

Concluding Remarks

Liturgy is the public worship of the Trinity. The active participation of the baptized in the liturgical rites – the summit and source of all Christian living – is the goal of all Christian formation and life.[39] For the Catholic educator, this active participation in the liturgy is also at the core of all professional growth and the liturgy, with its cycle of fasts and feasts, underpins the Catholic school's identity as both a pastoral and educational community. The Catholic Church continues to develop its liturgical practices and we are currently witnessing a rediscovery of many liturgical practices which had fallen out of favour in recent years. We know, for example, that Pope Benedict XVI is keen to restore the Church's rich repertoire of liturgical music, especially Gregorian Chant. He has written eloquently in favour of the practice of kneeling for communion. In some places there is a partial return to the ancient practice of the priest facing east during the Eucharistic prayer.[40]

Whatever happens in the years to come, we hope that Catholic educators will continue to find ways in which a profound and rich liturgical understanding can be integrated fully into catechesis in parishes and Religious Education in Catholic schools. This will provide a solid doctrinal and pastoral basis for the mission and identity of the Catholic school in the twenty-first century.

---

[39] SC 10.
[40] Tracy Rowland, *Ratzinger's Faith The Theology of Pope Benedict XVI* (Oxford: Oxford University Press, 2008) pp. 123–43.

Further Reading

Hahn, Scott, *The Lamb's Supper The Mass as Heaven on Earth* (London: Darton Longman Todd, 2003).

Lebon, Jean, *How to Understand the Liturgy* (London: SCM Press Ltd, 1991).

Vitz, Evelyn 'Liturgy as Education in the Middle Ages' in R. Begley and J. Koterski (eds), *Medieval Education* (New York: Fordham University Press, 2005).

Chapter 6

The Sacraments

John Bollan

'A symbol of something sacred, a visible form of invisible grace, having the power of sanctifying.'[1]

Introducing the Sacraments

We navigate our way through life with the help of signs. Even the printed words on this page are themselves part of the complex process of looking, deciphering and attributing meaning which lies at the heart of communication. From the moment we begin to interpret signs – from the pictures above our coat hooks in nursery to the reading of theology books – we are engaged in the work of making sense of our world. The Christian faith is clear about the nature of this reality which surrounds us: we are part of a creation which is 'seen and unseen'. Moreover, this mix of visible and invisible applies to us as well; every human being is a composite, a marriage of matter and spirit in a way which escapes easy definition. It is a truth of faith that there is more to us than meets the eye.

Given our spiritual and physical nature, it is fitting that God chooses to share with us his life (which is spiritual) through channels which are physical, rooted in the world of things. This is what we usually mean by the Sacraments. The pages of the Old Testament are full of stories where God catches the attention of his people through the use of striking signs which advertise his presence or make his purpose clear. Following in this tradition, we see the prophets being inspired to take ordinary things and make them eloquent symbols of a deeper reality. Christians believe that this tradition reaches its high point in the preaching and teaching

---

[1] Council of Trent, Session 13:3.

of Jesus who is 'light from light, true God from true God'. In other words, he is 'the image of the unseen God'[2] and, through him, the mystery 'which has existed from the beginning, which we have heard and seen with our own eyes, which we have looked at and touched with our hands'[3] is revealed to our senses:

> When God takes a symbolic or ritual form and fills it with his own presence, the symbol then becomes an extension of his Incarnation as a man among men.[4]

We can read the Gospels as accounts of Jesus' opening this mystery to the Apostles and 'mere children';[5] his activity of teaching, healing and raising the dead are really signs, rather than mere miracles. Those who see these wonderful things are invited to look beyond the surface to perceive something even more wonderful. After Jesus has taken his leave of the Apostles, part of the mandate of the young Church is to continue this work of making the unseen presence and action of Christ a felt reality. And so the Church herself becomes the Sacrament of Christ;[6] she becomes the agent for Christ's continuing presence as expressed through those sacramental signs which flow from his ministry. Over the course of time, these signs have become embedded in rituals which have a defined shape and whose performance takes on a particular quality. There is an element of doing, of celebrating these sacramental signs. It is a central plank of Catholic sacramental theology that the sacraments are effective in channelling grace simply by virtue of being performed. Beneath the prosaic Latin formula *ex opere operato* ('by the work being carried out') is a belief that Christ is faithful even when the minister conferring the sacrament is not. The grace of the sacrament is objectively present, although the subjective attitude of the person receiving the sacrament can limit its effectiveness.

[2] Col. 1:15.
[3] 1 John 1:1.
[4] Statford Caldecott, *The Seven Sacraments* (New York, Crossroad, 2006), pp. 12–13.
[5] Matt. 11:25.
[6] CCC 1118.

Form and Matter

When we are describing a sacrament, a classic distinction has been made between the sacramental word and the sacramental sign. As we have seen, the celebration of a sacrament involves a precise form of words which cannot be arbitrarily changed: for example, we cannot add or subtract words from the formula accompanying baptism or the words of consecration at the Mass. These words are intrinsic to the sacrament itself and are often referred to as the form of the sacrament.

Along with the 'word element', there is also the 'sign element'. Most sacraments make use of physical things which are given a precise function in the celebration of the sacrament. So, to take the example of the Anointing of the Sick, the sacramental sign resides both in the oil and the action of anointing the sick person. This is what is meant by the matter of the sacrament. In some sacraments both form and matter are essentially words – such as in the confession of sins or the giving of consent in marriage.

Sacraments and the Christian Life-Journey

One other important aspect of the Sacraments is the way in which they map onto the life-journey of the Christian at its crucial moments:

> The seven sacraments touch all the stages and all the important moments of Christian life: they give birth and increase, healing and mission to the Christian's life of faith. There is thus a certain resemblance between the stages of natural life and the stages of the spiritual life.[7]

Sacraments are not, however, merely Christian 'rites of passage': their true focus is not the individual who receives them (at whatever stage) but Christ himself. Each of these signs is intimately connected with the person of Jesus who becomes ever more present in the life of the Christian through the grace of the Sacraments.

So, in summary: the Sacraments are the channels by which God communicates and shares his life with us using visible signs. These signs, which are founded on the ministry of Jesus, are entrusted to the Church to give grace and strength to individual Christians. The

[7] CCC 1210.

gift of his life which God shares with us, usually referred to as grace, makes us grow in holiness. Through these sacramental actions 'mundane realities are permeated by grace and become conductors of God's life and love'.[8]

The Sacraments of Initiation: Baptism, Confirmation and Eucharist

We have already used the word 'mystery' in the context of the Sacraments. If we look back two thousand years to the beginning of the Christian era, we see that many 'pagan' religions were essentially mystery cults whose members had to be initiated into the worship of the god (or goddess) through secret ceremonies. The Early Church grew up in this environment and, in order to make sense of itself to the outside world, borrowed this language of mystery and initiation. A crucial distinction for the Christian community was that the mystery they were entering was not an escape from the world but the immersion in a new life which transformed and redeemed it.

Baptism

The use of the word 'immersion' is a deliberate one: the first – and key – sacrament involves the symbolic immersion of the Christian into the death and resurrection of Christ. Although the word itself implies 'a going down' (the Greek *baptizein* means 'to plunge'), for St Paul it implied a going into the tomb with Christ.[9] The power of the resurrection is the energy that fuels the life of the Christian which is, by its very definition, a sacramental life.

Early Christians preserved this close link with the idea of resurrection by celebrating the sacrament of baptism at Easter; the form of the rite echoed the practice of 'new baptism' as performed by John the Baptist in the waters of the Jordan. Candidates for baptism (catechumens) were literally immersed in the waters of the font to underscore the new life into which they emerged reborn. However fleetingly, the new Christian was plunged into a realm which could not sustain life before being lifted up into the realm of light and air. Just as the water is symbolic of cleansing

---

[8] John Bollan, *The Light of His Face* (Dublin: Veritas, 2007), p. 90.
[9] Rom. 6:3–5.

from the dirt and wounds of the old life, it is also a powerful symbol of the old life itself: one which inevitably leads to death.

Death, understood in spiritual terms, is the result of sin and sin is a rejection of God's love and grace. All forms of sin spread from one root: the 'original sin' which dates from the first pages of the human story recorded in Genesis. According to the biblical account, this most ancient sin consists in a failure to trust God and respect the boundaries that have been set for our wellbeing and flourishing. By falling for a lie about God, the woman is quickly seduced into a false understanding of who she is – both in relation to God and the man – and soon the relationship between all three begins to unravel. Each of us is born into a world which bears the scars of this original sin; everyone is 'damaged in relationships' as a result of this wound in our nature.[10] The chief effect of baptism is the cleansing of this 'stain' on our character. Without this healing, we remain compromised in our ability to form relationships with others based on true freedom and generosity. That is why baptism is regarded as essential to our salvation: only God can do this for us. We rely on his love and goodness to make us 'whole' again. It is important that we understand this notion of original sin properly: if we are not careful, we might end up with the notion of an angry God who excludes us from his love on account of a sin for which we have no personal responsibility. To think that would be to fall for another 'lie' about God, as devastating at the first.

We believe that Jesus died on the Cross to break the stranglehold of sin and death:

> His self-sacrifice is uniquely effective because it is done with the love of which only God is capable. Love itself cancels out all the suicidal self-love of the human race and inaugurates a fresh beginning, a new relationship between the Creator and His creatures.[11]

The water and blood which flow from the pierced side of Jesus on the Cross[12] are 'read' as symbols of the new life of the sacraments, especially Baptism and Eucharist. Thus the sacraments radiate from the heart of the Paschal (Easter) mystery of the passion, death and resurrection of Christ.

Although the Catholic Church still cherishes baptism as the Easter sacrament par excellence, the current form of the baptismal

[10] Cf. Joseph Ratzinger, *In the Beginning: A Catholic Understanding of Creation and the Fall* (London, Continuum, 2005), p. 73.
[11] Ian Ker, *Mere Catholicism* (Steubenville, Emmaus Road, 2006) p. 45.
[12] John 19:34.

celebration extends the symbolism of the paschal season through-out the liturgical year. The basic symbol of the sacrament is still water, although the widespread practice of infant baptism means that immersion has been largely replaced with the less traumatic pouring of water over the child's head. A new identity is conferred on the Christian and this is emphasized in the gesture of anoint-ing. Strictly speaking a preparatory ritual which may precede the rest of the ceremony, the candidate is first anointed with the oil of Catechumens. This is meant to mark the transition from the dark-ened, 'unenlightened' world into the world that has been redeemed by Christ. The knowledge associated with this enlight-enment is briefly summarized in the words of the Creed, which the candidate (or the parents and godparents) is invited to affirm. After the ritual cleansing in the waters of the font, the newly-baptised's identity as 'another Christ' is sealed in the anointing with holy Chrism. It is this fragrant oil, the most precious oil used by the Church, which is a feature of those sacraments which confer a permanent character on the Christian: baptism, confirmation and Holy Orders. The paschal candle also features prominently in the ceremony, symbolizing the light and life of Christ which is passed on to the new Christian in the form of the individual baptismal candle. Once again, the link is made between the rituals of the Easter Vigil and its 'replay' in the baptismal liturgy.

Overall, the celebration of baptism is a privileged teaching moment for the Christian community as it gathers to welcome new members into the Church. Not only are the symbols eloquent in themselves, but the structure of the rite allows the celebrant to offer something of a catechetical commentary – provided that this commentary complements the symbols rather than suffocating them with a surfeit of words. The same would be true in a class-room setting.

Baptism can be administered by anyone – even an unbaptised person – provided that they share the same intention as the Church. In normal circumstances, however, baptism is celebrated by a bishop, priest or deacon.

Confirmation

Basically put, confirmation is the sacrament which completes the work of baptism. Indeed, it is so closely associated with baptism that it is sometimes a struggle to distinguish them; in the Rite of Christian Initiation of Adults (RCIA) and in infant baptism in the Eastern Churches, both sacraments are conferred at the same liturgy. Perhaps the best way to approach confirmation is to see it as the sacrament which gives the Christian, who has already been 'claimed for Christ' in baptism, the necessary grace to live a life of courageous witness and faithful service in the world. In other words, the Holy Spirit is called down to strengthen (con-firm) the candidate's living out of the baptismal commitment to walk always as 'a child of the light.' For this reason, the Profession of Faith is renewed and the child's baptismal candle is pressed into fresh service to 'reignite' the grace of baptism with the sevenfold gift of the Holy Spirit. This individual 'tongue of fire' also evokes the descent of the Spirit on the Apostles in the upper room at Pentecost. In confirmation a successor of the Apostles calls down this 'fire of love' on the Church today.

The bishop, who is the usual minister of the sacrament, prays for the candidate(s) in these words:

> All-powerful God, Father of our Lord Jesus Christ,
> by water and the Holy Spirit
> you freed your sons and daughters from sin
> and gave them new life.
> Send your Holy Spirit upon them
> to be their Helper and Guide.
> Give them the spirit of Wisdom and Understanding,
> the spirit of Right Judgment and Courage,
> the spirit of Knowledge and Reverence.
> Fill them with the spirit of Wonder and Awe in your presence.

These seven gifts, which often go by subtly (and sometimes confusingly) different names, are all dimensions of the Christian character. Essentially – to use the language of educational theory – they address the fields of cognition and performance. In order to act properly in the world, we must be able to 'read' it; these spiritual faculties impress upon us the need to go deeper and further in our relationships. This requires wisdom and courage, as well as inviting an attitude of reverence and so on.

The key moment of the celebration comes with the anointing of the candidate with the oil of Chrism – indeed in the Eastern Rite churches it is the oil which gives its name to the sacrament: *chrismation*.[13] Oil has been used for millennia in the conferring of special rank or a new identity: it has precisely this function in baptism. Here too, in Confirmation, it seals that new identity with

---

[13] Cf. Scott Hahn, *Swear to God: The Promise and Power of the Sacraments* (London: Darton, Longman and Todd, 2004), p. 45.

a permanent character. In many (but not all countries) this element of taking on another layer of identity is made more obvious by the adoption of a 'confirmation name'. As a result, a popular feature of sacramental preparation among school-age children is the carrying out of a research project into the life of their 'confirmation saint'. This is always worthwhile, provided that the candidate is aware that they are called to be ever more Christ-like and that it is by following the example of their patron that they can attain this goal.

Alongside the completion of baptism is the equally important dimension of mission. Every gift is given with a purpose; the gifts of the Holy Spirit confer a mandate 'vis-à-vis the mission, worship and social action of the Church'.[14] Every confirmed Christian is called to be committed to the life of the Church in all its dimensions.

Eucharist

The purpose of sacramental initiation is to become part of Christ and to share more fully in God's life. An essential feature of this process is to be received by the Body of Christ (the Church) through the act of receiving the Body of Christ (the sacrament of the Holy Eucharist). One becomes a full member of the Church by entering into full communion with it. That word 'communion', which is often interchangeable with 'Eucharist', is more accurately the description of a state we enter rather than something which is received by us. In the same way, the word Eucharist itself is derived from an action – literally 'thanksgiving' – rather than a thing.

Once again, the Early Church regarded the celebration of the Eucharist as the definitive moment in a triptych of sacramental scenes: from the Jordan to the Upper Room where both the Eucharist was instituted at the Last Supper and the Church was born at Pentecost. Although all three were compressed into the Easter liturgy, special prominence has always been given to the moment where the Church returns to her origins in the Paschal Mystery. Over the centuries, the celebration of this particular sacrament has become the principal liturgy of the Church and 'the Mass' is regarded as 'the source and summit of the Christian life'.[15]

Although it is meant to be sacrament which creates the unity of the Church, it is, unfortunately, the point from which the fault-

---

[14] Aidan Nichols, *Epiphany: A Theological Introduction to Catholicism* (Collegeville: Michael Glazer, 1996), p. 290.
[15] Vatican Council II, *Lumen Gentium*, 11.

lines of Christian disunity radiate. Different interpretations of what
the Eucharist means have led to historical divisions in the Body of
Christ. For Catholics, the celebration of the Eucharist is an event
which transcends time; in this privileged moment we see the sacrifice of Jesus made present in our midst. Just as he offered himself
at the Last Supper and on the Cross, so that act of sacrifice is
renewed for us 'and for many for the forgiveness of sins'. The
Church teaches that, from the moment of consecration onwards,
the bread and wine undergo a change in their substance to
become the body and blood of Christ. Although nothing changes
about the physical properties of the bread and wine, what they are
in themselves (the 'breadness' and 'wineness' of these elements)
does undergo a transformation 'because something can only really
be one thing at a time'.[16] The technical term for this change is
transubstantiation; much of the theology of the Eucharist derives
from an attempt to explain how such a process works – especially
in the face of theological objectors who have dismissed this idea as
crude nonsense. While this is an understandable objective for
theology, there is always a risk that too much explanation of the
Eucharist actually ends up weakening it. As Jesus breaks the bread
and passes the cup to his disciples, he does not tell them in what
way this is his body and blood; rather he emphasizes what it is for
– the 'why' rather than the 'how'.

What is most important for the Catholic is the belief that
worthily receiving the Eucharist gives real nourishment to the soul.
Coupled with this is the conviction that it is in the Eucharist that
Jesus most clearly fulfils his promise to be with us 'to the end of
days'. Jesus is truly and substantially present in the Eucharist or, in
a phrase that was once better known than it is today, really present
in his 'body and blood, soul and divinity'. This presence is an
enduring one: after the celebration of the Eucharist, consecrated
hosts are reserved in the Tabernacle as a focus for prayer and
adoration. Catholic churches are usually distinguished by the
prominence they give to the Blessed Sacrament (as the reserved
sacrament is called): the Tabernacle is usually at the heart of the
sanctuary, marked by the ever-burning lamp.

So the Eucharist operates at different levels: it is a sacrament
which is received (perhaps on a daily basis), celebrated in a specific
liturgical context (the Mass) but which allows for ongoing worship
and prayer (through Eucharistic devotion). By the same token, the

---

[16] Francis Selman, *The Sacraments and the Mystery of Christ* (Oxford and
Birmingham: Family Publications and Maryvale Institute, 2009) p. 122.

act of receiving Holy Communion is not just a simple act of saying 'Amen' or 'yes' to the gift of Christ's body and blood which is offered to us in the Eucharist. By saying 'Amen' we are also affirming our communion in faith with the rest of the Church at local and universal levels. That is why sharing in the Eucharist is the clearest way of showing our unity in belief and why we are unable to share it with those who do not hold that same faith.

Since the Eucharist is understood, theologically at least, as the step which completes Christian initiation, there is a sense in which baptism and confirmation are directed towards it. Baptism is celebrated as a pledge of new life in Christ which must be nurtured through the Eucharist which is 'real food and real drink'.[17] The gifts of the Holy Spirit are brought to bear in the living of a life which is 'Eucharistic' in its shape: modelled on Christ's offering of himself, gifted with spiritual wisdom and understanding, marked with a sense of wonder and reverence for the things of God. Among the challenges of sacramental preparation is the development of a vocabulary which is both accessible to fairly young children but which still kindles a spirit of reverence; all too often the word 'special' becomes the default terminology for all things Eucharistic. There is also a balance to be struck in the proper emphasis placed on 'First Holy Communion' whilst ensuring that subsequent 'communions' are recognized as being no less wonderful. Teachers also need to be aware that, for all its importance, receiving communion is not the most important part of the Mass: it is the consecration in the Eucharistic Prayer which is the core of the celebration.[18]

From its very beginnings, the Eucharist has been the celebration of the visible communion of the local Church with its bishop. With the expansion of the Christian community, bishops delegated their role as presider at the Eucharistic liturgy to presbyters (priests) who did so 'in the person of Christ' and 'in the name of the Bishop'. The proper ministers of the Eucharist are, therefore, the bishop or a priest.

---

[17] John 6:55.
[18] Cf. Kenan Osborne, *Sacramental Guidelines: A Companion to the New Catechism for Religious Educators* (New York: Paulist Press, 1995) p. 75; CCC 1352.

The Sacraments of Healing: Penance and Anointing of the Sick

While the Sacraments make us aware of the beauty of the world, they also recognize its fragility. We, as part of this created order, are also vulnerable: we are susceptible to 'wounds', both spiritual and physical.

We have already encountered sin and the role of baptism as the root sacrament of healing; but once the wound of original sin has been addressed, our ability to resist the temptations of selfishness is still compromised. Like St Paul, we are often frustrated by our inability to act upon our good intentions and the ease with which we slide back into lazy, sinful routines:

> I can will what is right, but I cannot do it. The good thing I want to do, I never do; the evil thing which I do not want – that is what I do.[19]

Paul, like many great saints, found his 'alter-ego' as a sinner to be one of the most troubling mysteries of all. Each of us has to deal with the *mysterium iniquitatis* – the mystery of sin and injustice – around us and within us.

> Sin is an offence against reason, truth, and right conscience; it is failure in genuine love for God and neighbour caused by a perverse attachment to certain goods. It wounds the nature of man and injures human solidarity. It has been defined as 'an utterance, a deed, or a desire contrary to the eternal law'.[20]

The Catechism definition leads us towards an understanding of sin as an action which violates 'reason, truth and right conscience': we go against our better nature when we sin. Moreover, 'it wounds the nature of man and injures human solidarity'. The language of the Catechism is one of harm inflicted upon oneself and one's neighbour; it is important to recognize the social dimension both of sin and the sacrament which brings forgiveness and healing.

Penance

The sacrament of penance (also known by the action associated with it, confession, or its result, reconciliation) always has a social

[19] Rom. 7:18–19.
[20] CCC 1849.

dimension. Although it is usually celebrated in a private encounter between the penitent and the minister of the sacrament, it is always an action of Christ and the Church. The minister, usually a priest, will act in the person of Christ (*in persona Christi*) but is also exercising that ministry in the name of the Church. In this way he is representing 'the other', the community which is wounded by sin. The sacrament is part of that ministry of 'binding and loosing' entrusted to the Apostles by Christ.[21] In the early centuries of the Church's life, baptism was the sacrament of reconciliation: all past sins were washed away in the 'fountain of rebirth'. It was only over time that the very real problem of what do to about sins committed after baptism came to prominence. It was by returning to the Gospels that the Church Fathers found both the justification for and the outlines of the Sacrament which was to emerge. The shape of the sacrament as we know it today bears the imprint of Eastern and Western Christianity.

Like all sacraments, penance is embedded in a ritual form; unlike other sacraments, there is no obvious 'matter'. The closest we might come to the raw substance of this sacrament is what Psalm 51 calls 'a humbled, contrite heart'. It is this sense of knowing what we have done wrong and feeling sorry for it which gives the impetus to our desire to be reconciled with God and the Church. A necessary preparation for the sacrament is the examination of conscience; this is the process whereby we sift through our thoughts, words, deeds and omissions in order to identify where we have fallen short of the standards of Christian life as enshrined in the Gospel. The Ten Commandments also offer a helpful framework for this process, but the subtleties of sin mean that sometimes we need to go beyond the words of the Commandments to gain access to their meaning in a contemporary context.

Ideally the sacrament, even when celebrated individually, should involve some reflection on Scripture. The Word of God is meant to illuminate the words which pass between the parties to this sacred conversation. It is sad – and damaging – when this conversation deteriorates into a perfunctory recitation of sins or, worse still, an interrogation. Although the rite of penance requires us to be specific in acknowledging the nature and frequency of our sins, this has nothing to do with humiliating ourselves. On the contrary, the ability to be honest with God and ourselves is a sign that we are able to take responsibility for our lives and take back control of them.

---

[21] Matt. 18:18.

While the sacrament takes place in a well-defined context – and indeed under an unbreakable seal of confidentiality – there is a sense in which it is open-ended. The minister (a bishop or priest) may offer some advice or direction for the future and certainly encouragement to persevere in love. The penance which is given is, strictly speaking, imposed but is rather more helpfully conceived as a medicine which is prescribed. It is by carrying out this action (either through prayer or a work of service or reparation) that we help ourselves 'get better'. We 'do' penance in order to restore the lost balance in our lives and to (at least) begin the healing process. Like all sacraments, we are sent out from confession with a mission: to sin no more and witness to the power of God's love.

As always, the best summary of the sacrament of Penance is given in the liturgical formula which crowns it, the Prayer of Absolution:

> God, the Father of mercies,
> through the death and resurrection of his Son
> has reconciled the world to himself
> and sent the Holy Spirit among us
> for the forgiveness of sins;
> Through the ministry of the Church
> may God give you pardon and peace,
> and I absolve you from your sins in the name of the Father,
> and of the Son, +
> and of the Holy Spirit.

This prayer which literally loosens the penitent from the bonds of sin and guilt draws us back to the source of the Sacrament. Once again we are reminded that is the Paschal Mystery of Christ's death and resurrection which ignites the Sacraments. His saving death has brought about the reconciliation between God and humanity, and between peoples: 'For it is he who is our peace. Through his death he made both groups one by tearing down the wall of hostility that divided them'.[22] In breathing out the Holy Spirit on the Apostles,[23] the risen Jesus gave them the explicit power to forgive sins; this same power is given to the Church in its ongoing ministry of reconciliation. It is in his name that absolution is pronounced.

The last word – or words – on this sacrament should be given to its effect in our lives: pardon and peace. We are acutely aware of

[22] Eph. 2:14.
[23] John 20:22.

how 'wrong' it feels when we are conscious of betraying another person or indeed going against our better nature by deliberately choosing something that is harmful to us. God is also wounded by these actions and it is really his voice which calls us back to wholeness. Like the father of the lost son,[24] God is actively watching for us to turn back to his mercy. It is his will, striking a chord in our deepest selves, that we might come to our senses and be led by our hunger for forgiveness to seek his merciful embrace. Pardon brings peace. 'Peace' is synonymous with that restored relationship with the Father and our brothers and sisters in Christ: to find that peace is to be restored to the Father and our true selves.

Anointing of the Sick

If a sense of peace accompanies spiritual healing, then we should be aware of the various kinds of dis-ease which can afflict both body and soul.

> Illness and suffering have always been among the gravest problems confronted in human life. In illness, man experiences his powerlessness, his limitations, and his finitude. Every illness can make us glimpse death.
>
> Illness can lead to anguish, self-absorption, sometimes even despair and revolt against God. It can also make a person more mature, helping him discern in his life what is not essential so that he can turn toward that which is. Very often illness provokes a search for God and a return to him.[25]

With this in mind, 'the sacrament of the sick' addresses the radical unity of the human person and the very spiritual challenges which physical illness can bring. In Christ's ministry we detect a strong connection between the healing of the body and the cleansing of the soul. The widespread belief in his day was that many physical conditions were signs – or punishments – for sin. When the disciples ask Jesus about the blind man and whether it was his own sin or that of his parents which caused him to be born without sight,[26] such a question was not unreasonable by the standards of the day. Although he distances himself from such a mindset, Jesus is nevertheless acutely aware of the connection between the life of the body and the spirit. Moreover, while we see instances of his healing

[24] Luke 15:11–31.
[25] CCC 1500–1501.
[26] John 9:2.

people by a 'word of power', there are other times when Jesus is keen to touch the sick person. Here again Jesus challenges the established practices of his time: fear of contagion and the ritual taboos surrounding many physical conditions forced many sick people to live on or beyond the margins of normal, healthy society.

The Anointing of the Sick is the sacrament in which the healing touch of Christ is conferred upon those who are most in need of healing. Since the liturgical reforms initiated by the Second Vatican Council, the Church has carried out its own reassessment of this sacrament. Until these reforms were set in motion, the Anointing of the Sick had been regarded as the last sacrament, sending the soul on its final journey 'fortified by the rites of Holy Mother Church'. The standard nomenclature – Extreme Unction – said it all: this was not really a sacrament intended for the living, but for the soon-to-be-dead. Part of the Council's fruitful reflection on this sacrament was the restoration of its significance for the life of Christians who were not quite ready for their journey out of this world. Naturally the experience of sickness awakens in us an awareness of our limits and the possibility of death: a rounded view of this sacrament requires us to be hopeful of recovery but also accepting of the possibility that only death will bring an end to suffering.[27]

The scriptural roots of the sacrament are, as we have said, grounded in the healing ministry of Jesus himself. Yet one of the defining characteristics of this ministry is the way in which it is shared with his disciples and indeed anyone who worked in the name of Jesus.[28] St James offers us perhaps the most succinct account of a 'first generation' sacrament in action:

> Is any one among you sick? Then he should call the elders of the church to pray over him and anoint him with oil in the name of the Lord. And the prayer offered in faith will make the sick person well; the Lord will raise him up. If he has sinned, he will be forgiven.[29]

We should note here, once again, the link between sickness and sin: while not suggesting a narrow 'causal nexus' between the two, it is worth considering the possibility that 'the man whose soul is not at rights' flags precisely because there is a gap between the condition of his heart and the condition of his physical wellbeing.

[27] Cf. Anselm Grün, *The Seven Sacraments* (London: Continuum, 2003), p. 253.
[28] Mark 9:38.
[29] James 5:14–15.

The brief account offered by St James draws our attention to two key features which more or less conform to the form and matter of the sacrament today: the praying over and the anointing. Much of the Early Church's ritual practice was inherited from the Jewish community from which it had sprung. Those who were sick were routinely brought before the rabbi to be prayed over and anointed with oil. In Christian terms this 'praying over' came to be identified with the *epiclesis* (the calling down of the Holy Spirit) signified by the laying on of hands. Oil has long been used as an ointment, but its role in the sacrament involves a yet deeper function as a symbol of that same Holy Spirit: soothing, calming, rendering supple once again. The Catholic Church sees this sacrament as an exercise of the 'elders' – the presbyters or priests of the Church – who have had this task entrusted to them by the bishop. That is why the blessing of the Oil of the Sick takes place at the Mass of Chrism at which the Oil of Catechumens and the Holy Chrism are also consecrated.

> God of all consolation
> you chose and sent your Son to heal the world.
> Graciously listen to our prayer of faith:
> send the power of your Holy Spirit, the Consoler,
> into this precious oil, this soothing ointment,
> this rich gift, this fruit of the earth.
>
> Bless this oil + and sanctify it for our use.
>
> Make this oil a remedy for all who are anointed with it;
> heal them in body, in soul, and in spirit,
> and deliver them from every affliction.

The bishop sends this healing oil from the cathedral church to each parish in his diocese to be used in bringing comfort and healing to the sick who are anointed with it.

The Sacraments of Commitment: Matrimony and Holy Orders

Christian life is directed outwards as well as inwards: the inner life of grace is cultivated so that we might more effectively love and serve God in one another. The so-called 'sacraments of commitment' are linked by their vocational outlook. We believe that God calls us to respond to his initiative of love by leading fruitful lives.

In speaking of these sacraments, the Catechism imagines them 'at the service of communion':

> Holy Orders and Matrimony are directed towards the salvation of others; if they contribute as well to personal salvation, it is through service to others that they do so. They confer a particular mission in the Church and serve to build up the People of God ... Those who receive the sacrament of Holy Orders are consecrated in Christ's name 'to feed the Church by the word and grace of God.' On their part, 'Christian spouses are fortified and, as it were, consecrated for the duties and dignity of their state by a special sacrament'.[30]

There are, of course, other forms of service and commitment which build up the Church; if they are not accompanied by a 'special sacrament' that is no indication of their value as vocations or their contribution to the life of the community. What marks these specific commitments out for sacramental status is their necessity to the life of the Church. Although we shall explore each in greater detail, the necessity of matrimony (more frequently called marriage) lies in its role in the creating 'mini-churches' which give life to future generations and the necessity of Holy Orders resides in its service of the Church, most notably in proclaiming the Gospel, celebrating the Eucharist and the other sacraments.

Marriage

Marriage, like all sacraments, finds its origin in the mystery of Christ. Even the Book of Genesis, perhaps better known for its account of the Fall, is, more fundamentally, a theological narrative of the origins of human relationships. Although wounded and compromised by the sin which broke apart the relationship between man and woman, the memory of that original blessing endures. In the Church's nuptial (wedding) blessing, marriage is described as 'the one blessing that was not forfeited by original sin or washed away in the flood'. It is this sense of blessing which informs Christ's teaching about marriage. In responding to the Pharisees' question about divorce, Jesus recalls the 'original' sense of marriage as the coming together in one flesh of man and woman according to God's original design: 'What God has joined together, let no man put asunder' (Matthew 19:6). In this light, the

---

[30] CCC 1534–1535.

Catholic Church regards the two fundamental characteristics of Christian marriage to be *unity* and *indissolubility*. The covenant established between the man and woman unites them in an exclusive, lifelong bond. They must, therefore, remain faithful to each other and allow no one to usurp the other's place in their hearts or in the physical expression of their love. By the same token, no human authority has the power to set aside a marriage which has been validly contracted and consummated. In refusing to accept divorce, the Catholic Church is merely recognizing the limits of state or ecclesiastical power to interfere in a sacramental bond which 'belongs' to God, not man. While affirming this principle, we are all called to show compassion and support to those whose marriages have ended in difficulty.

There are, of course, inevitable tensions surrounding an institution which has legal, social, economic and religious dimensions. The debates around the various identities of marriage have been influenced by society's prevailing attitudes and preoccupations. It can be difficult to discern the spiritual core of Christian marriage beneath the other layers of gloss applied to it. St Paul's words to the Ephesians remain an important reference point for us in approaching what he calls 'the great mystery' of marriage:

> Husbands, love your wives, just as Christ loved the church and gave himself up for her to make her holy, cleansing her by the washing with water through the word, and to present her to himself as a radiant church, without stain or wrinkle or any other blemish, but holy and blameless. In this same way, husbands ought to love their wives as their own bodies. He who loves his wife loves himself. After all, no one ever hated his own body, but he feeds and cares for it, just as Christ does the church – for we are members of his body. 'For this reason a man will leave his father and mother and be united to his wife, and the two will become one flesh.' This is a great mystery – but I am talking about Christ and the church.[31]

Paul takes Christ's words and applies them to the relationship between the Church and her Lord. This vision of the spousal bond between Christ and his mystical bride is theologically and spiritually dense. Husbands and wives should see in their own relationship a mirror of that sacramental mystery which indissolubly unites Christ and the Church in self-giving love. As a result, the Church's theology of marriage is unabashedly lofty. The

[31] Eph. 5:25–32.

couple are called upon to share in the unfolding of Paul's 'great mystery':

> Of this salvation event marriage, like every sacrament, is a memorial, actuation and prophecy: 'As a memorial, the sacrament gives them the grace and duty of commemorating the great works of God and of bearing witness to them before their children. As actuation, it gives them the grace and duty of putting into practice in the present, towards each other and their children, the demands of a love which forgives and redeems. As prophecy, it gives them the grace and duty of living and bearing witness to the hope of the future encounter with Christ.'[32]

It is fitting that the spouses themselves have such a central role to play since they themselves are the ministers of the sacrament. By virtue of their baptism, the parties to the marriage confer the sacrament upon each other; the role of the Church's ordained minister is to receive the couple's consent and ratify it with the church blessing.[33] The grace of the sacrament is meant to help them face the demands and use wisely the gifts of marriage in an unselfish way. Although there are many things in contemporary society which conspire against the spirit of commitment, love and sacrifice required for successful marriage, with God's help there is no reason why that ancient blessing should not continue to bear fruit in our world.

Holy Orders

The sacrament of Holy Orders is best understood in light of Christ's actions leading up to (and including) his Passion. He had already gathered a group of followers with whom he had shared his public ministry and to whom he allowed a privileged insight into the mysteries of the Kingdom.[34] As the events of Holy Week intensified, Jesus drew his Apostles into a deeper experience of what following him would entail. The liturgy of Holy Thursday, centred on the institution of the Eucharist, focuses our attention on the illuminating gesture of Christ washing the feet of his disciples.[35] This striking example of service – in which we see the self-emptying (*kenosis*) of Jesus – reveals the heart of the Eucharist and

[32] John Paul II, Post-Synodal Exhortation, *Familiaris Consortio* (1996), 13.
[33] CCC 1630.
[34] Matt. 11:25.
[35] John 13.

makes explicit its connection with Christ's sacrifice on the Cross. After the resurrection, the Risen Jesus returns to his disciples so that they might be strengthened in their task as witnesses 'to the ends of the earth'.[36] This witness involves not only their personal testimony to the Gospel but their fulfilment of Christ's mandate to baptise all nations. From its inception, the Church has been engaged in this mission of Word and sacrament.

Word and sacrament do not reside in a vacuum: the community which receives these gifts must also be changed by them. Christ's example of service must also shine through this ministry. Early on, the young Church had to meet the twin challenges of providing spiritual sustenance while at the same time ensuring sufficient material support for the poor and needy. This very real problem met with a response which was as spiritually creative as it was practically minded. Following Christ's practice of associating others with his ministry, they selected a group of men to help them in their work of caring for the poor. These helpers, traditionally regarded as the first Deacons, were attached to the apostolic group through a ritual of prayer and laying on of hands.[37] Thereafter a pattern was established whereby the Apostles 'unpacked' the grace attached to their mandate and shared it with others, so that the Church could continue to grow and flourish. A key instance of this was the ministry of pastoral leadership which came to be entrusted to the 'heads' of local churches. As it became clear that the work of the Apostles would not be completed in their lifetime, so the need to ensure authentic and authoritative oversight of the churches also became apparent. These overseers (*episkopoi*) became the successors of the Apostles in their shepherding of the Christian flock; the order of bishops is, therefore, a sacramental extension of Christ's invitation to follow him. As we have already seen, this overflowing of the sacrament to meet fresh needs led to a further extension of the apostolic ministry in the form of presbyters chosen to deputize for the bishop at the table of the Eucharist. Priests are an indispensable part of the unfolding of the mystery of Christ which expresses itself in the signs and symbols we have been exploring in this chapter.

It is fitting that we conclude with a sacrament which is essential to the Church precisely because it is so wedded to the sacramental life. The prayer of consecration at the ordination of a bishop

[36] Acts 1:8.
[37] Acts 6:6.

reminds us that the core duty of the Bishop is in continuity with that of the Apostles:

> May he be a shepherd to your holy flock, and a high priest blameless in your sight, ministering to you night and day; may he always gain the blessing of your favour and offer the gifts of your holy Church.

> Through the Spirit who gives the grace of high priesthood grant him the power to forgive sins as you have commanded, to assign ministries as you have decreed, and to loose every bond by the authority which you gave to your apostles.

The building up of the Church through the celebration of the sacraments is his key concern; with the heart of an apostle it is his responsibility to work with the clergy (the priests and deacons) and the lay faithful in ensuring that the Mystery of Christ continues to shape future generations. It is in this mosaic of sacramental word and action that the world sees the face of its Redeemer.

Chapter 7

Catholic Moral Teaching: An Approach from Christian Anthropology

John Keenan

Introduction

The Second Vatican Council explained that, in Jesus, we do not only see who God is and his plan for us but, in the wise and gracious way he lived on earth, we are given the perfect example of what it is to be authentically human. Anthropology is the study of what it means to be human and both philosophy and science tell us a lot about who the human person is. In the light of Christ, however, we see most perfectly who we are from the perspective of God the Father's loving plan for humanity. It is only in reflecting upon mankind in the light of Jesus, or what we call Christian anthropology, that we really know the fullness of who we are.

In ancient times, when catechumens were preparing to enter into the Church, they were introduced to the four pillars of the Catechism, or the foundations on which they could see their Christian lives being built.

The first pillar they studied was the Creed. Reflecting upon this they came to know what Catholics believed. This profession of faith contained the essential beliefs of the Christian. It was the Christian's passport. Believing the truth contained in this test of faith allowed everyone to present themselves validly for entry into the Christian community.

The second pillar was the sacramental system of the Church. Here the catechumens learned about the seven sacraments of the Church. In the Creed they learned who God is, what he has done for us and the life he offers us in his Son, Jesus, by the working of the Holy Spirit. It is in the Liturgy of the Eucharist and the other sacramental rites of the Church that we accept and receive his salvation, not just as a set of ideas or a philosophy, but as grace that transforms our being, flesh and spirit, from within. In the sacraments we receive and share God's own life, the life he has lived in himself from all eternity. This life, expressed as divine love and mercy for us, gives us forgiveness, consolation, new life, strength and joy to live up to our calling as his disciples.

It is only because we know him and his Son, Jesus Christ, and have received the divine life of the Trinity as a grace that recreates us that we are able to resist the temptations and lies of evil and to do all that God asks us to do in this world. This is the third pillar and it comes to us in the Ten Commandments of God and the Beatitudes that Jesus revealed to us on the Sermon on the Mount. These instruct us in how to live a moral life. Here we gradually discover what is a good life and where to find true happiness.

Living this life we begin to live more for God and others and less for ourselves. We praise him and look out for his will. We find encouragement to ask him for all that we really need. We find in ourselves a deeper desire to live in an environment of mercy and we become wise to the danger of temptation and the horror of evil. All of these hopes and fears we take to God, meeting him in a personal encounter where we become true friends. This is the fourth pillar. It is how to pray and it is at its best when it comes from true faith in God, the experience of his life-giving love in the sacraments and the assurance of living out our Christian dignity in a good moral life.

Morality and happiness

In professing the Creed we declare that God is the Creator of all that is, seen and unseen. This includes me and you. In fact the Book of Genesis goes much further. It reveals to us that the human person, uniquely in the material world, is made in the image and likeness of God. After God had created the heavens and earth, the land and sea, the fruit and vegetation on the earth, the beasts, birds and fish that team in the oceans, he paused and took a deep breath. Then he said, 'Let us make man in the image of ourselves.'[1] And so in the image of God he created them, male and female. This is the source of all human dignity; that we are made like God. This is why we associate rights with the human person that belong really to God. We say that the human person has a dignity that is absolute, inalienable and inviolable: absolute because this dignity

[1] Gen. 1.

admits of no exceptional circumstances to undermine it; inalienable because we cannot give it away; inviolable because it cannot be taken from us. But why should humans have such dignity if we are just clever apes or the highest and most developed of the animals? An animal is just an animal after all. Such dignity as we have enshrined in human rights belongs only to God. It can be ours only if there is something divine about us, something God-given and that is his image and likeness.

The Book of Genesis goes on to say that God made us by taking clay from the earth, breathing his breath into our nostril and creating us male and female. The clay represents our flesh, God's breath means our spirit or soul and male and female represent our sexuality. In all of these aspects we are called to find the image of God.

Traditionally Catholic doctrine focused its attention on the soul as being in the image of God. The old 'Penny Catechism' said, in fact, that the image of God was chiefly in our souls. It is in our souls that we think and choose. The thinking aspect we call the reason and the choosing aspect we call the will. We are confident about the healthiness of these faculties of our souls. So we know that, even though we often make mistakes, our reason basically gets to the truth of things. Similarly, while we experience that we often do bad things, our wills still point us more strongly in the direction of what is good.

Moreover, our moral reasoning seems to come with a basic programming. It tells us that we are supposed to do what is good and avoid what is evil. We can go a little further. Our moral compass also outlines for us what are the basic goods of human existence that are to be protected and promoted and that we should guard against anything that threatens these. All we have to do is to look at the development of all the societies and cultures from the beginning of history until now. In one way or another they all progressed to a belief in the value of the following: religion, strict rules around sexuality and family relations, protection of life, the value of education into truth and goodness, certain rights of property and regard for the common good of all. They most certainly did not all have the same rules and their systems had many errors but their general sense about what was good for the human person and society was tied up with promoting the same basic values and protecting them from threat by means of rules and laws or force and penalty, if necessary.

The Good Foundations of Moral Philosophy

In time the first Western philosophers from Greece were able to outline the range and limits of human reason in reaching truth and goodness. According to them the human mind, under its own power, was able to know the existence of God, the immortality of the human soul, that the human person was fundamentally free in choosing his destiny and that he was able to work out and feel obligations towards a natural moral law, as outlined above. That is, he was capable of coming to recognize that he was accountable for how he lived, that his happiness or wretchedness in life was determined on these grounds and that he may well encounter some kind of eternal reward or punishment on that basis. Living a good or virtuous life tended to lead to happiness and leading a life of vice tended to cause unhappiness. Experience did not always back this up but it did remain the fundamental conviction of the philosophers.

All of this was important because the whole point of life was to attain happiness. Everyone strove for this end. At first sight it seemed that happiness was simply the pursuit of pleasure and the avoidance of pain. You could be mistaken in thinking that this was a licence for doing whatever you wanted and doing whatever it took to get it. Some philosophers, called hedonists, held this. But a set of philosophers called the Stoics soon saw that this kind of life enslaved us in our passions and destroyed our inner being and character. They went to the opposite extreme and said that happiness lay in avoiding all feelings; never be so attached to anything that it makes you either happy or sad. Accept everything with equanimity and tranquillity. Yet the philosophy of the Stoics seemed to miss out so much of what was dear about being human. It is only human to feel joy and pain and it is quite inhumane to feel immune to these.

Instead, the great philosophers like Socrates, Plato and Aristotle offered a way to happiness on the basis of our capacity to know certain goods and choose them. They pointed out that the more we do the right thing the easier it becomes. We develop good habits (virtues) and avoid bad habits (vices). The basic virtues, called cardinal virtues, were prudence, fortitude, justice and temperance. With the virtue of justice we learned to give to each their proper due, not unduly favouring one over the other. With prudence we learned that the means to the end were as morally relevant as the end itself. For example it is always good never to lie but sometimes I need to be prudent as to when and to whom I divulge the truth. With fortitude we train ourselves to keep going in our pursuit of the good even when it gets tough and the end seems far away. With temperance we learn to enjoy good things in moderation and not to excess.

The more virtuous we become the better our judgement gets. Our inner sense of right and wrong becomes clearer and keener, less confused and affected by our desires. This inner sense, called conscience, was seen as a divine spark in us, like the voice of God telling us what to do. But the soul had to be still, like calm waters, to hear that voice.

In the end, the possession of self that these virtues brought about gave us true freedom over our passions. We were masters of ourselves rather than tossed about here and there by our unruly passions and desires. In this freedom our peace, well-being and happiness thrived.

The Good Fulfilled in the Gospel

The philosophers made important progress in working out what was the good life that led to happiness for the human person. This progress, however, was slow and not all the explanations they gave made perfect sense. Moreover they did not all agree. They did not find the clarity and certainty that was necessary for societies to have such confidence in them as to be safe and secure in their growth in virtue.

From the point of view of our faith we can understand this. Although we were created good by God, in his own image, and with minds capable of attaining the truth clearly and choosing the good perfectly, we chose to disobey him. The account of our rebellion is told in the story of Adam and Eve and their Original Sin. This sin causes terrible damage. In our relationship to God we who were friends make ourselves his enemies. Our harmony with each other is ruptured so that Adam blames Eve instead of standing by her. Our relation to Creation does not remain unaffected. So, while God had commissioned us to be stewards of the earth, taking care of it, we now use our power over it to exploit and damage the earth. In our inner being, perhaps above all, we experience something dysfunctional. St Paul, in his letter to the Romans, sums it up best of all. He talks of a certain law he finds in himself such that the good he really wants to do he often finds he leaves undone and the evil things he makes such resolution to avoid he finds himself just too weak to resist.[2]

---

[2] This is a good example of what Christians understand as 'The Fall'. See CCC 385–418.

It is important, however to be accurate about the effect of the Fall in human nature. At times we are inclined to deny our brokenness outright and presume we are perfectly capable of knowing what's right and choosing what's good. At other times we can just as easily exaggerate it and think that humans can never do anything good or right in the world. The truth is somewhere in between. Even after Original Sin human nature remains generally intact. Our minds still have the capacity to reach the truth but now it is like trying to see its reflection in a very blotchy and distorted mirror; it is difficult to make out the truth and quite easy to err. Similarly our will still seeks what is good but now a tendency in us to selfishness makes us weak in choosing it and all too ready to find excuses.

God, who knows us best, knows we need help to find and follow the truth and to seek and choose the good. Moreover he knows that this is what makes us most free and happy and so he himself provides us a means to it. One of the prayers at Mass puts it very well. It says to God:

> Even when we disobeyed you and lost your friendship you did not abandon us to the power of death but helped all men to seek and find you. Again and again you offered a covenant to man and taught him to hope for salvation.

At the end of the story of the Fall, in fact, God promises a definitive victory for humanity through Eve's offspring. Christians see in this a prophecy of Jesus Christ, the Son of God himself, made man to save us.

The Bible tells the story of God's plan for our salvation. Through Abraham he created a new people, called Israel. He had personally selected the Jewish nation to teach them how to live a good and holy life so that, in time, they would become the teachers of all people, leading all humanity into the virtuous life.

After Abraham God called Moses to lead the people and through Moses he gave the people the Moral Law in the form of Ten Commandments. The first three treat of our proper relation to God; he should have first place in our lives and we should show this by respecting holy things and keeping the Sabbath. The final seven concern our relationship with each other; we should honour our family ties, respect human life, uphold marriage, be truthful, respect others' property and serve the common good of all. Most of these make good sense. Indeed we have already seen how the ancient philosophers discovered most of them. Yet, because sin has undermined our clarity and confidence in holding these, God has revealed them so that we can be sure.

The Ten Commandments were a great gift of God to humanity in showing us the way. It is one thing to know the way. It is quite another, however, to choose it and keep it. The history of God's people in the centuries after they enter the Promised Land, however, seems to be one of doing their best to avoid the Commandments and often breaking them in all their respect, both in respect to their right relation with God and their correct relationships with each other. Their unfaithfulness, in the end, leads only to unhappiness. God sends prophet after prophet to remind them of the way and encourage them to follow it but, usually, without much success. Usually the prophets are rejected. Often they are banished and put to death.

As the Old Testament comes to a close two things are obvious. The first is that God has revealed to the People of Israel more than any other the knowledge of the way to the moral life. The second is that he does not seem to have given them in their wills and choosing the capacity to follow it. In effect the Law becomes a curse. Just as much as showing them what they should do, the Commandments remind them of their fault and condemnation in not following them. They need more help.

In fact God promised them through the prophet Jeremiah that he would come to the rescue of their weak wills. 'I will, write my law in their hearts.'[3] He fulfils this promise in sending his Son, Jesus Christ.

The crowds recognize Jesus not just as a rabbi but as Saviour. As a rabbi he will teach them the wisdom that comes in the perfect completing of the Commandments. As Saviour, however, He will also let them share in his strength, his spirit, so that they can keep the Law. His disciples soon see that Jesus is not just a special ethical teacher who gives them the right ideas about the perfect moral life. He also has this unique power, whereby he grants the strength or grace to live this life as authentically as he does. This is something quite new.

In his Sermon on the Mount, Jesus (the rabbi) teaches the people about the most excellent way of living the good life.[4] It is more than a happy life. It is a truly blessed or saintly existence and, in living it, we open ourselves up to another world. We become transformers of the world, recreating it with him into the Kingdom

---

[3] Jer. 31:33.
[4] Matt. 5–7.

of God on earth. The virtues to which his blessed disciples give witness are: humility of spirit; pure focus on God's will; compassion for the needy; peace-making presences amid conflict; sensitivity to the pain of all that is wrong in the world; working tirelessly for justice; witnessing to faith and true religion; being ready to suffer persecution from evil forces so that the Gospel flourishes.

Putting the Kingdom of God first often means putting our own wishes last. It means going the extra mile for those who need us in order for them to begin to believe in goodness. It means being charitable to those who hurt us.

Above all Jesus taught this good way in the example of his own life. He was the Son of God, faithfully obedient to his Father's will and he was the Son of Man, the faithful servant of mankind to turn us from all that harmed us and lead us to true flourishing, personally and as a society, in spirit and body.

Especially in his Passion and Cross he gave an excellent example of what it means to be good and holy. In the Garden of Gethsemane he chose obedience to his Father over his own desire: 'Not My will but Thine be done.'[5] On the Cross he chose loving service of all humanity, even his enemies. For his followers 'Greater love has no man that he lay down his life for his friends';[6] for his enemies: 'Father forgive them for they know not what they do';[7] and to the Good Thief: 'Today you will be with me in Paradise.'[8]

As he died he breathed forth his Spirit and soon afterwards, when the soldiers pierced his sacred, side, there followed out blood and water. This breathing forth of his Spirit, giving of his body to death, and pouring out of his blood as a fountain, complete the work of the Last Supper. As these are offered to and accepted by his Father, there is poured out into the hearts and flesh of all humanity his transforming grace. This is divine strength that heals our souls and strengthens them so that, at last, we are able to see the truth and choose the good. At the Last Supper, ordaining his apostles into his priesthood, He commissioned them to 'do this in memory of me'.[9] Thus he initiated the Eucharist and Sacraments of the New Covenant as channels of this grace so that all God's people receive this means of interior strength to keep the commandments they know to be true. God's new people not only know his plan for the true life more perfectly

[5] Mark 14:36.
[6] John 15:13.
[7] Luke 23:24.
[8] Luke 23:43.
[9] Luke 22:19.

than their fathers of old but are given the strength of soul to live by them.

This interior strength, which Jesus imparts to the Church in giving up his Spirit, to the Father on Calvary and then to his Apostles on the day of his Resurrection, makes him our Saviour in the order of grace and not just a good example in the fashion of a teacher. In essence the Gospel reveals to us that it is impossible for us to copy Jesus' example and follow his teaching without this grace. It is only possible to live the good or blessed life with the grace of the Holy Spirit. This active, interior help he gives through the Church and the sacraments. That is why it is so important to be baptized and grow strong through the nourishment of the sacramental life of the Church, especially through Sunday Mass, regular receiving of the Eucharist and faithful practice of the sacrament of confession.

Theology of the Body

We have already mentioned how, traditionally, Catholic teaching focused on our souls and how the old catechism taught that the image of God was chiefly in our souls. This is true. Yet the careful formulation, stating how this image is in our souls left open and begged a question that, more recently, the Church has been able to consider and answer. If God's image is not exclusively in my soul but only mainly there, I am encouraged to ask where else in me is that image shining.

The story of the Creation of Adam and Eve indicates the answer. As God carries out his plan to create Adam in his image he lifts up into his hands clay from the earth and into this he breathes his Spirit. So we discover that this image is not just in our souls but actually breathed into our flesh. The image of God is in our bodies too. Also interesting is the form of God's declaration to create us. We hear him say, 'Let us make man in our own image' and then the conclusion of his creative action is given in the words, 'So in the image of himself God created man, male and female he created them'. There is a lot in these words.[10] First of all God is revealed simultaneously, as 'He' and 'us', or as person and also as a community. Secondly his image is expressed both in humanity on its own and in male and female together. It seems that the image of God, then, is also in our sexuality. In short, the story of the

[10] Gen. 1.

creation of humanity suggest that the image of God is in everything that we essentially are; in our souls, in our bodies and in our sexuality.

At first glance this is a problem! Certainly it was for the People of God in the Old Testament. They could understand how the image of God was in their spirit because God was the pure, infinite and uncreated Spirit. But how could his image and likeness be in human flesh if God had no flesh to provide a template? How, similarly, could this image be in human sexuality when God was above the differentiation of gender. Or, if he were male, how could his image be in the female? We will now consider the image of God as reflected in human sexuality.

God is a Trinity

This problem remained unresolved and irresolvable throughout the Old Covenant days. The answer is possible only when Jesus comes and reveals to the world who God really is. Throughout his public ministry Jesus spoke of God as his Father. He also introduced his disciples to the Holy Spirit, whom he would send from the Father. Finally, he announced that he, himself, was the only begotten Son of God.[11] Indeed in the days of his Passion Jesus completed the revelation of God to the people as a Trinity. From all eternity God has been Father, Son and Holy Spirit. So, as Jesus revealed that God is Love, He simultaneously showed that God is 'Persons-in-Love', an eternal Community or Family. This does not mean that God is not One. Instead Jesus completes the revelation his Father had given to Abraham. God is One but he is Three Persons in this One Divine God. This teaching, of course, begins to make sense of God's identity in the first pages of the Bible, in the story of Adam and Eve. References to God as He and Us veil only thinly his triune identity.

It is not good for man to be alone

Now we can understand why, after creating Adam and observing him in the garden, God can reach the conclusion that it was not good for man to be alone. This is indeed an odd thing to read. Probably a better translation would be that God saw it was no longer good for man to be alone. Adam's first stage of original solitude, alone or by himself in Creation, was a beneficial one to him.

---

[11] 'The Father and I are One.' John 10:30.

Adam's first solitude was certainly a rich and informative experience. In this solitude God brought him all the animals for him to name. So it was an experience that taught him about his uniqueness in all of Creation. He was so special that nothing else compared to him. That was why he felt alone. But he did not feel alone before God. He had a solitude before God, a sense of himself as unrepeatable in God's eyes and heart. The effect of naming all the other animals was that he discovered he was not able to give himself a name. Only God could do that. Only God understood Adam's real identity.

From this solitary task Adam grew in knowledge and self-awareness. God taught him to value his capacity to reason and work things out. In this solitude Adam also learned that he had to work to understand the world and himself. He did not know who he was except by working it out in understanding the other beasts. At this stage he was also introduced into the tree of the knowledge of good and evil. He could eat of the fruit of all the other trees of the garden but not this one. In his solitude he was given choices, and introduced to the reality of his freedom and the drama of his self-determination. God laid down principles of their life together in the garden; what Adam may and may not do, how to use his freedom in a responsible, humane and holy way. In appealing to Adam's gifts of reason and freedom God set down the arrangement whereby he and Adam would be blessed partners in a covenant for the well-being and development of Creation.

I will make him a helper

Adam learned much about himself in his original solitude. But he learned much more fully about himself through his second creation as male and female. He is opened up to an experience of original unity or communion when God divided him and created out of him a helper, Eve. This helper – the same word used when Jesus promises the Holy Spirit to the Church as another helper or advocate – will draw out of his aloneness the experience of companionship. From this point onward human existence is male and female. Solitude has made Adam ready for a partner, for flesh from his flesh. Together with the woman he is now a unity in nature in the complementary duality of sexuality. Alone with God he had experienced himself as created as a good, valued and loved in and for himself. But now that Eve has appeared before him he immediately recognizes that he has become an even greater value or good for someone else, whom he already loves. Sexual attraction to Eve had the basic meaning of inspiring him to overcome the barrier of his solitude. Its effect was to lead him to a new unity and communion of persons, in and through which he experienced a quite ravishing and superabundant fulfilment. It is not that this new communion overran his solitude or subsumed it. It remains in him as his sanctuary where he must often return to be alone with God and as the perennial wellspring out of which flows the source of his meaningful, free, loving and conscious opening to the other.

The real point, of course, is that it is only in this dual experience, both of solitude and of communion, that humanity really becomes fully the image of God. For God, in the solitude of the each of His Persons, is himself a unity in the communion of the Three.

This, in the end, is the deepest meaning of sexuality. God could have created humanity sexless. Each of us would have been perfectly complete, bearing the fullness of our nature in ourselves. Instead he chose to create half of us one way and half the other. In so choosing, God ensured that none of us would feel complete in ourselves. If I am male I am not female and vice versa. In order to discover the fullness of humanity in and for himself man needs to go out of himself to find another, in Adam's case a spouse, with whom he enters into a relationship of love. In this way the one humanity, in the loving union of persons, becomes complete. It is complete because it is the image of a God who is one and yet made so in the union of Three Persons united by love. So my sexuality is the sign to me that I am not complete in myself but made complete only by another, whom in a loving relationship, I am likewise called to make complete. In the end the image of God is not fully to be found in any of us. Since God is Love, his image can be found only in the love between and among other human beings. Only in love do we become like God and find the name we had ever been searching for in ourselves. As Pope John Paul put it in his very first letter to the world:

> Man cannot live without love. He remains a being who is incomprehensible to himself; his life is meaningless unless he encounters love, participates intimately in it and makes it his own.[12]

When Adam first sees the woman, surprisingly to our ears, he calls her flesh. This is not because he is reducing her to some object of carnal desire. To him her body revealed her humanity. The image of God was breathed into her body. When Adam saw Eve he saw

---

[12] John Paul II, *Redemptor Hominis* (1979).

God: to Adam, Eve's body was a sacrament. What does this mean?

We could think here of the Eucharist for example. In the Eucharist there is really present the Person of Jesus in his body and blood under the elements of bread and wine: in seeing the elements of bread and wine we really do see Jesus. To Adam, Eve's flesh was a double sacrament. It was the radiant presence of God to him through her and represented the gift of the whole of Creation that God has given him. It was also the sacrament of Eve's own person or spirit. In seeing Eve's body, Adam saw her. He recognized her as a person in a way – female – that called out to him for a communion that would complete both of them.

In the communion of their persons, to which they had been called by God in the vocation of marriage, vows consummated, they were set to be a kind of incarnation of God in the world. Their human love, word of promise made to each other and become flesh in the marital act, was to be a sacrament of God's love in the sense that it signified God's love and gave it meaning in the created order. Even more, it expressed it and realised it; sacramentally it made God's love real in the natural world. Moreover, reflecting God's love that, of its essence gives life, their communion both providentially and naturally gave life to each other and beyond them in the family of the human race.

Original Sin and the Call to Purity of Heart

Of course this story did not have its immediately planned happy ending. The devil tempted Adam and Eve and they ate of the forbidden fruit. The original innocence of their natural state is broken at once and God's good and gifted Creation is deformed by an alien logic of grasping and lust. They encounter new experiences. Gone is their original sense of solitude, communion, innocence and harmony in their bodies. In their place are new experiences of lust, fear and shame, contradiction, opposition of the sexes, and hardness of heart. In fear and shame they made clothes of fig leaves and hid. They are afraid of God and of each other. Now they are ashamed of being naked in front of each other because they know they have lost something of the pure love they gave to each other. They have lost control of their bodies which now no longer perfectly reflect their love as gift but, instead, rebel and break away in lust that steals something from the other. In sinning Adam chose for himself and Eve for herself against God. From now on they will act in the same against each other. Adam will choose for himself when with Eve and so dominate her. Eve will react by choosing herself against Adam and seek to possess him by all sorts of seductions of his will. In the end, in their self-seeking souls and naked flesh they are a threat to each other that needs, for the time being, to be covered up.

The Redemption of the Body

God's grace, however, does not just cover up what is wrong. In Jesus he comes to heal our bodies. There is no way for humanity to return to the natural state of innocence in Eden. Jesus does, however, offer the possibility of healing or redemption of our bodies. He provides us with both grace and wisdom that allows us to restore the correct dynamism of person and body. We are able to turn around our tendency to self-gratification and face in the proper direction of the other, offering ourselves as sincere gifts in love and truth, in lives lived for the good and holiness of the other. By the supernatural gifts of faith, hope and love, as well as the gifts the Holy Spirit offers in joy, peace, patience, kindness, goodness, gentleness and self-control, together with the accumulation of the natural virtues of temperance, prudence, justice and fortitude we are able to re-establish our control over the lust of our flesh and to rediscover the freedom to love in the real way whereby we are a genuine gift to each other. The grace of God, in Jesus, adminis-tered in the sacraments of the Church, gives us the strength to rise beyond lust so as to reach the heights of real love.

Two virtues are worthy of special mention. First, abstinence or self-control, which includes and safeguards purity. Abstinence is so important in developing the real freedom necessary to this authen-tic love. In fact no love is possible without genuine freedom. Being free, first of all, means being free from slavery to ourselves; our needs, wants and passions. While out shopping, the parents of a little child may allow him a packet of crisps if he asks. If he asks a little while later they may let him have an ice lolly. But they will say, 'No!' to any further demand for chocolate. It is not really that they fear he may be sick. It is because they know that, giving him every-thing he wants or demands, will spoil him. That is, he will be so ensnared to his own will and way that he will never be happy unless he gets it. Perhaps, at the back of their minds, they know that in a few decades he will hope to stand before the altar of God and say, 'I do' to a lovely young woman! Saying yes to her means saying no to every other woman; and in this capacity to say no to all else is his hope of true love, freedom and meaning. To say yes to his bride means to make himself an irrevocable and total gift to her. But he cannot give what he does not possess. He has to possess himself in order to give himself. And the way to possessing himself is by getting into the habit of saying no to himself and his desires in order to say yes to something worthier. It has to start somewhere and it might as well start when he is a little child with no chocolate.

A second, forgotten, virtue is piety. Piety is really reverence for God and his Creation. It involves trusting that what God has done is good. It means listening to his Son and his voice in the teachings of the Church. It means accepting that God is Our Father, whose laws are only out of love and for our good. This sense is a special help to purity. It means accepting that the way he has formed our bodies, especially in their sexuality, signifying total and lifelong commitment and orientated to fertility is good. Together with purity, this reverence for God's Creation and Word brings fullness to our body's dignity. In this regard St Paul calls our bodies temples of the Holy Spirit. Such reverence for them allows God's glory to fill the human body and allows the Spirit to manifest his power in his temple.

Concluding Remarks

In the Creed we profess our belief in the Holy Spirit, the Holy Catholic Church, the communion of saints the forgiveness of sin and the resurrection of our bodies. What makes the Christian claim unique – some say absurd – is our belief not only in the immortality of our souls but in the final resurrection of our flesh. If we are blessed enough to get to heaven we will live there in our bodies renewed and glorified. This is why the Christian sense of the moral life and of our ultimate goodness and happiness is so caught up in the meaning of our bodies and in living with them according to God's plan. We are happiest when most fulfilled and thriving as a person, made to love in the true image of God, worked out in the giving of our bodies like the sacrifice of his Son; and this is most perfectly accomplished in his body, broken and given for us all and in his blood poured out for the life of the world.

In the Eucharist Jesus issues the most perfect act of goodness and the most perfect vow of love when he says 'This is My Body for you, and this in My Blood shed for all so that sins may be forgiven.'[13] Jesus came so that we might have life and have it to the full. He freed us so that we could be free. His Church tells the

---

[13] Matt. 26:28.

world of him so that its own joy in him can be passed on and the world can be made complete in joy. This is the good life, the right and happy way to live. It was seen darkly but really by the philosophers of old and, in the Gospel, has become the Light of the World.

Further Reading

Butler, Brian, Evert, Crystalina and Evert, Jason, *Theology of the Body for Teens: Discovering God's Plan for Love and Life* (Ascension Press, West Chester, PA, 2006).

West, Christopher, *Theology of the Body Explained: A Commentary on John Paul II's 'Gospel of the Body'* (Leominster, Gracewing, 2003).

——, *Theology of the Body for Beginners: A Basic Introduction to Pope John Paul II's Sexual Revolution* (Ascension Press, West Chester, PA, 2003).

Chapter 8

Catholic Social Teaching

John Deighan

Introduction

Since the earliest days of Christianity the way we treat other people has been a core concern of the Church's teaching.[1] The New Testament bears witness to the importance of charity and Our Lord gave particular emphasis to service of others: he cured the sick;[2] he satisfied want;[3] he had particular concern for those suffering.[4] Just as the Early Church showed its spirit of service for the sick, the imprisoned, the widow and the orphan, the contemporary Church continues to follow that example by making charitable activities an essential aspect of its mission.[5] Indeed the Church publicly articulates a 'preferential option' for the poor owing to the reality that the poor are more vulnerable to the threats that life in the world poses.[6] The history of the Church's influence throughout the ages has been one of advancing civilization and encouraging support for the weak whilst reminding all of their duty to adhere to truth and justice.[7] In recent times, the Church's approach to such issues has been categorized as 'Catholic social doctrine'.[8] Pope Leo XIII's encyclical *Rerum Novarum* (1891) is widely recognised as the launching of modern social teaching as a distinct body of church doctrine. The document dealt with the pressing social conditions of the time and the deplorable injustices

[1] Pope Benedict XVI, *Deus Caritas Est* (2005), 20.
[2] Matt. 10:8.
[3] John 6:5–13.
[4] Luke 9:37–42.
[5] Pope Benedict XVI, *Deus Caritas Est*, 22.
[6] Pope John Paul II, *Familiaris Consortio* (1981) 47.
[7] Pope Paul VI, *Populorum Progressio* (1976), 12; 85.
[8] Pontifical Council for Justice and Peace, *Compendium of the Social Doctrine of the Church* (2006), 87.

arising from a faulty relationship between capital and labour. It also provided a model which was to be used by subsequent popes who re-addressed the issues raised by Pope Leo and built on his work

Important principles and advice on responding to the difficulties of our own times have arisen in these teachings. For example Pope John XXIII promoted the famous principle of 'See, Judge, Act' to ensure Catholic social teaching did not remain merely a theoretical pursuit.[9] The Church's social teaching has now been systematically drawn together in the *Compendium of the Social Doctrine of the Church* produced by the Pontifical Council for Justice and Peace in 2004.

In this chapter we will examine the scope and principles of Catholic social teaching in order to provide an understanding of the structure of society and the various ways in which people and organizations contribute to our lives on earth and interact with each other. In particular we aim to outline the main principles and values which provide the foundations of Catholic social doctrine. The Church has a vision of society which arises from God's creation and we wish to understand how that society should operate. This is essentially about identifying the principles and values of the Christian message and applying them to social relations such that we can assist society in operating effectively and can have a level of guidance for making decisions about our own personal, social and political activities.

The Nature of Human Society

An understanding of the nature of the human person will help us understand how society ought to be organized.[10] The recognition of the dignity of the human person, the need for justice, respect and charity can then provide principles which can be applied to the situations which confront people in the communities to which they belong and the problems that face our fellow human beings around the world.

It should be noted first of all that the Church's social teaching does not provide the answer to all the challenges of living in the world. Rather it provides the principles which we should use in evaluating these concerns and their possible solutions. The

[9] Pope John XXIII, *Mater et Magistra* (1961), 236.
[10] CCC 1879.

Catechism of the Catholic Church states that 'The Church's social teaching proposes principles for reflection; it provides criteria for judgment; it gives guidelines for action.'[11]

The Human Person

The person is made in God's image and for that reason is of inestimable worth.[12] Intrinsic to human nature is the ability to know and understand, i.e. human beings are rational creatures. In addition to this, each person has the radical capacity to choose his own actions based on reason. This sounds straightforward in that we may conclude that it is possible to know the right thing to do and therefore choose to do it. However, each person is also subject to the influence of human passions and appetites which affect the capacity to reason.[13] That is, we can know the right thing to do and even wish to do it but owing to a weakness in our will we may fail to follow through on a decision we make.[14] Everyday experience affirms the reality of human fallibility in maintaining our resolve particularly when pressured by events and moods which draw us in competing directions.

The human person is social in nature. We seek out the company of other people. This is a reflection of the divine nature of the Trinity which is intrinsically social; the attraction we have to other persons is part of the attraction to God made present in the human person.

Among the relationships which arise from the social nature of humanity is that between a man and a woman who choose to commit themselves to a life together. This relationship is of huge significance; as spouses they make possible the creation of new life.[15] This forms the first social unit, that is the family, which is identified by the Church as the 'basic cell' of society.[16]

The Family

It is in the family that children first learn the values that guide their lives.[17] This is where they experience the love and support of their

---

[11] CCC 2423.
[12] Second Vatican Council, *Gaudium et Spes* (1965), 26.
[13] Pope Pius XII, *Quadragesimo Anno* (1931), 132.
[14] *Gaudium et Spes*, 10.
[15] Pope Pius XI, *Casti Connubii* (1931), 11.
[16] *Familiaris Consortio*, 46.
[17] Ibid., 42.

parents and siblings and learn the virtues necessary to live together. For this reason the Church describes the family as 'an intimate community of life and love'.[18]

The Church identifies four general tasks of the family: forming a community of persons; serving life; participating in the development of society; sharing in the life and mission of the Church.[19] The importance of the family is so crucial that the Church emphasises that the health of families is necessary for the health of wider society.[20] It is, therefore, understandable that the Church defends the family from laws or policies which threaten it.

The full development of the human person is not fulfilled just in the family. It is necessary for families to assist others to facilitate their mutual advancement.[21] Thus families form the foundation of communities which, for example, need to cooperate in the exchange of goods, creation of educational and cultural opportunities, building communications infrastructure and so on. This interconnecting web of relationships forms what is known as civil society.

Civil Society

People co-operate in civil society to meet the needs of everyday life. In so doing, individuals have the opportunity to flourish by applying and developing their talents in the variety of activities in which they participate. The interests of different organizations in society lead to a need to coordinate and regulate the activities of civil society and to help manage competing interests.[22] That means that society needs the exercise of a level of authority to make it possible to live together in an ordered way.

It is important to remember that civil society precedes political society and is not to be absorbed by political authorities as occurs in totalitarian systems. Rather, the State should serve civil society and seek to ensure its wellbeing. Members of society should, therefore, be able to exercise freedom in their social activities and have their personal rights recognized.[23]

---

[18] Ibid., 17.
[19] Ibid.
[20] Pope John Paul II, *Christifideles Laici* (1988), 40.
[21] *Familiaris Consortio*, 45.
[22] Pope John XXIII, *Pacem in Terris* (1963).
[23] *Compendium of the Social Doctrine of the Church*, 419.

Political Society

The Church teaches that political society arises directly from the social nature of the human person; it is that element of a community dedicated to the governance and oversight of social interaction.[24] The trappings of power can often make political society a particularly susceptible area for exposing human weakness. Consequently selfishness and the misuse of power can tarnish the reputation of politicians. It is also understandable that history has been greatly influenced by the struggles of finding an effective way of organizing political authority to avoid corruption or tyranny and so on. For the Church, however, these facts do not undermine the principle that political authority has an esteemed status.[25] In fact political authority is, in a way, a reflection of divine authority, because political authority is divinely ordained as necessary for human societies.[26] Logically therefore it is reasonable that human societies find a way themselves to allocate political authority. The legitimacy of that authority is strengthened by the consent of those who are governed.

A Christian conception of society can be thought of as the layers of family, civil and political life which interact with each other. A strong civil society is important because it provides the balance to political society as well as providing the free environment in which persons and families can flourish.[27]

The State is the element of political society which possesses sovereignty; we identify this as the government in contrast to the wider community of political participants, such as political parties, which comprise political society.

Principles to Regulate Social Relations

The Common Good

Arising from the recognition of the dignity of each human person is the concept of the common good which can be defined as 'the sum total of social conditions which allow people, either as groups or as individuals, to reach their fulfilment more fully and more easily'.[28] This ought to be a guiding notion in our social interac-

---

[24] Ibid., 393.
[25] *Pacem in Terris*; see also Rom. 13:1–7.
[26] *Pacem in Terris*, 46.
[27] Pope John Paul II, *Centesimus Annus* (1991), 48.
[28] CCC, 1906–9.

tions such that we always bear in mind the wellbeing of other people in general. That is, we should live in such a way that we contribute to a better life for all persons.[29] Closely linked to this idea is that of the 'universal destination of goods' which is really a recognition that all people, for all generations to come, depend on the goods of the earth for their sustenance and wellbeing.[30] God, in creating the world, did not designate the lands or contents of the earth to any particular individual, generation or nation and therefore it belongs, in a way, to all.[31] This needs to have some practicable application, it cannot simply be a pious wish and, therefore, the Church does not demand some form of communism where no one has personal property. Rather it insists that the system for distributing the earth's resources, produce and wealth (i.e. the economic system) should permit all people to receive what is adequate for their needs.[32] For this reason economic activity must be regulated to ensure it serves the needs of the human person.[33]

Property has a social dimension. In the use of our possessions we should bear in mind that in absolute terms they belong to God and we are administrators of what we own, therefore we should use our possessions wisely and with concern for others.[34]

The Church emphasizes that the human person is, alongside the earth, man's greatest resource,[35] and in light of the fact that economic life increasingly incorporates a knowledge economy; there is a duty to meet the needs for educating and training people to participate effectively in economic life.[36]

Solidarity

A concept which encapsulates our commitment to the common good is that of solidarity. In solidarity we show not just a commitment to justice but also a willingness to bear the burdens of our fellow human beings.[37] This principle is seen in action in the myriad of charitable works that the Church, through its members,

[29] *Pacem in Terris*, 99.
[30] *Compendium of Social Doctrine*, 171.
[31] *Laborem Exercens*, 14.
[32] *Populorum Progressio*, 22.
[33] *Compendium of Social Doctrine*, 331.
[34] Ibid., 23; see also *Mater et Magistra*, 19.
[35] *Centesimus Annus*, 32.
[36] Ibid.
[37] *Sollicitudo Rei Socialis*, 40.

participates in across the globe. It is shown in less dramatic ways simply by our contribution to the communities in which we belong: in our participation in the school board or the community council; in organizing soup kitchens for the poor or sports clubs for children, and so on. Solidarity also requires a concern to pass on the spiritual benefits of the faith and initiatives like catechism classes provide a great witness of our concern for the spiritual wellbeing of others.

Solidarity needs to recognize a balancing principle which ensures that our attempts to meet the needs of others do not lead to the smothering of their initiative and talents; that balancing principle is called subsidiarity.

Subsidiarity

Subsidiarity is the recognition of the autonomy of persons or societies to act without interference from a higher authority. It effectively means that we should try to maximize the individual freedom of the person.[38]

The implication of this is that individuals should be permitted to direct their own lives as much as possible and likewise their families should be free from unwarranted interference from other groups in civil society (intermediate societies) or state authorities. Any intervention in lower societies should be that which is necessary to support the lower society when it is not capable of achieving a particular objective on its own or if the wellbeing of a person necessitates it. An example would be the case of neglectful parents where authorities step in to ensure the welfare of a child is protected. An individual person will inevitably give a greater commitment to his own endeavours. Subsidiarity, therefore, is not only a principle which respects the dignity of a person's freedom but supports greater assiduousness and the fulfilment of potential.

The balancing of subsidiarity and solidarity is not always clear and straightforward and is often at the root of many political disputes. For example, those who give greater emphasis to solidarity may intervene more readily in the support of families which are struggling financially whilst those who give greater emphasis to subsidiarity may hesitate to provide support to a similar family for fear of the family losing its independence. The Church does not provide the definitive answer to these dilemmas; it is possible to err in both directions and the choice at where the balance is set needs

---

[38] CCC 1884.

to be evaluated periodically to ensure that the adverse effects of getting the balance wrong are avoided. Issues around welfare dependency and children being born into poverty are both testimonies to the struggle to get the approaches to solidarity and subsidiarity right. The danger of not doing enough is that people may suffer poverty and deprivation whereas the danger of doing too much may lead people to become over-reliant on others and in consequence not do justice to their own talents.

The principles of subsidiarity and solidarity do not apply only in terms of political policies but in all our social interactions. Within the family a wise parent knows when to let a child develop his or her talents by trying to achieve some task independently. Some parents may not permit their child to develop adequately and effectively smother the child with kindness. In the long run such behaviour is not kindness at all but a hindrance to personal development. Within a business, permitting employees to exercise responsibility fosters not only the individual but can help the business by unleashing greater application of talent from employees of the business.

Authority

We have noted already that there is a need for the exercise of authority in society which arises from human nature. The Church teaches that directing and obeying are two ways of serving the common good. Authority ought to serve but it does so with a power to bind consciences.[39] That is we are morally bound to obey legitimate authority by adhering to validly constituted laws. Such a manifestation of authority in fact reflects divine authority. The Church has continued to uphold this principle which has been recognized since Old Testament times and affirmed forcefully in the New Testament.[40] Those in authority have a duty to exercise power in conformity with the moral law.[41] There are times when political powers introduce laws which are unjust – laws permitting abortion are an obvious example. Such laws are not binding in conscience and in fact there is a moral duty to oppose such laws, by campaigning to have them rescinded or by voting against them when one has the opportunity to do so.

A particular dilemma which has confronted peoples throughout society is what to do in the face of an unjust government. The

[39] *Pacem in Terris*, 49.
[40] Rom. 13:1–2, 7; 1 Peter 2:13–16; 1 Tim. 2:1–2.
[41] Ibid., 47.

Church has identified that it can be licit to resist a tyrannical leadership but it has been careful to identify principles to ensure that the overthrowing of an unjust leader does not give rise to greater harm to society.[42]

Given the importance of the State and its legitimate authority, the relationship with church authority has been a perennial source of tension. The Church recognizes that the Church and State have their own areas of competence. Christ, of course, taught us to render unto Caesar the things that are of Caesar and to God the things that are God's.[43] The implication of this teaching was historically formulated at the beginning of the Middle Ages by Pope Gelasius I (died AD 496) who recognized the priestly and kingly roles to be performed by Church and State respectively: the Church being subject to the temporal authority of the Emperor but the Church retains moral authority. The principle is encapsulated in the following observation of Pope John Paul II:

> The Church respects the legitimate autonomy of the democratic order and is not entitled to express preferences for this or that constitutional solution. Her contribution to the political order is precisely her vision of the dignity of the person revealed in all its fullness in the mystery of the Incarnate Word.[44]

The authority of the State, although it has a binding authority, should primarily be used as a moral force rather than a coercive one. It is not possible for the State to force people to be good but it can create a framework where individuals are more likely to be good. On the other hand, it has a duty to restrain the evil actions within society which are unduly harmful to the common good.[45]

Participation

The social nature of the human person leads people to participate in society. This helps each of us to improve ourselves by exercising and developing our talents. It also provides the opportunity to fulfil our duty of upholding and contributing to the common good. Each person, of course, has particular talents and has a unique contribution to make on behalf of the whole Church in

---

[42] *Populorum Progressio*, 30–31; see also *Compendium of the Catechism of the Catholic Church*, 401.
[43] Matt. 22:15–22.
[44] *Centesimus Annus*, 47.
[45] Pope John Paul II, *Evangelium Vitae* (1995), 71–2.

making the world a better place.[46] Some may feel drawn to political office whilst others may feel that their interests and talents are most fully exercised in the family or local community. Nonetheless, we all have some responsibility for the exercise of authority in the communities in which we live and must ensure that we influence this when we can. This means, for example, that we must vote for good leaders, that we keep ourselves reasonably informed on the issues that affect the societies of which we are part and so on.

The twenty-first century continues to witness the emergence of political structures which operate at an international level, such as the Council of Europe, the European Union and the United Nations. In this global society we have the duty to influence issues at world, continental, state, national, regional and community level. Decisions now adopted at United Nations and European levels influence nations and communities and families and we need to take responsibility to some degree for these decisions.

Pope Benedict XVI has commented on the need for such a global authority with 'real teeth'.[47] The lessons of the Second World War highlighted that sovereign states cannot simply be permitted to define right and wrong according to their own particular worldview. There are universal values which arise from an understanding of the dignity of the human person and which are accessible to human reason. The Universal Declaration of Human Rights, created by the United Nations after the Second World War, encapsulates much of the dignity proposed by Christianity and shared by other faiths and cultures across the world. The intervening years have seen some of these truths obscured and both the sanctity of all human life and the importance of the traditional family are under fierce opposition at an international level.

From our previous consideration of political society we can see that democratic forms of governance are most closely reflective of the participatory principles of Catholic social teaching and have been explicitly recognized as such but the Church recognizes the right of nations to choose their own political solutions to issues.[48]

Values

To reiterate some of the points above, the social doctrine of the Church arises from an understanding of the dignity of the human

---

[46] *Christifideles Laici*, 20.
[47] Pope Benedict XVI, *Caritas in Veritate* (2009), 67.
[48] *Centesimus Annus*, 47.

person made in the image of God and leads to an understanding of the structure of society: family, civil and political.[49] The interaction of persons in society is guided by principles, notably: the common good, subsidiarity, solidarity, authority and participation. The Church further contributes to the wellbeing of society by promoting the values which should permeate society and interact with the principles identified. These values are principally those of truth, freedom and justice.[50]

When it comes to deciding what is right and wrong it is often attractive to many that truth is relative, that is each person can decide what is good and what is evil. The Church, on the contrary, holds that there are values which can be known with absolute certainty. This for some is seen as an imposition or a threat and it is realistic to identify the concern which lies behind these fears. Some have in the name of truth imposed their will, with the most terrifying of consequences for others. For example, in the days of the great ideologies, the 'truth of communism' was to be implemented and opposition crushed.[51] The Church, however, welcomes truth from any branch of human knowledge confident that the truth cannot contradict itself.[52] The Church also holds that truth, far from a threat, is a safeguard. Without the truth we are at the mercy of those who claim to be arbiters of what is right and wrong. This ultimately means that it is the powerful who will impose their will. The real truth recognises the dignity of the human person and stands firm even when powerful forces claim that some people do not really deserve to be recognized as persons. Pope John Paul II famously warned that 'If there is no ultimate truth to guide and direct political activity, then ideas and convictions can easily be manipulated for reasons of power.'[53] This in turn creates the conditions for democracy to turn into a 'thinly disguised totalitarianism'.[54] (Totalitarian regimes exercise oppressive control over the lives of citizens even to the point of crushing the conscience of its citizens. It is not difficult to see similar tendencies even in our liberal western societies.)

The Church safeguards truth by respecting the dignity of the human conscience which is manifest particularly in the protection

---

[49] CCC 1700.
[50] *Compendium of the Social Doctrine of the Church*, 197.
[51] Pope Pius XI, *Divini Redemptoris* (1937), 9; see also *Evangelium Vitae*, 70.
[52] John Paul II, Address to the Ponitifical Academy of Science, 22 October 1996.
[53] *Centesimus Annus*, 46.
[54] Ibid.

of religious freedom. In a certain sense, the source and synthesis of these rights is religious freedom, understood as the right to live in the truth of one's faith and in conformity with one's transcendent dignity as a person.[55] This respects each person's freedom to consider what is really right and wrong and contribute to public discourse which in turn contributes to the creation of just laws and a justly ordered society.[56]

The democratic method allows the wisdom of the community, and of generations gone by, to be applied to the concerns of the day thus arriving at informed and rational solutions to the challenges we face in society. The importance of freedom, which is the second value promoted by the Church's social teaching, is obvious in this regard: freedom is the way in which human persons most closely reflect the nature of God, in that they can freely choose to direct their actions and not be directed by mere instinct or external influence.

The third value is justice which has several forms but is, most essentially, recognition of an individual's right to receive what is his due. The Church identifies social justice which is a duty to support the community; distributive justice which is a right to receive a sufficient share of the earth's resources to support a satisfactory lifestyle; and commutative justice, which recognizes the right to be given a fair price in an exchange of goods, for example, a worker should receive a fair wage and an employer should receive a fair day's labour for that wage.

Contemporary Challenges

Issues of particular contemporary interest include the crisis of the family, the 'culture of death' and the advance of secularism, each of which pose particular challenges to the creation of a society consistent with a Christian vision. These issues are in fact interrelated and merit some comment.

Family Crisis

Recent years have witnessed dramatic changes in family life and how marriage is recognized in society. Laws which permit 'no-fault divorce', recognize cohabitation and same-sex unions as being

---

[55] *Centesimus Annus*, 47.
[56] *Caritas in Veritate*, 4.

morally equivalent to marriage are widely supported by politicians and many in society.[57] The confusion over family composition is typified by claims from politicians that it is not right to incentivize particular forms of relationship. Such a claim is essentially a way of saying that marriage will not be supported. This is, in fact, a serious error and a failure to adequately uphold the common good.[58] It is based, to a great extent, on a misunderstanding of marriage in terms of its social function and also of its intrinsically religious dimension in that it is created by God.[59] Marriage is a social institution which has been recognized throughout time, across cultures and in societies in the most diverse stages of development. This fact reflects the reality that marriage corresponds with a need arising from human nature and the inherent complementarity of the sexes which leads to procreation.[60] For all societies the fact of the birth of children and their need to be raised and socialized needs to be dealt with. It has been dealt with by ensuring that children will be born into a family where the biological parents can take responsibility for the birth of the children and the provision of care for the children. Marriage publicly binds a man and woman and thereby ensures that a man will father children in the context of a relationship where that child can be best cared for. Sociological evidence, in fact, affirms the natural law analysis of family composition and confirms the wisdom of divine revelation. The married family is found to provide the environment in which children are most likely to fair well. This is found in relation to drug and alcohol abuse, educational attainment, mental and physical health, promiscuity, criminality, of forming stable relationships and, in fact, in any social indicator which can be tracked.

An understanding of the proper role of the family will be a necessary contribution, and one that should be made by those familiar with Catholic social teaching, to the success of society and the advancement of children's welfare.

The 'Culture of Death'

Another important contemporary issue is that which has been identified as the 'culture of death'. It identifies a mindset which permeates an increasing numbers of countries. This culture has

---

57 Pope John Paul II, *Ecclesia in Europa* (2003), 90.
58 *Casti Connubii*, 52.
59 Ibid., 5.
60 *Casti Connubii*, 18.

made it acceptable to destroy human life when it is found to be an inconvenience.[61] It has grown from the practice of abortion on an industrial scale, to encompass the instrumentalization of human life in practices which degrade or destroy life, for example, embryo experimentation, *in vitro* fertilization and human cloning. The instrumentalization of human life has encouraged the notion that some life, when it is no longer productive or of an arbitrarily set quality, can be eradicated through regimes permitting euthanasia or assisted suicide.[62] This mindset coincides with an exaggeration of efficiency in our time, such that lives which are deemed non-productive are no longer valued.[63] These features break down the notions of charity and the commitment to solidarity which ought to permeate society and therefore, as well as permitting grave injustices against the fundamental right to life, undermine the values which make the flourishing of society possible.[64] This has contributed to an enormous demographic shift which now calls into question the viability of western societies which can no longer sustain their populations because birthrates are so low.

Dictatorship of Relativism

In light of the preceding two issues it is of little surprise that a third issue, secularism, is an important concern to the Church. This phenomenon has generally been identified by successive Popes as a threat not just to the Church but to society itself. At the heart of secularism is a detachment of freedom from morality. Modern secularism demands the removal of religious values from society and does so with increasing aggressiveness and intolerance.[65] The irony that it is promoted under the veil of tolerance is lost on its proponents. Cardinal Ratzinger prior to being elected as Pope Benedict XVI, identified a 'dictatorship of relativism' which demands that values held by people of religious faith are inapplicable in public life; thus arguments against an array of social evils are dismissed as belonging to the private world of faith.[66] Freedom of conscience has become a casualty of this form of secularism which demands, for example, that Catholic adoption agencies

---

[61] *Evangelium Vitae*, 12.
[62] Ibid., 15.
[63] Ibid., 23.
[64] Ibid., 8.
[65] *Caritas in Veritate*, 56.
[66] Cardinal Joseph Ratzinger, *Votive Mass for the Election of a New Pope*, Homily, Rome, April 2005.

place children with unmarried and same-sex couples, pharmacists prescribe contraceptives and abortifacients and doctors participate in directing women to abortionists. The philosophical roots of this mindset are found in the belief which emerged during the period in the eighteenth century known as the Enlightenment. In this mindset, it was believed that humanity could gain dominion over its destiny through the application of reason and scientific knowledge.[67] The need for a redeemer, therefore became superfluous and faith could be displaced from public life.[68] The emphasis on reason and freedom at the time of the Enlightenment underpinned the notion of progress and these became the new sources of hope. This notion gained a political manifestation which ushered in revolutionary forces to build a society without God. Secularism has unfortunately 'poisoned[ed] a wide spectrum of Christians who habitually think, make decisions and live, "as if Christ did not exist"'.[69] Catholic social teaching has warned that a society without God cannot be sustained. Without God there can be no stable morality and confusion over morality threatens the existence of society itself.[70]

Concluding Remarks

The challenges outlined in this chapter present a particularly serious threat because they have the potential to destroy society from within. Societies can often face great external threats successfully when they are strong internally, but when they are critically weak they are susceptible to collapse from within, such as that which happened to the Soviet Union.[71] From the comfort of Western society which, even at times of financial difficulty for many, is marked by over-consumption and indulgence, the thought that society cannot continue as it is may seem far-fetched but the problems outlined above have created problems in the stability of our most basic society, i.e. the family, which stretch the resources of the rest of society to deal with. The lack of commitment in marriage and the spread of the culture of death have made the survival of this society and its present way of life impossible in numerical terms due to the low birth rate. The removal of firm

[67] *Spe Salvi*, 16.
[68] Ibid.
[69] *Ecclesia in Europa*, 26.
[70] *Mater et Magistra*, 217.
[71] *Centesimus Annus*, 22.

standards of right and wrong makes the identification of solutions to these social problems extremely difficult. In fact the law is used to ensure calls for solutions, such as support for marriage, are regarded as being out of step with equality principles and are deemed to be a form of discrimination against other forms of relationship.

The Church has, however, repeatedly encouraged the formation of Catholic laity to enable them to imbue society with the values that can make society prosper.[72] This is the challenge facing the present generation and the extent to which Catholics, and those who share our social values, respond will potentially determine the future prospects or our nations. The post-modern world has lost sight of many of the values which are necessary for its survival. It has particularly distanced itself from God and has established sceptical and relativistic values that threaten even to trick and confuse Christians. Our Lord asked that we be salt and light of society and at present many areas of our society are in a sort of darkness where they fail to distinguish good and evil clearly. We can especially see this in the values and behaviour in our television shows, films, magazines and newspapers. The everyday reality, that the life of many people in communities and families is scarred by violence, crime, addiction and infidelity, highlights that Christian values urgently need to be restored to society. This requires that each of us continually learn from the Church's teaching and introduce it to the part of society in which we operate. Only then will our faith meet the demands set by Jesus Christ. A society cannot rely on structures to maintain its existence, it needs to be filled with good mothers and fathers, good teachers. Workers in all professions and trades need to imbue their workplaces with a Christian spirit and give those they encounter the opportunity to receive the saving message of our faith.

---

[72] *Pacem in Terris*, 149.

Further Reading

The Social Agenda of the Catholic Church: The Magisterial Texts, Foreword by by Archbishop Francois-Xavier Nguyen Van Thuan, 2002. This document is available here: http:/www.thesocialagenda.org

Charles, Rodger, *Introduction to Catholic Social Teaching* (Oxford: Family Publications, 1999).

——, *Christian Social Witness: The Catholic Tradition from Genesis to Centesimus Annus,* vols 1 & 2 (Leominster, Gracewing, 1988).

Part Two
Application to Context

Chapter 9

A Rationale for Catholic Schools

Stephen J. McKinney

Introduction

The contemporary concept of education is very broad and encompasses many different forms and processes of teaching and learning sometimes categorized as formal, non-formal and informal.[1] The contemporary understanding of education, then, includes formal learning such as schools, further education and higher education. It also includes the non-formal learning that takes place in everyday home life and in working environments and informal learning such as non-certificated adult and continuing education.[2] The concept of Catholic education is equally broad and can also be understood to include formal, non-formal and informal learning. Catholic education encompasses Catholic schools, Catholic colleges and Catholic universities, everyday home life and work and non-certificated adult and continuing education.[3] As a consequence of this breadth of understanding of the concept of Catholic education, Catholic schooling is not, and cannot be, synonymous with Catholic education.

There are Catholic schools in many parts of the world, within different religious and cultural contexts. This chapter will be restricted to the discussion of Catholic schools in the contemporary English-speaking world. This includes Australia, New Zealand, the United States of America, Ireland, Scotland and England and

---

[1] These categories are very general and more porous than they may appear, but help to illustrate the point. Zurcher discusses a range of models of learning: http://www.infed.org/informal_education/informality_and_formalization .htm.

[2] Ibid.

[3] Second Vatican Council (1965) *Declaration on Christian Education* 1, 3, 5, 8, 10. See Stephen J. McKinney, Communicating faith through adult education in J. Sullivan, *Communicating Faith* (CUAP, 2010).

Wales, though the chapter will focus primarily on the United Kingdom.[4] While it is important to note the long history, variety and impact of the models of Catholic schooling that were established and existed alongside Catholic institutions such as monasteries, cathedrals and parish churches, the contemporary networks, or systems, of Catholic schools in the English-speaking, western world are a relatively new phenomenon.[5] The establishment of the Catholic schools in the western English-speaking world in the nineteenth and twentieth centuries, that are the foundation of these contemporary networks, pre-dated or were contemporaneous with the establishment of national systems of state-funded compulsory schooling.[6] The funding arrangements and the relationship between the Catholic schools and the state vary from country to country (and sometimes varies within different administrational authorities contained within countries) and are usually the result of complex historical negotiations and accommodations.[7] Catholic schools are distinctive models of schooling but can be identified as one type of faith school (sometimes referred to as faith-based schools or religious schools). There are other forms of faith schooling in the English-speaking world that are also Christian (Church of England, evangelical) or of other faiths (Jewish, Muslim).[8]

This chapter will begin by examining the contemporary rationale and vision for Catholic schools, contextualizing the work of Catholic schools within the salvific mission of the Catholic Church. The chapter will continue by discussing the distinctive Christ-centred nature of the Catholic school in some detail, and, further, the importance of the role of the Catholic teacher for the success

[4] For a useful introduction to this history consult Gerald Grace and Joseph O'Keefe (eds), *International Handbook of Catholic Education Part One and Part Two* (Dordrecht: Springer, 2007).

[5] CCE (1988), *The Religious Dimension of Education in the Catholic School*, section 44; Thomas A. Fitzpatrick, 'Catholic Education' in H. Holmes (ed.), *Scottish Life and Society: A Compendium of Scottish Ethnology volume 11* (East Linton: Tuckwell Press, 2000) pp. 435–55.

[6] Mass compulsory state-funded schooling in the western English-speaking world was initially established in the nineteenth century and structurally consolidated in the late nineteenth and twentieth century. M. Miller, 'Historiography of Compulsory Schooling', in Roy Lowe (ed.), *History of Education Volume II* (London: Routledge, 2000), pp. 156–7.

[7] Stephen J. McKinney, 'Mapping the debate on faith schooling in England', in Stephen J. McKinney (ed.), *Faith Schools in the Twenty-First Century* (Edinburgh: Dunedin Academic Press, 2008).

[8] Ibid.

of the Catholic school. Finally the chapter will conclude by exploring some of the contemporary challenges that are faced by Catholic schools.

Rationale and Vision for Catholic Schools

The best starting point to discuss the contemporary rationale and vision for Catholic schools is the Vatican II document *Gravissimum Educationis* (1965).[9] While acknowledging that there are important prior documents on Catholic education and Catholic schooling emanating from the Catholic Church, this short and closely written document sets out a systematic overview of Catholic education and Catholic schools that was to prove to be highly influential for subsequent documentation, Catholic academics and educationalists.[10]

Gravissimum Educationis begins by positioning Catholic education within the context of the mission of the Catholic Church. The Catholic Church continues the work of Jesus Christ by proclaiming the message of salvation to all people. This is essentially continuing the work of evangelization. This mission of the Church to all people means the Church must be concerned with all aspects of the life of humanity, including education.[11] *Gravissimum Educationis* states that education per se is an inalienable right for all people – they are entitled to education. The aim of true education is to form the human person to achieve his or her potential and to contribute to the good of society.[12] These egalitarian aspirations are not exclusive to the Catholic Church, but are shared with other major institutions in the western world (for example, the United Nations in its Declaration of Human Rights).[13] *Gravissimum Educationis* further states, however, that all Christians have a right to a Christian education that will help them to grow and develop a mature Christian faith.[14] There are a number of key partners who

---

[9] Second Vatican Council, 1965.

[10] CCE (1977), *Catholics Schools*; CCE (1982), *Lay Catholics in Schools; Witnesses to Faith*; CCE (1988), *The Religious Dimension of Education in the Catholic School*; Congregation for Catholic Institutions (1998), *The Catholic School on the Threshold of the Third Millennium*; CCE (2007), *Educating Together in Catholic Schools*.

[11] Second Vatican Council (1965), Introduction.

[12] Ibid., 1.

[13] United Nations (1948), *The Universal Declaration of Human Rights*, available online at. http://www.un.org/en/documents/udhr/.

[14] Second Vatican Council (1965), 2.

contribute to this Christian education. Parents have an important role to play as they are expected to be the first educators of their children and are called to create a Christian family 'animated by love and respect for God and man'. Civil society is also expected to play a role in the education of children as it strives to achieve its goal of promoting the common good in society. Finally, the Church has a duty to educate in order to proclaim the message of Christian salvation and she has a responsibility to support the Catholic parents and families in the religious formation of their children.[15]

Catholic education, as has been mentioned above, can take a variety of forms but *Gravissimum educationis* argues that Catholic schools have a 'special importance'.[16] The Catholic school offers a distinctive and enriching opportunity within the pluriformity of school possibilities.[17] Catholic schools, like other schools, have a duty to engage with culture and form the youth, but they also have a responsibility to create a 'special atmosphere animated by the gospel spirit of freedom and charity'.[18] This highlights the Christocentric nature of Catholic schools, that is, that Jesus Christ is at the heart of the Catholic school. This theme would be developed in subsequent documentation. Another important theme that is introduced in this document is the crucial role that teachers play in Catholic schools, through their commitment and witness to Christ and Christian values.

Perhaps a helpful way to understand Catholic schools is to consider that all schools are concerned with epistemology and ontology.[19] By epistemology we mean that schools are concerned with knowing, the knower and how to know things. By ontology, we mean that schools are also concerned with what it is to be human, to be a mature human being who attains his or her potential, leads a good life and contributes to society.[20] The Catholic Church states that it is Jesus Christ who lies at the heart of epistemology and ontology in Catholic schools. All knowledge is ultimately rooted in

---

[15] Ibid., 3.

[16] Ibid., 5.

[17] CCE (1982), 14.

[18] Second Vatican Council (1965), 8.

[19] Drawing from some ideas from Thomas Groome. See Thomas Groome 'What Makes a School Catholic?' in Terence McLaughlin, Joseph O'Keefe, J. & Bernadette O'Keeffe (eds), *The Contemporary Catholic School* (London: Falmer Press, 1996) pp. 107–25.

[20] There is a plethora of initiatives in education designed to enable young people to fulfill their potential, lead a good life and contribute to society.

God, and, since the Enlightenment, may be sometimes recognized more implicitly than explicitly. In a Catholic school, being for the Catholic school community (teachers, pupils, other staff) is being in, with and for Christ. This is not necessarily an introverted understanding of being but a being that welcomes others and invites them to share, in as much as they wish to, the richness of this theological vision of education. The concept of a Catholic school community, then, is a theological concept, rooted in Christ, rather than a sociological community.[21] Repeatedly, Catholic documentation advises that the Catholic school is conceived as an outward looking Christian community that should 'promote respect for the state', 'an awareness of international society' and contribute to the well-being of society.[22] The Catholic school, for example, should respond to Church appeals for those in need but should also be prepared to respond to calls for assistance from organizations such as UNESCO and the United Nations.[23]

Having explored some of the key ideas in this influential document, the chapter will continue by examining the development of these ideas in subsequent documentation and in the relevant academic literature, but using a thematic approach rather than a systemic discussion of each document. These themes are: the nature of the Catholic school and the Catholic teacher. The chapter will then discuss some of the contemporary challenges for Catholic schools

The Nature of the Catholic School

In the *Catholic School* (1977) Jesus Christ is stated to be the foundation of the Catholic school.[24] Christ is the perfect man and within him 'all human values find their fulfillment and unity'.[25] The Catholic school is committed to the development of whole people and bases this on the example of Jesus Christ. This is a high ideal and the Catholic school is called to ensure that it pursues this ideal, maintains its identity and sustains itself with 'constant reference to the Gospel and frequent encounter with Christ'.[26] This

---

[21] CCE, (1988), *The Religious Dimension of Education in the Catholic School*, 31.
[22] Ibid., 45.
[23] Ibid., 46.
[24] CCE (1977), *Catholic Schools*, 34.
[25] Ibid., 35.
[26] Ibid., 55, 66.

means that the Catholic school must be nourished by the 'saving word of Christ', as expressed in scripture, tradition, liturgy and sacraments and in the lives and witness to Christian life.[27] There are interesting implications that arise from these statements. The Catholic school aims to enjoy frequent encounters with Christ, but this cannot be delegated or limited to the Religious Education classes.[28] If this were to occur there is a strong possibility that the vision and purpose of the Catholic schools would not be realized throughout the school day and week, but within a specific time slot several times a week. This would substantially diminish the Christian self-actualization of the Catholic schools and the Catholic school community, and weaken the role of the school in the religious formation of the children.

The frequent encounter with Jesus Christ is one that must be experienced by the school, then, and this is accomplished, in the first instance, through reading of the scriptures, especially the Gospels. This will enable the members of the school community to become familiar with the teachings of the Gospel, understand these teachings and enact them together within the school context and within other spheres of their lives on a daily basis. Ultimately, those who work and learn in a Catholic school should be prepared to immerse themselves in the scriptures and be nourished individually and collectively by the Word of God. The Catholic school is also expected to honour the tradition of the Church and celebrate the liturgy and the sacraments. The school community is called to participate in the liturgical and sacramental life that nourishes the spiritual life of the school community and co-joins the school with the larger body of Christ.

The dual task of the Catholic school is described as a 'synthesis of faith and culture and a synthesis of faith and life'.[29] This first synthesis refers to the integration of knowledge in the light of the Gospel. In the pursuit of the integration of knowledge, there is no desire to conceive curricular subjects as adjuncts to faith or as a means for apologetics.[30] In as much as study in any curricular area is a genuine search for truth, it will ultimately lead to 'the discovery of Truth itself'.[31] This is based on a fundamental belief in a world that has been created by and for God and, ultimately, all

---

[27] Ibid., 53.
[28] Stephen J. McKinney and Robert L. Hill, 'Why Scripture is important for Catholic Schools,' in *Le Cheile* 13, May 2010, p. 7.
[29] CCE (1977), *Catholic Schools*, 37.
[30] Ibid., 39.
[31] Ibid., 41.

knowledge will lead back to God. The role of the teacher is crucial in the endeavour to help the pupils see beyond truth to the Truth. The second synthesis refers to the growth of Christian life. The integration of faith and life is concerned with the Christian formation of the pupils.[32] The children have commenced a lifelong journey to Christian maturity.

It is important to note at this point that the Catholic school is only a stage on this journey and, sometimes, local Catholic communities can have unrealistic expectations of Catholic schools and the progress of the children in their faith development. The school children are on an early and important stage of this faith journey and once they leave school must continue on that journey. This is not to minimize the importance of Catholic school and this stage of Christian formation, but school is not the end of the formation process and the next stages of young adulthood and adulthood which are expected to consolidate and progress on the work of the Catholic schools (and other early forms and loci of faith development) are also very important.

There can be creative tensions for the Catholic school as it strives to undertake this dual task of the two syntheses of faith and culture and faith and life in its daily operations as both a civic institution, a place of learning like other schools, and as a Christian community, a site for religious formation.[33] These two aspects (civic institution and Christian community) of the work of the Catholic school need to be kept in harmony and, at times, this can be challenging. In some respects this distinction between the two aspects could be interpreted as a conceptual distinction only but, as dicussed above, the religious aspect of the Catholic school should permeate all aspects of Catholic school life. Sometimes, however, this conceptual distinction can become a real distinction if there is an imbalance in the harmony. If a Catholic school places a greater emphasis on the role of the Catholic school as a civic institution, there is a disjuncture in the harmony as the Catholic schools becomes more like other places of learning. The result is that the Christian community and the religious formation may suffer, jeopardizing the Christian identity of the Catholic school. Conversely, if greater emphasis is placed on the religious dimension of the Catholic school, the position as civic institution and learning may suffer. In this circumstance, the consequences could be that the children are insufficiently prepared for employment or

[32] Ibid., 46.
[33] CCE (1988), *The Religious Dimension of Education in the Catholic School*, 67.

to continue their education into Further and Higher education and to fulfill their potential as citizens and contribute to society. The balancing of this harmony may be particularly acute in those places where Catholic schools receive a high level of state funding and, as such, would be expected to participate in national, or state, educational initiatives that may require some adaptation for the Catholic school to ensure this harmony.[34]

The Religious Dimension of the Catholic School returns to the importance of the relationship between the Catholic schools and the parents and families of the children. The Catholic school has a responsibility to work in close partnership with parents, the first and primary educators of the children, and the families of the pupils. Again a balance is required, as this partnership should focus on both the religious formation of the children and their academic profile and progress. *The Religious Dimension of the Catholic School* comments that, at times, the Catholic school will have to avail itself of opportunities to engage parents in dialogue about their responsibility as the primary educators in the faith and raise their awareness of this key role.[35] The partnership and collaboration is especially important when dealing with 'sensitive issues such as religious, moral or sexual education'. *The Truth and Meaning of Human Sexuality* (1995) states that parents should provide timely education in moral and sexual matters within the context of education for love. When these issues are discussed in the Catholic school context (or any school context for those families who have no access to a Catholic school) this must take place under the attentive guidance of the parents.[36] In practical terms, parents should be consulted and advised of the content and delivery of any school-based programmes in morality and sexuality.

The Catholic Teacher

The rationale and role of the Catholic teacher is explored in some depth in another document from the Congregation for Catholic Education *Lay Catholics in School – Witnesses to Faith* (1982). In the first instance, it should be recognized that anybody who is

---

[34] A good example of this would be the inclusion of the Catholic sector in Scotland in the national 5–14 curricular guidelines (early 1990s) and the 3–18 Curriculum for Excellence curricular framework (launched 2010).
[35] CCE (1988), *The Religious Dimension of Education in the Catholic School*, 42–3.
[36] The Pontifical Council for the Family (1995), *The Truth and Meaning of Human Sexuality*.

engaged, in some way, in 'integral human formation' can be described as an educator.[37] This acknowledges the importance of all of those who are involved in the formation of young people (family, friends, clergy). Once again it is important to remember the central importance of the parents. This recognition of the wide scope of those who could be described as educators acknowledges the importance of the role of those who co-operate or assist with the teachers in the school and all of those who support the administration and organization of the school.[38] Nevertheless, as has been stated, the Catholic teacher is perceived by the Church to be crucial to the success of the Catholic school (and has an important role to play in other forms of schooling).[39] The Catholic teacher in a school context has adopted the specific profession of teaching, though the concept of a Catholic teacher cannot be reduced to that of a 'professional' who imparts knowledge (limited to the epistemological functions of schooling). The Catholic teacher must also necessarily be an educator – one who is concerned with the formation of human persons (focus on the ontological) and the communication of truth leading to the Truth.[40]

The Catholic Church has high expectations of the Catholic teacher. She or he is understood to be a person who is enriched with 'both secular and religious knowledge'.[41] The Catholic teacher would be expected to undertake appropriate formation and possess the appropriate qualifications. There is an educational requirement that they are engaged in on-going professional formation throughout their careers.[42] There is also a need for the Catholic teacher to be engaged in a permanent process of personal religious formation.[43] In other words, they are called to continue and persevere on their own faith journey. The Catholic teacher is called to be a person of hope and charity.[44] The teacher is supported by their faith, the word of God, the sacraments and the prayer of the Church, but there is an awareness of how difficult it can be to be a Catholic teacher.[45] It may be useful, then, to explore

[37] CCE (1982), *Lay Catholics in Schools: Witnesses to Faith*, 15.
[38] Ibid., 32.
[39] Ibid., 14.
[40] Ibid., 16.
[41] Ibid., 60.
[42] Ibid., 67.
[43] Ibid., 64–6.
[44] Ibid., 72.
[45] Ibid., 72.

this idea of the Catholic teacher as a person of faith, hope and charity, and this brings us back to Jesus Christ and the question of what it is to be human (Christian anthropology).[46]

As a baptized person, the Catholic teacher is a person of faith, a member of the People of God, the body of Christ.[47] This is a life-long journey of discipleship. The Catholic teacher is called to witness to their Christian faith on a daily basis within the school.[48] The Catholic teacher is a person of hope in a number of senses.[49] The contemporary world is beset by enormous social and economic problems, and this is acknowledged in a number of Catholic documents.[50] The Catholic teacher is the one who lives and expresses the hope that the world and people can be changed and improved by the 'principles of the Gospel'.[51] Bernard Lonergan coined the phrase 'realistic optimism' to describe the Catholic Christian understanding of humanity.[52] While there is a 'realistic' approach to life and the challenges of life, the accent is on 'optimism'. The Catholic teacher has hope, for example, that the faith development of their students will continue beyond school and that they will develop into mature Christians.[53] The Catholic teacher is in need of charity to love each of the students, recognizing in each one that they are individuals who have been 'created in the image and likeness of God'.[54] This statement helps us understand the true distinctiveness of Catholic schools and the relationship between the Catholic teacher and her pupils. All school teaching necessarily involves some form of relationship with the pupils. Teachers often have a great love and care for their pupils (this is a characteristic of the 'exemplary' school teacher), but a Catholic teacher is called to love and care for the pupils because they recognize that the children have been created by God in his image and likeness – this goes beyond a shared humanity and

---

[46] Ibid., 18 There are, of course, different conceptions of what it is to be a human and these will influence the way in which human formation is conceived and implemented.

[47] Ibid., 6.

[48] Ibid., 40.

[49] Ibid., 72.

[50] Congregation for Catholic Institutions (1998), *The Catholic School on the Threshold of the Third Millennium*, 1–3; Congregation for Catholic Education (2007), *Educating Together in Catholic Schools*, 1.

[51] CCE (1982), *Lay Catholics in Schools: Witnesses to Faith*, section 19.

[52] Quoted in Thomas H. Groome, *Educating for Life* (Allen Texas: Thomas More, 1998) pp. 74–5.

[53] CCE (1982), *Lay Catholics in Schools: Witnesses to Faith*, 72.

[54] Ibid.

benevolence that can be discerned in many forms of non-faith schooling.

Contemporary Challenges for Catholic Schools

There are many serious contemporary challenges for Catholic schools, but this section will be restricted to examining three major challenges. The first is the secular challenge to the right of a Catholic school to exist in the public forum. The second is the effect of the vicissitudes of twenty-first century life on the outlook, psychological wellbeing and faith of the young people who attend Catholic schools. The third is the closely related challenge of the increasing isolation of the Catholic school as the only site of religious formation for many young people.

Sacred and secular

Catholic schools exist, as schools, in the public forum in a number of ways. They are located in buildings that have a physical presence in a local neighbourhood. They also exist as a reminder of the historical and contemporary influence of Christianity in the western world. Whenever there is a level of state funding, the Catholic schools also exist as a sector within some form of national or state educational jurisdiction. Catholic schools can be valued and validated in the public forum, but, especially when there is some form of state funding, the aims and operationalization of Catholic schools can be misunderstood and distrusted and they can attract opposition and even hostility. In the face of any such opposition or hostility, those who support Catholic schools and their continued existence must be able to articulate a clear account of the contribution of Catholic schools to the public polity and also identify and understand the arguments and positions adopted by those who oppose Catholic schools. There are strong counter-arguments to the existence of Catholic schools. Catholic schools, like all forms of faith schooling, are perceived to be an unacceptable use of public resources, exclusive, socially and religiously divisive, inhibiting rational autonomy, privileging the right of parental choice and restricting the rights of the child.[55]

[55] These arguments are drawn from the British Humanist Association website: BHA Education Policy – a summary. These arguments are analyzed and discussed in chapter one of S. J. McKinney, *Faith Schools in the Twenty-First Century* (2008). http://www.humanism.org.uk/education/education-policy.

Many of these counter-arguments are rooted in alternative views of the nature of society and education. The Humanist view is useful as an illustration because it is consistent, coherent and well-articulated. The Humanist view advocates the creation of a secular state, a complete separation of state and religion, and, consequently, a secular state-funded school system for all children that would aim to ensure equality of opportunity.[56] This secular system would aim to help all children, from a plurality of backgrounds whether religious or secular, understand themselves and their relationship with others, the world and its diversity, their role in this world and, ultimately, realize their potential. There would be no Catholic schools, and no other forms of faith schooling. There would be no forms of religious observance or 'collective worship' but inclusive school assemblies – practice of religious belief would be consigned to the private sphere of life. The Humanists propose further that the subject of religious education should become be broadened to be more inclusive of non-religious beliefs and should probably be re-titled 'Belief and Values Education, or Philosophy, or (as in Scotland) Religious and Moral Education / Religious, Moral and Philosophical Studies'.[57]

While the different arguments concerning Catholic schools are argued and counter argued, and the dialogue continues to develop, the Catholic viewpoint and the secular viewpoint (as expressed by the Humanists) are polarized positions and can never be reconciled. The concept of Catholic schooling is constructed within a Catholic Christian belief system that positions God at the heart of its epistemology and ontology. The secular viewpoint believes in the goodness of humanity and strives for the flourishing and progress of humanity, but within an epistemological and ontological framework that is founded on humanity and rejects any possibility of a deity.

Disorientation of the young

As the Church vision of Catholic schools develops through the late twentieth and early twenty-first century, it is grounded in a realistic appraisal of the changes in contemporary society, culture and lifestyles, and the effects of these changes on the young. These

---

[56] British Humanist Association: BHA Education Policy – a summary.
[57] British Humanist Association website: Religious Education. http://www.humanism.org.uk/campaigns/religion-and-schools/religious-education.

changes include greater urbanization and industrialization in some places – accompanied by the influence of an 'all-pervasive mass media'.[58] The young live in developed societies characterized by a rise in 'subjectivism, moral relativism and nihilism', often societies where Christianity has become increasingly marginalized.[59] The Church identifies a poverty and instability in family and societal relationships that results in young people becoming depressed and disaffected.[60] The young people are anxious when confronted by the complexity of the problems faced by contemporary societies (e.g. unemployment, war, poverty) and can be disorientated and struggle to discern meaning and value in contemporary life.[61] Some turn to drugs, alcohol or sex to escape loneliness or find meaning in life.[62] Some young people reject the gospel values espoused by the Catholic school. There is a growing number of children who come to the Catholic school from a disaffected family background. These children have little or no previous knowledge of Christianity and Christian lifestyle and a general lack of religious literacy. They will have very little contact with the local parish community.

The Catholic School as the Only Site of Religious Formation

When the Catholic school is the only place where Catholic children receive a religious formation, an immediate disjuncture in the actualization of the vision and rationale for Catholic schooling is created. The Catholic school is perceived to be in partnership with the parents and families and the local church to help the children on their journey of faith. When there is little or no input from the families and little or no contact with the local parish community, the responsibility for the religious formation of the children falls to the Catholic school. Church documentation, recognizing the weakening of the support system, calls upon the local parishes and church organizations to engage in self-evaluation of their efficacy and be more aware of their role in the religious formation of young people.[63] Nevertheless, in many situations, the Catholic

---

[58] CCE (1988), *The Religious Dimension of Education in the Catholic School,* 8–9.
[59] CCE (1997), *Catholic Schools,* Introduction.
[60] CCE (1988), *The Religious Dimension of Education in the Catholic School,* 10–11; Congregation for Catholic Education (2007) 1.
[61] Ibid., *Educating Together in Catholic Schools,* 12; Congregation for Catholic Education (2007), *Educating Together in Catholic Schools,* 1.
[62] CCE (1988) 13.
[63] CCE (1988) 17.

school is often the only site where the disaffected and religiously illiterate children will experience the opportunity for encounter with Jesus Christ through the scriptures, tradition and liturgical and sacramental celebrations. The role of the contemporary Catholic school in introducing these children to encounter with Christ for the first time (or re-introducing them and attempting to re-engage them) becomes crucial.[64] This can be very challenging, especially in those Catholic schools that include significant numbers of children who have no family experience of Christian life and faith or children who are disaffected. There are further serious implications for the ongoing religious formation of these children as they become young adults (and adults) and leave the Catholic school, the only site of religious formation for them. They may not enjoy, or have any access to, ongoing support in their religious formation once they have left the Catholic school.

In response to these challenges, more recent church documentation calls for Catholic schools to have a renewed awareness of their rationale and purpose and work towards their aims with vigor. *Educating Together in Catholic Schools* emphasizes the multi-layered concept of 'communion' as a fundamental principle for the identity of the Catholic school and elaborates this concept as *educating in communion* and *for communion*. The *education for communion*, consistent with the outward-looking vision of Catholic schooling, is not just for communion with Christianity but, ultimately, for communion with 'man, events and things'.[65] The importance of the role and the formation of the Catholic teacher are reiterated and they are called to play their part in the creation of the communion of the Catholic school.

Concluding Remarks

This chapter has outlined the contemporary rationale and vision for Catholic schools, focusing on the nature of the Catholic schools and the role of the Catholic teacher. Some of the serious contemporary challenges for Catholic schools have been addressed. Despite the challenges, Catholic schools continue to be successful in a number of ways. In the last ten years, Catholic schools have

---

[64] Stephen J. McKinney and Robert J. Hill, 'Reflection for the Catholic Secondary School on the Parable of the Father and his Two Sons', in *Journal of Religious Education*, 57 (2009), 4, p. 44.
[65] CCE (2007), 39, 43.

experienced publicly articulated support from a number of political parties and governments that is unprecedented.[66] There is an ongoing academic debate about the educational effectiveness of Catholic schools and while they may not enjoy significantly higher results in public examinations than their non-faith schools counterparts, they appear to be as successful, if not marginally better at times.[67] Apart from the success in examinations and the opportunity for social mobility, Catholic schools are perceived by many parents to be 'good' schools that are based on Christian values and continue to have a mission to serve the poor. They have become a popular form of schooling, attracting not just families with a Catholic background, but providing a choice for parents and children of other Christian denominations, of other faiths and those from no faith background.[68] In all of these markers of success, the Catholic schools have a responsibility to retain a sense of their distinctive identity – the harmony between the civic institution and Catholic community has to be maintained and evenly balanced. The Catholic school community has to acquire a deep-rooted understanding of the Christ-centred epistemology and ontology that are at the heart of its daily operations.[69]

---

[66] Stephen J. McKinney, *Faith Schools in the Twenty-First Century* (2008).

[67] Ibid.

[68] While the Catholic school must respect the religious freedom of these students it also has a duty to proclaim the gospel (CCE (1988), *The Religious Dimension of Education in the Catholic School*, 6). This inclusion can create a tension in the Catholic school. For a helpful discussion see Maurice Ryan 'Including students who are not Catholics in Catholic schools: problems, issues and responses', in S. J. McKinney (2008) (ed.) *Faith Schools in the Twenty-First Century*.

[69] 'The Catholic teacher is called to be a person of faith, hope, charity and love, a person with a realistic optimism and, in these challenging times, a person of courage.' Stephen J. McKinney, 'Christ at the Centre of the Catholic School' in *Networking*, vol. 10, 2009 issue 5, pp. 18–19. 5.

Chapter 10

Contemporary Approaches to Religious Education

Leon Robinson

The relationship between religions and education is difficult. Attempting to make sense of the shared spiritual experiences of humankind, and the many traditions which have sought to interpret it, is a path on which it is easy to start, but even easier to get lost.

In preparing for work in the classroom, the teacher is always required to consider what the children will encounter. What will they see, hear, smell, taste and touch? As well as this, teachers need to ask how, whether or why pupils might find this interesting, what they will make of it, and what they will gain.

The cultural context in which teaching and learning happens today needs to be taken into account. We are living in what can be described as a 'post-modern' world. What does this mean? Considerably more heat than light has been generated in arguments about 'postmodernism (see, for example, Lyotard's *The Postmodern Condition* and its myriad offspring, including Alan Sokal's infamous hoax for the *Social Text* journal and the creation of a 'postmodernism generator' which produces seemingly erudite, impeccably referenced nonsense at the click of a mouse).[1]

To clarify, 'modern' refers to the world view characterized by the belief that facts are discoverable, and truth is objectively knowable. This view is distinct from the pre-modern view, in which truths were revealed by God, in religious, infallible texts. The modern view gave the scientific method to the world, allowed the agricultural and industrial revolutions to transform almost every aspect of

---

[1] Jean-François Lyotard, *The Postmodern Condition* (Manchester: Manchester University Press, 1979).

modern life, and contributed to the development of almost every piece of technology that we in the West consider indispensable.

Unfortunately, many of those who subscribed to this in many ways uncontroversial Modern view also subscribed to assumptions about the proper ordering of society. At its most simply caricatured, this would be a society dominated by white, heterosexual, able-bodied men, who were firm in their belief that women, people of other races, sexual preferences or physical abilities were not only different, but inferior, disordered or wrong. There were understandable reasons for this – the able-bodied white men had, at least on their own terms, succeeded in demonstrating to their own satisfaction, their superiority, and had mistaken this hegemony for moral superiority.

For a number of reasons beyond the scope of this chapter, this hegemony has been challenged, and it is now widely acknowledged that the supposed objectivity of the modern world was to an extent compromised by the perspectives of the dominant. The degree of distortion is still disputed, and is likely always to remain so. What has emerged of value, however, is the insight that different perspectives have both value and validity. History is understood very differently by the victors and the victims in any dispute, but both perspectives will provide valuable insights.

Hence the post-modern world, in which a wide variety of perspectives can seriously be considered, whether or not they agree with the consensus or dominant view of the world. Postmodernism is not necessarily characterized by the belief that all truths are subjective, and that 'Truth' is nowhere to be found. The assumed polarities and mutual exclusivity of the modern and postmodern positions are not necessary. Frameworks of understanding and interpretation, all of which are subjective to some extent, will include varying degrees of objectivity in their picture of the world. This does not destroy or undermine the objectivity of the truth – it does, however, explain how and why people disagree about so many things.

How does this apply to the RE classroom?

There is value in taking an approach to religions which takes more than a single perspective into account. One view of a religion will be taken by insiders, those for whom the tradition provides the meaning, purpose and structure to their lives. Quite another may be taken by those who study the tradition from the outside. The view that 'religion is always a mystery to the outsider' is one which must be taken seriously. There is an understandable view from devotees of religious traditions that one can only understand the faith from within. In order to address this concern, and as a useful check on the temptation to judge rashly, or analyse traditions unfairly, the Canadian scholar Wilfred Cantwell Smith suggested that no statement made about religion can be considered valid unless an insider would agree with it.[2] This in itself raises questions as to who might be considered an insider to traditions which contain considerable differences and disagreements. This will be further explored later in this chapter.

Outsiders may be from different religious traditions, when the temptation will be to understand the alien in familiar terms. A Christian might interpret the Hindu concept of Brahman, for example, as God. If this interpretation involves the assumption that all the qualities of the Christian God, such as personality, relationship and activity in history, which the Christian concept carries with it, this would be a misunderstanding and a misrepresentation of the Hindu term. Likewise, there will always be the temptation for atheists to interpret religious experiences and artefacts in a materialist and reductive manner. To the non-believer, the sacraments are only water, bread and wine and believers are, therefore, mistaken about matters of fact, demonstrable through entirely unsuitable, although irrefutable, scientific experiments. These reductionist accounts of religion and their associated sentiments are of no use to the Catholic teacher, however. Adhering to the faith, religious sentiments in others must always be seen in terms of a search for truth, a response to God.

In the 1965 Declaration of the Relationship of the Church to Non-Christian Religions *Nostra Aetate*, the Catholic Church made clear for the first time her esteem for other religions:

> The Catholic Church rejects nothing that is true and holy in these religions. She regards with sincere reverence those ways of conduct and of life, those precepts and teachings which, though differing in many aspects from the ones she holds and sets forth, nonetheless often reflect a ray of that Truth which enlightens all men.[3]

---

[2] Kenneth Cracknell (ed.) *Wilfred Cantwell Smith: a Reader* (Oxford: Oneworld, 2001).

[3] Second Vatican Council (1965), *Nostra aetate*, 2.

A catechetical and evangelical approach which excludes any consideration of the value of other, different 'ways of conduct and of life ... precepts and teaching' should, therefore, not be used in Catholic schools. How the teacher negotiates the complexities of world faiths, in classrooms which may be composed of a variety of believers and non believers from a range of backgrounds, presents an interesting and difficult challenge in the twenty-first century.

The problem is, as argued by Robert Segal, whether or not reductionist interpretations themselves refute the reality of God – non-believers, as long as they are nonbelievers, can use only them.[4] His is a pressing concern for the RE teacher in the contemporary classroom, as there is likely to be a large number of secular pupils in all classrooms.

Contemporary Approaches

In his collection of case studies in the research and development of good pedagogic practice in Religious Education, Michael Grimmitt suggests we need to consider three questions:

- What kind of interactions between pupils and religious content does the model seek to promote?
- What procedures or strategies are employed in order to achieve this?
- What principles inform the procedures, including choice of content?[5]

These are questions that teachers should ask themselves in preparing schemes of work for Religious Education. The superficial question of 'what we are going to cover this term' is hardly sufficient when the subject matter in question concerns the very meaning of life, as understood by different cultures across space and time. The differing responses to questions of ultimate concern, about the nature, purpose and value of all things, continue to supply the world with beauty and horror, compassion and cruelty beyond measure. In approaching this subject matter,

[4] Robert Segal, 'In Defense of Reductionism', in *Journal of the American Academy of Religion* 51, 1, 1983, pp. 97–124.
[5] Michael Grimmitt (ed.), *Pedagogies of Religious Education: Case Studies in the Research and Development of Good Pedagogic Practice in RE* (Essex: McCrimmon Publishing, 2007).

the very least we as teachers should be doing is considering our reasons for teaching what we do.

There are unquestioned assertions and assumptions made about contemporary Religious Education that the classroom will be post-Christian, secular, indifferent if not hostile to religion as a source of meaning and value; either that, or so richly diverse as to offer a hothouse of inter-cultural opportunities for learning about different traditions in a multi-cultural kaleidoscope of enriching opportunities. The reality for many teachers in contemporary Britain is rather different. It should be remembered that, while the UK is remarkably mono-cultural in many areas, and not all classrooms are characterized by multi-culturalism, teachers must be prepared to respond to the particular needs of their classes, while preparing their pupils for the likelihood of encountering a wide range of beliefs, practices and traditions over the course of their lives. Christianity, while no longer being the almost universally held faith of the country which it once was, is still an important aspect of self-identity for the majority of UK households. How successfully this identity is transmitted to or understood by children of school age is a moot point. Where other faiths are present, they are often quite understandably concentrated in protective, insular communities, separated as much by language as by other cultural dimensions (including religion). Children brought up in a particular religious context may have inherited prejudices and preconceptions from their families and communities. Perhaps an even greater challenge is presented by the increasingly secular context in which many pupils have been brought up, in which they have not been exposed to religious language or concepts in anything other than mockery.

It is rare to find multiple cultures spread evenly like leaven in the social mix. Every area, every neighbourhood, every classroom will be different. It is in this context that the approaches to Religious Education need to be considered.

Critical Realist Approach

The challenges raised by the postmodern context led Nicholas (NT)Wright, later to be Bishop of Durham, to propose a form of critical realism. This is a way of describing the process of 'knowing' that acknowledges the reality of the thing known, as something other than the knower (hence 'realism'), while fully acknowledging that the only access we have to this reality lies along the spiraling path of appropriate dialogue or conversation between

the knower and the thing known (hence 'critical').[6] This acknowl-
edgement of the limitations of perception and understanding will
be useful to bear in mind when examining the various other
approaches suggested.

The Phenomenological Approach

The phenomenological approach, looking for the 'essence' of religion by looking at a variety of different expressions (such as Islam,
Buddhism, animism and so on) was a major development in religious studies, moving as it did away from the Christian-centred
critique which characterized earlier, more theological approaches
to the study of religion. It is entirely understandable that an
approach which takes seriously the expression of religious sentiments, and the exploration of religious questions beyond the
confines of Christian theology, should appeal to the increasingly
secular student of religion and philosophy. What works in religious
studies, however, is not necessarily suitable for religious education,
particularly in the context of Catholic schools. The phenomenological approach invites students to set aside all preconceptions,
bracketing them out of the picture, in order to learn about religious traditions empathetically, walking in the shoes of believers,
as it were, in order to understand how the world looks through
other eyes.

However, there are a number of distinct problems with this
approach. The assumption that it is possible to bracket out one's
own preconceptions is highly questionable, particularly with
regard to the use of language – the very words we use are culturally loaded, creating and reinforcing a conceptual and cultural
framework in which we make sense of our experiences and our
world. To suppose that the *dharma* traditions can be understood
using only English language, for example, is questionable in the
extreme, as there is not, nor can there be, a direct translation of
the cluster of concepts referred to as the *dharma*, into an English
word or phrase.

The phenomenological approach championed by Ninian Smart
and others became in the hands of less rigorous scholars and non-
specialist teachers in the classroom, distorted and diluted, despite
the best efforts of many involved in the design of RE curricular
documents, becoming in the end a transmission of mere facts about

---

[6] Andrew Wright, *Religious Education in the Secondary School: Prospects for Religious
   Literacy* (London: David Fulton, 1993).

religious traditions, paying little regard to the significance of these, or to the complexities of lives as lived, religious or otherwise.[7]

The new approaches to RE are in many ways attempts to redress the imbalances caused by the well meaning but doomed approach of phenomenology.

The Anthropological Approach

In order to learn about religions, a student might study books or other written sources, and get what might seem to be a firm grasp on the subject in all its complexity and exoticism. The problem with this method of study is that it rests on the assumption that the authors of the original texts knew what they were talking about, and gave an accurate representation of their subject. This has not always been the case, and many highly questionable books have been written, using only earlier books as the source of their information. The phenomenon of relying on texts rather than on other evidence is known as intertextuality. The dogged insistence repeated in many introductory texts on Hinduism, for example, that Hindus worship three main deities, all of whom are male, owes more to the lens through which the Indian religious traditions were initially viewed by Christian scholars than it does to Indian religious practices, where the worship of the goddess Devi in her myriad forms is almost universal.

In order to avoid this problem, the anthropological approach to study is suggested. Rather than studying from the comfort of the armchair, the anthropologist (following Malinowski) should make observations of what people actually do. The anthropologist can then 'make sense' of these actions, habits, rituals and engagements. There is clearly potential in this approach for much hilarity, (for example in Nigel Barley's account of his work in *The Innocent Anthropologist*) as the ideas and motives of people going about their daily business are rarely self-evident, and are liable to be understood within the conceptual framework brought along by the observer.[8] Hence the Hindu's morning salutation to the sun might be understood by the devout Muslim as idolatry, mistaking the creation for the creator. The Catholic's prayer to the Virgin might be similarly misunderstood. The difference between veneration and worship is subtle, and lost on many.

---

[7] Ninian Smart was a key scholar in Religious Education in the 1960s and beyond. His work is still influential today.

[8] Nigel Barley, *The Innocent Anthropologist: Notes from a Mud Hut* (Harmondsworth: Penguin, 1986).

The anthropology of a more philosophical bent, following Levi Strauss, advocates the critical examination of social structural forms, such as the rules regarding sex and marriage. This, too, is less than objective. There are important questions to be asked as to who has the better understanding of social structural forms – the insider-participant or the outside observer.

There are important questions to consider as to what sort of understanding is being sought in the RE classroom. Take, for example, the nature of the Catholic Church: what sorts of understanding are being promoted through a critical reappraisal of its history, taking in a line of highly questionable pontiffs, simony, patriarchal misogyny, resistance to science, and repression of dissent? Is a proper understanding of the Church best served by this historical critical approach, or by the testimony of a contemporary believer, for whom the Church provides solace and support, community and purpose?

The Church is no more likely to agree with the anthropology of Feuerbach or Durkheim, who maintained that religions are the creations of the societies in which they occur. It would be astonishing if the views of Marx, Freud, or Weber were to be given much room in the syllabus of the Catholic school. There are some approaches which are simply incompatible. What, then, would be the nature of a Catholic anthropological approach? The examination of concepts such as descent, relationships, matrimony, as building blocks of societies cannot, unless conducted by outsider perspectives, be properly described as 'anthropological'.

A non-judgemental, descriptive analysis is not possible while maintaining a faith perspective. Consider, for example, what an RE teacher is to make of couples who would like to get married in a church, with all the 'trappings' such as prayers and hymns, while at the same time rejecting the very existence of God. This appropriation of religious activities by the irreligious is not confined to the unthinking. The militant atheist scientist Richard Dawkins confesses to finding carol services 'moving' even while he attacks religions as 'child abuse' in *The God Delusion*.[9]

This raises a fundamental question which needs to be asked about the extent to which one can accord respect to those with whom one disagrees completely. While the Church is willing to extend respect to religious seekers of other traditions, to the extent that their faith practices will be studied (although seen as more or less misguided), no such respect is accorded to the atheist

[9] Richard Dawkins, *The God Delusion* (London: Transworld Publishers, 2006).

traditions, which are not to be studied. Is the assumption that there is no respectable tradition to study? Questions might be raised as to the reasons that no such tradition has been allowed to exist, given the history of intolerance of heretics and apostates that the Church has only recently in its long history seen fit to put behind it – and that not completely. Working on the assumption that one has the Truth, respect to those who differ can only ever be limited. In a country such as Scotland, where a very sizeable minority (nearly thirty per cent in the 2001 Census) declared that they had no religion, the refusal to countenance non-religious stances as being worthy of study hardly accords respect to all, nor does it provide evidence to support the claim that the Catholic school 'should support all children and young people in their personal search for truth and meaning in life'.[10]

An anthropology of the irreligious would certainly be challenging. It would be a difficult and problematic approach for any researcher to take, and it is far beyond the resources of the working RE teacher to undertake this sort of approach.

The Interpretive Approach

Another approach suggested in response to the perceived weaknesses of earlier efforts is the Interpretive Approach. Chief amongst the problems associated with the phenomenological approach, it could be argued, was the implicit assumption that religions were identifiable entities or groups, with memberships that were understandable, clearly defined and distinct. Thinking about any or all of the traditional groupings of religions studied in the UK, for example, Christianity, Islam and Hinduism, it soon becomes clear that there are questions as to how these traditions are to be represented. Should Islam be represented as Sunni, Shi'ite or Sufi? Is Christianity best understood by examining the traditions of the Catholic, Protestant or Orthodox? When studying the traditions grouped under the label 'Hinduism', are Shaivite, Vaisnavite or Shakta traditions to be examined? Even labelling such divisions implies that the divisions themselves represent clearly demarcated sects within the greater tradition, but this is far from being the case. Schisms and distinctions are made between dogmas, and the varieties of interpretations and lived experiences within any of the traditions are complex.

[10] Scottish Executive, *A Curriculum For Excellence Principles and Practice*, p. 1.

Using techniques from a range of disciplines, including ethnography, philosophy, cultural studies and psychology, the interpretive approach developed by Robert Jackson's team in the Warwick RE project from the early 1990s (and ongoing) reassesses the pedagogical principles in RE and has identified three key areas for consideration and attention: representation, interpretation and reflexivity.

The issue of representation places emphasis on the need to appreciate the diversity within the traditions studied. Consideration must be given as to which examples from the range of possible alternatives teachers will present as being representative of that tradition. In their early work, the Warwick RE Project produced a series of books in which the religious traditions were 'presented' by children of the tradition, of a similar age group to those being taught. There is a great deal to be gained from this, as pupils of no faith background will not be misled into believing that religion is something exclusively for old people.

Interpretation is seen as a necessary and inescapable process, and has to be undertaken consciously, oscillating between the perceptions of the tradition experienced by the outsider studying it, and the perceptions of the traditions experienced by the 'insider', the member of the community or faith tradition being studied. Just as one goes through a process of translating when learning a new language, unfamiliar religious ideas are, at first, interpreted in terms from more familiar traditions. The challenge is to gain the sort of understanding of religious ideas that a believer might have – a challenge complicated by the fact that many followers of faith traditions believe and belong with only the vaguest notion of what it is they believe in. Church pews have never been occupied solely by theologians, and the Hindu in the street is unlikely to be a scholar of Sanskrit. Quite what it is to understand a religious idea, as distinct from accepting or believing it, is still a matter of considerable debate. Does a student of Christianity, for example, understand what a devout Christian means when they say 'I know in my heart that my saviour lives'?

It is this tension between academic knowledge and personal affective understanding that is, to some extent, addressed in the third key area of concern in the interpretive approach. The issue of reflexivity recognizes that in the process of studying a subject, both the student and the subject will be liable to change, each under the influence of the other. While the impact of a class studying Islam will not have any impact on the Five Pillars of that faith, the consideration of questions about the faith, addressed to members of the tradition, may have a significant impact on that person's understanding of their own tradition. Equally, in examining the beliefs, practices and assumptions made about the nature and purpose of life in a different tradition may have a significant impact on the student of that tradition.

The result should be that not only do pupils learn about religions, they learn from them in doing so.

The Experiential Approach

Both the anthropological and interpretive approach may give the impression that religion is something which other people, perhaps a minority are involved in, and which may be of interest to study. Alister Hardy's research in the 1960s suggested that religious or spiritual experiences are very common.[11] He further suggested that, if we are to accept the truth of evolutionary theory (and he saw no reason not to) then the capacity for such experiences must have had a survival value for humans. In their work building on these insights and speculations, Hay and Hammond et al. suggested that in order for pupils to understand the nature of religions, they should be allowed to develop their awareness of the aspects of life which are traditionally of interest to religious traditions, particularly the experience of being in the moment, experiencing being alive and aware of what is happening, without the 'noise' of distractions that are almost always sought in our culture (information, music or other media, news, gossip, conversations, memories, anticipations and plans).[12] In the stillness of any moment, reality continues, and when other distractions are stilled, reality might be perceived. This is variously understood as meditation, prayer, or mindfulness.

The many ways in which religious traditions have understood and interpreted this reality might then be explored in a sympathetic and empathetic way. Without the opportunity to experience, pupils are dealing with abstract (and therefore to most, less interesting) ideas. The aim is to educate pupils' awareness of the processes of consciousness, of thinking as interpreting. In order to do this, exercises are suggested to encourage pupils to keep an

[11] Alister Hardy, *The Spiritual Nature of Man: a study of contemporary religious experience* (Oxford: Clarendon Press, 1979).
[12] John Hammond, David Hay, Jo Moxon, Brian Netto, Kathy Robson and Ginny Straughier, *New Methods in RE Teaching: An Experiential Approach* (London: Oliver and Boyd / Longman, 1990).

open mind, rather than jump to conclusions within their habitual cultural confines. A well known example used by Hay was to present a 'Necker Cube' – a deliberately ambiguous series of lines, usually read as a representation of a cube, which can be interpreted in many different ways. It has been observed that viewers become quite attached to their initial interpretation of the image, and are resistant to alternative interpretations. In examining these responses, divorced from any emotional or social content, we can learn a great deal about the mental habits and processes which may inform our attitudes to the unfamiliar, such as those we are exposed to in studying other faiths. Once pupils have experienced this phenomenon of their own innate resistance to different ways of seeing things, they may then be more able to explore more complex examples of different ways of seeing, and understand the many ways in which reality has been understood and interpreted throughout the history of the world.

In order to make meaningful explorations of different perspectives, a high degree of skill and sensitivity is required on the part of the RE teacher. For pupils to benefit from an experiential approach, the classroom must be a place of safety and trust. Pupils must know each other, and be certain that anything they share in the context of the class will not be used against them. For a school which has not addressed issues of bullying, for example, it would not be advisable or acceptable to attempt this sort of approach. Teachers must be honest in their appraisal of the individual situations of their classes and, importantly, listen respectfully to any concerns voiced by pupils. If pupils are unwilling to share experiences, there is probably a good reason for this. It would not be appropriate to discipline pupils who did not wish to share their thoughts or feelings.

Once a classroom environment of safety and trust has been established, the further activities in the experiential RE classroom will include raising awareness, through allowing pupils to 'be in the moment'. Attention needs to be drawn to the fact that awareness is embodied, realising that our experiences of the moment are informed and interpreted through our bodies, and our particular histories. The male and female experiences will differ for example, as will the experiences of those raised in secure and nurturing environments differ from those raised in homes characterised by confrontation, chaos, neglect or abuse. Awareness can then be extended, through the exploration of others' interpretations, through religious and other stories, for example. The sensed presence of another being may be understood by one tradition as an

angelic experience, by another as illusion, or yet again as a possible communication across the dimensions of a multi-verse. The
possibilities are endless, interesting and worth exploring.

Endings of such lessons need careful management. If pupils
have been taken on interior journeys, confronting deep personal
questions which may be profoundly moving for them, it would be
irresponsible to allow these experiences to end abruptly with the
intrusion of the end of session bell, hurling pupils straight into the
mundane and difficult world of the school corridor. Time for
appropriate adjustment and transition into the ordinary world
needs to be built into any such session.

The experiential approach can be used to supplement a
variety of other approaches to RE, as it adds another dimension
to learning.

RE as a Gift to the Child

Although the experiential approach requires considerable skill
from the teacher, and is an approach best adopted by RE specialists rather than those for whom RE is sometimes the 'filler' in their
timetable, it does represent an important development in the
pedagogy of RE. Centring on the developmental needs of children,
rather than on the need of the subject to be understood and
respected, John Hull and his team developed an approach to RE in
primary and lower secondary schools which was to enable the non-
specialist teacher to become confident in an approach to religious
topics, without necessarily becoming expert in religious topics.

Taking a range of religious articles ('numena', from Rudolf
Otto's *Idea of the Holy*), teachers could introduce children to articles of importance to faith communities, firstly inviting them in to
appreciate the unique qualities of the object, be this Our Lady of
Lourdes, Ganesha, the Call to Prayer or the story of Jonah, for
example, then to explore it, contextualize it, and reflect on it.[13]
This would be done through techniques firstly by 'entering' the
subject, becoming familiar with it, then through 'distancing
devices', learning that the article is of significance and sacredness
to particular communities. This would be done through the
introduction of materials about how a member of the faith community would approach, appreciate and understand the article in
question.

---

[13] Rudolf Otto, *The Idea of the Holy: an inquiry into the non-rational factor in the idea of
the divine and its relation to the rational* (London: Oxford University Press, 1929).

As with the interpretive approach, children from the communities are used as guides into the traditions. Appreciation of aspects of another's faith leads into reflection on articles and issues of importance to the individual child – questions of belonging, in particular, with all that means to children and their growing identities, are particularly powerful opportunities presented by this method.

The success of this approach depends largely on the ability of the teacher to use carefully selected materials in such a way as to bring children close enough to appreciate the tradition being studied, while maintaining the appropriate distance from it. This is comparable to the skills of a navigator or ship's pilot. It is one thing to get close enough to a waterfall to feel and appreciate its power – it is quite another to fall or be thrown into it.

The Narrative Approach

Also arising from the conviction that too much RE was 'content led', while insufficient attention was being paid to the abilities and experiences of pupils, the narrative approach to RE was developed by researchers Clive and Jane Erricker.[14] The approach is a reaction against the educational theories and policies dominant in the UK during the 1980s, where the competencies of skills, knowledge and understanding were, and to a great extent still are, seen as the only suitable (or possible) measures of learning having taken place. It is important to understand the full import of the context in which this arises, where questions concerning the legitimacy of RE as a subject to be studied at all are repeatedly raised by those who would prefer to see religion consigned to the dustbin of history. In seeking to justify itself as a subject worthy not only of study, but suitable for examination, religion is at something of a disadvantage in comparison to the material sciences, or the disciplines of history, languages or literature. As soon as facts become the focus, the purpose of religions is lost. Concerns were also expressed by educational and cultural critics as to the extent to which Christianity should be the focus of RE – was this an attempt to include moral education in schools, or an attempt to make that moral education specifically Christian in character?

---

[14] Clive Erricker and Jane Erricker, 'The Children and Worldviews Project: A Narrative Pedagogy of Religious Education', in Michael Grimmitt (ed.), *Pedagogies of Religious Education. Case Studies in the Research and Development of Good Pedagogic Practice in RE* (Great Wakering, McCrimmons, 2000), pp. 188–206.

The narrative approach attempts to give more weight to what matters in the lives of pupils, rather than what is understood by teachers to matter. This must not be seen as an approach entirely determined by the interests and preconceptions of children, but rather involving the learners in the shaping of the material which is learned. Instead of the classroom being the place where a curriculum is delivered, it is a place where children and young people are listened to and responded to in a nurturing way, through sensitive, guided and well-informed conversations. Taking children's spirituality seriously is central to this approach. The Errickers' convictions that religions represent 'grand narratives' which tend to silence the smaller narratives of individuals, however, lead them to the untenable conviction that children are better off working out their own responses to 'the struggles and joys of faith, the difficulties and successes of constructing values and community without recourse to simply presenting them with the sanitising ideological platitudes of religious tradition.'[15] It may seem that the Errickers give rather more respect to children than they do to their adult professional peers, and in doing so present an unbalanced account of what religious education consists in. It is one thing to value the small narratives of individual experiences, interpretations and value judgements. It is quite another to discard the wisdom of the world's religions in favour of the insights of any and every child who is given a few minutes in the classroom. Without significant input and appropriate guidance from the teacher, it is unlikely that children, particularly those from backgrounds without a religious vocabulary, will develop anything but the most naive and uninformed views. We should be wary of encouraging uninformed naivety in the name of education, as this is the very ground in which intolerance and prejudice thrive.

The chief concern about the narrative approach is that, in discarding any sense of Truth in favour of 'narrative pragmatics' (a phrase coined by Jean François Lyotard in *The Postmodern Condition*), teachers and pupils alike are leaving themselves undefended against intolerance. Far from being an enrichment of the learning experience, an unrestrained relativism leaves open the door to the very repressive 'grand narratives' of racism, sexism and homophobia that have too often been associated, accurately or otherwise, with religious traditions. It is unlikely that these attitudes are any less repugnant in the mouths of individuals than they are in the ideologies of organized religions. Their power to convince may be diminished, but the offence is the same.

[15] Ibid., p. 204.

On a practical level, responding to all learners as unique individuals clearly raises considerable challenges for the classroom practitioner. To engage thirty or more children in personally meaningful individual conversations over a forty-minute period is not an achievable goal. This should not dissuade teachers from moving away from a content-centred approach and towards an approach which valorizes the individual learner's contribution, but the fundamental relativism advocated by the Errickers is unlikely to provide a workable pedagogy in the contemporary RE classroom.

The Religious Literacy Approach

A balance needs to be struck between the content driven 'facts about religions' approach and the radical relativism suggested by the narrative approach. An approach which attempts to find this balance is advocated by Andrew Wright, Roger Homan and Philip Barnes, amongst others, developing what they refer to as religious literacy. Andrew Wright makes his concerns about the naive egocentrism of the narrative approach. 'Religious understanding is achieved not by any pre-linguistic introspection, but through the mastery of language that derives its meaning from public traditions.'[16] This is a form of the critical realism advocated by Nicholas Wright, explicitly rejecting the isolated, solitary image of the human being in general and the learner in particular, in favour of a more humane understanding of our condition. We are not dislocated individuals, creating our more or less coherent meanings from fragmented and chaotic personal narratives. 'Critical realism has challenged this image of dislocation; to be genuinely human requires a recognition of our reciprocal relationships within the world. We do not stand god-like above reality, but indwell the world of nature and culture.'[17]

It is important in introducing ideas of religious literacy through the exploration of religious language that the richness and mystery of this language is preserved and valued. 'The banking of fragments of information without the opportunity to apply them in a real context is a phenomenon of the culture of the trivial and the superficial' warns Homan, in a scathing critique of the trend towards reductive and closed glossaries that are increasingly used

[16] Andrew Wright, 'Language and Experience in the Hermeneutics of Religious Understanding', in *British Journal of Religious Education*, 18:3, 1996, pp. 166–80.
[17] Ibid.

in curricular documents, in text books, and consequently in class-rooms.[18] A literacy approach must be enriching for the learner.

> The mark of the religiously educated child within such an approach would be his or her ability to think, act and communicate with insight and intelligence in the light of that diversity of religious truth claims that are the mark of our contemporary culture.[19]

In order to accomplish this literacy, pupils should be encouraged and supported towards an appropriately challenging encounter with the wealth of religious texts, their beauty and mystery intact. Homan is particularly critical of some modern translations of the Bible, seeing the style of some as being 'worthy of the civil service rather than appropriate to use in worship. 'A literacy strategy which diminishes the literary quality of text and deprives its clients of the experience of the power and poetry of religious language sells them short.'[20]

RE specialists should resist the temptation to simplify, bowdler-ize or tidy up religious texts as simple language and pictures may resolve mysteries and ambiguities that are better left untouched.[21] To imagine the resurrection of Jesus is probably a lot more reward-ing than to see the literal, pious and, to many, laughable representation of the event in, for example, Mel Gibson's *Passion of the Christ.*

This is far removed from the narrative approach, and brings with it considerable challenges, particularly in classrooms where pupils are not well disposed towards religious ideas or language. Ironically, many young people may have been put off religious language and imagery by exposure to lifeless readings of over familiar texts, either in classrooms or in chapels. Nevertheless, only by mastering the language of religions can proper sense be made of the widespread experiences of the numinous.

> Intellectual, moral, aesthetic and religious development here requires the appropriation of public forms of language as a means of understanding, ordering, and responding appropriately in a way freed from the tyranny of self-reliance.[22]

[18] Roger Homan, 'Religion and literacy: observations on religious education and the literacy strategy for secondary education in Britain', in *British Journal of Religious Education,* 26:1, 2004, pp. 21–32.

[19] Ibid.

[20] Ibid.

[21] Ibid.

[22] Andrew Wright, 'Language and Experience in the Hermaneutics of Religious Understanding'.

The Constructivist Approach

It should be clear that the contemporary social context of the UK requires approaches to RE which are creative, take account of the learner as much as the subject content, and are open to the unexpected, the creative and the individual. Making things relevant to learners does not require the rejection of anything that does not have an immediate and obvious bearing on the lives and interests of pupils. The project is to expand and enrich their lives, not to confirm preconceptions, entrench habits or valorise limitations.

Partly in an attempt to draw on all the strengths of various approaches, while doing justice to the insights of postmodernism, Michael Grimmitt suggests a constructivist approach to RE. Constructivism is a way of understanding learning through the careful examination and analysis of how people make sense of things. It started with the insights of Piaget, who saw learning as a process in which individuals would place new knowledge of the world, gained through personal experiences, into 'schemas' or cognitive structures in which the world could make sense. The approach advocated by Grimmitt favours a social constructivism, deriving from the work of Vygotsky, who suggested that knowledge was constructed socially, rather than individually. The approach can be emancipating, as it allows pupils and teachers to challenge accepted 'truths' through an active critique of assumptions and received wisdom. Whether or not this approach needs to take on the radically sceptical approach suggested by von Glaserfield for whom there is no objective reality, only 'an order and organisation of a world constituted by our own experience' is beyond the scope of this chapter.[23] Grimmit explains that the sequence of learning is always from encouraging egocentric interpretations of experience within '*situated thought,* through *alternative contextualised interpretations* (as represented by interventions from pupils or the teacher), to *evaluative judgements* about the interests which each interpretation serves and expresses' [Grimmitt's original italics].[24]

Many pupils may never have had the opportunity to consider the deeper meaning of things, or seriously considered the nature and purpose of their lives. There is little to encourage reflection and consideration of these matters in a culture characterised by instant gratification through endless purchasing and consumption. The

---

[23] Ernst von Glaserfield, 'Why Constructivism Must Be Radical' in Marie Larochelle, Nadine Bednarz and Jim Garrison (eds), *Constructivism and Education* (Cambridge: Cambridge University Press, 1998).

[24] Michael Grimmitt (ed.), *Pedagogies of Religious Education.*

very acts of not purchasing, not consuming, not moving immediately on to the next novelty as soon as things get difficult or dull, need to be considered as having value, and can themselves be acts of subversion and emancipation.

Concluding Remarks

Whichever approach or approaches we take to teaching RE, the focus should always be on how our teaching might enrich pupils' lives and point them towards spiritual possibilities.[25] The essentially mysterious, numinous quality of religion and religious experiences will in all probability continue to resist categorisation, will, like the faerie, flit away from direct observation. Whatever you look at, you will miss the thing you are looking for. In attempting to solve a related problem, namely Maria in *The Sound of Music*, the Mother Superior might have suspected that some things are simply not amenable to exploration through close examination: as soon as you attempt to hold a wave upon the sand, it ceases to be a wave.

---

[25] John Rudge in ibid., p. 108.

Chapter 11

The Use of Story in Catholic Religious Education

Mary F. Lappin

Introduction

> Teachers should help students begin to discover the mystery within
> the human person, just as Paul tried to help the people of Athens
> discover the 'Unknown God' ... that human history unfolds within
> a divine history of salvation; from creation, through the first sin, the
> covenant with the ancient people of God, the long period of waiting
> until finally Jesus our Saviour came, so that now we are the new
> people of God, pilgrims on earth journeying toward our eternal
> home.[1]

While recognizing storytelling as a skill and an art, this chapter will
explore the theological and educational value of using story in
Religious Education. Naturally, the newly qualified teacher prac-
tises and develops the skill of storytelling until it matures into an
art form. The effective telling of stories requires patience, hard
work and practice, for when a story is not told well it can lose its
emotive impact. Assumptions are made in this chapter that the
teacher will develop his or her own skill and techniques and
instead will concentrate on the theological and educational significance of story within Religious Education.

Story, like painting, sculpture, poetry and dance, is always an
experience of aesthetic emotion whereby heart and head, thought
and feeling merge into a meaningful experience. The greater the
emotional charge, the more memorable the experience. Aesthetic
emotion blends what we know with what we feel; story encourages
us to look at meaningfulness in the present, as it is happening. This

---

[1] CCE (1988), *The Religious Dimension of Education in a Catholic School.*

differs from reflection on one's life, situation or event, which becomes meaningful with reflection in time. Parables, for example, invite us to reflect in the here and now, for the setting, plot and characters are secondary; it is what the characters do that is of prime importance and that action brings the same call to conversion as when first told – a conversion that goes beyond the present to the rest of one's life. Story in the classroom allows for inner monologues reflecting on 'what would I do?' Events cause reactions and insight is gained.[2] In other words, authenticity is required, not actuality. Authenticity can be dependent on the teller who is attentive to the atmosphere, true to the message, and engaging in presentation.

Story – a Pedagogical Device

Contemporary educational theory and practice encourage collaboration, active participation and self-directed learning experiences with an emphasis on connectedness to one's life, community and environment. The classroom of today is one of discussion, group projects and research, and, hopefully, moments of quiet reflection and thoughtfulness. Within pedagogy of story, teacher and pupils leave the language of instruction and correction and enter the world of imagination, to be confounded by mystery and touched by the sacred. In her work on storytelling as a therapeutic tool in working with children, Margot Sunderland claims that the natural language of children is that of image and metaphor; stories can speak to children in deep and immediate levels for they use the 'language of imagining', in a way that literal, everyday language fails to enter, due to their 'sensory dryness'.[3] Sunderland's work is concerned with helping children with feelings, particularly troublesome and distressing emotions, whereby the child and adult engage in therapeutic narratives to enable understanding, growth and healing. Nevertheless she gives food for thought on the richness of experience and engagement that comes as a result of good storytelling.

A good story that enhances learning and teaching presents the archetype and is never stereotypical. Whilst primarily for screen

---

[2] Aristotle, 'Probable impossibilities are preferable to implausible possibilities' in *Poetics* (England: Penguin Books, 1996).
[3] Margot Sunderland, *Using Story Telling as a Therapeutic Tool* (UK: Speechmark Publishing, 2003), Chapter 1.

writers, Robert McKee's text book on '*Story. Substance, Structure, Style and the Principles of Screenwriting*', gives helpful guidance on the art of storytelling, warning against a tight focus on formula but rather stressing that a good story is a story worth telling and one that the world wants to hear.

> The archetypal story unearths a universally human experience, then wraps itself inside a unique, culture-specific expression. A stereotypical story reverses this pattern: it suffers a poverty of both content and form. It confines itself to a narrow, culture-specific experience and dresses in stale, non-specific generalities.[4]

Stories teach much about life, reality and our world. The primary classroom envelops children in myth, fairy tales and legends, providing a framework for children to understand and interpret the world as they develop language acquisition and expression. Communication skills, language appreciation, critical thinking and emotional literacy can be enhanced when story is used to nurture, provoke curiosity, encourage empathy and allow for child-centred, effective learning and teaching. The school curriculum involves pupil understanding of cognitive content, engagement in problem-solving, development of a capacity for memorization, articulation of the views, experiences and questions, wrestling with complex concepts, dissonance and mystery, learning about scientific theories, participation in philosophical conversations, forming of reasoned arguments and ethical viewpoints and the development of physical, emotional and social well-being. Clearly then, a significant challenge for the teacher is the assurance of effective learning and teaching in an ever-expanding curriculum. A central educational objective is the acquisition of knowledge and information. Naturally, stories can pass on factual information and knowledge set within a narrative, plot, setting and characters. Comprehension, or depth of understanding, come as a result of engagement with the narrative, with teacher and pupil interpreting, analysing, synthesizing and drawing conclusions or evaluation of issues and concerns.[5] Knowledge and understanding are not in themselves such simple terms as first appears. There is ambiguity in the term '*know*' within Religious Education and distinction is

---

[4] Robert McKee, *Story, Substance, Structure Style and the Principles of Screenwriting* (London: Methuen Publishing, 1999).

[5] Susan M. Shaw, *Storytelling in Religious Education* (Alabama USA: Religious Education Press, 1999), Chapter 6 for an exploration of Harold Bloom's 'Taxonomy of Educational Objectives' in relation to story.

required between knowledge as a disposition and knowledge as a process. Knowledge as disposition can refer to 'I know that Jesus was born in first-century Palestine ... I know the story of the Lost Sheep ... or I know about Scriptures, religious festivals, key events ...' In other words, 'I can repeat this information, or I remember and can retell the details, content and so on.' Knowledge arising from experience involves process and faith. There is clearly a distinction between 'I know about the Christian God' and 'I know, or rather I am coming to know, God'. One is phenomenological in approach while the other is confessional. The classroom teacher in the Christian-faith school has a contractual duty to teach pupils about religion and an obligation, or indeed vocation, to provide opportunities for his or her pupils to come into relationship and communication with God.

Distinction between religious understanding as a scholarly or cognitive activity and understanding as an affective activity or experience presents similar ambiguity. Understanding may or may not require commitment to a faith tradition and is a debate beyond the scope of this chapter.[6] Suffice it to say that understanding through looking on is quite different from understanding through personal experience; it is a matter of degrees or depths of understanding as well as what is being understood and who is doing the understanding. Clearly, students of Religious Education can gain a scholarly understanding of doctrine, practices and Scripture, yet teachers with a responsibility for faith development and growth leading to a faith professed and a faith lived, require thoughtful engagement and catechetical skill. The language of metaphor, allegory, parable and story allow the teacher to navigate her pupils through the truths and nuances of a faith that is professed and lived.

In telling a story, it is not uncommon for the classroom teacher to be met with the question, 'Is this true?' While this question may be posed as an opening for further discussion and exploration, it misses the central point. At the heart of the pedagogy of story is the question; 'Is it true for us?' Story is not life in actuality, just because something actually happened does not necessarily bring us close to truth. The Book of Genesis tells us the story of Creation. To ask if the world really was created in seven days is limited for it inevitably leads to a dead end. Rather, our questioning of why God states 'Let

---

[6] For further exploration of cognitive and religious understanding see Barbel Inhelder and Jean Piaget, *The Growth of Logical Thinking* (London, Routledge & Kegan Paul, 1959).

there be ...' and investigation into 'Why does each act of creation end with God's approval ...?' encourage a reflection on the nature, power and majesty of God. The answers to, and reflections on, such questions aid us in understanding the concept of deity, as well as an appreciation of the writers' intent. The Bible is an anthology – a collection of works written by many authors over many centuries. Much of the language of the Bible is metaphorical and allegorical and an understanding of such language is a complex yet necessary activity. Metaphors are not easy to define and for the young child fairly challenging to understand; essentially one concept is understood in terms of another. Allegory presents events and characters as symbols to express an idea. As pupils respond to the stories and biblical narratives in classroom, the teacher is mindful of the possibilities for meaningful understanding than literal utterances. The teacher will tell, and pupils will respond, to many stories, from varying traditions and cultures, but his or her intention and purpose is always apparent: to engage in effective learning and teaching within Religious Education, enhancing knowledge and understanding of faith beliefs, traditions and practices.

The Power of Story in Religious Education

One must not be misled into limiting the art of storytelling to serving as mere pedagogical device. Storytelling certainly allows for learning and teaching opportunities, providing a language, structure and form through which to unpack abstract or ethical concepts. Stories can have a life of their own, potentially causing disturbance or resonance, remaining alarmingly or reassuringly present in our consciousness well after the event. They engage the conscious and unconscious, transporting one into the presence of mystery. They are used not primarily to impart information or knowledge but rather for revelation of truth and, in the case of religious storytelling, a possibility of an encounter with the sacred and the holy.

The use of story as a key pedagogical tool in Religious Education enables the teacher to present and invite pupils to join him or her and the Christian community on a 'holy journey'. Stories can be, in one way or another, our story for they are ultimately about us and the choices we make: the dilemmas we encounter, the inner and outer landscape we inhabit and the cry of the heart for love, freedom and fulfilment. William J. Bausch's book *Story telling, Imagination and Faith* is a useful text for any teacher or catechist.

He presents thirteen characteristics of story, and uses narratives, legends and myths to illustrate his claims. Bausch reminds us that, stories engage the heart, provoke curiosity, nourish the imagination and can potentially promote unity, healing and wholeness validating our life experience and the self as interconnected and bound to 'all of humankind, to the universal, human family.'[7] Stories in Religious Education not only enable familiarity with religious language and symbol but can further develop religious literacy including a capacity to articulate religious experience, appropriate liturgical practice and an ability to describe, share and defend one's faith, belief and practices. The passing down of stories, from which our faith and theological understandings have emerged, provides a means for our pupils to encounter their faith tradition and continue to grow cognitively, behaviourally and religiously.

The central story, or the story above all stories, is that of Jesus Christ, Son of God. Mark, most probably the first of the evangelists, opens his Gospel with the words, 'The beginning of the Gospel of Jesus Christ, the Son of God.' He states his intent unequivocally and yet to dare speak of the good news of the Son of God must lead to the language of metaphor, poetry, myth and story. The evangelist is not intent on supplying information but rather meaning, inspiration, calling and commitment. The call is not so much to know about Jesus Christ, but rather to know him. The demonstration of our commitment comes in following him. The Gospel narratives present, not an account, but meaning enveloped in real events and interpreted to show divine intervention, revelation and incarnation. Sacred stories and biblical narratives highlight the human condition and areas of human experience, and then go beyond to reveal the face of God. Likewise, in the teaching of Catholic Religious Education the teacher as catechist, artist and storyteller embodies lessons with a narrative, a story – the story of Jesus Christ.

The stories Jesus told and the miracles and healings he performed reveal something of his nature as human and divine as well as his teachings on the truths and values of the Kingdom of God. They inspire and compel us to embrace the Good News. It is precisely their power that enables the reader or learner to be informed, formed and transformed as a disciple of Christ.

---

[7] William Bausch, *Storytelling, Imagination and Faith* (New London, CT: Twenty-Third Publications, 2002).

Parables

While myths are stories that aid us in recognizing our world, parables often subvert and can challenge our worldview. They call for a
renewed way of seeing; the story begins in a familiar setting and
presents conventional expectations, yet goes on to create a space
for the listener to re-orientate and explore an alternative response
or way of living. The parables of Jesus are universal in their
message and invitation and central to his message and preaching.
In his book 'Journey towards Easter' Pope Benedict XVI (then
Cardinal Ratzinger), gives a profound reflection on the parable of
the Prodigal Son, sometimes known in the classroom as the
'Forgiving Father'.[8] Benedict suggests it might also be called the
'Parable of the Two Brothers'. This parable is often used by teachers, catechists and clergy in preparing pupils for the sacrament of
Reconciliation to emphasize the mercy and compassion of God. It
is a multi-layered story, unashamedly optimistic, and profoundly
'*metanoein*' (change of heart). The two brothers are metaphors for
human nature, while the dialogue and actions of the father reveal
to us the face of God. The teacher tells the story of reckless behaviour and lost dignity while highlighting one of the central
sentences in the story: 'But while he was still at a distance his father
saw him. And had compassion and ran and embraced him . . .' thus
showing the compassionate, ever-watchful face of a loving God.[9]
The teacher does not limit the exploration to a one-dimensional
event or message but rather engages in reflection on the meaning
and challenge of the parable primarily for the self and all believers.
The son who lives as a stranger in a strange land, in the *regio
dissimilitudinis* (a phrase that generally means a place of dissimilar-
ity, remote from God, the self and from what it means to be
human) finds healing, belonging and love. The elder son who has
obeyed his father's commands and already has '*all that is mine is
yours*', is also challenged to inner conversion. In telling this well
known parable, the teacher engages the pupils in Religious
Education. His or her theological insight, prayerful reflection and
ability to tell a good story, enables the teacher to not only inform
pupils of the stories Jesus told but also allows for a depth of learning.
   The parables Jesus told were oral events and as a narrative they

---

[8] Pope Benedict XVI, *Jesus of Nazareth* (London: Bloomsbury, 2007).
[9] Luke 11:20–1.

are less threatening than lectures, confrontations or corrections, for the listener is likely to be drawn into the story and surrendering to its plot. Ironically, confrontation can exist but it becomes self-confrontation; the status quo or the conventional establishments are subverted, opening up glimpses to a new way. The educational and theological value of Jesus' parables is the exploration of the Kingdom of God. The study of one parable, however robust, does not fully describe or define the Kingdom of God for each parable has its own context and its own message. Parables do give a glimpse or a certain insight into how one can participate as builders of the Kingdom of God. They can be considered eschatological in nature and message, although Pope Benedict suggests that an interpretation in terms of imminent eschatology can only be imposed artificially.[10] This is a valid point, for Benedict goes on to clarify that an over-emphasis on the parables' eschatological theme risks exaggeration and loses sight of their Christological significance. Undoubtedly the early followers of Jesus expected the imminent end of the world and the coming of God's kingdom within their lifespan, and yet as the Christian communities develop generation after generation we link the mystery of the kingdom of God and its values with the person of Christ. His teaching on the Kingdom of God is eschatological and Christological, interpreting all the parables as hidden and multi-layered invitations to faith in Jesus as the Kingdom of God in person.[11] Essentially, the teacher also tells his or her pupils Jesus' parables because of their Christological significance with an emphasis on something hidden now which is to be revealed more clearly in the future. In telling the parables of Jesus the teacher or catechist opens, reveals and proclaims the Word of God. It is for this purpose that story becomes a central tool in the catechetical, evangelical and educational tasks of the teacher.

At the heart of parables are ethics, relationships and values giving direction on how to engage with others and the values that underpin this engagement. The parables then enable ethical consideration and decision-making to become matters for classroom learning and future action. Obviously, collaboration of the learner is necessary for ethical action, as the dynamic and seductive story remain words on the page without transformation and self transcendence. The parables show us what to do, who we are and who we are to become. This is most obviously seen in the Parable

---

[10] Benedict XVI, *Jesus of Nazareth*, p. 186.
[11] Ibid., p. 188.

of the Good Samaritan in Luke10:29–37 and the Parable of the Two Debtors in Luke 7:41–3. 'Who is my neighbour?' and what it means to find, love and serve him is a topic of endless speculation, classroom learning, teaching and debate. The paradox is, of course, that when we seriously seek to find our neighbour and choose to love we in turn often experience ourselves found by him and loved by him; the stranger becomes a friend, the spirit of the law surpasses the letter, and justice, service and compassion become central and active ingredients in the renewal and trans-formation of society.

Story and Education

The educator of children and the curriculum in schools asks for consideration of, and planning for, the moral development of the child.[12] Story is a tool that serves moral growth, cognitive explo-ration and affective consideration of the great themes of life, loss, love, good, bad, light and dark. Fairy tales touch many themes and provide an avenue for the young child to safely navigate through conflict and fear, and the triumph of good over evil. Myths, alle-gorical tales and parables enable child and adult alike to navigate through moral ambiguity, moral themes and moral choices. Naturally, the teacher and significant adults can be moral models for the child, providing moral examples in word, action and deed. The educator is aware that the child passes through a series of moral developmental stages dependent on capacity for reasoning. Piaget maintains the child can be trained to act in particular ways but it is the reasoning for doing so that indicates the stage of devel-opment.[13] Arguably, his work suggests a certain level of cognitive development is required to become a fully moral person. Kohlberg continued Piaget's work to a certain extent and focused on inves-tigating the processes through which people make moral decisions. He was concerned with exploring moral thinking (not acting) and claimed that the child, adolescent and adult go through a series of developmental levels towards moral maturity. Fidelity to God and the dignity of human being is the driving force

---

[12] For further reading on the moral development of the child see Richard H. Hersh, Diana P. Paoliltto and Joseph Reimer, *Promoting Moral Growth: From Piaget to Kohlberg* (New York: Longman, 1979).

[13] Jean Piaget, *The Moral Judgement of the Child* (Free Press: Universal Digital Library, 2001).

for any Christian moral and religious education. Well-educated Christians will be in a position to make a worthwhile contribution to the well-being of society with an emphasis on the common good.

The great story of the People of Israel, the covenants and promises made with Noah, Abraham, Moses, David, and the fidelity of God in his relationship with the chosen people and in turn their lack of faithfulness, whether in exile and captivity or in times of prosperity, are rich narratives to be explored in the classroom. The Gospel portraits of Jesus are presented to the child through hearing stories about Jesus and through hearing the stories he told. The use of such sacred stories in the classroom allows for appreciation, understanding and recognition of a people, not unlike us in their flawed humanity, on a journey to wholeness and holiness and to the 'Promised Land'. Sometimes it is appropriate to use a Children's Bible in the telling of Old Testament and New Testament stories, yet great care must be given to ensuring a theologically and educationally appropriate version with fidelity to the original text. Equally important is the manner within which stories are told: children understand story in their own way and cannot be expected to understand in an adult capacity. The teacher then must use skill in opening up Scripture for the child to understand something of the historical setting, context and meaning within. This does not mean an adult interpretation should be imposed; rather it enables the child to identify with the narrative, experience the wonder and awe of God's power, majesty and love of his people as well as allowing the word of God to be heard within the heart of the child. The creative and skilful teacher can enable pupils to experience the message and presence of God: the seed can fall on fertile ground, grow and produce fruit.[14]

In conclusion, the teacher as storyteller is someone who tells and retells a story, whether fictional or fact, giving meaning to experience. Within Religious Education the teacher receives the narrative, primarily from Scripture and relates this to his or her pupils, setting it within context, attentive to its seductive power, aware of the needs and stage of the audience, and, on occasions, proclaims the Word of God.

---

[14] See Monica Brown, *Embodying the God we Proclaim* (Australia: Emmaus Productions, 1996) for insights into presenting Gospel narratives and parables within educational and parish communities.

Chapter 12

Exploring Theology through Art

Catherine O'Hare

Artistic representations, like metaphor, are powerful ways into understanding religion.[1]

Introduction

The use of visual images in the classroom is a well-established methodology in Religious Education. At its most basic level an image can illustrate what is being addressed and focus attention. It can also be used as a means to develop skills of observation and language. Yet, in the right hands it provides so much more, as exploring an image becomes a process of enquiry, developing thinking skills, deepening understanding and encouraging reflection. As Dillenberger points out:

> Our first acquaintance with a painting is like our first meeting with a person. We may feel immediately interested and attracted, or we may feel indifferent or hostile. But experience teaches us to question these initial responses, for often further acquaintance reverses our attitude. With paintings as with people further acquaintance is essential for full enjoyment and appreciation. The more we know about the painting, the richer our experience of it will be.[2]

In his book *The Intelligent Eye*, David Perkins points out that 'Looking at art requires thinking – art must be thought through.'[3]

---

[1] Brenda Watson, *The Effective Teaching of Religious Education* (Harlow: Longman Group, 1993), p. 125.

[2] Jane Dillenberger, *Style and Content in Christian Art* (London: SCM Press, 1965), p. 15.

[3] David N. Perkins, *The Intelligent Eye: Learning to Think by Looking at Art* (Los Angeles: Getty Publications, 1994), p. 3.

To this end he characterizes some key features of art which lend themselves to the development of thinking skills that go beyond the look and see approach. These features are sensory anchoring, instant access, personal engagement, dispositional atmosphere, wide-spectrum cognition and multiconnectedness.

In the context of the classroom, using an image/object provides an anchoring for the senses. It focuses the attention immediately. Such an image/object can also be kept on display allowing constant access which in turn can stimulate new reflections and insights. This is particularly useful in terms of using works of art in Religious Education as not only is the art a focus for constant reflection but the concept being explored is also a visible fixture in the classroom. Best of all, a work of art encourages a personal engagement and provokes a deeply personal response even if that response is initially a negative one. Because art demands such thoughtful attention it encourages 'thinking dispositions'.[4] Although viewed as primarily developing skills of looking and observation, art involves 'wider spectrum' cognition. It can appeal to the imagination and the creative but also to the analytical and problem solving mind. In addition connections can be made between art and other areas offering an ideal approach to cross-curricular teaching and learning.

In terms of Religious Education, art has always been recognized as an excellent medium for teaching and learning. Certainly the Early Church saw its value as a vehicle for religious education as well as for broader human and faith development.[5] In passing on doctrine to a population, for the most part illiterate, the Church made ample use of visual images to communicate and reinforce its message and a great deal of Western European art stands as testimony to centuries of Church patronage and influence. The advantage of this for the classroom teacher is that resources are plentiful and easily accessible.

In his wonderful *Letter to Artists* John Paul II quoted the Polish poet, Cyprian Norwid, in extolling the link between beauty and art. 'Beauty is to enthuse us for work.'[6] The inherent beauty in a work of art can also enthuse us to reflect and study when used as a stimulus in teaching and learning. In the hands of a good teacher a work of art can encourage interest and motivation in a theme to be

---

[4] Ibid., p. 5.
[5] Joseph A. Komonchak (ed.), *The New Dictionary of Theology* (Dublin: MacMillan Ltd, 1987), p. 60.
[6] Pope John Paul II (1999), *Letter to Artists*, 3.

explored. Art can have many purposes whether it is used to encourage the devotional, to aid reflection on the spiritual or to enhance teaching and learning through a more cognitive approach. It also encourages a visual literacy; the clues are in painting, and when using religious images, encourage a religious literacy.

There are many themes that can be explored using this medium. However, by way of example, and for the purpose of this chapter, the focus will be on Mary and how Marian theology can be explored through works of art. The intention is to provide a means of engagement with theological perspectives through paintings, which will allow the teacher to consider the value of adopting such an approach in the classroom while at the same time deepening his or her own understanding.

A Case Study: Mary In Christian Thought

> What the Catholic faith believes about Mary is based on what it believes about Christ and what it teaches about Mary illumines in turn its faith in Christ.[7]

To trace the role of Mary in Christian belief would require a book, or several books. So necessarily this chapter must be selective. In line with Catholic doctrine this chapter takes as its central thesis that belief in and devotion to Mary are always truest in a Christological context. What has been written in the New Testament and what has been said officially by the Church about Mary has always been primarily about her son and not about herself and devotion has tended to become suspect when people have divorced her from that context and treated Mary in isolation.

New Testament

In St Paul's Letter to the Galatians, Mary has no name. She is simply a woman.

> When the fullness of time had come, God sent his Son, born of a woman, born under the law, so that we might receive adoption as children.[8]

---

[7] CCC 487.
[8] Gal. 4:4–5.

Paul does not seem to be interested in Mary herself. He is making a point about Jesus. The fact that Jesus is born of a woman is a sign that he is human himself, sharing the same humanity with the people Paul is writing to, the people to whom he promises that they will share with Jesus the status of adopted children and heirs of God. In Paul's presentation the 'woman' is not a person in her own right, someone to be the centre of attention: she is used to make a point about her son, she is a symbol of humanity.[9]

In the Gospels too the presentation of Mary underscores something about her son. Mark's Gospel mentions Mary on only two occasions. In chapter 3, as in Paul's Letter to the Galatians, she has no name and is simply referred to as 'his mother', appearing along with his brothers and she seems to be considered of no special importance as Jesus said: 'Whoever does the will of God is my brother and sister and mother.'[10] As Rahner remarks, 'During Christ's public life (starting about AD 27) she maintained, as Jesus wished, an attitude that shows that what is most important, even in her motherhood, is not merely physical motherhood as such, but the fulfilment in faith of God's will.'[11] Mary's physical relationship to Jesus gives her no higher status than any other believer. The second reference to Mary appears to be similarly dismissive. 'Is not this the carpenter, the son of Mary and brother of James and Joses and Judas and Simon.'[12] The reaction of the people is that they see Jesus as just another normal human being and their knowledge of his mother simply reinforces this. Mark's preoccupation is to suggest that there is something more to him than this. But Mary's role is to represent that human element. She is not presented as a figure in her own right. She is not even presented alone, she is always part of the family unit. She represents the very humanity of Jesus which the people find to be a stumbling block (*skandalon* in Greek), preventing them from accepting the divine in him.

Matthew and Luke also present the person of Jesus as human and more than human but they go beyond Mark through the development of the infancy narratives. Here they expand on Mark's bald statement that Jesus is the Christ, the Son of God. The sonship

---

[9] This point is reinforced by Joseph Fitzmyer who explains that the phrase 'born of a woman' is a frequently used Jewish expression to designate a person's human condition. See Raymond Brown et al. (eds), *Mary in the New Testament* (London: Geoffrey Chapman, 1978) pp. 42–3.

[10] Mark 3:35.

[11] Karl Rahner, *Mary, Mother of the Lord* (Hertfordshire: Anthony Clarke Books, 1974), p. 1.

[12] Mark 6:3.

is expressed as a union between the human (Mary's contribution) and the divine (the power of the Spirit). Here again Mary is the symbol of humanity, but a humanity which responds to the impetus of God, a willing co-operation in the incarnation. The stories of the conception and birth of Jesus set a context in which readers are invited to understand the figure of Jesus. Mary does not understand the message of Luke's angel but is ready to say yes. The figures of wise men and shepherds, innkeepers and soldiers, also represent responses to God and to the son Mary bears. The genealogies set Jesus and his life and work in the context of a human history and experience of God, from Abraham (for Matthew) or from Adam (for Luke). But it is interesting that this background is presented by both writers as coming through Joseph: Mary simply represents the humanity that says yes to God. According to the eminent Church historian and Yale professor, Jarislav Pelikan,

> If historians of art or of the church were to follow the example of their colleagues in the natural sciences by compiling a 'citation index' ... of the themes that have captured the attention of painters and sculptors throughout history, and especially if they were to prepare such an index together, it seems clear that among all the scenes of the life of the Virgin Mary that have engaged the piety of the devout and the creativity of the artists, the annunciation has been predominant.[13]

Images of the Annunciation, taken from the Gospel of Luke, present the moment where Mary is made aware of her role as the mother of Jesus. The central figures are normally Mary herself and the angel Gabriel. The Holy Spirit is symbolized in the form of a dove. Artists have used such depictions to explore Mary's reactions to such a revelation, from fear to puzzlement to humble acceptance. While Mary is visually the central focus of such works the point of the story is to say something about Jesus and Incarnation and some paintings attempt to provide a theological insight in to this through the visual medium.

One example is the painting of *The Annunciation* by the Dominican Friar, Fra Angelico. Mary, seated, bows before the angel in humble recognition of his divine source while the angel echoes her posture in recognition of her role as the mother of Christ

---

[13] Jarislav Pelikan, *Mary through the Centuries – Her Place in History and Culture* (London: Yale University Press, 1996), p. 81.

Incarnate. On her lap is a book representing the Word of God, upon which Mary has been meditating and which, through her acceptance of God's will, she will bring to life in a unique way. In the background the artist has depicted the expulsion of Adam and Eve from the Garden of Eden. Eve's disobedience brought sin to the world and this is paralleled with Mary's obedience by which Jesus, through his death, will atone for the original sin of Adam and Eve. Because of this, Mary is sometimes referred to as a second Eve.

The symbol of the Holy Spirit, the dove, can be seen in the ray of light that moves towards the figure of Mary. The small bird, a swallow, which can also be seen, is a symbol of incarnation and also of resurrection. In the centre of the portico, between Mary and the angel, is carved the face of God.

The artist here has not simply painted an illustration of the New Testament scene but has used his imagination and his knowledge of theology to present a view of Incarnation and what it means in a creative way: a visual theology. Being able to recognize and interpret the symbols used is key to understanding. This type of image can add great depth to classroom teaching taking it beyond a mere superficial recognition of key characters and events but moving to explore the meaning behind such events.

The Infancy Narratives in Matthew and Luke also allow artists to focus on Mary as a young mother. Such images can reinforce the sense of shared humanity, the tender bond between mother and child. Two examples illustrate this:

- In Luis de Morales' *Virgin and Child,* mother and child share a look of mutual tenderness. Mary's hand cradles the infant's head protectively and gently as he reaches towards her. Such a loving and intimate moment will resonate with any mother who has held a child in her arms and this is part of the popular appeal of such images. Such images highlight the humanity of the characters, while the sometimes sorrowfulness of Mary's expression reminds the viewer of the fate awaiting this particular child.
- Artemisia Gentileschi's portrait *Madonna and Child* shows Mary as an ordinary mother feeding her child in a manner that is refreshing in its naturalness. Such images of *virgo lactens* were at one time very popular emphasising as they do the intimacy, humanity and humility of both mother and child, they fell out of favour over time. However by rediscovering such works we can rediscover the essential beauty of the human condition of motherhood.

Both these images focus on the humanity of Mary and thus of her son. Her role as a mother includes a physical intimacy with her child which is touching and down to earth. There are many paintings available which depict such a scene and these can be used effectively in the classroom as a way of reinforcing Mary's motherhood and link to her son's humanity.

The Gospel of John takes the image of Mary in a different direction. She is presented metaphorically as the mother of the Church. She is with her son at the start of his active ministry and at the end she shares in his suffering, standing at the foot of the Cross. Mary's unwavering loyalty and courage in the face of such suffering provide not only the model for faithful discipleship but also inspiration, hope and consolation for humanity. The image of the 'Mater Dolorosa' that John presents would become one of the most compelling of all Marian images.[14] It is more than mere filial concern that prompts Jesus to say to Mary 'Woman, behold your son,' and to John, 'Behold your mother.'[15] The bestowal of Mary to John is symbolic in so far as John represents all disciples and all men and women. Thus by adoption Mary becomes mother of this community, the Church. Mary's connection with the Church is through her connection with her son, who himself is connected to the Church, in Paul's words, as head to body. This presentation of Mary's link with the Church is also in keeping with Luke's mention in Acts of Mary's presence among the community of disciples at Pentecost (Acts 1:14–2:4).

Van der Weyden's *Deposition* shows Mary in all her grief as the body of her son is removed from the Cross. The connection between mother and son is highlighted by the similarity in posture. Mary's pose echoes that of her son. Pain, suffering and death are part of the human condition. Just as the artist sought to convey something of Mary's reactions in the face of the will of God in depictions of the Annunciation, so he uses the Gospel account of the crucifixion to communicate something about human suffering. Some paintings show Mary standing at the foot of the Cross passive and stoical, a model of quiet courage and fortitude. Her eyes focus on the figure of her son with that same intimate gaze that can be seen in images of the young Madonna and child. In others she is supported in her overwhelming grief by John.

The image of Mary holding the body of her son has inspired

---

[14] 'Mater dolorosa' is a Latin term which means sorrowful mother and is used to describe images of Mary as the mother of the crucified Jesus.
[15] John 19:26–7.

artists through the centuries. This type of work known as a 'Pieta' can provoke an emotive response in the viewer as they are encouraged to reflect on the moment. In comparing two works by Bouguereau, his 'Madonna and Child' (Madonna of the Roses) and his 'Pieta', it is interesting to note some similarities in the way Mary holds her son, living and dead, protectively close to her. In his 'Pieta', Mary's gaze is not on her son but instead she looks directly at the viewer drawing us in to the picture and to her sorrow. Mary as Mother of Sorrows became a powerful image for suffering humanity to identify with. The artist Giovanni Battista Salvi da Sassoferrato in his work *The Madonna in Sorrow* focuses solely on the face of Mary to convey her sense of sadness in an understated manner.

It is important to note that the New Testament writers were not concerned with spreading the Good News about Mary but rather the Good News about Jesus. But by giving space to Mary and particularly by doing so through the infancy stories and the picture of Mary at the foot of the Cross, they left an image of Mary which was going to capture the imagination of future generations and which would develop both theologically and in popular devotion. Thus they opened the door on Mary as a potential point of focus whose cult would develop a life of its own through popular imagination and piety.

Mary as *Theotokos* – the God-bearer

In the centuries following the establishment of the canon of the New Testament, thinking about Mary and devotion to her continued to grow. The pivotal moment in the development of Mariology came with the Council of Ephesus in AD 431. Here Mary was given the title *Theotokos* (God-Bearer), which, in the West, was translated as Mother of God. The purpose of the Council of Ephesus was to provide a Christological statement about the divinity and humanity of Jesus. Mary's title, Mother of God, was used as a theological definition in its own right to defend the fundamental Christian belief in Jesus as the incarnation of the divine Son of God. By declaring Mary to be the Mother of God, and not just the mother of the humanity of Jesus, the Council stressed the complete union of human and divine in the person of Jesus. The Fathers of the Council made it clear that Mary did not give Jesus his divine nature; she is not the mother of divinity but she gave birth to a divine person. She gave birth and a human nature to the Son of God.

Mother of God, not that the nature of the Word or his divinity received the beginning of its existence from the holy Virgin, but that, since the holy body, animated by a rational soul, which the Word of God united to himself according to the hypostasis, was born from her, the Word is said to be born according to the flesh.[16]

Mary is thus the intimate source of God's involvement with humanity, 'giving to God incarnate all that a mother gives to her children – blood, bone, nerve and personality'.[17] The Council of Ephesus refused Mary any divine attributes – she is no goddess. In giving her the title *Theotokos* and not simply *Christotokos* it intended to emphasise the total unity of the divine and the human in the person of Jesus. The statement is carefully crafted as a statement about Jesus and not about Mary and this is achieved through the affirmation of the motherhood of Mary.

An icon is a sacred image presented in a stylized form. The intention is to draw the viewer into spiritual contemplation. Some icons of Mary as *Theotokos* show her with arms spread to reveal the figure of Jesus encircled in her womb to underline the message that she is the bearer of the human and the divine. Such beautiful works of art are a useful resource in the classroom as they combine a deep theology with a sincere devotion.

Apocryphal Accounts

As the only human parent who gave Jesus his human nature it seems a natural progression that Mary's own humanity should become a focus for discussion, debate and devotion. Later doctrines would seek to address this issue but even before any of these doctrines emerged popular piety had begun to produce stories. Such apocryphal narratives sought to address the perceived shortfall in New Testament texts about Mary. Prominent among these is the Protevangelium of James which gives names to Mary's parents, Anne and Joachim, and details events in her upbringing. It is from sources such as these that we get stories about Joseph being an elderly widower with children from a previous marriage and so on.

---

[16] Council of Ephesus in DS 251 cited in CCC 446.
[17] Eamonn Duffy, *Madonnas that Maim* (Glasgow: Blackfriars, 1996), p. 4.

And the priest said to Joseph, 'You have been chosen by lot to receive the virgin of the Lord as your ward.' But Joseph answered him, 'I have sons and am old: she is but a girl ...'[18]

Such works, while feeding popular imagination and curiosity, projected a Mariology that was a mixture of folklore, legend and religious sentimentality. While such stories were not included in the canon of the New Testament the early Fathers of the Church were apt to quote such works in their own writings. Artists also drew on such sources for creative inspiration and images of the girlhood of Mary, the marriage of Mary and Joseph and other events were depicted to assuage popular demand. While some of these would not be of immediate use in the classroom they do convey a fascination with Mary herself and are interesting to explore. Titian portrays the apocryphal story of Mary as a child being taken to live at the Temple and despite her tender years she negotiates the steep stairs with ease and confidence. She already displays an innate sense of purpose and destiny. Ghirlandaio depicts episodes of Mary's life from her conception and birth which are displayed in the Church of Santa Maria Novella in Florence. Images of Mary with her mother, St Anne, are varied and plentiful and show Mary herself as part of a human family.

Rossetti's *Girlhood of the Virgin* is full of symbolism that points to Mary's future role as mother of Christ incarnate: the Angel, dove, lily, books, the colour red and more symbolize her role and allude to the fate of the son she will bear.

Mary as One Set Apart

By the end of the patristic period in the seventh and eight century, a double tendency had come to characterize Marian doctrine and devotion. One tendency emphasized Mary's close association with her son. The other tendency could be called the transcendence of Mary, where Mary became a celebrity in her own right by popular demand. Her motherhood became a secondary consideration as the focus on her condition (i.e. her virginity) increased. The shift from Mother of God to Virgin Mary is highlighted by Duffy when he considers the imagery of the modern cult of devotion to Mary.

---

[18] Protoevangelium IX, 1–2 in Montagu R. James (ed.), *The Apocryphal New Testament* (Oxford: OUP, 1980).

Citing examples of Our Lady of Guadalupe, Lourdes, Fatima, Garibandal and Medjurgorge, he notes that these appearances (some approved by the Church, others not) are not of a mother and her child but of a beautiful and refined young woman.[19]

Removing Mary from her son and her earthly role as mother with all that motherhood entails and focusing instead on her condition as chaste young virgin, exposes a tension, which is characteristic of certain aspects of Christian spirituality, between the reality of the world as experienced and the looking towards another dimension outwith that reality. While the distinction between earthly and heavenly is an important one in Christian thinking, what is dangerous in this context is the equation of motherhood with the earthly, and by implication less sacred, and the virginal with the heavenly, or the better position, which is also unattainable. Even the title 'Our Lady' applied to Mary is reminiscent of the courtly love poetry of the thirteenth century, in which the object of affection and desire is clearly beyond the grasp of the poet. The contrast between the earthly and the heavenly is paralleled in hymns that set the purity and beauty of Mary against the sordidness of the world and those sinners in it. Mary is thus seemingly removed from the human condition that God became involved in through the incarnation.

Using images that focus on Mary's role as mother of Jesus helps keep things in perspective and avoids removing Mary too far from her close connection with her son. Of course we are all familiar with images derived from various apparitions and these can be displayed but not necessarily to the exclusion of all else.

Teachers can look for a variety of images which will reinforce their teaching and to do this they need to be clear about exactly what it is they want their pupils to understand. A lovely example is Rembrandt's portrayal of *The Holy Family*. Here we see a close family unit. However, angels, representing the heavenly and the divine, indicate that while this may look like an ordinary family, it is anything but. Joseph is present but stands apart in the background signifying his role as protector of the family though not as father. He had no part in the conception of this child. Without the angels bringing a sense of the heavenly, this could be a typical family domestic scene. The artist has attempted to convey something about the humanity/divinity of Jesus. Here humanity is represented by the ordinariness of the setting, the characters and earthy tones. The mother figure, Mary, is solid, earthly and natural

---

[19] Eamonn Duffy, *Madonnas that Maim*, pp. 4–5.

and holds a book which is in fact a bible while a Divine light illuminates her and her child.

The Immaculate Conception

In considering the way in which the Church's theology has responded to popular devotion, Pelikan argues that Marian doctrine is a prime example of spirituality leading theology, not vice versa, for it has been popular devotion which has run ahead of official dogma and lead to official papal pronouncements about Mary, most notably her Immaculate Conception (1854) and her Assumption into Heaven (1950).[20] While this is true to an extent, the effect of the papal statements when they did appear was to reinstate the Christological context which a lot of popular devotion had underplayed or forgotten.

The first of these pronouncements was made in the Apostolic Constitution, *Ineffabilis Deus* issued by Pope (Blessed) Pius IX after consultation with the whole Church:

> We ... pronounce and define that the doctrine which holds that the Blessed Virgin Mary, from the first moment of her conception, was, by the singular grace and privilege of Almighty God, in view of the foreseen merits of Jesus Christ the saviour of the human race, preserved immune from all taint of original sin, is revealed by God and therefore firmly and constantly to be believed by all the faithful.[21]

For centuries the Church had reflected on the life and character of Mary and her role in God's plan for salvation. It is understandable that Christian tradition should have looked towards Mary as a figure who could be a fitting channel for the birth of the incarnate Son of God, a person in a way set apart from the rest of humanity. But as a human being Mary, like everyone else, was dependent on the death and resurrection of Jesus to be saved from original sin, that negative aspect of the human condition which is a part of the inheritance shared by all. Had she not been, she would have been a kind of super-human being and the humanity she gave to her son would not have been the humanity shared by the rest of mankind. So one important element in the

---

[20] Jarislav Pelikan, *Mary Through the Centuries*, p. 210.
[21] Pius IX (1854), *Ineffabilis Deus*.

proclamation of *Ineffabilis Deus* is to avoid the semi-deification of Mary. She is not above the need for redemption but is preserved by the same merits of Christ which are believed to be necessary and effective for all people.

> Her life, poor, insignificant, modest, sorrowful, gives us solace after all, and the strong hope that we are more than merely sinners, that God's grace is doing in us what it did in her.[22]

To define the Immaculate Conception in this way has, therefore, two significant implications. First the release from the consequences of original sin, already effective in Mary from the moment of her conception, is a pledge of salvation offered to all through the merits of Christ. Redemption is thus not an ungrounded promise but a reality declared to have been achieved in one like the rest of humanity. In addition to this, the declaration that Mary was preserved from the moment of her conception makes it clear that the salvation that was hers could not be linked to any merit of her own. In this way *Ineffabilis Deus* makes it clear that God's gift of salvation is totally gratuitous, unmerited – it is God's grace that is at work.

These two profound theological statements, which are not about Mary but about her son, ensured that popular devotion, with its tendency towards an exaggerated glorification of Mary, was recalled to the sound doctrine of redemption through the grace of God and the merits of Jesus Christ.

Spanish art was more successful than most in portraying the difficult concept of the Immaculate Conception. References to a young woman clothed in the sun with the moon at her feet and a crown of twelve stars comes from the Book of Revelation (Chapter 12) and has been used as a symbolic representation of Mary by some artists. Works by Zurbaran and Murillo are full of deep symbolism and beauty.

The Assumption of Mary

The proclamation of the Assumption of Mary was also the result of centuries of popular devotion bearing fruit in a Magisterial pronouncement. This consistent devotion prompted Pius XII first

---

[22] Karl Rahner, *Mary: Mother of the Lord*, p. 82.

to consult about then, in the Bull *Munificentissimus Deus*, to declare
as a doctrine of the Church that:

> The Immaculate Virgin, preserved free from all stain of original sin,
> when the course of her earthly life was finished, was taken up body
> and soul into heavenly glory ...[23]

Any assertions about Mary's actual death are significantly absent
from the document which focuses instead on Mary as a sign of
hope and consolation for humankind. What Jesus did for his
mother, as a reward for her faithful discipleship, is the reward
awaiting, at the end of time, all who respond as she did.[24] Mary was
the first human to be assumed by God into Heaven but would not
be the last. The emphasis here is not so much on Mary as on the
message to all members of the Church about the redemptive
effects of her son's death and resurrection.

Caravaggio's *Death of the Virgin* was controversial in its depiction
of Mary's death. Surrounded by the Apostles and a weeping Mary
Magdalen, the lifeless body of Mary, mother of Jesus, is the focus of
their grief. Mary's swollen stomach is a reminder of her role as a
mother. But this is ultimately about a human death.

Duccio's version of the scene includes not just the earthly death
of Mary but also points to her Assumption by including the heavenly in the angelic figures and that of Jesus, who carries her soul
which is depicted as a small version of Mary herself.

Both Carracci and Poussin portray the bodily Assumption of
Mary with Carracci including the Apostles, surprised as they mourn
at Mary's tomb while she can be seen rising from her grave suggesting that she had experienced death and undergone burial. Poussin
meanwhile omitted all other human figures together with any
sense of death and the grave and focused on Mary being supported
by angels to her heavenly home where she will be reunited with her
son.

Mary's role as Queen of Heaven is portrayed by Velasquez in his
Coronation of the Virgin. Here the Trinity of Father, Son and Holy
Spirit are united in glorifying Mary who is shown sitting slightly
below these figures but above the angels. This image also says
something about Mary's place in worship. Church teaching has
traditionally made a distinction between *latria* (adoration) that is
due to God alone and *dulia* (reverence given to the saints). Mary

---

[23] Pius XII (1950), *Munificentissmus Deus*.
[24] CCC 974.

being less than God, could not be accorded *latria* yet, being more than any other saint, was, in the eyes of the Church, entitled to super-reverence (*hyperdulia*). The intention behind this distinction was to accord Mary her rightful place within the Church's worship while at the same time avoiding any exaggerated worship of Mary herself.

Throughout the history of Mariology it has been through the language of devotion that sentiments about Mary could more easily be expressed. Such language spoke to and from the heart and fuelled the imagination. Using images drawn from Scripture along with some drawn from apocryphal narratives, artists, poets, preachers and musicians created a Mariology that both drew on and influenced popular devotion and belief. This was to prove more appealing and more enduring than any official Church teaching to the extent that many remained and remain unaware of official Church pronouncements and accept or reject Marian devotion in a very uncritical way.

As the works of artists such as Botticelli, Raphael and Michelangelo illustrate the figure of Mary has inflamed the imagination of artists through the centuries as they seized on scenes from the New Testament to create imaginative and enduring images of the Annunciation, the Nativity, the classic Madonna pose and the Pieta. In the eastern churches the stylized icons, rich in symbolism, extolled Mary's role as God-Bearer. In the west Madonnas for a time became less stylized and more earthly and human. They were depicted embracing, tending and suckling their infant, exuding maternal warmth. Here Mary's image was depicted in the fullness of the human condition. Her enduring appeal lies in her embodiment of motherhood, the mother intimately connected with her son. As such she brings a richness to Christian spirituality. As Duffy says: 'Christianity without Mary somewhere at the centre of it, is quite literally, unimaginable.'[25]

Concluding Remarks and Some Implications for The Classroom

It is a well-worn maxim in teaching that you cannot give what you don't have! Using works of art in Religious Education requires

---

[25] Eamon Duffy, *Madonnas that Main*, p. 19.

both a knowledge of the medium and a knowledge and under-standing of the theology being presented. It is certainly noticeable that the artists knew their theology. Bringing together these two disciplines should add something to the quality of the teaching and learning experience that goes beyond a mere nod in the direction of cross-curricular activities. However, to use this effectively in the classroom, the teacher has to carry out his or her own research. There are countless images to choose from which, thanks to modern technology, are easily accessible.

When choosing which images to use it is important to consider them carefully. How does it relate to the teaching? What point is being made? In regard to Mary, there are many paintings available for use and the teacher must be discerning in his/her choice. It is well worth considering, in addition to the above, how the image relates to an aspect of Mary. What does it say about humanity? Her maternal role? Her role in Christian thought and teaching? Womanhood? What is the underlying message?

Art, like religion, communicates through the use of symbols. Recognizing these and being able to interpret such symbolism, both artistic and religious, helps deepen understanding. Shape, colour, objects are just some of the ways art can communicate meaning.

One of the advantages of using a work of art in the classroom is that it elicits an immediate personal response. Whether favourable or unfavourable, it provokes a reaction and the teacher can draw upon this in order to engage pupils more fully in the learning process. It can also encourage an emotive response. These can be used as a starting point for further exploration and so begins a process of enquiry. For example:

- consider Bouguereau's 'Pieta'. Why has the artist chosen to paint Mary this way? Why is she looking out of the picture? Compare this with other versions of this type of painting. Are they all the same?
- images of Madonnas abound, from the naturalistic to the ethereal and to the sentimental. Consider which you prefer and why? What does that reveal about your own understanding of Mary?

Throughout the school year there are plenty of opportunities to introduce various images of Mary in line with the Church's liturgical year. Celebrating the key Marian feast days presents a context for teaching and learning about Mary and provides an opportunity to select a particular image for examination and also for prayer and reflection. For example, 25 March is the feast of the Annunciation. The Annunciation is covered briefly in the lead up to Christmas but can be considered again later. There are many artistic representations of the story which deal with a number of aspects and so provide a number of teaching points. The story may be the same but the art can be varied and this allows the teaching to be varied as well.

For those who want to make connections to the area of global citizenship it is worth considering that many cultures have depicted Mary in a manner that conveys something of the culture itself.

Finally, before using works of art as a basis for teaching, teachers first have to find and research such works. This can be an enlightening and enjoyable process which, while extending knowledge and deepening understanding, provides a good opportunity to gather a wide range of resources. The first step is to start by simply looking, whether in church, in a gallery, in books or online. Once that first step is taken, the rest follows quite naturally.

Reference list of Marian Images

Title	Artist	Location
The Annunciation	Fra Angelico	Museo del Prado, Madrid
Virgin and Child	Luis de Morales	Museo del Prado, Madrid
Madonna and Child	Artemisia Gentileschi	Spada Gallery, Rome
Pentecost	El Greco	Museo del Prado, Madrid
Deposition	Rogier Van der Weyden	Museo del Prado, Madrid
Pieta	Adolphe-William Bouguereau	Private Collection
The Madonna in Sorrow	Giovanni Battista Salvi da Sassoferrato	Galleria degli Uffizi, Florence
Madonna of the Roses	Adolphe-William Bouguereau	Private Collection
Birth of Mary	Ghirlandaio	Tornabuoni Chapel Church of Santa Maria Novella
The Presentation of the Virgin in the Temple	Titian	Galleria dell'Accademia, Venice
The Virgin and Child with Saint Anne	Masaccio and Masolino	Galleria degli Uffizi, Florence
The Virgin and Child with Saint Anne	Leonardo da Vinci	The Louvre, Paris
The Girlhood of Mary Virgin	Dante Gabriel Rossetti	Tate Gallery, London
Holy Family	Rembrandt	The Hermitage, St Petersburg

The Immaculate Conception	Diego Velasquez	The National Gallery, London
The Immaculate Conception	Francisco de Zurbaran	Museo del Prado, Madrid
Our Lady of the Immaculate Conception	Bartolomé Esteban Murillo	Museo del Prado, Madrid
Death of the Virgin	Caravaggio	The Louvre, Paris.
Maestà – The Death of the Virgin	Duccio di Buoninsegna	Museo dell'Opera del Duomo, Siena
Assumption of the Virgin	Annibale Carracci	Santa Maria del Popolo, Rome
The Assumption of the Virgin	Poussin Nicolas	Louvre, Paris.
The Coronation of the Virgin	Velasquez, Diego	Museo del Prado, Madrid, Spain

Chapter 13

Contributing to the Pastoral and Spiritual Life of the Catholic School

Roisín Coll

Nemo dat quod non habet[1]

Introduction

Being a Catholic teacher in a Catholic school is a wonderful privilege, but it can be challenging. By very nature of its title, the role of the Catholic teacher is significantly different from that of any other teacher in any other school. From the day a Catholic decides to embark on a career in the teaching profession there is an expectation of a commitment to faith, and transmission of that faith (and not merely religious knowledge), on the part of the individual. In fact, reaching the 'decision' to teach is not considered by the Church to have been a journey embarked on by the individual alone but rather has been arrived at though the direction of the Holy Spirit in response to a particular 'calling' to teach. Catholics believe that teaching is not a job or career choice but rather a response to a call from God: a vocation.

For decades, teaching has been described as a *vocation* in both pedagogical and andragogical contexts.[2] Indeed today this description is extended to many occupations and groups and is often used

---

[1] 'You cannot give what you do not possess.'

[2] M. E. Englander, 'A psychological analysis of vocational choice: teaching', in *Journal of Counselling Psychology* 7 (4) (1960) pp. 57–264; Wayne C. Booth, *The vocation of a teacher: rhetorical occasions 1967–1988* (Chicago: University of Chicago Press, 1988); Michael Collins, *Adult Education as Vocation: A Critical Role for the Adult Educator* (New York: Routledge, 1991).

interchangeably with the term 'profession'.[3] However, Schwarz argues that there is a distinction between the two terms claiming that it is the ethical considerations, such as pastoral contexts and notions of service, that make teaching vocational rather than simply professional.[4]

'Vocation' comes from the Latin *vocare*, meaning 'to call'. This concept of calling is rooted in the Christian experience and understanding and God's plan for his people. Historically its context was specifically Christian and is what distinguishes vocation from occupation. It is, therefore, of interest to explore the concept of vocation within the context of Catholic education in general and the Catholic teacher in particular.

Much has been written about the vocation and role of the Catholic teacher and it is widely accepted in the Church that Catholic teachers are called to be 'authentic' and 'authoritative' witnesses to faith: authentic in how they live their lives and authoritative through the accurate knowledge that they impart.[5] In doing so, they affect the pastoral and spiritual life of the school in which they teach. The purpose of this chapter is to explore some of the areas Catholic teachers should consider in terms of teaching in a Catholic school and identify the contribution they can make to the pastoral and spiritual life of the Catholic school.

[3] P. R. De Lacey and R. L. Pryor, 'Senior High-School Pupils' Aspirations for Teaching and Other Professions', in *Asia Pacific Journal of Teacher Education*, 4 (3) (1976), pp. 252–5.
R. Broome and H. Tillema, 'Fusing experience and theory: The structure of professional knowledge', in *Learning and Instruction* 5 (4) (1995), pp. 261–7.

[4] G. E. Schwarz, 'Teaching as vocation: enabling ethical practice', in *The Educational Forum*, 63 (1) (1998), pp. 2–29.

[5] Thomas H. Groome, 'What makes a school Catholic?' in Terence McLaughlin, Joseph O'Keefe & Bernadett O'Keeffe (eds), *The Contemporary Catholic School: Context, identity and diversity* (London: Falmer, 1996); Terence McLaughlin, 'Distinctiveness in the Catholic school', in James C. Conroy (ed.), *Catholic education: Inside out, outside in* (Dublin: Lindisfarne Books, 1996); Gerald Grace, *Catholic Schools: Mission, markets and morality* (London: Routledge Falmer, 2002); John Bollan, *The light of His face: spirituality for Catholic teachers* (Dublin: Veritas, 2007); Roisín Coll, 'From Theory to Practice: The Experience of Catholic Probationary Teachers', in *Journal of Research on Christian Education*, vol. 18 (2), (2009).

Part 1

A Teaching Church

The Catholic Church uses the Sacred Scriptures to formulate the basic principles of Christian pedagogy. It claims that the New Testament is rich in educational wisdom and is a support to any Christian educator. There, Christ can be found establishing a teaching Church; during his three-year period in active ministry he is engaged in daily conversations with his Apostles, those appointed by him to follow him and to carry on his work. The Gospels report Christ being addressed by his Apostles as Rabbi – which means 'teacher': we observe him educating them, supporting them, clarifying their thinking during special 'seminars' and illustrating how to teach others.[6] After his resurrection, Christ gave his mission to his Apostles; he commissioned them to go and 'teach all nations' authentically and authoritatively and to observe all of his commands. Jesus promises that they will never be alone since he will always be with them, 'to the end of time'.[7]

The mission of the Church, then, is considered a continuation of the mission of Christ. 'As the Father has sent me, so I send you.'[8] From the very beginning, the recognition of this fact by Christians has moved them to give public witness to their faith in Jesus Christ and to teach the Gospel of the Kingdom of God. Today, all Christians are expected to play their part in that same mission.

> I have called you friends, for all that I have heard from the Father I have made known to you. You did not choose me but I chose you and appointed you that you should go and bear fruit and that your fruit should abide.[9]

Education in the faith is considered part of that mission. The Church considers the narrative of Christianity and its expansion as a record of the Apostles' achievements as teachers and of their ability to ensure the continuation of a teaching office. In the Acts of the Apostles and the Epistles of the New Testament the educating activities of the early Christians are evident where the teachings of Christ are passed on with passion and conviction. They are found advising, converting, catechizing, evangelizing and teaching

---

[6] John 1:38.
[7] Matt. 28:19–20.
[8] John 20:21.
[9] John 15:15–16.

with authority the messages proclaimed by Christ in the name of God, whom he claimed to be his father.[10] The successors of the Apostles and those charged with the responsibility of continuing to teach in the name of Christ were referred to as the 'elders' or 'bishops' – the Greek *episcopos* literally means 'overseer'.[11] That title has remained unchanged and the main duty of the bishop in the Catholic Church today honours Christ's expectation of his followers: to teach authentically and authoritatively. The Pope and bishops' interpretation of what they believe to be the 'truth' is known as the 'Magisterium' – the teaching authority of the Church – and these teachings are transmitted to followers.

The Congregation for Catholic Education has the responsibility to advise and guide Catholic teachers on matters of education. The Church relies heavily on its members to assist in the transmission of this 'truth' and its Catholic schools, and those teaching within them, are central to the proclamation of Christ and his teachings.

When addressing an audience in the Catholic University of America in Washington DC, Pope Benedict XVI referred to the Catholic school as 'a place to encounter the living God who in Jesus Christ reveals his transforming love and truth'.[12] This echoes what was said in his address to the Diocese of Rome, when he explained that Catholic education should allow a child to 'meet Jesus Christ and to establish a lasting and profound relationship with him' which is central to the 'formation of a person to enable him or her to live to the full and to make his or her own contribution to the common good'.[13]

The Church has affirmed the Catholic school as being at its heart and has increased awareness of its ecclesial identity in the modern world. Where decline in Sunday Mass attendance in the UK and elsewhere continues to be observed, Catholic schools – worldwide – remain full[14] and so as 'a genuine instrument of the Church,' these schools are expected to fulfil their vocation and provide a genuine experience of Church for Catholic children.[15]

---

[10] 1 Cor. 12:9; 1 Tim. 4:1–5; Titus 3:8.

[11] Titus 1:7–9.

[12] Pope Benedict XVI, *Meeting with Catholic Educators* Conference hall of the Catholic University of America in Washington DC, 17 April 2008.

[13] Ibid.

[14] Helen Johnson & Michael Castelli, 'Catholic Head Teachers: the importance of culture building in approaches to spiritual and moral development and the transmission of faith tradition' in *International Journal of Children's Spirituality*, 5 (1) (2000), pp. 75–90 .

[15] CCE (1997), *Catholic Schools*, 11.

Unsurprisingly then, the role of the teacher is considered by the Church as central to the success of the Catholic school in fulfilling its mission. Literature from the Church's Magisterium will now be presented in an attempt to outline its expectation of the Catholic teacher.

The Catholic Teacher

There are numerous official Catholic documents detailing the role of the Catholic teacher. Consideration of these documents presents those choosing to embark on a career in Catholic education with a clear 'job description', indeed a vision of Catholic education. The Church recognizes that Catholic teachers, like all teachers, should have the best possible academic qualifications, a thorough knowledge and understanding of their subject and competence and skill in the transmission of that knowledge. However, an additional expectation of these teachers exists, one that focuses on their personal identity and disposition, an expectation of which they should be aware. The Second Vatican Council's *Declaration on Christian Education* states:

> Let teachers realise that to the greatest possible extent, they determine whether the Catholic school can bring its goals and undertakings to fruition. They should, therefore, be trained with particular care so that they may be enriched with both secular and religious knowledge ... Bound by charity to one another and to their students, and penetrated by an apostolic spirit, let them give witness to Christ, the unique Teacher, by their lives as well as by their teachings.[16]

In *The Catholic School on the Threshold of the Third Millennium,* the importance of the contribution of teachers to the continued promotion of the faith is presented once more:

> In the Catholic school, 'prime responsibility for creating this unique Christian school climate rests with the teachers, as individuals and as a community' ... Moreover, we must remember that teachers and educators fulfil a specific Christian vocation and share an equally specific participation in the mission of the Church, to the extent that 'it depends chiefly on them whether the Catholic school achieves its purpose.'[17]

[16] Second Vatican Council, *Gravissimum educationis* (1965), 8.
[17] CCE (1997), *Catholic Schools*, 19.

The centrality of the teacher is further demonstrated in the following statement:

> Teaching has an extraordinary moral depth and is one of our most excellent and creative activities. For the teacher does not write on inanimate material, but on the very spirits of human beings.[18]

Pope Benedict XVI has spoken of the challenges facing Catholic educators but reminds them of the promise of the permanent abiding of Christ with his Church and thus with his teachers, until the end of time.[19]

> We must always be aware that we cannot carry out such a task with our own strength but only with the power of the Spirit. We need enlightenment and grace that come from God and act within hearts and consciences. For education and Christian formation, therefore, it is above all, prayer and our personal friendship with Jesus that are crucial: only those who know and love Jesus Christ can introduce their brothers and sisters into a living relationship with him.[20]

The Catholic teacher accompanies children on their journey of faith and, in order to do so effectively, must give witness to their own faith and continue on their personal faith journey. According to Benedict XVI, the 'figure of witness and role of witnessing is central' to Catholic education, since a witness is not simply involved in the transmission of information but is personally engaged with what he believed is the truth, 'and through that coherence of his own life, becomes a dependable reference point'.[21] Benedict stresses the importance of the Catholic teacher's relationship with Christ and God the Father, explaining that this is the 'fundamental condition' for carrying out their responsibility in educating effectively. However, the role of the Catholic teacher in educating in the faith is not to refer to him or herself, but rather to Christ, and so an 'authentic' educator is one who models himself or herself on 'Jesus Christ, the witness of the Father who said nothing about himself but spoke as the Father had taught him.'[22]

[18] Ibid.
[19] Matt. 28:20.
[20] Pope Benedict XVI, 'There is talk of a great educational emergency', *Address of his Holiness Benedict XVI to the Diocese of Rome*, Basilica of St John Lateran (11 June 2007).
[21] Ibid., 6.
[22] Ibid.

'*I do nothing of my own accord. What I say is what the Father taught me.*'[23] According to the Code of Canon Law of the Roman Catholic Church, Catholic teachers in Catholic schools should be *outstanding in true doctrine and uprightness of life.*[24]

In summary, the Church's expectation of the Catholic teacher is clear. It is someone who knows and loves Jesus Christ; is inspired by the Apostles; believes in the mission of the Church; develops their own faith; is engaged in prayer; will give witness to Christ as role model; accepts their vocation within that mission; is prepared to accompany their students on their journey of faith; is committed to helping children get to know Jesus Christ and develop a lasting relationship with him.

Part Two

Putting the Theory into Practice.

Recent research has tracked the development of thirty newly qualified Catholic teachers in both primary and secondary schools in Scotland.[25] Amongst many findings that emerged from that study, one of the most significant was that while all participants were anxious to some degree about their 'faith' responsibilities, those who were aware of their Catholic faith as being central to their own identity and who were actively embracing and living it (via personal prayer, Mass attendance and/or additional faith related activities) were much more confident, and indeed able to be authentic and authoritative witnesses to their faith.[26] While such a truism is often associated with the world of finance, it applies perfectly in the context of the Catholic teacher in the Catholic school. If teachers want to be in a position to feel supported in their work as Catholic educators and to be able to be effective witnesses to their faith, then their own faith dispositions must necessarily become a personal point of focus.

What also emerged from the study was that a need to refocus on personal faith and sometimes even a return to the Catholic faith, is

---

[23] John 8:28.
[24] Codex Iuris Canonici (1983), *Code of Canon Law. Latin-English Translation.* Washington DC, No. 803.
[25] Roisín Coll, 'The struggle for the soul: implications for the identity of Catholic teachers', in *Journal of Religious Education* 55 (3) (2007) pp. 45–53 .
[26] Of course, this isn't surprising as the title of this chapter tells us '*Nemo dat quod non habet.* – You cannot give what you do not possess'.

indeed a reality for many Catholic teachers, many of whom have lapsed from the practice of the faith. Apprehensions about lack of knowledge or ability to 'witness effectively' emerged from such individuals but so did a commitment to reversing that and to developing faith. But what does 'refocus on faith' or 'return' to it mean and how does a teacher 'witness effectively', a phrase that has been repeated throughout this chapter?

Teaching From and Through Faith

Thomas Groome's account of what faith is summarizes a relatively recent shift in an understanding of it.[27] Groome claims that faith, in the past, was often considered to be very much concerned with an intellectual understanding of doctrine or truths but is now considered to be a human *response* to this through witness, worship, knowledge and actively sharing this with others.[28] Indeed the *Catechism of the Catholic Church* is very helpful in its guidance to Catholics as it is divided into four parts, each focusing on different dimensions of faith: faith believed, faith celebrated, faith lived and faith prayed. These are often referred to as 'pillars of faith' and the guidance contained within each are to be considered of equal importance and interrelated. But what does this mean for the Catholic teacher in the Catholic school and the manner in which he or she should educate their pupils? Essentially, being a Catholic teacher in a Catholic school is not just about 'teaching faith' or teaching what the Church says about faith but rather is providing an education for Catholic children through a 'faith medium' where they are immersed in a lived faith; everything they are taught, and all of their experiences, are underpinned by the teachings of the Gospel of Jesus Christ, through the direction of, and experiences provided by, the teacher. Academics have alluded to this in the past and there are many references to the concept of a 'permeating Catholic ethos' in a Catholic school, that is, a faith that is not simply confined to the Religious Education lesson but one that is believed by the teacher and has an impact on all actions and words. While this is a credible and commonly accepted position amongst Catholic educators it is sometimes misinterpreted, and so what is being suggested here is subtly different: a Catholic

---

[27] 'Faith is a way of believing, a way of worshipping, and a way of living: it is cognitive, affective, and behavioural, engaging people's minds, emotions and wills.' Thomas H. Groome, 'Hope for Dirty Hands', in *The Furrow* (April 1998), p. 225.
[28] Jim Gallagher, *Soil for the Seed* (Essex: McCrimmon, 2001).

ethos permeating all aspects of school life could arguably imply that school life exists first and that the permeation of the Catholic ethos follows. Instead, using the concept of a 'faith-medium school', the philosophy is that the starting-point at all times is the Catholic faith and that what is taught and how it is taught and all aspects of school life emerge from and through that. There is a definite distinction here and one that Catholic teachers should consider.

A prime example of this approach is prayer. From a Religious Education perspective prayers can simply be taught. For example, very often in the Catholic school the teacher encourages the children to learn prayers such as the Our Father, the Hail Mary and many others. Some of these can be given a scriptural context and their origins studied in detail. However it is the regular action and experience of *praying* that generates and sustains a lived faith that permeates children's experience of school. The 'morning offering' prayer at the start of the day in the Catholic classroom exemplifies this, where the children – and the teacher – are presenting to God their daily work as prayer.

Prayer

Prayer can be a very simple and practical way for the teacher to positively contribute to the spiritual and pastoral life of the school. Praying with children and talking to them about their own prayer life or giving them examples of the way they pray are powerful illustrations of how a teacher can give witness to Christ and help children get to know and develop a lasting relationship with him. Without a doubt, some of the most effective prayer sessions occur when the teacher joins with the class in their prayer task and shares his or her own prayer with the children. Hearing the personal petitions or prayers of thanksgiving from the teacher indicates to a child many things: my teacher also prays; my teacher has a relationship with God and it makes her happy; my teacher knows that there is always someone to talk to and who listens when she is worried or happy; my teacher puts her trust in God; and my teacher writes/says her prayer in that particular way and that I can learn from that too. Praying *with* children is significantly different from simply teaching and reciting prayers. Letting them see that prayer is important to their teacher, as an equal member of their community of faith, is an example of being an effective and authentic witness.

In the Catholic school, prayer should not be viewed as a duty but rather as a natural expression of what it means to be Catholic.[29] The key to making this successful is to work with children when creating prayer time and not for them, ensuring that the prayer is theirs and that it is their minds and hearts that are raised to God, which is ultimately what the Catholic teacher should strive to achieve. But how is this done? There are three main principles that are suggested to ensure that teachers provide the best possible opportunity for children to develop a relationship with God. These are: ownership; tradition; focus. Each will be considered in turn.

Prayer: Ownership

Inviting the children to work with the teacher when preparing classroom or school prayer ensures that their ideas, experiences and concerns will be shared and ultimately the prayer experience will be what it should be – a communication between themselves and God. For example in a Catholic primary school individual classes can be asked, in turn, to lead the school weekly prayer assembly. Week after week well-rehearsed assemblies are presented, where prayers are recited by children in a competent and polished manner and particular hymns are chosen that tie in with the theme. These assemblies are fine but do they raise children's hearts and minds to God? The content of most of these assemblies is usually written (often at the last minute) by the teacher and certain 'able' children are chosen to read. In addition, leading the assembly is often viewed by teachers as being a 'burden' or even something that is dreaded as 'their time' draws near. This is unfortunate. Some of the most exciting and powerful prayer opportunities that classes can encounter are occasions, such as this. These can be approached very differently: ownership is the key.

For example, the simple act of gathering a class together to discuss what the theme or focus of the assembly could be is an important stage in achieving ownership of such a prayer event. Simple questions could be asked to establish what the children want to pray for and what the 'theme' of the assembly could be. For example:

> What is happening in school/the playground/ in our local community at the moment? What is the good news we may want to thank

---

[29] Roisín Coll and Ed Hone, *All Together: creative prayer with children* (Dublin: Veritas, 2009).

God for? What is the bad news that we may want to pray about? Where in the liturgical year are we? For example, Lent, Advent, the month of May?'

From such directed questions children are provided opportunities to share their concerns, experiences and thoughts and collectively arrive at an appropriate theme or focus for the assembly. From the very start then this prayer is theirs – they, with some direction from the teacher can choose the theme and instantly have ownership of this prayer experience. What would follow then is the planning of the different elements of the assembly in more detail, which adhere to a simple, but effective, structure. Having scripture at the start and as the focus is important (with the children choosing a relevant narrative they know or being exposed to a different scripture passage with which they could engage); the children teasing out a particular message from this scripture via music, drama, faith sharing, or through their own written prayer (in a variety of forms) again, with many the ideas coming from themselves; ensuring that there are times during the prayer in which all in the school would be able to participate, through the inclusion of traditional forms of prayer and well known and appropriate hymns or the invitation to do something else. The teacher's role is to lead the children by asking them questions, helping with ideas and keeping them focused. Ultimately the decisions and direction would be a collective responsibility. When the assembly occurs, the children understand why they are praying to God, how they are to do it and they know that it is their prayer – both the teacher's and the children's.

Allowing Religious Education time to devote to this also enables catechesis to take place – the children *learn* as they prepare for their assembly. The overall experience may also assist them when engaging in personal prayer away from school – anytime, any place. Ownership is key.

Prayer: Tradition

The Catholic Church has a rich tradition of beautiful prayers and hymns that have existed for hundreds, even thousands of years. It is our responsibility as Catholic teachers to let our children hear these, to pray them together, uniting our children with other Catholic children no matter where they are in the world. Not only are the words of these prayers poetic, historic and powerful, but knowing that they unite us with others worldwide is a wonderful reminder to children that they are part of a much wider community of faith. Passing on tradition from generation to generation is an important part of identity and letting children hear, learn and pray traditional prayers in English (and Latin too) is very much a part of that. These need not be elaborate and, of course, should be age appropriate, but their inclusion in the prayer life of the class and school should be encouraged to be as much a part of the children's prayer as their own personal communication with God.

On the principle of *lex orandi, lex credendi* ('as we pray, so we believe'), not to be overlooked is the importance of prayer in educating about faith and expressing the content of faith.

Prayer: Focus

The third and final principle to consider when providing prayer opportunities for children is to stay focused. This has been alluded to earlier. The official prayer of the Church has a daily focus. Each Mass that is offered has a particular focus. For example, those involved in music in the liturgy look to the readings of the Mass and choose hymns that are linked to that theme. In the same way our prayer with children should have a focus. Essentially, in any given prayer experience, children should be encouraged to develop their relationship with God. If it is a prayer activity at the end of the lesson, ensure the children are given clear directions as to what to they are focusing on. An instruction to simply write a 'prayer' (about anything) can be so vague that the opportunity to maximize effective communication with God is lost. In addition, challenging the children, depending on their stage of development, to consider what they want to say to God should also be a consideration.

If the prayer experience is a dedicated 'prayer time' (for example, a classroom prayer service or a school assembly) try to ensure that it also has a focus or theme. One way of doing this is to have a line of scripture as the root and all the subsequent parts of the prayer service relating to that. Effective prayer services often have one phrase repeated at different times throughout, keeping all of those participating focused. Focus is also concerned with what the prayer is trying to achieve for the person praying. For example, is it to give praise, to give thanks, to ponder, to explore, to share concern, to motivate?

Listening is also an important part of prayer. It must be a two way conversation between the faithful and God and so providing opportunities to actually listen to and hear what God may be saying should be an integral part of prayer. Silence can be one way of doing this and it is good to allow the children to become used to silence in their day for this reason. There are other ways too that can tap into children's own culture: imagining they are on their mobile/Facebook/MSM to God – what do they say to him and what is he saying back? Regardless of how it is done, letting them listen to what God, might be saying to them in response to their prayer focus is an integral part of the prayer experience.

Outside the school environment some children have no one in their lives whom they can trust and many of them are unaware of the parish community of which, by nature of their baptism, they are members. Revealing to them the ability to find space to pray and be listened to and heard amidst their sometimes turbulent home life, can be a source of strength to them. And those with happy and secure childhoods, where their faith is celebrated regularly in both the family and parish environment, opportunities such as these can enhance their prayer life as they mature in faith.

This spotlight on differing family backgrounds of children introduces the final section of this chapter, which draws the Catholic teacher's attention to home, parish and school links, particularly in an era where the bonds between all three have weakened.

Home, school and parish – the catechetical trio

Historically for the Catholic Church, strong elements of shame were often attached to lack of observance and, those choosing not to go to Mass often considered this as, in effect, a severing of ties with the Church and their faith. In our much more global and cosmopolitan society, there is evidence to suggest that these sources of shame have on the whole been normalized and that people still consider themselves to be 'of faith' but are less fixated on religious observance and worship, but more concerned with values and dispositions. Martin remarks that, 'Loyal identification does not entail agreement with ecclesiastical pronouncements and lay Christians make their decisions in terms of what makes moral sense in the life-world.'[30] Many parents of children in Catholic schools fall into this category and while there are still those who do practise their faith in the traditional sense, it is important for the Catholic teacher to understand that children come from a very wide range of backgrounds and that the children's lifestyles mirror this.

---

[30] David Martin, 'Secularisation and the future of Christianity', in *Journal of Contemporary Religion*, 20(2) (2005), pp. 145–60.

The traditional catechetical trio is now recognized as the ideal rather than a constant reality. Thankfully, that ideal exists for many children where the message and instruction they receive at home is built on at school and in the parish and vice versa. For others however, the only experience of Church that they will ever get is in school and from their teacher. The Catholic school has been referred to as the new pulpit, that is the only place where many hear the Word of God being proclaimed or are taught the message of the Gospel.[31] This is indeed a significant responsibility for the Catholic teacher and many recognize this as part of their vocation, accept it and excel in their role.

There is, however, a temptation for teachers to react differently to this modern day reality, something that has been referred to as 'the temptations of commonality'.[32] With children from a range of faith backgrounds in their classroom (and Catholic schools with children from different non-Christian religions) many teachers feel uncomfortable teaching aspects of church doctrine or conveying the Church's position on moral issues such as marriage and sex. In addition, others have felt the need to dilute the Church's teaching on issues such as sin for fear of embarrassing children because of their family context. In this terrain Catholic leaders encourage vigilance since, as a result of engaging with contemporary culture, there is often the 'temptation to prevent attention being given to the specifically religious concepts and perspectives which a properly balanced perspective on the Catholic tradition of faith and life require'.[33] Geoffrey Robinson (Auxiliary Bishop of the Archdiocese of Sydney) further illustrates the point. He questions the modern image of God promoted in some Catholic schools:

> This new God is full of love, tenderness, compassion, kindness, and warm feelings. This God permanently consoles, never challenges, doesn't forgive because there is no such thing as sin and thus nothing to forgive, and often doesn't even encourage, for encouragement could imply challenge.[34]

A balanced grasp of both faith and life is called for to avoid superficiality and ambiguity.

---

[31] Roisín Coll, 'The Struggle for the Soul'.
[32] T. McLaughlin et al., *The Contemporary Catholic School*, p. 77.
[33] Ibid., p. 85.
[34] Geoffrey Robinson, *Travels in sacred places* (Blackburn, Australia: Harper Collins, 1997).

The Catholic teacher is recognized as – and expected to be – a beacon of faith, a guide for Catholic children accompanying them on their journey of faith. Dilution of this, in any form, is not an option. Catholic parents have many choices for the education of their children and choosing the Catholic school is making a clear statement about how they expect their child to be taught. For many children, the catechetical trio of home-school-parish is still strong but for others the Catholic teacher will be its only constituent part.

Conclusion

This chapter has explored some of the issues that affect the contribution of a Catholic teacher to the spiritual and pastoral life of the Catholic school. While the expectations of the vocation of Catholic teacher can be daunting, the Catholic teacher should never underestimate what he or she can bring to the classroom by virtue of their own faith background. Accompanying children on their journey of faith does not mean always getting it right – it means being an example of faith to them, sharing with them aspects of your own faith journey and demonstrating how your love and God's love for them can change their lives.

Remember your leaders . . . Consider the outcome of their way of life and imitate their faith.[35]

[35] Heb. 13:7.

Notes on Contributors

John Bollan, a priest of the Diocese of Paisley, has been lecturing in Religious Education at the University of Glasgow since 2004. He also has responsibility for spiritual and pastoral formation across the School of Education's Initial Teacher Education programmes for those intending to teach in Catholic schools. He is the author of *The Light of His Face: Spirituality for Catholic Teachers* (Dublin: Veritas, 2007) and several articles in the fields of education, spirituality and homiletics. His other principal area of research is religion and politics in late Republican Rome.

Roisín Coll is a lecturer in Religious Education at the University of Glasgow where she also leads the Bachelor of Education programme in Primary Education. She has taught and written widely on Catholic Education in Scotland, Catholic school leadership, faith education, the faith development of teachers, the professional development of teachers and the use of prayer in schools. Teacher education is her central research focus and, in particular, the continuing professional development needs of those teaching within a faith context. Roisín has a long association with the Congregation of the Most Holy Redeemer (Redemptorists) and is currently youth coordinator for its London province.

John Deighan has worked since 1999 for the Bishops' Conference of Scotland in the role of Parliamentary Officer. His work has involved him directly in a variety of social and moral issues giving him many years of experience in presenting and explaining the Catholic Church's social doctrine in a political context. His work has covered issues such as abortion, bioethics, family life and sexuality, social justice, nuclear deterrence, religious freedom, human rights and euthanasia.

He has previously worked as a lecturer and started his career as an engineer in the nuclear industry. He is married to Angela and has seven children.

Leonardo Franchi teaches Religious Education in the School of Education at the University of Glasgow. He is involved in the theological education of students preparing to teach in Catholic schools. He has wide experience of teaching in schools and Higher Education. His principal research interests are the relationship between catechesis and Religious Education and early Christian education. He has a particular interest in St Augustine of Hippo's contribution to Catholic educational thought. He is the editor of *An Anthology of Catholic Teaching on Education* published by Scepter in 2007.

Victoria S. Harrison is Reader in Philosophy and Director of the Centre for Philosophy and Religion at the University of Glasgow. She came to Glasgow in 2005 from the University of Colorado at Boulder. Previously she taught at Birkbeck College (University of London), the University of Notre Dame's London Centre, the Muslim College (London), and Kingston University. Her publications include: *The Apologetic Value of Human Holiness* (Kluwer, 2000) and *Religion and Modern Thought* (SCM, 2007). Her current work is concerned with theories of religious and ethical pluralism and the relevance of these to the philosophy of religion.

Mary Lappin teaches in the School of Education at the University of Glasgow. She specializes in Religious Education. She works extensively with educators throughout Scotland providing curriculum and professional development. She was a co-writer of the Scottish National Catholic Religious Education curriculum. Her research interests include Grief and Loss Education and the impact of significant loss on the education and wellbeing of young people. Mary provides courses and training in education, health and social work within the field of Bereavement, Grief and Loss.

John Keenan was born in Glasgow and obtained a Law degree from the University of Glasgow. He obtained a theology degree and Philosophy Licence from the Pontifical Gregorian University in Rome. On his ordination he was appointed Assistant Priest in Christ the King, Glasgow and served in that capacity from 1995 until 2000. While there he was also the chaplain to Holyrood RC Secondary School, Glasgow. He was subsequently appointed as a teacher of philosophy in the National Seminary, Bearsden. From

2000 until the present he has been the Catholic Chaplain to the University of Glasgow and an associate lecturer in the School of Education at the University.

Thomas Kilbride is a priest of the Archdiocese of Glasgow. He was ordained in 1996. Having studied philosophy at the University of Glasgow and Theology at the Pontifical Gregorian University, Rome, he gained a Licence in Sacred Scripture from the Pontifical Biblical Institute. He was a school chaplain for seven years, and is currently a parish priest in Glasgow. He is Archdiocesan Director of Religious Education, supporting teaching of RE in Catholic schools, the professional development of teachers, adult formation and parish catechesis. He is also involved in the ongoing formation of priests locally and nationally. From 2003, he was lecturer in New Testament at Scotus College, the National Seminary in Scotland, until its closure in 2009.

Stephen McKinney is a Senior Lecturer in the School of Education, University of Glasgow and a former Head of the Department of Religious Education. His research interests include faith schools and Catholic schools and he has published widely on these topics in journals and books, including his own edited collection from 2008: *Faith Schools in the 21st Century* (Dunedin). He has presented over forty papers at national and international conferences. He is an Executive member of the Scottish Catholic Education Commission and a member of the Editorial Boards of the *Journal of Moral Education* and the *Journal of Beliefs and Values*.

Catherine O'Hare teaches in the School of Education at Glasgow University. She teaches on a range of courses in Initial Teacher Education and, in addition to areas of Education and Religious Education, she is responsible for devising and teaching the Specialist Course 'Exploring Theology and Exploring Spirituality through Art' which includes an annual field trip to Florence.

Leon Robinson was born and raised in Liverpool, gained a joint Honours degree in philosophy and theology from Oxford University before embarking on a series of adventures in theatre, music, writing, art and academia, experimenting with a wide range of graduate employments; his ventures have included alternative pantomimes, animated films, site-specific sculptures, and window cleaning. He has taught widely, in schools, colleges, universities and Adult Education. He is currently Programme Leader in

Religious and Philosophical Education at the University of Glasgow, a four-year undergraduate professional qualification for those wishing to teach RE in secondary schools.

Philip Tartaglia was born in Glasgow in 1951. In 1975, he was ordained a priest for the Archdiocese of Glasgow. He studied Theology at the Pontifical Gregorian University, Rome, where he completed doctoral studies in 1980. He taught systematic theology in the Catholic seminary in Glasgow from 1980 to 1997, and was for a number of years a visiting lecturer at the Faculty of Divinity of the University of Glasgow, teaching a course on the history of the doctrine of the Trinity. He was parish Priest at St Mary's, Duntocher, Clydebank, from 1995 to 2004. He was Rector of the Pontifical Scots College, Rome, from 2004 to 2005, when Pope Benedict XVI appointed him Bishop of Paisley.

Karen Wenell is lecturer in New Testament and Theology in the Department of Theology and Religion at the University of Birmingham. She previously contributed to teaching for the B.Ed. and the MA in Philosophical and Religious Education as lecturer in the School of Education, University of Glasgow. She has been one of the editors of *The Expository Times: International Journal of Biblical Studies, Theology and Ministry,* and is the author *of Jesus and Land: Sacred and Social Space in Second Temple Judaism* (Continuum, 2007). She recently co-edited a book of essays in honour of John K. Riches: *Paul, Grace and Freedom* (Continuum, 2009).

Index

Village London

Village London

ANDREW DUNCAN

ORIGINAL WALKS THROUGH
25 LONDON VILLAGES

NEW
HOLLAND

First published in 1997 by
New Holland (Publishers) Ltd
London • Cape Town • Sydney • Singapore

24 Nutford Place
London W1H 6DQ
United Kingdom

80 McKenzie Street
Cape Town 8001
South Africa

3/2 Aquatic Drive
Frenchs Forest, NSW 2086
Australia

ISBN 1 85368 944 0

Commissioning editor: Jo Hemmings
Editor: Helen Varley
Assistant editor: Sophie Bessemer
Copy editor: Geraldine Christy
Designer (colour section and jacket): Alan Marshall, Wilderness Design
Design consultant (text): Penny Mills
Cartographer: ML Design
Indexer: Alex Corrin

Reproduction by Dot Gradations
Printed and bound in Singapore by Kyodo Printing Co (Singapore) Pte Ltd

Photographic Acknowledgments
All photographs by the author with the exception of the following:
Martin Charles/Dulwich Picture Gallery: Plate 26; English Heritage Photographic Library:
Plate 4; Oliver Lim: Plates 5, 7, 8, 11, 19, 21, 22, 23; Norman Plastow: Plate 35;
The William Morris Gallery: Plate 18.

Front cover: Golden Square, Hampstead, photographed by Oliver Lim.

Contents

Preface

Village London? Sounds like a contradiction in terms, but outside its historic centre of City, Westminster and West End, London is, in fact, a collection of villages, gobbled up when the capital expanded on the backs of the railways in the 19th century.

Many of these once quiet country villages were wiped out by the advancing tide of bricks and mortar. But for various reasons – a powerful preservation society perhaps, or a local shift in the centre of commercial and administrative activity – many also survived. While the surrounding countryside was transformed into a featureless landscape of suburbia, they managed to hang on to their visual identity and historical distinctness.

Were London's villages still to be in the traditional rural setting they once enjoyed, many of them would feature in guide books, and draw hordes of trippers at weekends in search of a good pub lunch and a stroll in the fresh air. But engulfed in London as they are, their charms are overlooked, their delights ignored and the good things they have to offer are left to the locals to appreciate and enjoy.

In a bid to bring their attractions to a wider audience, *Village London* explores 25 of the best of them – I won't say *the* best because there is an element of subjectivity in the choice. Six of the villages are paired with neighbours so there are 22 entries in all. A glance at the map of London villages on pages 12–13 will show that they cover the whole city, north, south, east and west, extending from Kensington and Rotherhithe close to the city centre to Monken Hadley and Carshalton right out on its fringes.

The central London villages – hilly Hampstead with its heath and winding lanes and alleys, Chiswick with its beautiful Mall, Kew with its perfectly preserved 18th-century green – are inevitably slightly less unknown than some of the outer London ones. But anyone who makes a trip out to Carshalton with its ponds forming the source of the Wandle, to Pinner with its wonderful High Street and half-timbered farmhouses, to Mitcham with its historic cricket green, to Petersham with its farm selling eggs and honey, and to Bexley with its beautiful riverside mansion, is in for a whole succession of extremely pleasant surprises.

I have thoroughly enjoyed writing this book, and I hope you get just as much pleasure out of reading and using it. 'Using' is the operative word for the only way to see London is on foot. So get out those trainers and hit the trail: you've only got 25 villages and 65¾ miles to go!

Andrew Duncan
Kensal Green

Introduction

About the book

Each village entry contains two main features: an historical introduction giving a brief account of the origins and development of the village up to the time when it was absorbed into the greater London conurbation – usually sometime in the mid to late 19th century – and a guided walk. The walk explores the old village centre and points out not just the features that survive but also the location of such things as rectories and manor houses that have long since disappeared.

Each entry also has its own essential information listing and a detailed map. The information listing covers distance from central London, rail and Underground connections, main sights, local events, and details of where to eat and drink. The map shows, in addition to the route of the walk and the main sights, the location of public toilets. The maps are detailed enough to make an A–Z atlas of London unnecessary, but it is always a good idea to have one along, if only to identify any places mentioned in the text which are not included in the walks.

Choosing a walk

During the writing of this book I have often pondered on how people will use it. Will they start with the first village and then work through to the end? Will they visit villages close to where they happen to live? Or will they choose those that are easiest to get to? Maybe some museum or historic house will be the deciding factor. And what about visitors to London who do not know the city at all? How will they make their choice?

To help all readers – whether they are capital residents or visitors – I have produced on pages 9 and 10 a set of lists which group villages according to certain categories, for example riverside villages and villages with cricket clubs (a match on a weekend afternoon in summer provides an excellent focal point for a walk in the same way that a museum or historic house does). Using these lists, even the most undecided village explorer should be able to choose which place to visit without too much difficulty.

Further information

At the back of the book further information is provided for the walks. The opening times section starting on page 148 gives addresses, telephone numbers and opening times for places included in the walks which are open to the public. You will know when to consult this section because all the places which have entries in it are highlighted in the body of the book – both in the text and on the maps – in **bold type**. Tourist information centres also appear in the opening times section. These and local libraries have free leaflets on local places of interest, booklets for sale, and collections of books, photographs and other material on local history. In addition, local councils and local history societies often display information about parks, gardens, cemeteries and places of historical interest on notice boards at the entrance. Libraries are listed village by village starting on page 154.

Walking in London

All the walks start and finish at Underground or rail stations for maximum travel convenience. I urge all walkers to use this form of transport. Not only is it much better for the city, but with a bit of planning it is also much easier than going by car, and it adds to the element of adventure in the outing. I have not included bus information because I have found from experience that it soon goes out of date. For the latest information and full advice on routes the easiest thing to do is ring London Transport's 24-hour information service on 0171 222 1234.

The walks range in length from just under 2 miles (3 kilometres) to just over 4 miles (7 kilometres). The average is roughly 3 miles (about 4.8 kilometres). A list of walks in order of length appears on the next page. I find that a 3-mile (4.8-kilometre) walk takes approximately two hours at a gentle pace, not including stops. But of course different people walk at different speeds. Mine is quite quick so slower walkers might find they need more time. Either way, there's never any point in rushing a walk. You never know when you will want to stop and linger, or for how long. My advice is to turn each walk into a day trip, or in summer a long afternoon/early evening excursion. That way you'll really be able to savour the outing and make it an event to remember.

The walks can be done on any day of the week, but bear in mind that the villages will be liveliest on weekdays when all the shops will be open, and that the recreational areas – parks, gardens, commons and other open spaces – will be busiest at weekends, especially in summer.

Walking in London is not like walking in the country. The endless traffic and hordes of people (except in the quietest sections, of which there are fortunately many in the book) are surprisingly tiring, and of course tarmac is a lot harder on the feet than turf. So again, my advice, especially for those not as young as they were, is to take things easy and have frequent stops for rest and refreshment (the refreshment listings at the beginning of each village entry should help here).

On many of the walks you will see coloured wall plaques commemorating people, places and events. The most common are the circular blue plaques first put up by the old Greater London Council and now by English Heritage. Other plaque-providing organizations include local councils and history societies. A surprising amount can be learned from these plaques, some of which are pointed out on the walks.

Choosing villages to visit

Villages by distance from central London (miles/kilometres from Charing Cross)

mi	km	
3	4.8	Kensington
3¾	6	Rotherhithe and Bermondsey
4½	7.2	Hampstead
5	8	Dulwich
5½	8.8	Barnes
5½	8.8	Chiswick
5½	8.8	Greenwich
5½	8.8	Highgate
6½	10.4	Blackheath
7½	12	Kew
7½	12	Walthamstow
7½	12	Wimbledon
8	12.8	Brentford
8½	13.6	Mitcham
9	14.4	Ham and Petersham
10	16	Carshalton
10	16	Isleworth
10½	14.2	Harrow-on-the-Hill
11	17.6	Chipping Barnet and Monken Hadley
11	17.6	Enfield
12½	20	Bexley
13	20.8	Pinner

Villages by length of walk (in miles/kilometres)

mi	km	
1¾	2.8	Hampstead
1¾	2.8	Harrow-on-the-Hill
2	3.2	Kew
2¼	3.6	Kensington
2½	4	Chiswick
2¾	4.4	Carshalton
2¾	4.4	Ham and Petersham (5¾ miles/9.2 kilometres if you walk to and from Richmond)
2¾	4.4	Pinner
2¾	4.4	Walthamstow
3	4.8	Blackheath
3	4.8	Enfield
3	4.8	Isleworth
3	4.8	Mitcham
3	4.8	Barnes
3¼	5.2	Bexley
3½	5.6	Brentford
3½	5.6	Greenwich
3½	5.6	Highgate
3½	5.6	Rotherhithe and Bermondsey
3¾	6	Wimbledon
4	6.4	Chipping Barnet and Monken Hadley
4¼	6.8	Dulwich

Villages beside the River Thames

Barnes
Brentford
Chiswick
Greenwich
Ham and Petersham
Isleworth
Kew
Rotherhithe and Bermondsey

Villages with views

Chipping Barnet and Monken Hadley
Dulwich
Greenwich
Hampstead
Harrow-on-the-Hill
Highgate
Wimbledon

Villages with cricket clubs

Bexley
Kew
Mitcham

Villages beside heaths and commons

Barnes
Blackheath
Chipping Barnet and Monken Hadley
Dulwich
Greenwich
Ham and Petersham
Hampstead
Highgate
Mitcham
Wimbledon

Villages by Underground line/railway station/steamer pier

Underground

Circle Line	Kensington
District Line	Chiswick
	Ham and Petersham
	Kensington
	Kew
	Wimbledon
Docklands Light Railway	Greenwich
East London Line	Rotherhithe and Bermondsey
Metropolitan Line	Harrow-on-the-Hill
	Pinner
Northern Line	Chipping Barnet and Monken Hadley
	Rotherhithe and Bermondsey
	Hampstead
	Highgate
Piccadilly Line	Brentford
	Chiswick
Victoria Line	Walthamstow

Rail

Cannon Street	Greenwich
Charing Cross	Bexley
	Blackheath
	Greenwich
	Enfield
Kings Cross	Enfield
Liverpool Street	Walthamstow
London Bridge	Dulwich
	Wimbledon
Marylebone	Harrow-on-the-Hill
	Enfield
Moorgate	Ham and Petersham
North London Line	Hampstead
	Kew
North London Line	Walthamstow
Victoria	Carshalton
	Dulwich
	Mitcham
Waterloo	Barnes
	Brentford
	Ham and Petersham
	Isleworth
	Kew
	Mitcham
	Wimbledon

Steamer

| Charing Cross Pier | Greenwich |
| Wesminster Pier | Kew |

Key to Route Maps

Each of the walks in this book is accompanied by a detailed map on which the route of the walk is shown in green. Places of interest along the walks – such as historic houses, museums and churches – are clearly identified. Those that are open to the public appear in **bold type** (as in the text). Opening times are listed village by village at the back of the book, starting on page 148.

The following is a key to symbols and abbreviations used on the maps:

Symbols

	route of walk
	footpath
	railway line
	railway station
	Underground station
	major building
†	church
	public toilets
	viewpoint
	wood

Abbreviations

APP	Approach	PH	Public
AVE	Avenue		House
CLO	Close		(Pub)
COTTS	Cottages	PK	Park
CT	Court	PL	Place
DLR	Docklands	RD	Road
	Light Railway	S	South
DRI	Drive	SQ	Square
E	East	ST	Saint
GÐNS	Gardens	ST	Street
GRN	Green	STN	Station
GRO	Grove	TER	Terrace
HO	House	UPR	Upper
LA	Lane	VW	View
LWR	Lower	W	West
MS	Mews	WD	Wood
MT	Mount	WHF	Wharf
N	North	WLK	Walk
PAS	Passage	WY	Way
PDE	Parade		

Map of London Villages

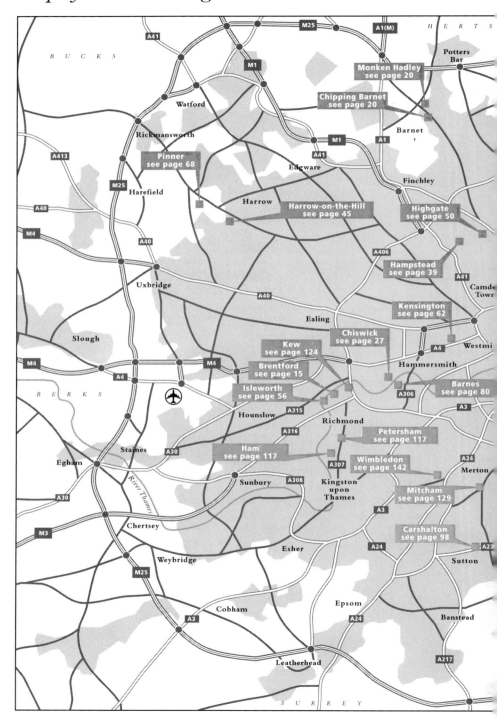

HERTS

A1(M)

Potters
Bar

Monken Hadley
see page 20

Chipping Barnet
see page 20

Barnet

Finchley

Highgate
see page 50

A406

Hampstead
see page 39

A41

Camde
Towr

Kensington
see page 62

Westmi

Chiswick
see page 27

A4

Hammersmith

Barnes
see page 80

A3

Kew
see page 124

Brentford
see page 15

Isleworth
see page 56

A306

A315

Hounslow

Petersham
see page 117

Richmond

A316

Ham
see page 117

A307

Wimbledon
see page 142

A24

Merton

Kingston
upon
Thames

Mitcham
see page 129

A3

Carshalton
see page 98

A24

A23

Sutton

Esher

Epsom

A24

Banstead

A217

Leatherhead

SURREY

BUCKS

A41

M25

A1

M1

M1

A41

Watford

Rickmansworth

Pinner
see page 68

Edgware

A413

M25

Harefield

Harrow

Harrow-on-the-Hill
see page 45

A40

A40

A40

Uxbridge

Ealing

M4

A40

Slough

M4

A4

BERKS

Staines

A30

Hounslow

Sunbury

A308

Egham

River Thames

A30

M3

Chertsey

Weybridge

M25

Cobham

A3

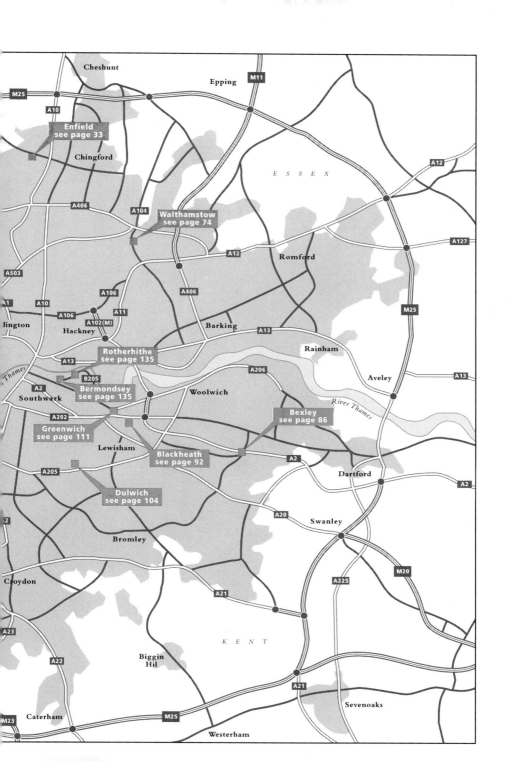

Villages North of the River Thames

Brentford

Location	8 miles (12.8 kilometres) west of Charing Cross.
Transport	Boston Manor Underground Station (Piccadilly Line). Brentford Station (overground trains from Waterloo) can be used if more convenient: it is on the walk and being closer to the village centre cuts out the longish walk between Boston Manor Station and Boston Manor House.
Features	**Boston Manor House**; The Butts estate of late 17th-century town houses; the Grand Union Canal; the wharves and working waterfront and the remains of Brentford Dock; views of the River Thames.
Refreshments	*High Street* cafés, pubs, fish and chip shop, pizza restaurant, bakery; *overlooking the marina* (on the walk) bar/restaurant; *wharf area* (on the walk) Brewery Tap pub; *near The Butts* (on the walk) White Horse (with a riverside garden). *St Paul's Church* (see map page 17 for location) morning coffee and cheap hot lunches.

Standing at the confluence of the rivers Brent and Thames, Brentford – or more properly New Brentford to distinguish it from nearby Old Brentford – clearly takes its name from a ford over the Brent, but some people think it also refers to a ford over the Thames. The Thames ford is supposed to have been the the lowest on the river and may well have been the one used by Julius Caesar during his invasion of England in 54BC. Later it was the scene of two battles: one in 1016 between Edmund Ironside and King Canute; and another during the Civil War in 1642, when the Royalists defeated the Roundheads.

Despite its strategic importance as a fording place, Brentford was not a particularly populous place and in the Middle Ages was therefore not a parish in its own right but an outlying settlement of the parish of Hanwell. Hanwell church was two miles away, however, so from an early date Brentford had its own church, which was dedicated to St Lawrence. Brentford at last became a parish in 1749. Fifteen years later, when the radical political writer Horne Tooke was parson, the bulk of the church was rebuilt in brick next to the original 15th-century stone tower. Rationalization during this century led to its closure in 1961. Plans to convert it into a theatre in the 1980s fell through and now the building stands redundant beside the busy High Street.

Boston Manor

Although the village was not a parish in the Middle Ages, it was a manor; but it was known as Bordestone and later Boston, rather than Brentford. The manor belonged to the priory of St Helen Bishopsgate in the City of London. After the dissolution of the monasteries it passed into secular hands. The Reade family rebuilt the manor house, which lay about three-quarters of a mile (1.2 kilometres) to the north of the village on the east bank of the Brent, in 1623. Half a century later James Clitherow, the fourth son of Sir Christopher Clitherow of Pinner, bought it and remodelled it following a fire. James's descendants owned the Boston Manor estate right down to 1924 when the advent of the Great West Road induced them to sell up. **Boston Manor House** was bought by the council and is now (partially) open to the public, together with its gardens and surrounding parkland.

About the time the Clitherows moved to Brentford, the village – or town, rather – was beginning to develop as a commercial and industrial centre. Inns and shops lined the High Street, serving travellers on the original Great West Road out of London. Corn and garden produce from orchards and market gardens were traded in the market place. To the south, industry (including several breweries and distilleries) crammed into the narrow space between the High Street and the waterfront, and the waterfront was lined with wharves. Here also lived Brentford's working population. Meanwhile, the increasingly prosperous middle classes migrated north to The Butts, an enclave of handsome new houses built in the late 1600s and early 1700s. The Butts survives more or less unspoilt today and features in the walk.

The canal

From the 1790s the construction of the Grand Union Canal between Brentford and Braunston in Northamptonshire linked London with the industrializing Midlands via the Thames This inevitably increased the economic significance of Brentford dramatically. So did the arrival of the railways, especially when the famous engineer Isambard Kingdom Brunel built a large dock at Brentford and connected it to his Great Western Railway by a branch line leading north to Southall. Brentford Dock has now been closed for over 30 years, but the canal and busy waterfront remain and the land between the High Street and the waterfront is still packed with boat-building firms and many other small businesses. The walk explores this area, as well as the manor house and grounds, The Butts and the old village centre.

THE BRENTFORD WALK

Start and finish Boston Manor Station.
Distance 3½ miles (5.6 kilometres).

Come out of the station and turn right down Boston Manor Lane. After about 200 yards (180 metres) you come to the gates of Boston Manor House. Turn in here and make your way round to the left of the house to the garden front with its stately old cedars. Today the view is of the M4 flyover, but originally the house looked over parkland to the River Brent and, beyond, to Osterley Park, former home of the Child banking family. Before the area was built up Brentford was surrounded

BRENTFORD

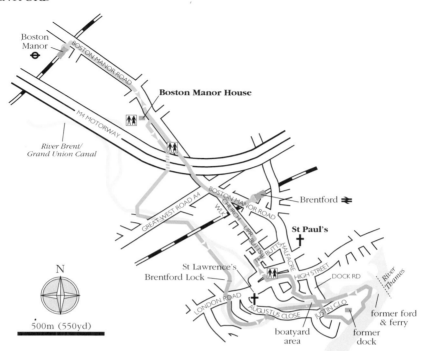

by a whole string of country mansions: Syon House, Osterley Park, Boston Manor House, Gunnersbury House (home of the Rothschild family) and, south of the river, Kew Palace. Remarkably, all survive today and all are open to the public.

Turn left down the broad tarmac walk, aiming for the tall office blocks. At the bottom by the toilets and the little car park, turn right and walk down the gently sloping hill towards the canal at the bottom. Here, in fact, the canal is no more than the canalized River Brent. At Hanwell, about 1 mile (1.6 kilometres) north of here, the river and canal diverge. The canal heads off east towards Uxbridge, while the river makes its way northwest to its source near Barnet. Cross over the footbridge and turn left, heading in the direction of the Samsung tower and the Great West Road bridge. Beyond the bridge you go round a corner and under a railway bridge before passing through a covered dock. Now you can see, ahead left, the old village centre on the far bank of the Brent with the spire of **St Paul's Church** rising up behind. The wide loop of the Brent here was cut off by the canal partly as a short cut and partly to create a backwater basin.

St Lawrence's Church and Brentford Lock
Carrying on, St Lawrence's Church comes into view straight ahead through the trees and beyond the Brentford Lock. Looking back just after you pass the lock, you

17

get a good view of The Butts area of the old village, laid out on high ground to protect it from flooding. The poorer areas were not so lucky: serious inundations were not infrequent in the days before the development of water management techniques. Turn left over the bridge on the site of the original Brent ford and then immediately right and down the steps to continue the towpath walk (signposted). Having flowed south until now, the canalized river here turns sharply east as it nears the Thames. Over on the far side, the trees denote the grounds of the Duke of Northumberland's Syon House. On this side new houses and offices are being built among the small factories and workshops that crowd what is called The Ham – a former piece of riverside common. When you reach the bridge that once carried the railway to Brunel's dock, you have to turn left onto the road to pass underneath it. A flight of shallow up-and-down steps brings you back onto the towpath and into the main waterfront and boatyard area.

Brentford Dock

Cross the footbridge and once you are on the other side do not go back down to the towpath but continue along the riverside, keeping to the tarmac (and do not go up the ramp). Good views of the basins and boatyards open up to the left. When you reach the lock, turn right on Dock Road and go under the arch by the dock management office. Carry on over the road and up the steps, now walking on red tarmac with flats to your left and a little car park on the right. You are now in the former dock, built on an islanded spit of land called Old England. The dock basin could accommodate boats up to 300 tons and all around were loading bays, warehouses and railway sidings. Like London docks downriver, Brentford Dock closed in the 1960s and was subsequently redeveloped with flats, houses and a marina for pleasure boats.

Turn left at the small fountain. Go under the walkway into a garden area and then up the steps ahead onto the terrace of the marina bar and restaurant. Cross the terrace diagonally to the right, go down the bank and turn left along the gravel walk by the river. Kew Gardens is surprisingly close on the right. Ahead, in Old Brentford, rises the graceful campanile of Kew Bridge Steam Museum, formerly the Grand Junction Waterworks Company.

Cross the entrance to the dock basin and follow the path round to the right, up the steps and back onto the red tarmac. From the viewpoint here you can see, away to the right, George III's Kew Palace, and near to the left, the entrance to the ferry basin. The King's ferry operated between here and the Surrey bank of the river, carrying horses and carriages as well as people, from at least the mid-17th century.

Soap and starch

To the left of the ferry basin there used to be a large soap factory which, as early as the 1820s was the biggest hard soap factory in the southeast of England. Production at the works – which, apart from the dock, was the largest enterprise in Brentford – ceased in 1961. Turn sharp left back along the entrance to the canal, which strictly speaking starts at the lock crossed by Dock Road. Cross the lock on the blue-painted footbridge and walk back along the canal. First you cross a weir and then a pair of disused floodgates called Dr Johnson's Lock after Dr William Johnson, the proprietor of a starch mill in Catherine Wheel Yard in the 18th century. Turn right by the Brewery Tap pub and walk up Catherine Wheel Road (the Catherine Wheel was an inn). When you reach the High Street turn left and cross at the lights into the Market Place. Both the High Street and the Market Place have been dramatically altered in the 20th century to allow the main road to be widened and to provide more up-to-date shopping facilities. The market was forced to move in the 1850s when the new courthouse was built. It went first to Old Brentford and then, in 1974, to Heston.

Pass to the right of the courthouse. To the left of the White Horse, the artist J.M.W. Turner spent four years as a boy living with his uncle, a local butcher, before going on to study at the Royal Academy. The White Horse has been here since at least 1603, though it has, of course, been rebuilt since then. Beyond the White Horse you come to The Butts.

The Butts
Originally common land used since at least the 16th century for compulsory archery practice (a butt is a target, hence the name). The Butts was enclosed and sold off for building in 1664. Most of the houses around the square date from soon after that time. Throughout the 18th century, and for much of the 19th, the elections for Middlesex's two MPs were held here. Local traders benefited enormously from what was effectively a two-week jamboree, but the reputation of the town suffered badly from the concomitant bribery, brawling, drunkenness, and even violence.

Make your way across to the far right-hand corner of the square. Here there is a wide avenue leading from the square to Half Acre. The houses on either side are rather later in date than those in the square. On the left side at least, this is because until well into the 19th century this was the site of Ronald's Nursery, one of the largest in the area and a supplier to Kew when the botanical garden was being developed. St Raphael's Convent takes up most of the avenue's right-hand side.

Exit the square via Upper Butts. At the end turn right into Somerset Road and then left into the continuation of Upper Butts. Go straight on down to the end (now Church Walk) and cross the bridge over the railway line, constructed through Barnes in 1849. When you reach the road you can either turn left, cross the Great West Road and continue up Boston Manor Road to Boston Manor Station, or turn right for Brentford Station (entrance over bridge) for trains to Waterloo.

Chipping Barnet and Monken Hadley

Location	11 miles (17.7 kilometres) north of Charing Cross.
Transport	High Barnet Underground Station (Northern Line).
Features	**St John's Church**; **St Mary's Church**; six almshouses; Elizabethan grammar school; Georgian mansions; Hadley Green and Common; **Barnet Museum**.
Refreshments	*Barnet High Street* variety of cafés, pubs, restaurants and fast-food outlets; *Hadley Highstone* (furthest extremity of the walk) Windmill pub; *Wood Street* (see map page 22) Black Horse pub.

Chipping Barnet and Monken Hadley sit on top of a 400-foot (122-metre)-high hill overlooking the valley of the Pymmes Brook to the east. South of Monken Hadley, Chipping Barnet also looks south over the valley of the Dollis Brook. On clear days there are therefore good views from the walk in both directions.

East Barnet, down in the valley of the Pymmes Brook, was the original Barnet village and remained for centuries the centre of the parish. Chipping Barnet grew up to the west of the village at a point where the Great North Road breasted its first major hill on the way out of London to York. Being a natural place for travellers to stop and change horses, it developed in the 18th century as a great coaching centre, with fine large inns and fleets of horses standing ready for the harness. By the end of the century at least 150 mail and stage coaches were passing through the village daily, not to mention post-chaises, private carriages, carts and wagons.

The old pre-suburban village of Chipping Barnet consisted of little more than the High Street and Wood Street, with the local church at their intersection. No new roads were added till the 1830s, by which time the growth of the coaching trade had generated some pressure for development. Woods, commons and fields lay all around. To the north was Hadley Green, and to the west was Barnet Common, stretching all the way from the Black Horse inn to the village of Arkley. Hadley Green, as you will see on the walk, is still open space, but Barnet Common has all disappeared save for a patch of manicured park in Wood Street.

Barnet horse fair

In the Middle Ages Chipping Barnet belonged to St Albans Abbey. The Abbey was granted the right to hold a market in 1199, hence the village's name ('chipping' means market). Four hundred years later in 1588, by which time the manor had passed into lay hands, Elizabeth I gave permission for two fairs a year to be held. One – the September horse fair – acquired an international reputation as dealers came from all over Europe to buy and sell. Horse-racing naturally developed as an offshoot of the fair, and for a time racing at Chipping Barnet rivalled the great Newmarket meeting. But the races, which were held first on the common and then, after the common was enclosed, in fields southeast of the village, ceased when High Barnet Station was built in 1871. The September horse fair is still held, however, usually in a council-owned farm in Mays Lane, but it is inevitably a shadow of its former self. The market survives, too. It is held in St Albans Road every Wednesday and Saturday.

The Wars of the Roses

The biggest event that has ever taken place in Chipping Barnet is the battle in 1471 between the Yorkists and the Lancastrians during the Wars of the Roses. After being deposed and forced into exile by Warwick the Kingmaker, Edward IV returned to England in March 1471, captured Henry VI and then defeated and killed Warwick at Barnet one foggy day in April, though backed by only 2,000 men. This victory, plus another one at Tewkesbury shortly after, established him securely on his throne for the rest of his life.

High place in a wood

Unlike Chipping Barnet, Monken Hadley, half a mile (0.8 kilometres) to the north has preserved its identity as a pretty country village with a church, a manor house, a rectory and cottages. The village was originally a clearing in a vast tract of woodland, hence the name Hadley, which means 'high place cleared in a wood'. In the 1130s Geoffrey de Mandeville, Earl of Essex, founded a hermitage in the village and gave it to the Monastery of Walden in Essex. The Monastery owned the village all through the Middle Ages and so it acquired its prefix of Monken, a corruption of 'monachorum' meaning 'of (i.e. belonging to) the monks'.

After the dissolution of the monasteries, Monken Hadley passed into lay hands, but like Chipping Barnet, no one family owned it for long enough to establish a squirearchical dynasty. The village developed as a retreat for wealthy merchants and professional men from London, however, and so besides the manor house, Monken Hadley has as fine a collection of gentlemen's residences as you will find anywhere in the Greater London area. In fact, Monken Hadley is one of those villages, like Petersham near Richmond, where the grand houses of the rich outnumber the humbler homes of the poor. And, as at Petersham, they stand in a fine rural setting, provided by the green on one side of the village and the common on the other.

THE CHIPPING BARNET AND MONKEN HADLEY WALK

Start and finish High Barnet Station.
Distance 4 miles (6.4 kilometres).

Turn right out of High Barnet Station and walk up the hill to the High Street. Turn right here and carry on up the hill. Crossing Meadway you can see down into the valley of the Pymmes Brook. The first railway in the area was built in the valley in 1850, 20 years before High Barnet Station was opened. Meadway was originally the

CHIPPING BARNET AND MONKEN HADLEY

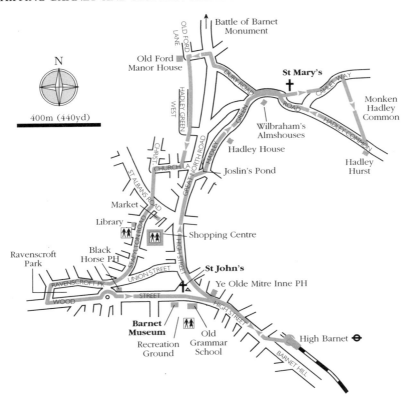

footpath made to link Chipping Barnet with that first station. Further up the High Street on the left, the Dandy Lion pub occupies part of the site of the Red Lion, probably the biggest and grandest of the old coaching inns in Chipping Barnet. The fine inn sign protruding way out over the street is a relic of the original inn. A few doors up on the right you come to Ye Olde Mitre Inne, dating from the century before the Red Lion and obviously more typical of an earlier age. It is the oldest pub in Barnet and one of the few 17th-century buildings to survive in the village.

Follow the High Street round to the right as it passes between **St John's Church** and the shops through a bottleneck called The Squeeze. Round the corner the street is much wider. The market was once held here, though it has now moved to its own site on the far side of The Spires shopping centre.

The Battle of Barnet

Walk all the way up the right-hand side of the street until you come to Hadley Green and open country. The 24-acre (10-hectare) Green, an ancient tract of common, is reputed to be the site of the Battle of Barnet in 1471, though whether it took place exactly here or somewhere nearby is now impossible to say. Bear right by the garage, cross East View and continue between Joslin's Pond and Ossulstone House. By the time this house was built in the 1760s (by John Horton, a sugar refiner) Chipping Barnet was connected to Monken Hadley by a row of houses of this type, reflecting the area's popularity with wealthy businessmen from London.

Thackeray's grandfather

Beyond Ossulstone House and The Cottage there is now a gap in this row. Here, formerly, stood an old house that once belonged to the grandfather of the novelist William Thackeray. Thackeray knew Hadley quite well because his cousin was rector here. By that time his grandfather was dead and the house had passed into other hands. Between 1829 and 1934 Hadley's lords of the manor lived in the house. The last lord of the manor, Miss Rhoda Wyburn, gave the fields behind the house to the public and after her death in 1935 the house was demolished to provide access to the new open space. The former fields are now crossed by a bridle path connecting Hadley Green with East Barnet.

Dr Livingstone

After World War II the gap in the row was a lot bigger because three of the houses on the far side (The Elms, Mercers and Thackeray House) were destroyed by bombs. Since then, however, they have been rebuilt exactly as they were before and now it is almost impossible to tell from looking at them that they are not genuine. Beyond the new-old houses you come to Hadley House, the grandest house in the row and the original manor house of Monken Hadley. Beyond the manor house are Fairholt and Monkenholt, both dating from the mid-18th century, and then Monken Cottage followed by Livingstone Cottage. The latter was the residence of the famous explorer, Dr David Livingstone, in 1857–8. He had just come back to England from Africa for the first time and it was here that he wrote *Missionary Travels and Researches in South Africa*. Although the time he spent here was very short, it was nevertheless one of the happiest periods of his life for he had his family with him all the time, a rare occurrence in the great traveller's life. The plaque was put up by his daughter in 1913 on the centenary of his birth.

Trollope's sister

After Livingstone Cottage, keep right. Beyond Hollybush House, Grandon has connections with another great novelist of the 19th century, Anthony Trollope. In January 1836 Trollope's consumptive sister, Emily, moved here hoping that the healthy situation would help cure her condition. It did not, however, and before February was out she was dead. Go past Sir Roger Wilbraham's almshouses, which were founded in 1612, and follow the road round to the right into the centre of Monken Hadley village. When you get to White Lodge, cross the road and enter **St Mary's** churchyard, where Emily Trollope and Thackeray's grandparents, among many others, are buried.

Above the west door of the the medieval church the date 1494 denotes when it was substantially rebuilt. The coats of arms close by, put up when the west door was renovated in 1956, represent the Archbishop of Canterbury and the Bishop of London and their respective provinces at the time. In the church there are various brasses and old monuments, the most striking of which is the portrait of Sir Roger Wilbraham and his wife Mary, carved by the well-known Jacobean sculptor, Nicholas Stone.

Monken Hadley Common

Pass between the church and the flint-faced Pagitt's almshouses on the right. Justinian Pagitt founded this almshouse in 1678: the plaque was put up on 3rd October, 1978, to mark its tercentenary. The path through the churchyard brings you out on Monken Hadley Common with Hadley Wood ahead down in a dip. Monken Hadley grew up on the western edge of a huge medieval hunting park called Enfield Chase. When the Chase was split up and enclosed in 1779, the village received the land that is now called Monken Hadley Common as compensation for loss of grazing and other rights in the old Chase. Today the Common covers 190 acres (77 hectares) and stretches east nearly 2 miles (3 kilometres) as far as Cockfosters.

Hadley Hurst

Turn left along the road. At the entrance to the Church of England primary school, the original village school founded in 1832, turn right across the road and head across the Common, bearing slightly left along a path leading towards a red-brick house on the extreme left with two superb cedars in front. This is just one of many fine houses on the south side of the common and approaching them from this direction is the best way of admiring them. When you reach the red-brick house – Hadley Hurst, built around 1705 – turn right along the path worn in the broad verge. The white house called Hurst Cottage is a slightly earlier and slightly less grand house than Hadley Hurst. Attached to it on the left is a small house rather more recognizable as a cottage. This one was built in the 16th century and is probably the oldest building in the village, apart from the church.

Further on along the row, Gladsmuir was the home of the Quilter family from 1736 until early this century. More recently it belonged to the novelist Kingsley Amis and it was during his tenure that the poet Cecil Day Lewis died in the house in 1972. Carry on back towards the village, passing the rectory on the right and then going through the Common gates. Retrace your steps through the centre of the village, this time on the right-hand side of the road and passing the 17th-century Pagitt's Almshouses. Beyond St Mary's Church you pass two large neo-Georgian houses set well back from the road in their own grounds. These were built in the early 1960s and replaced the so-called Hadley Priory, the largest house in the road leading from Hadley Green to the church. Although the house was built in the 16th century it was never a priory, but it was made to look like one around 1800 when the owner attached a sham Gothic front to it and gave it its religious-sounding name. The Priory was demolished in the 1950s.

When you reach the Green, again turn right along Dury Road, named after a family that lived in the vicinity in the 18th century. There are more Georgian houses here, but there are many more Victorian cottages, reflecting the expansion of the

Plate 1: *Boston Manor House, Brentford: the west front (see page 16).*

Plate 2: *Hurst Cottage and pond on Monken Hadley Common (see page 24).*

Plate 3: *Monken Hadley's 17th-century Wilbrahams almshouses (see page 23).*

Plate 4: *The Gallery in Chiswick House, one of several sumptuously decorated rooms in this early Palladian mansion (see page 30).*

Plate 5: The riverside terrace at Strand on the Green between Kew and Chiswick is a popular place for a stroll and a drink on a summer's day (see page 128).

Plate 6: A shady stretch of Gentlemans Row, Enfield (see page 36).

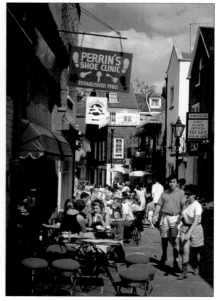

Plate 7: Perrin's Court, one of several narrow side streets off Hampstead High Street (see page 40).

Plate 8: The Keats House museum in Hampstead was once the home of Romantic poet John Keats (see page 43).

Plate 9: Harrow-on-the-Hill's winding High Street (see page 48).

Plate 10: Harrow School tuck shop just off the High Street (see page 48).

population at that time – and also the presence of Hadley Brewery. From at least 1770 this stood by the larger of the two ponds (the one with the wall along one side). Beer was brewed here until 1938. After World War II the old brewery became a distribution centre – latterly for Whitbread's Breweries – until it was demolished in 1978.

Hadley Highstone

At the end of Dury Road, turn right on the Great North Road and then, opposite the Old Windmill pub, cross the road into Old Ford Lane. As you do so, look right and you can just see a junction of roads and a patch of green. This is the site of the stone monument to the Battle of Barnet which was put up in the 18th century, supposedly on the spot where the Kingmaker fell, and which later gave its name to this part of Hadley, Hadley Highstone.

When Old Ford Lane bends right by the golf club (the clubhouse is a Regency house extended, in the Barnet direction, in the 1920s), turn left past Old Ford Manor House. Old Ford Manor was part of South Mimms, a village a couple of miles (about 3 kilometres) northwest of here. The moat of the original medieval manor house survives on the 18th tee of the golf course. This later house was built sometime around the middle of the 18th century.

Follow the path beside the green all the way back to Chipping Barnet. When you reach the junction of Gladsmuir Road and Christ Church Lane, turn right into the latter, passing on the left one of the old pumping stations of the East Barnet Gas and Water Company. When the road bends right, turn left into Christ Church Passage. At the end cross St Albans Road diagonally left and enter Stapylton Road. Walk all the way down this road, passing the library and the shopping centre. At the bottom Stapylton Road joins Union Street, one of the new roads built in Chipping Barnet in the 1830s. At the end of Union Street, turn right, past the Victorian almshouses of the Leathersellers' Company, one of the City livery companies, and then go left into Ravenscroft Park. The developer of this road, Thomas Smith, offered in 1880 to pay for the conversion of the last remaining patch of Barnet Common into the park here. Ravenscroft Park is sunken because it used to contain two large ponds that were only drained in 1992. The boundary stone at the end of the railings by the park marks the western limit of both Barnet parish (beyond it is South Mimms) and the long-defunct Whetstone and Highgate Turnpike Trust, which was once responsible for maintaining the main roads in the area.

Mrs Palmer and the Barnet poor

At the end of Ravenscroft Park turn left into Blenheim Road. At the junction with Wood Street you see the old tollgate-keeper's cottage across the road, and on the right the almshouses founded by Mrs Eleanor Palmer, the daughter of Henry VII's treasurer. Mrs Palmer left property in Kentish Town in 1558 to provide an income for the relief of Barnet's poor, but it was not until 1823 that the first almshouses were built with her money. They were subsequently rebuilt in 1930 and then modernized in 1987. About 100 yd (90 metres) beyond the almshouses you can see the junction with Wellhouse Lane. This leads – eventually – to the old chalybeate spring (the waters of a chalybeate spring contain dissolved iron salts) developed in the 1650s as a medicinal spa and visited by Samuel Pepys twice in the 1660s. Today the spring, in Well Approach and covered by a mock-Tudor well house, is surrounded by a 1930s housing estate.

Turn left along Wood Street. Bells Hill on the right shows you how steeply the ground falls away to the south into the valley of the Dollis Brook. The historic part of Wood Street really starts beyond the Black Horse pub and the roundabout. On the right the Elizabeth Allen free school functioned from 1824 until 1973. Local woman Mrs Allen actually left money for the school in 1727, but until the National School was set up in 1824 her bequest was used for the old grammar school seen later in the walk. The former Allen school building now provides sheltered accommodation for the elderly.

Barnet Museum
On the left is another almshouse, this one founded by John Garrett in 1728 for six elderly widows. A little further on from the Garrett almshouse and on the same side of the road is the fourth and last of Chipping Barnet's almshouses, the Jesus Hospital, founded by James Ravenscroft in 1679. Ravenscroft, of a prominent Barnet family, graduated from Jesus College, Cambridge, and went on to become a lawyer and a merchant. Just before the Registry Office, No. 31 Wood Street on the right is the **Barnet Museum**, run by the local history society. Ahead, Barnet church became a parish church in its own right in 1866. Since the Middle Ages until that time, it had officially been no more than subsidiary to the main parish church down in East Barnet. A wealthy brewer called John Beauchamp paid for the rebuilding of the original church in 1420. Then that 15th-century building was rebuilt and enlarged in the 1870s. Many of the old monuments were preserved, the best being that to James Ravenscroft's father, Thomas, who died in 1630.

Opposite the church and set back from the road is the last of Chipping Barnet's historic buildings to be seen on the walk. This is the Elizabethan grammar school, built in 1573 and the main school in the village until the 19th century. It was to this school that Elizabeth Allen's money was devoted for the century following her original bequest. The school moved to new premises in 1932. The old building, now part of Barnet College, is occasionally used for public concerts and other events.

Outside the old schoolhouse, cross back over the High Street to the north side and turn right. Make your way back down the hill past the Mitre and eventually to the station, where the walk ends.

Chiswick

Location	5½ miles (8.8 kilometres) west of Charing Cross.
Transport	Turnham Green Underground Station (District and Piccadilly Lines), Stamford Brook Underground Station (District Line).
Features	**St Nicholas's Church**; **Chiswick House and grounds**; **Hogarth's House**; old houses on Chiswick Mall; Church Street; riverside walk and views.
Refreshments	*Turnham Green Terrace/Chiswick High Road* (start of walk) variety of bars, restaurants and cafés; *in village* (on Great West Road) George and Devonshire and Mawsons Arms pubs; *grounds of Chiswick House* (halfway round walk) café/restaurant; *Chiswick High Road* (end of walk) Café Flo, Pitcher and Piano bar, Nachos Mexican restaurant.

Chiswick established itself on the north bank of the Thames a few miles west of London. Its one and only street – Church Street – led north away from the river towards the main road heading west out of London. At the river end of Church Street stood the church and vicarage (as they still do) and a cluster of cottages. A little to the east lay the manor house, called the prebendal manor house because the estate belonged to the Dean and Chapter of St Paul's Cathedral in the City of London, and its revenues were used to support one of the prebends, or members, of the Cathedral Chapter.

The river

'Chiswick' means something like 'cheese farm', but the village tended to regard the river rather than the land as its main livelihood and the occupations of its inhabitants were therefore generally river-related: fishing, boat-building, ferrying and so forth. The parish church was dedicated to the patron saint of fishermen – Nicholas – and a ferry ran from the foot of Church Street until 1934, the year after Chiswick Bridge opened.

From as early as the mid-15th century Chiswick was known to city-dwellers as an attractive and healthy place to live. The Russell family, later Earls and now Dukes of Bedford, lived at Corney House west of the village from 1542. In 1570 the still-existing Westminster School leased the old manor house as a retreat during times of plague. And about 1610 Sir Edward Wardour built the first Chiswick House to the north of Corney House. In the late 17th and early 18th centuries, people also began to build fine houses in Church Street and along the riverside lane leading from the church to the manor house. In time the whole of this lane to the manor house was built up to form a one-sided street called Chiswick Mall. Today Church Street, though mutilated at its top end, is one of London's most picturesque streets, while tranquil Chiswick Mall is one of its finest riverside promenades. Both feature on the walk.

Boot polish

Chiswick's riverside location attracted industry as well as wealthy and titled residents. In the 18th century there were two big breweries behind the Mall. Then, during the 19th century, when pollution killed off the fishing industry, came the Thornycroft shipbuilding yard and the Chiswick Soap Company, inventors of the famous Cherry Blossom boot polish. Polish and ships have both long since departed, but Fuller, Smith and Turner's Griffin Brewery, home of London Pride and Chiswick bitters, is still very much in existence (and often gives off a powerful smell of brewing to prove it).

As well as the village of Chiswick, the parish of Chiswick contained three other settlements: Strand on the Green, Little Sutton and Turnham Green. Like Chiswick, Strand on the Green was a riverside fishing village that later developed as a gentlemen's retreat. It is now another fine riverside promenade (see page 128). Little Sutton was a manor in its own right and in the 15th century boasted the king as tenant. It is now buried beneath suburbia. Turnham Green serviced traffic on the busy Great West Road. By 1700 it was as big as Chiswick itself and in the 19th century, boosted by the arrival of the railway, far outstripped the original village. Today most people think of Turnham Green as Chiswick. The old village is generally referred to as Old Chiswick.

Largely unscathed by its industrial past and cut off from modern Chiswick/Turnham Green by the new Great West Road built in the 1950s, Old Chiswick today is a peaceful and elegant backwater. Getting to and from it from the Underground line is not a particularly pleasant experience, but the village, with its old houses, luxuriant riverside gardens and fine river views, more than compensates.

THE CHISWICK WALK

Start Turnham Green Station.
Finish Stamford Brook Station.
Distance 2½ miles (4 kilometres).

Come out of Turnham Green Station and turn left under the railway bridge. Walk down to the lights and then go right on Chiswick High Road and immediately left into Devonshire Road. Towards the far end turn right into Bennett Street. Looking across the busy main road at the end you can see **Hogarth's House**, the little country house the painter and engraver, William Hogarth, used every summer from 1749 until his death in 1765. In those days it stood by a country lane surrounded by fields and market gardens. A local benefactor saved it from destruction early this century and it later opened as a museum with a large collection of the artist's well-known prints.

Turn left along the main road (here called, with unconscious irony, Hogarth Lane). The modern office block on the right stands on the site of the old Cherry Blossom polish works, originally founded as a soap works by brothers Dan and Charles Mason in 1878. Production ceased on the site in 1972 when Reckitt and Colman, who bought the company in 1954, transferrred operations to their main factory at Hull. Cherry Blossom is now owned by a private company called Grainger International.

At the roundabout go down into the subway. Take the first exit on the right if you want to visit Hogarth's House. Otherwise continue to the end and walk up the steps on the right. You come out opposite Chiswick Square, often billed as the smallest in London. At the far end stands Boston House, dating from the 1680s and named after Viscount Boston, later the Earl of Grantham, by whom it was extended

CHISWICK

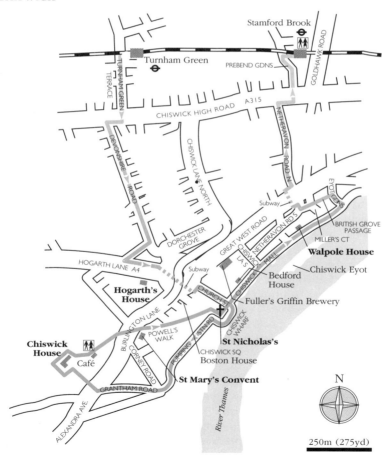

250m (275yd)

and refaced in the 1740s. Either side are two smaller houses. The one on the left has a plaque on its side relating to an incident in William Thackeray's novel *Vanity Fair,* of which more later when we reach Walpole House on Chiswick Mall.

The Lamb Brewery

Now turning to your left, you pass the George and Devonshire pub and enter Church Street, the high street of Old Chiswick. The street always curved round to meet you like this, but until the building of the new Great West Road in the 1950s it had shops, houses and a pub on the left-hand side where the entrance to the roundabout is. As you follow Church Street round to the right, you can see the bell tower of the old Lamb Brewery, in business here from 1790 till the 1950s. The Sich family founded it and owned it until 1920, and one member of the family still lives on Chiswick Mall. Beyond Ferry House the two old houses either side of the former brewery entrance were once Lamb Brewery pubs. Lamb Cottage was the Lamb Tap. The Old Burlington, built in the 16th century and the oldest building in Chiswick (apart from the church tower), was the Burlington Arms. Both became private houses in the 1920s. Opposite the Old Burlington, the Guardship acquired its name when it became a sea scouts headquarters in the 1920s. The nautical adornments were added by a later artist resident.

Walk on down Church Street between the Old Vicarage on the left (built in 1658 and refronted in the 18th century) and **St Nicholas's Church**. At the narrowest point notice the tablet in the churchyard wall saying that the wall was built in 1623 by Francis Russell to keep pigs out. Russell was one of the Corney House Russells and in 1627 succeeded as fourth Earl of Bedford. At the bottom of the street is the old ferry slipway. A gate just to the right leads to a riverside walk from which there are good views up- and downstream.

Chiswick Wharf

Turn right now into Chiswick Wharf. On the right at this point until 1950 stood the old village charity school, which was founded in 1707. On the left were the old fishermen's cottages, generally known as Sluts Hole and later as Fisherman's Corner. Now the modern development built over the site, which was cleared in the 1930s, is called Fisherman's Place. Further on along this road, which soon turns into Pumping Station Road, more modern housing is being built on the site of Thornycroft's Shipyard. Founded by sculptor's son, John Thornycroft, in 1864, the firm specialized in high-speed vessels, first launches and later torpedo boats and then torpedo-boat destroyers. It moved to Southampton in 1909 because it was building ever-bigger ships and finding difficulty in sailing them out into open waters.

Chiswick House

When you reach the roundabout (the approximate site of Corney House, demolished in 1832), take the second right by the off-licence – Grantham Road. This brings you out onto Burlington Lane, directly opposite the main entrance to **Chiswick House**. Go through the gates and walk towards the house. Modelled on Palladio's Villa Capra near Vicenza and one of the first Palladian houses in England,

Chiswick House was designed by its owner, the third Earl of Burlington, in the 1720s. The gardens, a pioneering naturalistic landscape, were laid out by Lord Burlington's friend, William Kent. Whereas in the 17th century the Russells had dominated Chiswick, in the 18th and 19th centuries it was the occupants of Chiswick House – first the Burlingtons and then the Dukes of Devonshire – who were the de facto squires of the village. The Devonshires, who also had a town house in Piccadilly, finally sold up in 1929.

Pass round the left of the house (with the lake to your left) and then turn right along the north front. Just before the gateway turn right and follow the path round to the left past the restaurant. This eventually brings you to a little lodge house. Exit the park by the little gate to the right of the lodge and turn left along Burlington Lane. At the lights cross over to **St Mary's Convent** and nursing home (here since 1897) and continue along the road. At the telephone box turn right into Powell's Walk, formerly a footpath connecting Chiswick House with the parish church. As you approach the church you pass the large railed tomb of 18th-century painter Philippe de Loutherbourg, a resident of Hammersmith Terrace just beyond Chiswick Mall. Several other artists are also buried here, including William Kent of Chiswick House (1748), William Hogarth of Hogarth's House (1765) and J. M. Whistler (1903).

Hogarth's tomb and grand houses

Turn right in front of the church tower (built in the 15th century – the rest of the church is Victorian) and then left through the south porch. Hogarth's tomb is the one with the urn on top on the right. Go down the steps out of the churchyard and carry straight on into Chiswick Mall. Beyond the Old Vicarage is the current vicarage. Soon after comes one of the two grandest houses on the Mall, Bedford House, now split into two. The original Bedford House, combining the current one and adjoining Eynham House, belonged to Edward Russell, a younger son of the earl who built the churchyard wall. Edward inherited Corney House but sold it and moved into the centre of the village in 1663. Years later, John Sich, founder of the Lamb Brewery, lived in the house until his death in 1836. Recent residents include the actor Sir Michael Redgrave, who lived there from 1945 to 1954.

More brewers

Further on, by the old draw dock, Belle Vue Cottage, Prospect Cottage and the warehouse on the corner of Chiswick Lane all belong to Fuller's Griffin Brewery. Belle Vue is the traditional home of the chief brewer. Next door to Belle Vue, Red Lion House was until 1916 a Fullers' pub, much frequented by reed cutters from the nearby island. Looking up Chiswick Lane you can see the entrance to the brewery and at the top on the left the Mawsons Arms pub. Thomas Mawson founded the brewery when he bought Bedford House's private brewhouse in 1701. The Fullers, Smiths and Turners all became involved in the 19th century. The Mawsons Arms pub, an early 18th-century building, was originally a private house and from 1716 to 1719 was the home of the poet Alexander Pope and his parents.

On the far side of the junction with Chiswick Lane, the Victorian villas stand where the manor house and College House stood until they were knocked down in 1875. College House, added to the manor house by Westminster School when it needed more room, was used by the school until well into the 18th century. From 1818 to 1852 it housed the Whittingham family's Chiswick Press, a printing firm famous for its hand-printed and finely designed books.

Inspiration for William Thackeray

A little further on near the end of the island you come to the second of the Mall's two finest houses. This one is called **Walpole House** and is named after a nephew of Prime Minister Sir Robert Walpole. Charles II's mistress, the Duchess of Cleveland, spent the last few years of her life in Chiswick, probably here. Much later the house became a school attended by the young William Thackeray in 1817. When he wrote *Vanity Fair* he is thought to have modelled Miss Pinkerton's Academy on it, though Boston House also claims that honour. The book starts at the academy, which is described as a 'stately old brick house' behind a great iron gate. Nowadays the house is home to members of the Benson banking family and the gardens are open each year as part of the National Gardens Scheme.

Passing more fine houses, you eventually come to modern Miller's Court, built on the site of a bakery, and, on the riverside, a row of small houses called Durham Wharf. Here, turn left into Eyot Gardens and then first left into British Grove Passage. Go past British Grove South and the entrance to Miller's Court. When you reach Netheravon Road South turn right and use the subway to cross the main road. Continue to the end of Netheravon Road North. At Chiswick High Road turn right and then left into Prebend Gardens. When you reach the railway viaduct go right through the station gates into Wilson Walk. This leads directly to Stamford Brook Station, where the walk ends.

Enfield

Location	11 miles (17.7 kilometres) north of Charing Cross.
Transport	Enfield Chase Station (overground trains from King's Cross and Moorgate via Finsbury Park); Enfield Town Station (overground trains from Liverpool Street).
Features	**St Andrew's Church**; Gentlemans Row; the New River; homes of the writer Charles Lamb; **Forty Hall** (not on walk – see map page 35).
Refreshments	*Church Street* pubs, fast-food outlets, Oliver's coffee house in shopping centre; *on the New River* (at halfway point of walk) Crown and Horseshoes pub; *Town Park* café.

Eight miles (13 kilometres) long by 3 miles (5 kilometres) across, Enfield was the largest parish in Middlesex after Harrow with Pinner. The village of Enfield, or Enfield Town as it became called, lay roughly in the middle. To the west was the 8,000-acre (3,250-hectare) royal hunting park known as Enfield Chase. To the east, open fields and later market gardens stretched down to the other parish settlement of Ponders End and the parish's eastern boundary, the River Lee. It was on the Lee that in 1804 the government established the arms factory that later produced the famous Lee-Enfield rifle.

In Enfield Town, settlement was restricted to just a few streets. Church Street was the high street, with the church and marketplace on one side and the manor house on the other. To the east London Road led south towards London and Silver Street led north to Forty Hill. The vicarage was in Silver Street and the rectory was a little to the north on the corner of Parsonage Lane and Silver Street's continuation, Baker Street. The ancient vicarage still survives in its original position, as you will see on the walk, but the rectory – which belonged to the Monastery of Walden in Essex up to the dissolution of the monasteries and to Trinity College, Cambridge, thereafter – was pulled down and its grounds were developed as Monastery Gardens in the 1920s.

The New River
At the west end of the village, the New River, an artificial canal constructed in the early 17th century to bring fresh water to the City of London from springs in Hertfordshire, divided the village from Enfield Chase. Along the village side of the river facing the Chase on the far side, a row of houses, many of them substantial,

grew up from the 17th century. In the 18th century it acquired the name Gentlemans Row. After 1779 when the old Enfield Chase was split up and enclosed, more houses, not so grand as the original ones, were built on the other side of Gentlemans Row, making it, at least for half its length, more like a regular street.

Royal connections

Many of the gentry who lived in Gentlemans Row's best houses and in other large houses in the village, notably Little Park and Burleigh House on the north side of Church Street and Chaseside on the south, were drawn to the village as much by its royal connections as by its proximity to London. For most of the Middle Ages the manor belonged to the de Mandevilles, Earls of Essex, and then to the de Bohuns, Earls of Hereford. But in 1421 it became part of the royal Duchy of Lancaster estate. Henry VIII's daughter Elizabeth inherited the manor after her father's death, along with Worcesters, the neighbouring manor to the north where she and her half-brother Edward – later Edward VI – spent a good deal of time as children. Elizabeth rebuilt Enfield's decaying manor house, but she is not believed ever to have visited it when Queen. She did, however, stay at the Worcesters manor house, Elsyng Hall, on a few occasions.

In the 17th century Sir Nicholas Rainton, a City merchant and twice Lord Mayor of London, acquired the Elsyng estate, pulled down the old house and built **Forty Hall** instead. This is now open to the public as the London borough of Enfield's local history museum, but it is unfortunately a little too far from the old village centre to be included in this walk.

Enfield's existence as a quiet country village came to an end in the mid-19th century when the railways arrived from two directions: first at Enfield Town Station in 1849 and then at Enfield Chase in 1871. In subsequent decades, and especially at the beginning of this century, the village lost its rectory, manor house and other fine houses, but it kept Gentlemans Row, the vicarage and the New River (which for a time was under threat). It also salvaged large tracts of gardens and orchards for use as a public park on the south side of the village and sports grounds on the north side, as you will see on the walk.

THE ENFIELD WALK

Start and finish Enfield Chase Station.
Distance 3 miles (4.8 kilometres).

Come out of the station and turn right under the railway bridge. Walk down the hill past the Wheatsheaf pub and Chase Green on the left. When Enfield Chase was enclosed in 1779, a portion was allotted to the villagers of Enfield as compensation for the loss of common rights in the Chase. When the common fields of Enfield were in turn enclosed in 1803, the allotment from the Chase, covering 12 acres (5 hectares), was preserved as Enfield's first public park. Cross Old Park Avenue and the bridge over the New River (more about the Old Park and the New River later). The gate into the Chase from Enfield stood just about here, on the village side of the bridge and at the entrance to Church Street.

ENFIELD

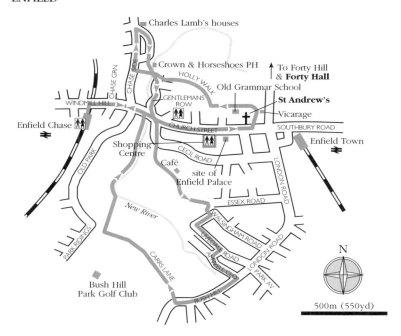

Cross Cecil Road and continue on into Church Street, the high street of the old village. Beyond Sarnesfield Road, Little Park Gardens on the left commemorates the old house called Little Park which, demolished in 1888, was one of the first of Enfield's mansions to fall victim to Victorian development. Burleigh House further on, commemorated in Burleigh Way, was knocked down in 1913. Opposite the marketplace, Pearson's department store on the right was built in the 1920s after Enfield's manor house, called the Palace because of its royal owner, was pulled down. As rebuilt during Elizabeth I's time, the manor was a two-storey gabled house with a central block and wings. Almost from the beginning it was let out, usually to royal servants. About 1670 Dr Robert Uvedale, who had been master of Enfield grammar school, opened a successful private boarding school in the manor, which survived right down to 1896. Destruction of the old house was finally completed in 1928. Nothing remains of it now except one panelled room with a fine plaster ceiling and a carved stone fireplace, re-erected in 5 Gentlemans Row.

Enfield market

When you reach Sydney Road, look across Church Street to the right-hand side of the bank and you will see the former parish beadle's house and lock-up, built in 1830. It later became the vestry house and is now a solicitor's office. Now cross Church Street to the marketplace. Although Enfield was first granted the right to hold a market in 1303, the modern one (on Thursdays, Fridays and Saturdays) was not started until 1612. From the beginning the proceeds were dedicated to parish poor relief. The original site of the market was a small green. Then it was enlarged by the acquisition in 1632 of a house called The Vine, which for a time served as the market house. The present octagonal market building dates only from 1904.

Fine memorials

From the marketplace go straight on into the churchyard. **St Andrew's** was the only church in the parish until 1831. Although it was extensively reconstructed in the 1820s, it retains its medieval appearance on the outside, and inside it has many of the monuments and memorials from the original structure. The best are in the northeast corner. One is a brass, said to be the finest in Middlesex, commemorating a soldier's wife, Lady Joyce Tiptoft, who died in 1446; the other is a fine 17th-century sculpture of Sir Nicholas and Lady Rainton, the builders of Forty Hall.

Make your way round the east end of the church. Now you can see to your left across the churchyard the original Elizabethan schoolhouse of Enfield grammar school. To the right is the handsome vicarage with its central Dutch-style gable. You can get a better view of it by standing on the plinth of the Mitton tomb next to the wall. Although the vicarage has all the appearance of a Georgian house, the oldest section of it, on the Silver Street side, is timber-framed inside and has been dated to the 13th century. Not many church houses of this antiquity survive in London, and certainly not still in church occupation.

Gentlemans Row

Walk on towards the churchyard gate. Just before you reach it, turn left along the footpath leading to the white house with black shutters. Continue past this house into Holly Walk. Follow this round by the car park on the left and the girls' school, founded in 1909, on the right. Keep right when the path forks. You now pass some cottages on your left, and on your right sports grounds bordered by the New River. Eventually you come out on Gentlemans Row. Turn right here, and at the end of the road by Brecon House turn left, cross the New River and carry straight on through the alley. You will emerge eventually on Chase Side next to Chase Green. Cross the road and turn right.

Development in this area started after the creation of Chase Green in 1803. After a while you come to an elegant terrace called Gloucester Place. The pretty little cottages here were built in 1823. At the end of the terrace look across the road to the white house (No. 87) and the brick house to the left of the white house (No. 89). Both these houses were successively home to the writer Charles Lamb and his mentally unstable sister Mary, and bear plaques to that effect. After retiring from the East India Company in 1825, Lamb occasionally took lodgings in Enfield. In 1827 he and his sister became tenants of The Poplars, the white house. After two years Mary's condition was so bad and she was away from home so much that Charles could not cope with the housekeeping and moved next door into Westwood Cottage to lodge with retired tradesman Mr Westwood and his wife. He stayed here for four years. In 1833 Charles and Mary left Enfield and moved to nearby Edmonton to live with Mary's keeper. Charles died there two years later.

Beer garden

Cross the road to the Lamb houses, turn right and walk along Cricketers Arms Road. Keep left into Chase Side Place and pass the modern Cricketers Arms pub. At the end of the Place turn left. Here you meet the New River again. Here also is the Crown and Horseshoes pub, which has a large beer garden behind. Turn right along the riverside. Having passed the wooden bridge, turn left across the next iron bridge (the one you crossed earlier in the other direction). Now you are at the top of Gentlemans Row. The next section of the walk follows the Row all the way down to its beginning in the centre of the village. The Row is lined with 18th- and 19th-century houses of varying sizes and styles, some cottages and some larger residences – Brecon House, for example, and a little further on, Archway, which arches over the entrance to Chapel Street, and which gave the Row its name.

Beyond Archway go left of the garden in the middle of the road and continue along the Row. Most of the houses have a special plaque indicating that they have been 'listed' (i.e. protected) by the local council. White-painted Clarendon Cottage, No. 17, was another of Lamb's Enfield homes (this was the one he occasionally rented before moving to The Poplars) and, like the other two, it bears a plaque recording the fact. At the end of the Row the biggest house provides offices for council services. To the right the New River flows through a pretty public garden. In the earlier section near the pub the river was roughly at the same level as the houses beside it. But here, as you can clearly see, it is several feet higher. This is because it was originally constructed to follow the 100-foot (30-metre) contour, a design constraint that produced some rather bizarre loops and diversions, including one all the way around Enfield village. In 1859 the Enfield section was straightened and then in 1890 piped underneath the village. Bypassed, the Gentlemans Row stretch then became superfluous and would have been filled in had there not been a public campaign to preserve it for its ornamental value. Today, therefore, the New River just here is not a river at all but a linear lake. The main channel still carries water to Stoke Newington, whence it is distributed via the mains.

Town Park

Gentlemans Row brings you out at the bus station. Turn right and then, in front of Trinity Church, go left across the road, using the zebra crossing. Walk on down Cecil Road and go straight on through the gates into the 27-acre (11-hectare) Town Park, created in 1903 out of the grounds of some large houses that formerly stood on the south side of Church Street. When the path forks, bear left beside the tennis courts. To your right you can see the embankment of the old New River course as it skirts the foot of Bush Hill.

Follow the path round to the right past the pavilion/café and then to the left towards the main gate. Just before you reach the main gate, cut right and go through the little gate leading into Walsingham Road. Immediately turn right. Follow the road round to the left (Uvedale Road) and then right into Whitethorn Gardens and left into Amwell Close (Amwell was one of the Hertfordshire sources of the New River). Keep to the high path on the right and then, when you reach the main road (Bush Hill), turn right and walk up the hill.

Bush Hill Park

At the top turn right at the Bush Hill Park Golf Club sign and join the footpath just to the right of the club gateway. The clubhouse, which you can see to your left at the end of the long straight drive, is in origin 18th century, but the history of the park in which it stands goes right back to before the Domesday survey of 1086. It is therefore much older than Enfield Chase, which was not emparked until a century or more later. After the restoration of the monarchy in 1660, Old Park, which was royal property, was granted to one of the major architects of the restoration, George Monck, Duke of Albemarle. Later the 550-acre (225-hectare) estate passed through many different hands before eventually coming into the possession of the Bush Hill Park Golf Club early this century.

The footpath goes straight through the middle of the golf course. When you reach the bollards at the end, turn right along the tarmac path leading down the hill back towards the New River. At the river go left (either side will do) and walk for some way beside the water. Eventually you come out back on Church Street. Turn left up Windmill Hill and make your way back to the station, where the walk ends.

Hampstead

Location	4½ miles (7.2 kilometres) north of Charing Cross.
Transport	Hampstead Underground Station (Northern Line), Hampstead Heath Station (overground North London Line trains).
Features	**St John's Church** and Constable's grave; **Fenton House**; **Burgh House and Hampstead Museum**; **Hampstead Scientific Society's Observatory** and meteorological station; High Street and **Antiques and Crafts Market**; Church Row and 18th-century houses; views of London; **Keats House** (not on walk – see map page 41).
Refreshments	*High Street and Heath Street* wide selection of cafés, bars, restaurants and pubs; *Holly Mount* (first half of walk) Holly Bush pub; *Well Walk* (second half of walk) Burgh House Buttery, Wells Tavern.

Hampstead was established a thousand or more years ago on the slope of the Northern Heights overlooking London to the south. At that time it belonged to the great Benedictine Abbey of Westminster. The abbot was the lord of the manor and he ruled the village through a bailiff based at the manor farm on the west side of the village. On the east the village was bounded by its great common, now Hampstead Heath. After the dissolution of the monasteries in the mid-1500s Hampstead passed into lay hands. Over the next 300 years it had a succession of lay lords, starting with a Tudor courtier, Sir Thomas Wroth. Descendants of the last lord, Sir Thomas Maryon Wilson, still own much property in the area.

From early times Hampstead was a pleasant resort for wealthy Londoners seeking a cool summer retreat or a refuge from the plague. Its slightly greater distance from the City and its hilly, uneven site meant that it did not attract quite the same quality of newcomers as Highgate, its neighbour across the heath. But what it lacked in quality it more than made up for in quantity. As early as the 1640s locals were complaining about outsiders taking over the village and forcing them out of their homes. Many of these outsiders must have built themselves fine houses, but thanks to wholesale rebuilding in the 18th century, none has survived – with the notable exception of the beautiful Fenton House, which is featured on the walk.

'Snowbound' village
Besides its healthily elevated position – the top of the village is 440 feet (135 metres) above sea level – Hampstead's other claim to fame in olden times was its water,

which was both abundant and unusually pure. No fewer than four rivers, the Brent, the Fleet, the Tyburn and the Westbourne, rose in the area, and the quality of their water was such that in the 1500s a significant number of Hampstead's women inhabitants earned their living by taking in washing from the city. So much linen was regularly hung out to dry that viewed from London the village appeared permanently snowbound.

Around 1700 a chalybeate (iron-containing) spring with medicinal properties was discovered on the heath next to the village and developed as a spa. In fact there were two spas, one following on from the other after a space of 20 years or so. Neither was hugely successful, but the spas nevertheless attracted a lot of people and money to the village and led during the course of the 18th century to its virtually complete rebuilding, and also to significant expansion and population growth. Many of the houses put up at this time – though sadly not the spa buildings – have survived. Thus modern Hampstead is largely a Georgian village, though the houses are mostly of mellow weathered red brick, not stone or stucco.

Writers and artists

At the time of the Romantic movement in the 18th century still-rural Hampstead, with its wild heath, was discovered by writers and artists – John Keats and John Constable to name but two. Two of Constable's Hampstead homes are seen on the walk. Keats' house in the hamlet of South End has been made into a museum and is only a few minutes off the walk (see map opposite). Thanks to Keats, Constable and the numerous fellow-workers that followed them, Hampstead acquired something of a bohemian reputation in the 19th century. In the 20th century – and particularly during the 1930s when Communism was fashionable – that reputation has gained a distinctly avant-garde, left-wing, edge. Today, although it has become hugely exclusive and expensive, Hampstead is still the archetypal trendy liberal's village and the spiritual home of the so-called chattering classes.

THE HAMPSTEAD WALK

Start and finish Hampstead Station.
Distance 1¼ miles (2.8 kilometres).

Come out of Hampstead Station and turn left down the hill. This, the very centre of Hampstead, is largely Victorian in appearance, having been rebuilt towards the end of the 19th century. Heath Street, above High Street, is much more as it used to be in the 18th century, as you will see later in the walk. Cross on the zebra, go a little further down the street and then turn right into Perrin's Court, a narrow lane named after a family that used to own land in the area. Since 1938 it has been the home of the local paper, the *Hampstead and Highgate Express,* familiarly known as the *Ham and High.* Halfway along the Court is an entrance (on the right) to the **Antiques and Crafts Market**.

At the end of the Court turn right into Heath Street, then immediately left into Church Row. Built at the beginning of the 18th century as Hampstead spa was developing into a fashionable resort, and designed to form a grand approach to the parish church, this is now the village's oldest and finest street. Many people of national significance have lived here, but the only plaque (No. 18 on the left) is to a local worthy, John Park, Hampstead's first historian. No. 14 is the rectory.

Bailiff's house

Just before you reach the church, a path called Frognal Way leads off down the hill to the left. This connects with a road called Frognal behind the church, and then continues on the other side of Frognal as Frognal Lane. At the junction of these two roads stood the manor farm and the bailiff's house in the last century and before. The farm has long since disappeared but the bailiff's house, rebuilt in the early 19th century and recently much restored, still survives as No. 40 Frognal Lane. There are many other fine old houses in large gardens in Hampstead's Frognal quarter.

Hampstead's medieval parish church of **St John** was cramped and dilapidated and hardly worthy of the village's new status as a pleasure resort, so in the 1740s the

HAMPSTEAD

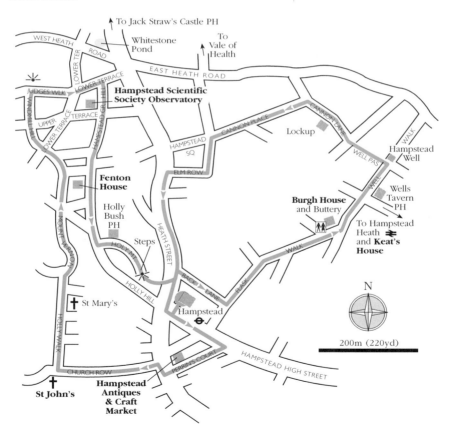

decision was taken to rebuild, leading to the construction of the present church. The churchyard is well worth exploring: tomb guides are available for a modest fee inside the church. The painter John Constable's tomb, surrounded by railings, is in the southeast corner and easily identifiable.

Holly Walk

From the church and Church Row turn right into Holly Walk. This part of Hampstead was developed in the early 19th century. First the churchyard extension was opened in 1812. Then, in succeeding years, came the little rows of houses at the top – Prospect Place, Benham's Place, Holly Place and Hollyberry Lane. St Mary's Catholic Church in the centre of Holly Place was built in 1816, mainly for French refugees, many of whom had settled in the village from the 1790s onward. The house on the corner of Hollyberry Lane served as the parish watch-house and lockup from 1830 until a proper police station was built nearer the High Street.

At the top of the hill Holly Walk meets Mount Vernon. The path left leads to Frognal. Looking back down Holly Walk there is a fine view towards London. Turning right into Mount Vernon, Abernethy House on the corner was built around 1820 as a parish girls' school. By the 1870s it had been converted into a lodging house and Robert Louis Stevenson, author of *Treasure Island,* stayed here several times for the sake of his health. Abernethy House faces the 18th-century Mount Vernon House, named after General Charles Vernon, and the former TB (tuberculosis) hospital, currently being converted into flats.

Constable's holiday home

Follow the road to the left behind Mount Vernon and descend to the green on Holly Bush Hill. On the left Frognal Rise goes down the hill to connect with Frognal. The walk goes straight on into Windmill Hill, named after the two windmills that used to stand in this part of the village. Follow Windmill Hill as it winds along the side of the hill past the gravelled back entrance to Fenton House, of which more later. When you reach Lower Terrace, a row of houses faces you across the green. The little one on the left with the blue door (No. 2) was Constable's summer home in 1821 and 1822. Constable first came to Hampstead for the sake of his family's health, but he found it such a wonderful place to paint that he returned every year for the rest of his life. He loved to study the great open skies and billowing clouds.

Cross Lower Terrace and continue on up Windmill Hill past Upper Terrace. Right at the top you come to Judges Walk, the place where the village ends and Hampstead Heath begins. Judges Walk is so called, it is believed, because of the number of lawyer tenants of nearby Branch Hill Lodge in the 18th century. In those days the view from the hilltop avenue was much better than it is today and the spot was one of Constable's favourites. Any of his pictures entitled *Branch Hill* would almost certainly have been painted from here.

Turn right along the gravel path and then cross the road and go straight on beside the reservoir on your right. Built in 1856 by the New River Company, this was Hampstead's first reservoir. Since 1909 it has provided an ideal base for the **Hampstead Scientific Society's Observatory** and weather station.

Fenton House

At the end of this small road look left and you will see the famous Whitestone Pond and beyond it a large pub called Jack Straw's Castle. The pond takes its name from the milestone standing in the bushes to your left ('IV miles to St Giles's pound' it says, i.e. roughly to the eastern end of Oxford Street). Turn away from the milestone and head off down Hampstead Grove back towards the village. Just beyond the junction of Admiral's Walk and The Mount Square you come to New Grove House, home of *Trilby* author George du Maurier until the year before his death in 1896. Opposite is the National Trust's **Fenton House**, a beautiful example of 1690s' architecture and the finest house in Hampstead. It is not known who built it but its name comes from Philip Fenton, the merchant who bought it exactly a century after its construction. Fenton is buried in the churchyard. His family subsequently played an early part in the long-drawn-out campaign to save the heath from developers. Fenton House is now owned by the National Trust.

Carry on down Hampstead Grove to the green on Holly Bush Hill. The weatherboarded house on the left was used as a studio by the artist George Romney at the end of the 18th century. Later it was turned into the village assembly rooms and used for meetings and lectures. In the 1930s it belonged to Clough Williams Ellis, builder of the resort of Portmeirion in north Wales. Go past the house and turn left into Holly Mount. Follow this hilltop cul-de-sac right to the end where there is a superb viewpoint to the south and west. To the left you can make out the British Telecom Tower in the West End. To the right the main feature is North Kensington's Trellick Tower, with its distinctive detached lift shaft.

Threepence a bottle

Go down the steps and cross straight over Heath Street into Back Lane. At the bottom is the Victorian version of The Flask pub. In the original one water from the spa was bottled and sold in London for 3d a bottle. Turn left on Flask Walk, the main route from the village centre to the spa. In the 19th century, after the spa had closed, this was a working-class area, as is indicated by the public baths and washhouse built near the end of the road in 1888 (they have now been converted into flats). Beyond the baths you come to the junction with New End Square. Here stands **Burgh House**, built in 1703 and residence of Dr William Gibbon, the official physician at the spa. A local trust now runs it as an exhibition centre and local history museum. New End was an extension of the village begun in the decade before the spa opened.

Keats museum

Go straight on from Flask Walk into Well Walk. The original village stopped here. All the streets down the hill to the right are suburban developments added in the 19th century. Right at the bottom is the early 19th-century Keats Grove, site of **Keats House**, where the poet lived from 1819 to 1821 and now a Keats museum.

On the left, post-World War II council flats stand on the site of the buildings of the second spa, which were bomb-damaged during the war and demolished in 1948. Crossing Christchurch Hill, you pass the imposing Wells Tavern and then a row of Georgian houses. No. 40 was rented by Constable in 1827. His wife died here the following year, but he stayed on with his seven children until his own death in 1837. Just beyond is the gated entrance to Gainsborough Gardens, the Victorian development laid out over the side of the first spa. Opposite the entrance on the left side of Well Walk is a Victorian drinking fountain that marks the site of the original chalybeate spring.

Squire's Mount

Turn left here up Well Passage. At the top cross Well Road (Hampstead Heath is to the right) and continue up Cannon Lane. On the way you pass the old parish lockup built into the garden wall of Cannon Hall and in use until superseded about 1830 by the one seen earlier in Holly Walk. The lockup is now part of a house built in the grounds of Cannon Hall. At the top of the hill you come to Squire's Mount and Cannon Place. Squire's Mount, named after Joshua Squire who built the house on the right in 1714, leads to Hampstead Heath and the Vale of Health. The Vale of Health is a little hidden suburb of Hampstead, first developed in the late 18th/early 19th centuries, when it was given its current name. Originally it was called Hatch's Bottom, but clearly that would not have been very effective in attracting prospective tenants to the somewhat out-of-the-way location.

Cannon Hall

Turning left into Cannon Place you pass Cannon Hall, named after old cannon brought here for use as bollards by a 19th-century resident. During this century the house's most famous residents have been the actor Gerald du Maurier and his writer daughter Daphne. Gerald was the son of George, whose house in Hampstead Grove you passed earlier.

Carry on right to the end of Cannon Place. Beyond Christ Church (1852), turn left into Hampstead Square and then right into Elm Row. Here there are many more early 18th-century houses, reflecting the development of the village east of Heath Street and High Street once the spa had started to attract visitors in large numbers. From Victorian times until well into the 20th century these older properties were relatively cheap, which is why so many impoverished writers and artists could afford to live in them. But now they are expensive again. In 1996 No. 1 Hampstead Square, dating from 1721, was on the market at £1.5m.

From Elm Row turn left on Heath Street, along with Hampstead High Street the main thoroughfare of the old village and still an extension of the High Street today. The station, where the walk ends, is down the hill on the left.

Harrow-on-the-Hill

Location	10½ miles (17 kilometres) northwest of Charing Cross.
Transport	Harrow-on-the-Hill Station (Underground Metropolitan Line; overground trains from Marylebone Station).
Features	**St Mary's Church**; **Harrow School and Old Speech Room Gallery**; Byron's Peachey stone; High Street; **Cat Museum**; views east and west; **Harrow Museum and Heritage Centre** (not on walk – see map page 47).
Refreshments	*High Street* French restaurant, Drift In tearooms (heavily used by boys from Harrow School), hotel and bar, tapas bar, Chinese restaurant, bar-brasserie; *West Street* Tea at Three tearooms, Castle pub; *Station Road Shopping Centre* (down by station) range of fast-food outlets.

Harrow-on-the-Hill must be the most conspicuous village in London. Perched on top of a high hill, largely bare for three-quarters of its circumference, it is visible for miles around. The 200-foot (60-metre) spire of **St Mary's Church** rising up above the trees further advertises its presence. In fact, the church is probably the reason why Harrow is here at all, for the name 'Harrow' is thought to be an ancient word meaning temple or sacred grove. In pagan times the summit of a hill would have been a natural site for a shrine or some other place of religious significance.

If this theory of the origins of Harrow is correct, it is all the more fitting that the Lord of the Manor of Harrow should have been the Archbishop of Canterbury. In 1094 Anselm, then archbishop, consecrated the first St Mary's Church. Nothing remains of that building, but sections of the existing church date from only half a century later. The chancel was constructed out of local oak in 1242. The nave and roof and the great spire – a landmark in every direction – were added in the 1400s.

The manor house of Harrow was reserved for the use of the archbishops when they came on a visit to their estate. Originally the manor house was at Sudbury Court down the hill to the east, but in the middle of the 14th century it was moved to Headstone northwest of Harrow and rather closer to Pinner. The moated manor house constructed at the time still survives and is now, with its huge tithe barn, the **Harrow Museum and Heritage Centre**.

Yeoman farmer

Big changes came to Harrow in the 16th century. First, having already shut down all the monasteries and seized their property, Henry VIII virtually forced the then

Archbishop of Canterbury, Thomas Cranmer, to hand over the Manor of Harrow to the Crown. Secondly, in 1572 a public-spirited yeoman farmer petitioned Queen Elizabeth I to allow him to found a free school at Harrow, funded by the rents from his various local properties, including his farm in the nearby village of Kenton. From this petition has grown the modern boys' public school of Harrow, second only to Eton in terms of social exclusivity and alma mater of such illustrious figures as Palmerston, Byron, Sheridan, Trollope and Churchill.

Since the 19th century, when numbers rose from under 70 to 500 and more, the school has dominated the village, and protected it from the pressures towards development that began to build up in Victorian times, especially when the railway arrived in 1880. The result is that the old village, centred on the High Street, Crown Street and West Street, still retains much charm. Also it remains islanded in a largely rural setting of parkland and playing fields, and even farmland. When the founder's farm at Kenton was sold for development in the 1920s, another small farm was created in the angle of Watford Road and Pebworth Road to replace it. The farm now adjoins the golf course and the school playing fields where games – including the unique Harrow football – take place most afternoons in term.

THE HARROW WALK
Start and finish Harrow-on-the-Hill Station.
Distance 1¼ miles (2.8 kilometres).

Take the south exit from Harrow Station, walk straight down to the end of the road and turn left with the rising ground of the park to your right. After a while turn right into Grove Hill and begin the climb up to the top of the hill. Just before the junction with Davidson Lane you pass between two large houses: Elmfield and The Copse. These are the first of the **Harrow School** boarding houses in the village. There are 11 in all. Another three are below you to your left on Peterborough Road. The remaining six are strung out along the High Street on top of the hill. Around the corner ahead you come to the main complex of school buildings, with more boarding houses on the left and the first classrooms on the right.

King Charles's Well
Just beyond the path on the right ascending to Church Hill there is a metal plaque high on the Art School wall recounting how Charles I stopped here in 1646 to water his horse and take a last look at London before going on to surrender himself to the Scottish Army. King Charles's Well, as the place came to be called, was just one of three places on Harrow Hill where villagers could obtain water until the Harrow Waterworks Company started piping in supplies in 1855. The difficulty of obtaining water on this hilltop site was an important factor in limiting the expansion of the village before the mid-19th century.

Speech Room
Opposite the massive Speech Room (assembly hall) built to commemorate the school's tercentenary in the 1870s, there is a plaque in the wall at the junction of

HARROW–ON–THE–HILL

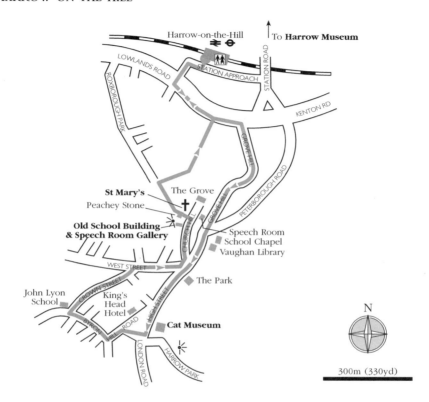

Grove Hill and the less steep road to the east, Peterborough Road. Headed 'Take Heed', it was placed here in 1969 on the 70th anniversary of what is thought to have been Britain's first fatal car accident, or, at least, Britain's first car accident in which the driver of the car died. Edwin Sewell was the man in question and the accident happened on 25 February 1899 when the brakes of his Daimler Wagonette failed as he was going down Grove Hill. He was killed instantly; his passenger died later. Peterborough Road had been constructed 20 years earlier to provide a less precipitous route up and down the hill – a pity he did not use it instead.

Passing the New Schools, the Vaughan Library and the Chapel on the left, you are now in the heart of the school. It is concentrated here at the north end of the High Street because this is where the school originally started, but all the buildings are much later in date, reflecting the great era of expansion and reconstruction in the mid- to late-19th century when Harrow transformed itself into a progressive, modern public school. As Church Hill joins from the right, you pass between two of the oldest boarding houses, Druries on the right, where Bryon and Palmerston lived, and Headmaster's on the left. The headmaster used to live here as well, but now has his own house elsewhere.

Flambards

Now you are in the High Street proper, dipping and winding along the crest of the hill in a north–south direction. At certain times of day it will be packed with boys in their straw boaters and blue blazers going off to eat or hurrying between classes. Beyond Headmaster's are the school bursary and bookshop. Opposite, at the beginning of West Street, are the outfitters and school tuck shop. On the far side of the bookshop are three more boarding houses: Moretons, Flambards and The Park. Flambards and The Park are connected historically because they are both relics in their way of another estate in Harrow that existed side by side with the Archbishop of Canterbury's. Flambards is the successor to the original manor house of this estate, named after the family that owned it in the Middle Ages. There are 14th- and 15th-century brasses to some of the Flambards in St Mary's Church. In 1797 James Rushout acquired the estate through marriage, but finding Flambards too small for him, proceeded to build The Park. The school acquired The Park as a boarding house in 1831.

The Cat Museum

In the little square ahead cat lovers should look out for an antiques shop called The Other Shop on the left-hand side of the road for they will surely not want to miss the **Cat Museum** here. Actually, it is not really a museum as such, more a private collection of feline memorabilia put together by the owner of the shop, Kathleen Mann, over the past 20 years and now, in response to public demand, put on show by her in the converted Victorian scullery beneath the shop. Admission is free, but the premises are rather cramped, so only two people can visit at a time.

The other Harrow school

After slipping into the private road called Harrow Park to see the easterly views from the first corner, exit from the square via the road going downhill next to the King's Head Hotel. The next section of the walk is a circuit that takes in Byron Hill Road, Crown Street and West Street to see the other old streets that have always been part of Harrow village. There are some pretty houses of varying ages and descriptions and some good views off to the west.

At the bottom of Byron Hill Road turn right into Crown Street. To the left now is the John Lyon School, another school set up with funds left by the founder of Harrow School, but long after the original Harrow School. John Lyon established the original Harrow School for local children, but also made some provision for fee-paying children from elsewhere. Over the centuries the fee-paying children gradually ousted the local children, even though the school tried to encourage local children to attend. In the end, following the passage of the Public Schools Act in 1868, Harrow School ceased to provide free places for local children and established the John Lyon School for them instead.

Workhouse and Old Schools

At the end of Crown Street turn right into West Street. The large white building on the left now is the former parish workhouse, dating from the 18th century, where poor people who could not maintain themselves were given spartan accommodation in return for their labour. When you get back to the High Street at the top of the hill, turn left and walk along the left-hand side of the road past Druries and into Church Hill. Now you are really at the heart of the school, for the building on the left with the clock on top is the original Harrow School building, called the Old Schools. John Lyon petitioned for permission to endow the school in 1572, but funds were not actually available for it until after both he and his wife were dead and that was not until 1608. Work on the new school then began and the building opened in 1615 with a single large classroom, masters' accommodation above and storerooms below. This Jacobean building is the left-hand section of the Old Schools and survives unchanged. Inside, every available surface in the classroom, known since the 19th century as the Fourth Form Room, is covered with the carved names of generations of pupils, including, close together, those of Byron and Sheridan. In 1820 the original school building was extended in identical style to the right. This now houses the **Old Speech Room Gallery** with its collection of school treasures. From the yard outside, where the game of squash was invented, there are wonderful views west as far as the North Downs and the Chilterns.

Byron's daughter
From the Old Schools make your way up Church Hill and into the churchyard (the big house up ahead is The Grove, another school boarding house, and there are good views east here, sometimes as far as Westminster Abbey and the British Telecom Tower). Byron's daughter Allegra, who died when she was only five, is buried somewhere in the churchyard and there is a little plaque to her fixed to the south porch. Inside the church there are various memorials to John Lyon and a large collection of brasses. The path takes you past the church to a famous viewpoint with a viewfinder to help you identify the various sights. This spot is also a place of pilgrimage for Byron lovers, for it is the site of the Peachey stone, the flat-topped tomb, now railed in, where as a boy the poet used to spend hours musing and gazing over the countryside.

If you go straight on here you will pass through the lower cemetery on to the western slope of Harrow Hill. But the route of the walk goes to the right to descend the northern slope. When you meet the road coming up the hill, take the signposted path to the right and follow it down to the main road. The station and the end of the walk is 100 yards (90 metres) or so to your left.

Highgate

Location	4½ miles (7.2 kilometres) north of Charing Cross.
Transport	Highgate Underground Station (Northern Line).
Features	**St Michael's Church**; **Highgate Cemetery**; Highgate School; High Street; fine collection of 17th- and 18th-century houses; Waterlow Park; Hampstead Heath and Highgate ponds (facilities for bathers); views of London.
Refreshments	*High Street* wide selection of pubs, cafés, bars and restaurants; *Waterlow Park* café/restaurant in Lauderdale House; *Highgate West Hill* (in the centre of the village and on the walk) The Flask pub.

Back in the Middle Ages the Bishop of London had a large hunting park, fenced to keep the deer in, on top of the hills to the north of London. In the early 1300s the then bishop decided to start charging travellers using the roads across the park. He put up three gates at various points and installed gatekeepers to collect the tolls and see to the maintenance of the roads. The most easterly gate was the most important because it controlled the main road from London to the northern counties. Here the gatekeeper and road-mender was a hermit. With pilgrims visiting the hermitage chapel, and thirsty travellers requiring refreshment and accommodation, a settlement soon grew up, centred on the road to the south of the gatehouse. In time, being on a hilltop site, the settlement acquired the name of Highgate.

At Highgate the Great North Road formed the boundary between the parishes of Hornsey and St Pancras. So to begin with Highgate was no more than an outlying hamlet of these two places. But as early as the 1500s it began to overtake its parent villages, and by the 1660s it had become the largest centre of population in both parishes. Even so, Highgate had to wait until 1834 before it became a parish in its own right.

Cholmeley's school

An important factor in Highgate's rapid development in the 1500s was its discovery by merchants and lawyers from London, attracted by its healthy position and fantastic views over the city a few miles to the south. One newcomer was Sir Roger Cholmeley, Lord Chief Justice in 1552. He first came to the village in 1536, living in a large house called Fairseat on the west, St Pancras, side of the High Street. After nearly 30 years in the village he began to evolve plans for the foundation of a boys' grammar school. It opened six years after his death in 1565, and like Harrow has since grown into a well-known public school.

In Elizabethan times aristocrats and courtiers began to settle in the village, particularly to the west of the High Street where there was a plateau offering good sites for houses. Here, beside the village green (now Pond Square), several great mansions were built on the edge of the escarpment looking west and south. All have since disappeared, but some largish houses remain, including Cromwell House, the finest early-17th-century house in London, plus whole rows of smaller 17th- and 18th-century houses in the High Street, Southwood Lane, North Road, Pond Square and The Grove. All these places are included on the walk.

Public open spaces

In the 19th century Highgate's hilltop position, and the fact that it was always able to attract the wealthiest and most influential residents, saved it from being engulfed by the tide of suburbia. Such development as there was occurred mainly on the east and less fashionable side. Here in 1813 was built a new and less steep stretch of the Great North Road, so giving the village a bypass. Here, also, the railway was built in 1867. Meanwhile, on the west and smarter side, the village benefited from the preservation of both Hampstead Heath and the private estate of Kenwood as public open spaces. To the north, the Bishops of London continued to own land until well into the 19th century. The site of the Bishops' hunting lodge in the medieval Hornsey Park is now covered by the 14th tee of Highgate golf course. Thanks to all these restraining influences Highgate is now one of the most elegant and best-preserved villages in London, as you will see on the walk.

THE HIGHGATE WALK

Start and finish Highgate Station.
Distance 3½ miles (5.6 kilometres).

Take the 'car park' exit from the Underground station and walk up to the junction with Shepherds Hill and Archway Road. The latter is the new road driven through a cutting in 1813 to avoid the steep slope up to Highgate village. Cross Archway Road into Jackson's Lane and walk on up the hill. Shepherd's Lane and Jackson's Lane are part of an old road connecting Hornsey and Highgate. Jackson's Lane gets its name from an early-19th-century fox-hunting colonel who lived in the house with the overhanging window which you pass at the top just before the junction with Southwood Lane.

Continue straight on along Southwood Lane towards the High Street, which comes into view as you approach the junction with Castle Yard on the right. On the left, detached houses once lined the road looking down the steep hill towards London. One, **Southwood Lodge**, survives in Kingsley Place: here you first see the panoramic views that have long been one of Highgate's main attractions.

Further along, on the right, are the village almshouses, founded by City goldsmith (i.e. banker), Lord of the Manor of Hornsey and Highgate resident Sir John Wollaston, who died in 1658. The almshouses, much decayed, were pulled down and rebuilt by Sir Edward Pauncefoot of Lauderdale House in 1722. In the rebuilding of them Pauncefoot doubled the accommodation to 12 and added a school for girls

HIGHGATE

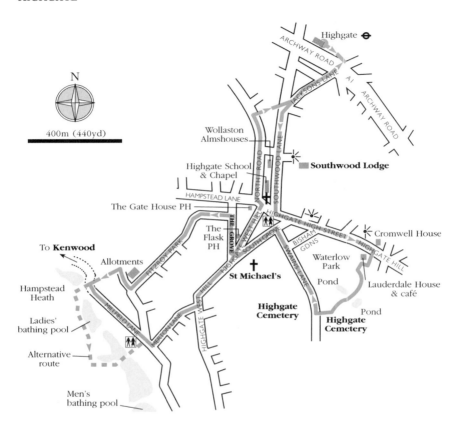

in the middle. The boys of Highgate had already been provided for by Sir Roger Cholmeley 150 years earlier. Cholmeley's school, much expanded, is behind the almshouses. Opposite the almshouses is Avalon, the childhood home of Mary Kingsley, writer and traveller, and niece of Charles Kingsley. She died in South Africa in 1900 while working as a nurse in a prisoner of war camp.

As you approach the village centre you pass on the right the main buildings of Highgate School and then, on the corner, the school chapel. The original chapel, which replaced the medieval hermitage chapel, doubled up as the village church until the early 1800s. By this time the village had grown so much that a new church was needed, but the school claimed ownership of the chapel and would not allow the village to rebuild it. So the village built a brand new church for its own use on a different site, which we will pass later.

Turn left into High Street, until you reach the opening of Archway Road, the Great North Road out of London. As you walk down it in the direction of the City, you can see what a gruelling climb it must have been for horses pulling heavily laden wagons and carts. With its restricted site, Highgate was a cramped village, hence the numerous yards – side streets really – leading off the High Street, particularly on the left-hand side. Townsend Yard, leading to a garden centre on the eastern slope of the hill, is a good example. It is named after a family of local builders called Townshend [sic] who lived in the 18th-century house on the south side of the entrance. Opposite the yard is the Prickett and Ellis estate agency, founded by John Prickett in 1767 and probably the oldest business in the village. Frederick Prickett, born in 1821, was the first historian of Highgate.

The Bank
Below Cholmeley Park you come to a raised road called The Bank, parallel with the main road. The first buildings belong to the Channing School, a private girls' school founded in 1885 (the large house on the other side of the road is the Channing Junior School). Then there is a row of fine 17th-century houses culminating in No. 104, Cromwell House, one of the very finest in the whole of London. Built about 1638 by the Sprignell family, it is certainly contemporary with Cromwell, but no one is sure why exactly it is now named after him. Possibly the Sprignells were admirers of the great Roundhead leader.

Lauderdale House and Highgate Cemetery
At the end of The Bank, cross the High Street and go through the gates into Waterlow Park, originally the grounds of Lauderdale House, which is now right in front of you. Go round to the left of the house and onto the terrace in front. Lauderdale House was built as the country home of London goldsmith Richard Martin in the 16th century. In the 17th century it was modernized by the Earl of Lauderdale, the 'l' of the ministerial grouping of Charles II's day called the 'cabal' (see pages 117–118). By the 19th century the house was part of the estate of Fairseat, the home of Sir Sydney Waterlow, head of the Waterlow printing firm and Lord Mayor of London in 1873. Waterlow generously donated the house and grounds to the London County Council in 1889.

From the front of the terrace go through the gap in the wall and then left and right down to the lakes. Cross the bridge over the cascade and continue along the main path. This brings you out of the park into Swains Lane, just by the entrance to **Highgate Cemetery**. The cemetery was opened on the other side of the road in 1839, just a few years after the new parish church. By 1856 it was already full, so an extension was consecrated on the eastern side of the road. It is in this new cemetery (entrance to your left) that Karl Marx is buried.

Turn right up Swains Lane. This ancient thoroughfare, more properly called Swines Lane, climbs steeply up to the village centre and brings you out on South Grove, west of the High Street. Immediately on your right is the Highgate Literary and Scientific Institution, founded in 1839 and the only surviving such organization in London. Ahead is Pond Square, the original village green. The ponds from which it takes its name were the principal source of water for the village's poorer inhabitants until piped water arrived in the mid-19th century. The old ponds – possibly former gravel pits – were then filled in.

Refrigeration experiments

Turn left along South Grove. Along here, right on the edge of the hill, used to stand the largest mansions in Highgate. The Old Hall, built in the 1690s, stands on the site of the most famous of them, Arundel House, built in the 16th century by one of Elizabeth I's courtiers, but from 1610 the home of the great art collector and connoisseur, Thomas Howard, Earl of Arundel. Many illustrious contemporaries stayed with Arundel here, including the lawyer, philosopher and scientist Francis Bacon. In fact, Bacon died in the house in 1626 after catching a chill while he was carrying out refrigeration experiments with a dead chicken and some snow!

Next door to The Old Hall Sir William Ashurst, Lord Mayor of London, built Ashurst House, also in the 1690s. Little more than a century later it was demolished and **St Michael's**, the new parish church, built on the site. The grounds were incorporated into the new cemetery.

The Grove

At the church, which stands exactly where Ashurst House stood, hence the fore-court in front, turn right across Highgate West Hill into **The Grove**. The first six houses were built on the site of Dorchester House in the late 17th century. At No. 3 the poet and writer Samuel Coleridge, by this time a laudanum addict, was looked after by Dr James Gillman and family from 1823 until his death in 1834. He was buried in the old churchyard and then re-interred in the new church in 1961. The author J. B. Priestley was a later resident of the same house.

No. 7 The Grove and following houses, obviously later in date, stand on the site of The Grove, demolished in the 18th century. At the end of this row of houses, turn left into Fitzroy Park. In the 18th century Charles Fitzroy, the first Lord Southampton, built himself a large house here with grounds laid out by Capability Brown. This road is the old drive to the house, demolished after barely half a century. Now it leads to houses of various dates, including some spectacular modern ones on the left-hand side.

Millfield Lane

At the second big left bend, turn right into a road leading along the foot of the allot-ments. At the end of the road carry on along the gravel path and then, just beyond some railings, go left down the bank and into Hampstead Heath. Follow this path down to the bottom of the hill where you join up with an old farm track called Millfield Lane, which leads up to **Kenwood** and Hampstead Lane. If you want to see more of the heath, go straight on across the bridge and then turn left beside the ponds (see alternative route shown on the map on page 52). Otherwise turn left on the lane, keeping the ponds to your right.

By damming the River Fleet, which rises near here, the Hampstead Waterworks Company created these ponds in the 1690s in an attempt to provide London with a reliable new water supply. There are six ponds altogether: the second, which you are passing now, is the ladies' bathing pool (the men's is number five). Millfield Lane passes the entrances to Fitzroy Farm (once the Fitzroy estate farm) and the Water House (the Waterworks estate farm) before – eventually – turning into a tarmac road by pool number four, the model boat pond. Here turn left up Merton Lane and then left again at the top into Highgate West Hill.

Royal thanks

On the right is the gated entrance to Holly Terrace, a long row of houses built about 1809 with its back sensibly to the main road and its front facing south to catch both the sun and the views. Opposite, No. 40 stands back at the end of the forecourt of the old Fox and Crown pub (see the plaque on the front). The landlord of the pub, James Turner, won heartfelt royal thanks in 1837 when he managed to prevent the young Queen Victoria's carriage careering down the hill out of control as she returned from a drive with her mother. Above the house on what must be Highgate's prime site stands, appropriately, the vast Witanhurst, reputed to be the largest house in London after Buckingham Palace. Millionaire soapmaker Sir Arthur Crosfield built it in 1920 as a platform for his young socialite wife, who had great ambitions to be a society hostess.

The Gate House

At the top of the hill, keep going along Highgate West Hill, passing the old Flask pub on the right and then the covered reservoir, dating from the 1840s, on the left. Beyond the heavily restored No. 47 at the end (the doctor's house in the 18th century) you come to the Gate House pub facing down the High Street. This stands on the site of the original gatehouse. Opposite is the old village churchyard and the Highgate School chapel of 1867, which stands on the site of the original hermitage chapel. Behind the chapel is the new school building, completed the year before.

Go round the corner by the pub. The sign shows what the gatehouse looked like before its demolition in 1769. Cross the zebra at the entrance to Hampstead Lane and carry on along North Road. As its name suggests this is the continuation of the old main road to the north. There are more 17th- and 18th-century houses here, including No. 17, Byron Cottage, where A. E. Housman lived from 1886 to 1905 and where he wrote his most famous work, *A Shropshire Lad*. Castle Yard on the right alludes not to a real castle but to the Castle Inn, which until 1928 stood at the right of the entrance to the road.

Highgate Wood

When North Road begins to lose height, cross over via the traffic island to the right-hand side. Here, No. 92 has a plaque commemorating the brief residence of the 20-year-old Charles Dickens in 1832. Continue on a few doors to the Wrestlers pub and turn right between it and the Indian restaurant into Park Walk. This brings you back to Southwood Lane and its junction with Jackson's Lane. The 'south wood' of the manor of Hornsey, now represented by Highgate Wood and Queens Wood, lies down the hill to the left. There are paths in Highgate Wood (and also a café) for anyone who has the energy for more walking. Otherwise, cross Southwood Lane and retrace your steps down Jackson's Lane to the station entrance, where the walk ends.

Isleworth

Location	10 miles (16 kilometres) west of Charing Cross.
Transport	Isleworth Station (overground trains from Waterloo).
Features	**All Saints Church**; Duke of Northumberland's River; boat-yards on the Thames; Ingram's Almshouses; historic London Apprentice pub; riverside walk and views; **Syon House** (walk passes entrance to park but not the house).
Refreshments	*outside station* burger bar/café, bistro and Chinese restaurants; *village centre* various pubs and cafés; *riverside* (and passed by the walk) Town Wharf pub (new), London Apprentice pub (old).

Isleworth is a riverside village on a great bend in the Thames opposite the Old Royal Deer Park at Kew. Originally it was no more than an enclosure belonging to one Gislhere; hence, apparently, the name. After the Norman Conquest of 1066 the manor was granted to the St Valery family of Picardy. In 1227 Henry III seized it and gave it to his brother Richard, Earl of Cornwall. Richard built himself a new moated manor house on the south bank of a little stream called the Bourne, just where it entered the Thames. Here the village grew up, with houses clustered around the manor house and the church, rectory, vicarage and manor farm on the north side of the stream. Further north and west lay the open fields of the manor. South at Railshead, where the River Crane entered the River Thames, there was a manorial corn mill for grinding flour and a salmon fishery (the stakes in the river forming part of the fishery gave Railshead its name). Further south lay the manorial hunting park.

Abbey and estate

In 1415 Henry V granted this park and the rest of the manor to a group of Swedish Bridgettine nuns who wished to found an English branch of their order. But the nuns preferred an alternative site to the north of Isleworth and it was here that they laid the foundation stone of their new abbey in 1426. Five years later they moved in and in 1488 the abbey church was finally consecrated. Half a century later, Henry VIII seized the abbey during the dissolution of the monasteries. It then passed into secular hands and was converted into a nobleman's mansion. The Earl of Northumberland acquired a lease of it from Elizabeth I in 1594 and the freehold from James I ten years afterwards. The now-ducal Northumberland family still owns the estate today and it is the last one in the vicinity of London to remain in the possession of its ancestral occupants.

Duke's river

After the dissolution of the Bridgettine convent the manorial corn mill moved to the mouth of the Bourne and a new channel was dug from the Crane to provide the Bourne with the extra water it needed to drive the mill. The new river was acquired along with the old abbey by the Northumberland family and inevitably became known as the Duke of Northumberland's River.

The extra power in Isleworth's river led to the building of several new mills upstream of the flour mill. At various times these turned out brass and copper, paper, dyes from mahogany imported from Brazil, and calico. Increased industrial output in turn stimulated the village's Thames-side wharves and in time Isleworth became quite a little port, complete with its own customs facilities. It handled not only local products but also swords and gunpowder from the nationally important mills on Hounslow Heath. More than once the village was badly shaken by gunpowder exploding in the wharf area.

Royal retreat

The impact of industrial development on Isleworth was not so great as to damage its attractions as a pleasant, healthy place to live. In the 17th and 18th centuries – and particularly when the royal family adopted Kew as a country retreat from the 1720s – it was a popular resort of courtiers and rich merchants. The whole area abounded in delightful country seats of all shapes and sizes. Most of the big houses have been demolished, but Gumley House, Isleworth House and Gordon House survive and are pointed out on the walk. Along with the big houses, much of the historic centre of Isleworth has also disappeared, a victim mainly of World War II bombing and of redevelopment, especially during the property boom of the 1980s when the old wharf area and Lower Square behind it were almost rebuilt. But there is still much to see – particularly the riverside grouping of church, pub and houses which is undoubtedly one of the prettiest sights on the Thames in the London area.

THE ISLEWORTH WALK
Start and finish Isleworth Station.
Distance 3 miles (4.8 kilometres).

Turn left out of the station and walk down through the car park to St John's Road. Turn left under the bridge and then second right by the Woodlands Tavern into Woodlands Road. After 100 yards (90 metres) or so you meet the Duke of Northumberland's River coming towards you from the Twickenham direction and then turning sharply east towards the centre of Isleworth and the Thames. Carry straight on, with the river on your left, and walk all the way along Riverside Walk (developed in the 1930s when the Middlesex County Council bought the river from the Duke of Northumberland) until you reach the bridge. Here, in the 18th century, there used to be two calico mills: a little further upstream near the disused railway embankment there is a road called Weavers Close.

Apart from the river there is not a great deal to see either on this or on the next section of the walk, but these suburban streets have to be negotiated in order to

ISLEWORTH

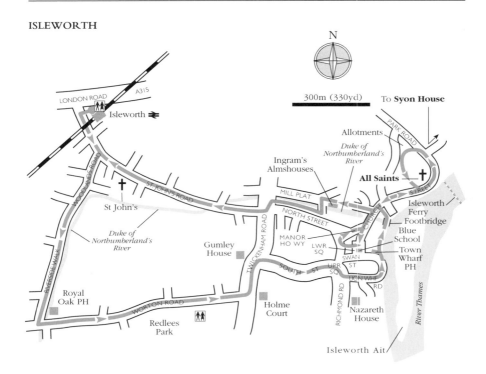

reach Isleworth village centre. Turn left over the bridge past the Royal Oak pub and carry on down Worton Road quite some way until, having passed the entrance to Redlees Park, you reach the junction with busy Twickenham Road. Holme Court, the old house on the far side of the road, is now an office but in the 1870s it was a Methodist boys' boarding school run by the Reverend J. S. Jones. In 1876–77 the young Vincent Van Gogh spent six months teaching here before returning to Europe and devoting himself to art.

Commissary-general

Cross Twickenham Road and turn left, passing Gumley House Convent School on the left. Gumley House, where the school started in 1841, is the large brick mansion straight ahead. It was built about 1700 by John Gumley, glass manufacturer, cabinet-maker and commissary-general to the army, after his marriage to Maria, daughter of Sir John and Lady Whittewronge of Isleworth. John and Maria's daughter later married the Earl of Bath, one of the aristocratic residents of 18th-century Isleworth.

Catholic centre

When you reach the road junction you will see, opposite Gumley House, the Roman Catholic church of Our Lady of Sorrows and St Bridget, built in 1909 to replace a small Catholic chapel on the riverside. After the Reformation Isleworth remained something of a Catholic centre. More Catholics came here from the 1680s onwards after James II built a Catholic chapel for his army encamped on Hounslow Heath. From 1744, by which time things were a little easier for Papists, a Catholic priest held regular services in the village.

Turn right at this junction into South Street, the beginning of Isleworth village proper. At the far end, the junction of roads – with a few original village houses on the left-hand side – is known as Upper Square. Shrewsbury Walk, to the right, commemorates Shrewsbury Place, where the Duke of Shrewsbury, an ex-Catholic, died in 1718. On the far side of Richmond Road, and away to the right, Nazareth House is another Catholic institution: a Poor Sisters of Nazareth convent and home for the elderly, founded in 1892 in Isleworth House. The house, once the home of Sir William Cooper, George III's chaplain, is still standing close to the riverside, but you cannot see it from this vantage point. Cooper enlarged his grounds both by buying up and demolishing houses north and south of Isleworth House and by diverting the Richmond road away from the riverside to its present course.

Lion Wharf

Cross Richmond Road and head off down Lion Wharf, the site of the Duke of Shrewsbury's house. From the riverside you can see the boatyard on Isleworth Ait (ait, or eyot, means island), reachable on foot at low tide. To the left there is a fine view of the old wharf area and, beyond the solitary surviving crane, the church and London Apprentice pub on the bend of the river. Turn left in this direction, walking through the Town Wharf pub. Beyond, look back for another fine view, this time of Gordon House, the residence of Lord and Lady Frederick Gordon in the 19th century and now part of the West London Institute of Higher Education.

Having passed the crane, cross the entrance to the Duke of Northumberland's River and then pass along beside the new houses covering the site of the old flour mill. As Kidd's Mill, it was bought by Rank in 1934 and immediately closed and then knocked down in the 1940s. Follow the path out – via the gate into this new development – into Church Street and turn right. Church Street has most of Isleworth's remaining original houses. Richard Reynolds House on the left (No. 43) commemorates a senior monk of Syon Abbey, executed in 1535 together with the vicar of Isleworth for resisting Henry VIII's attempt to make himself head of the English Church. Further on, No. 59 is called the Manor House, but is not really and is not even on the same site as the real manor house (which we come to later).

City apprentices

Here, by **All Saints Church**, you are in the most attractive part of Isleworth village. The old church is but a carcase of its former self, having been burnt down in 1943, not by German incendiaries but by two local, and youthful, arsonists. There is more about its history on the reverse of the signboard. To your right, the London Apprentice pub claims to date from the 15th century, but does not appear in the licensing records until the 1730s. The name alludes to the time when City apprentices used to row up river on their days off in search of recreation, exercise and, of course, beer. Church Wharf is a free draw dock, which means that boats can moor here free of charge. The wharf is also a ferry landing and the Isleworth Ferry uses it at the weekends during the summer months.

Carry on past the church and round the corner past the Headmaster's House and then the old Green School, a charity school for local girls. Ferry House, opposite, was the artist J.M.W. Turner's home from 1804 to 1806. Beyond Ferry House is the entrance to **Syon House**. On this side of the road you pass, first a pair of Syon estate cottages and then a house called The Limes. Immediately beyond The Limes, turn left into the lane by the allotments. Follow this round into the churchyard. At the top of the avenue leading up to the church there is a large yew tree on the left covering the mass burial pit of 149 victims of the Great Plague in 1665.

Blue School

Go right of the church tower and then exit from the churchyard, turning right on Church Street. Now retrace your steps along the street. When you reach the entrance to the riverside walk, carry straight on over the bridge and then keep going straight when the road bends right. You now enter Lower Square. Although it was comprehensively redeveloped in the 1980s, a few original buildings remain, notably the old village school in the centre. Founded as a charity school for boys in 1630, the Blue School (so called because of its blue uniforms) moved to another site at the end of the last century, but the school building, erected in 1841, continued to be used by the local elementary school until 1939.

Turn right by Waverley House – built as the Northumberland Arms in 1834 and an inn until 1983 – and exit from the square through the first arch on the right (by the sandwich bar). Head diagonally right across the green and then turn right along North Street (until around 1960 lined with houses at this point), with the relocated Blue School on your left. When the road turns left, turn right into Manor House Way, the site of Richard of Cornwall's medieval manor house.

Almshouses

At Church Street turn left, cross back over the bridge with the old mill sluice on your left and then turn left again into Mill Plat ('plat' just means a small piece of flat ground). This path eventually brings you to the oldest of the several sets of almshouses in Isleworth, Ingram's Almshouses, which were founded in 1664 by Sir Thomas Ingram, Chancellor of the Duchy of Lancaster, Lord Mayor of London and an earlier owner of the house later inhabited by the Duke of Shrewsbury. Each tiny single-storey almshouse has a bed-sitting room, a kitchen and a bathroom and, at the back, a little garden beside the river.

Silver Hall

When the path widens out, turn left, cross the river and then go right, through the gate, into Silverhall Neighbourhood Park, formerly the grounds of a handsome old North Street house called Silver Hall, demolished about 1950. Follow the winding riverside path to the main road, and then turn left and right into St John's Road. This is the final section of the walk and it takes you back to Isleworth station. The river is now behind the houses to your right. At Kendall Road it crosses underneath you and also joins with the Bourne, Isleworth's original stream, coming from the right. In the 'V' of land ahead between the river and St John's Road – where new houses are currently being built – the Isleworth Brewery stood until 1991. This was both the largest and the oldest commercial enterprise in the village. Founded in 1726, it gradually expanded to incorporate other mills on the river and was eventually sold to Watneys in 1924. Brewing ceased at Isleworth in 1952, although bottling continued till later.

St John's Church

Carry on up St John's Road. Copper Mill Drive on the right recalls John Broad's 16th-century brass and copper mill. Further on, St John's Church, paid for by the brewery owners and completed in 1857 along with almshouses, a parsonage and an infants' school, was needed by the growing population of the area brought in by the railway from 1849 onwards. On a site behind the houses on the opposite side of St John's Road, Pears soap was made between 1862 and 1962. The station, and the end of the walk, is up ahead on the right.

Kensington

Location	3 miles (4.8 kilometres) west of Charing Cross.
Transport	High Street Kensington Underground Station (District and Circle Lines).
Features	**St Mary Abbots Church**; **Kensington Palace**; **Commonwealth Institute**; **Kensington Roof Gardens**; **Leighton House Museum and Art Gallery**; Holland Park and remains of Holland House; Kensington Square and Edwardes Square; **Linley Sambourne House** (not on walk – see map page 64).
Refreshments	*Kensington High Street* pubs, cafés, sandwich bars and all manner of restaurants and fast-food outlets; *Holland Park* café and restaurant; *Kensington Church Street* Pierre Pechon's patisserie (and café).

The village of Kensington grew up at the junction of Church Street and High Street, the latter being a section of the Great West Road to the western counties. Traffic along this road accounted for most of the village's prosperity up to the 17th century. After that time it was the royal court and the capital itself that provided most local inhabitants with a living.

Throughout the Middle Ages the village was dominated by two owners. The larger of the two was the de Vere family, Earls of Oxford. Hailing originally from Vers in France, they came over to England during the Norman Conquest and added the manor of Kensington to their other estates before the end of the 11th century. The other landowner was the Abingdon Abbey near Oxford. One of the first de Veres granted a portion of Kensington to the abbey in the early 1100s out of gratitude for medical services performed by the abbot for a family member. From that time the abbey's property was a separate manor, distinguished by the name of Abbot's Kensington. The manor covered most, if not all, of the village of Kensington and gave its name to the local parish church, St Mary Abbots.

Sir Walter Cope's house
Following the destruction of Abingdon Abbey and sales by the de Veres, most of Kensington came into the possession of Sir Walter Cope around 1600. Choosing an elevated site a little to the west of the village, Cope built himself a fine country house with views south across the fields to the Thames glinting in the distance. This was one of the first modern country houses to be built on the fringes of London and it started something of a local trend. Lord Campden built Campden House up

on the hill behind the village, and on the London side Sir George Coppin erected a third mansion, later acquired by the Earls of Nottingham. Campden House disappeared long ago, but Cope's and Coppin's mansions survive respectively in Holland House (remains only) and in royal Kensington Palace.

Royal Kensington

In the 1680s Thomas Young, a carpenter, built a square in Kensington. Although people had already started to build them in London, it was probably a bit early to put one up so far from the West End. But Young was saved in 1689 when the asthmatic William III, unable to cope with the smogs and fogs of riverside Whitehall Palace, moved out to salubrious Kensington and transformed Lord Nottingham's house into a royal palace. Naturally he was followed by a huge retinue of servants, officials, courtiers and hangers-on. They soon acquired the empty houses in the new square and before long the High Street was buzzing with all kinds of new shops that catered to the wealthy new clientele. These were halcyon days for Kensington, but they did not last long: the palace was neglected after Queen Caroline's death in 1737 and deserted completely after her husband's demise in 1760. Thereafter, the village was thrown back economically on its traditional mainstay: its fertile nurseries and market gardens to the south.

Victorian suburb

Despite the departure of the court, Kensington never quite lost its reputation as a smart place to live. When London began to break out of its old historic confines in the 19th century, it became *the* Victorian middle-class suburb, home especially to the new rich of Victorian society, artists. Along with the middle classes came shops, and from these shops developed, from the 1870s onwards, department stores, notably Barkers. These stores, made accessible by the underground railway, which arrived in 1866, transformed Kensington into London's most fashionable shopping centre outside the West End.

Since those days, the 'old court suburb' as writer Leigh Hunt famously called it in the 1850s, has hung on to its reputation as a fashionable place to live and shop. But underneath the character of the old village survives, as the following walk shows.

THE KENSINGTON WALK

Start and finish High Street Kensington Station.
Distance 2¼ miles (3.6 kilometres).

Turn left out of the station down Kensington High Street and then cross Wrights Lane. Opposite Safeway, turn left through the arch into Adam and Eve Mews, which developed out of the yard and stables of a former inn. This was about as far as the high street of the original village extended before the era of expansion in the 19th century. Follow the mews round to the right at the bottom, then turn left by the Kensington Chapel (1854) – evidence of Kensington's expanding population – onto Allen Street. Go first right into Abingdon Villas, walk to the end and turn left into Earls Court Road.

Edwardes Square

Take the first right into Pembroke Square, walk to the end past Rassell's Nursery and the tennis court, and then turn right. Having passed the Scarsdale Tavern (named after a former mansion – Scarsdale House), turn left into Edwardes Square. This is the later of Kensington's two old squares. By the time it was begun in 1811, demand was building up locally for this type of house, but even so the developer took things steadily, building one side at a time. The north side, called Earls Terrace, was built first, then the east, west and finally the south sides, the latter completed in 1819. When you get to the little gardener's house halfway along, notice the artists' studios with their large north-facing windows on the left-hand side. First is a freestanding one used from 1940 to 1980 by the portrait painter Cowan Dobson. Then there is a purpose-built block of four, converted to offices. The East End is now the artists' quarter of London, no doubt because of lower property prices.

Artists' colony

Turn right at the end of the square and walk up to the main road, turning right by the lodge of Earls Terrace. The orientation of the terrace – facing the main road

KENSINGTON

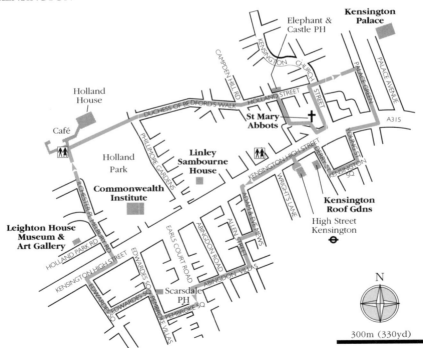

300m (330yd)

with gardens behind – proves that the developer was hedging his bets. It was only when the houses sold well that he proceeded with the square behind (perhaps it was even an afterthought). Cross the main road at the traffic lights, carry on a little way and then turn left into Melbury Road.

Attracted by the relatively clear air and the cheapish property, artists settled all over Kensington in the 19th century. The more successful congregated in the Melbury Road area, where they built themselves houses with studios attached. The sculptor G. F. Watts started the influx when he moved into Little Holland House on the edge of Holland Park. Before long there were no fewer than six Royal Academicians living in the colony. Chief among them was Frederick Leighton, president of the Royal Academy and the first painter to be made a peer. He lived in Holland Park Road where his house-cum-studio survives as **Leighton House Museum and Art Gallery**. Look left as you cross the entrance to Holland Park Road and you will see it with its glass-roofed studio sticking out at the back. Further on up Melbury Road, No. 18 carries a plaque to the Pre-Raphaelite painter William Holman Hunt.

When the road begins to bend round to the left, keep right into Ilchester Place. The house in the 'V' here was built for the artist Sir Luke Fildes, almost totally forgotten now, but a very successful painter in Victorian times. To the left, the house with the tower was the home of Cardiff Castle architect William Burges. He designed the house in the 1870s and made the inside – a riot of detail, colour and ornament that still survives – as medieval in style as the outside. Walking up Ilchester Place beside Fildes' house, look back to see the painter's huge studio, topped by a cupola, attached to the back.

Holland Park

Go straight on through the gate into Holland Park and walk up the hill towards the old stable block and garden arcade (the café is behind the arcade). Turn right here and walk eastwards across the park in front of the remains of Holland House (the green-roofed building away to your right is the **Commonwealth Institute**). The old Jacobean mansion was a private house until World War II, but it was badly damaged by bombs in 1940 and subsequently sold, with its surrounding parkland, to the local authority. Later the west wing was salvaged and converted into a youth hostel, which you can see today.

In the 18th century the house came into the possession of the Edwardes family, descendants of Sir Walter Cope. They sold it to Lord Holland, father of the famous Whig politician, Charles James Fox. During the time of Fox's nephew, the third Lord Holland, the house enjoyed several decades of fame when it served as the nerve centre of the Whig party, out of office almost continuously between 1784 and 1830. Later the Hollands, who were great entertainers, fell on comparatively hard times and had to start developing parts of their estate to make ends meet. The majority of the park survived, however, and, just as Holland House had been one of the first country houses on the fringes of London, so it was also the last private estate in central London to pass into public ownership. This belated transition helped protect Kensington's western flank from total obliteration by the developers. On the eastern side Kensington Palace performed a similar service.

The Phillimore estate

Having walked past the house, carry straight on out of the park into Duchess of Bedford's Walk. Phillimore Gardens on the right indicates that you are now entering the Phillimore estate, still privately owned after some 250 years. The Phillimores were one of the first Kensington landowning families to start developing their property. They began with a terrace of shops and houses on Kensington High Street in the 1780s. Then between 1812 and 1817 they built a group of seven country villas on the hill to your left. They intended these for markedly superior tenants, and got them, three dukes included. Immediately on your left stood the grandest of the villas, Bedford Lodge, which was the London home of the Duke and Duchess of Bedford.

Lesbian novel

Walk down to the end of Duchess of Bedford's Walk and cross over Campden Hill Road into Holland Street. Ahead the 250-foot (80-metre)-high steeple of St Mary Abbots Church rising above a row of gabled houses makes a picturesque view. Crossing Hornton Street and carrying on down Holland Street, you pass two of the many blue plaques in Kensington, a reminder of the large number of successful – often creative – people who have lived in the village over the past two couple of hundred years. Charles Stanford (terracotta house on the corner) was a leading English musician and teacher; Radclyffe Hall (No. 39 on the right) is best remembered for her lesbian novel *The Well of Loneliness,* published when she was living here and banned after an obscenity trial.

When you reach Gordon Place by the Elephant and Castle pub you are crossing the main drive that led left up the hill to Campden House, demolished about 1900. Beyond the pub you are in the oldest section of Holland Street and the heart of the former village. Further on, narrow lanes and passageways lead off the road on both sides and the houses almost all date from the 18th century. Take the first turning on the right – Kensington Church Walk – and walk on down to the churchyard. Most of it has been converted into a small park and playgrounds for the local school, but the section in front of the church's west door has survived. Turn in here and walk round to the right of the church, noticing the brightly coloured figures of the boy and girl high up on the wall of the school. The original parish school was designed by the architect Nicholas Hawksmoor, who was then clerk of works at Kensington Palace. It used to stand nearby on the High Street, with these charming little figures adorning its façade.

St Mary Abbots

The present **St Mary Abbots** is certainly the third and possibly the fourth parish church that has stood on this site. The arrival of the court led to the building of one new church in the 1690s; the coming of the Victorians, with their taste for Gothic, led to another nearly 200 years later. Fortunately, memorials from both replaced churches were preserved so that St Mary Abbots today, with its fine collection of over 250 inscriptions, is not unlike a miniature Westminster Abbey. The oldest memorial, dating from 1653 and commemorating Henry Dawson, MP and mayor of Newcastle, is on the west wall.

Barker's of Kensington

Leave the church by the covered passageway. This brings you out at the very centre of Kensington (the junction of Church Street and High Street) and presents you with a fine view of Barker's department store. Founded in 1870, Barker's gradually took over all its main rivals in Kensington and in the 1920s began work on this flagship store. But by the time the building was completed 30 years later, the firm had lost its independence and been taken over by the House of Fraser. Now it is merely a brand of another company, but its building remains a fine architectural adornment to Kensington's much rebuilt High Street.

Turn left and walk up Church Street as far as Holland Street and the traffic lights (Pierre Pechon's patisserie is on the left). Cross Church Street here and walk down York House Place, the name recalling another of Kensington's lost mansions. The path brings you out on Palace Green. Ahead is William and Mary's palace (or **Kensington Palace** where, later, Queen Victoria was born) and Kensington Gardens. To the right is the original palace coach house and stable. Either side of you are rows of vast mansions built in the mid-19th century as a Crown Estate speculation. Apart from a smattering of aristocrats, early tenants were mostly rich industrialists and businessmen. Today virtually every house is an embassy. Should you want to take a closer look at the palace, you can do so from the park, accessed by the gate in the park wall directly ahead across the green. Otherwise, turn right and walk down the hill to Kensington High Street.

Thackeray's novels

Turn right. Cross safely where you can and then take the first left into Young Street (the Victorian novelist William Thackeray lived in the house with bow windows on the right while writing *Vanity Fair, Pendennis* and *Henry Esmond*). Emerging in Kensington Square you are in Thomas Young's creation of the 1680s, the radical development only saved from disaster by the arrival of the court a few years later. Quite what Young thought he was doing building an urban square in a country village three miles (5 kilometres) from London is not clear, but that it was a premature development is surely proved by the fact that it backed directly onto open fields until as late as 1840. Then development started and the square's long-term future was at last assured. Turn right into the square. Except for those on the east side, most of the houses are original, but they have all been much altered and now each looks different from the rest. But this variety only adds to the square's charm.

Derry and Toms

At the west end of the north side, turn right out of the square into Derry Street. The Barker's building is on the right; the former Derry and Toms store, taken over by Barker's in 1920, is on the left. Should you want to see the famous **Kensington Roof Gardens** on top of what was Derry and Toms, the entrance is through the glass doorway marked No. 99. Otherwise, carry straight on to the end of the road and turn left into the High Street. The station entrance, and the end of the walk, is ahead on the left.

Pinner

Location	13 miles (21 kilometres) northwest of Charing Cross.
Transport	Pinner Underground Station (Metropolitan Line).
Features	**St John's Church**; High Street with 16th-century pubs and Georgian houses; timber-framed cottages and farmhouses scattered among suburban roads; views over park and farmland to Harrow Weald; **Harrow Museum and Heritage Centre** (not on walk – see map page 70).
Events	**Pinner Fair**.
Refreshments	*High Street* Italian restaurant, café/wine bar, Queen's Head and Victory pubs, Pizza Express; *Bridge Street* Oddfellows Arms pub, McDonald's, Wenzel's bakery and coffee house, Chinese restaurant, fish and chip shop.

Pinner. No name is more redolent of comfortable Home Counties suburbia. Yet few of London's villages are more ancient and picturesque. Pinner's chief glory is its wonderful High Street, a broad sloping thoroughfare stretching uphill from the River Pinn at one end to the parish church at the other. Lined with houses, shops and pubs built over the last four centuries or so, it is a wonderful lesson in architectural styles and building materials. Here, and in neighbouring Bridge Street, is held Pinner's famous fair, first authorized in 1336 and a regular annual event since at least the 18th century. Surrounding the old village centre, many of the timber-framed cottages and farms that once lay scattered about among the fields also survive. They are now embedded in more modern housing developments and the best of them feature on the walk.

South of the High Street in the early days lay the village's common fields reached by Rayners Lane. Traces of medieval ridge and furrow ploughing can still be seen in Pinner Village Gardens. East and west of the village were two outlying settlements called East End and West End. The sadly mutilated West House and Sweetman's Farm, a 16th-century timber-framed house, survive from the hamlet of West End in West End Lane.

Two lanes, Paines Lane and Moss Lane, stretched north to farms such as Waxwell Farm and Woodhall Farm. The former is included on the walk. At the latter, which still exists in Woodhall Drive, but which is a little too far to be included in the walk, John Claudius Loudon, the famous gardening writer, spent some time in the early 19th century convalescing from rheumatic fever and helping his tenant farmer father. A designer of elegant cottages and farm buildings, he also did some work on his father's farmhouse at the same time and it still bears his neo-Gothic Regency touches to this day.

High ground

On the high ground to the north of Waxwell and Woodhall farms – again, too far away to be included in the walk – lay more farms and, later, one or two large houses where Pinner's grander residents lived. From the 17th century, the village began to attract an increasing number of these types, usually City merchants and lawyers in search of country homes close to their London offices. The finest of these houses, Pinner Hill, a late-18th-century mansion, survives as a golf club.

Away to the east of Pinner – beyond East End – lie two large open spaces, Pinner Park and Headstone Manor Recreation Ground. Pinner Park, a former deer park and now a dairy farm, features on the walk. The Headstone Manor Recreation Ground, which surrounds Headstone Manor Farm, a moated medieval farmhouse with a massive tithe barn and an 18th-century granary, is unfortunately too far away. In the Middle Ages Headstone Manor was the manor house of Harrow. Pinner at that time was merely an outlying hamlet within both the manor and parish of Harrow. Harrow and its parish church were some distance away, however, so from early times Pinner had its own church. Today, Headstone Manor is home to the **Harrow Museum and Heritage Centre** and the Harrow Show takes place here over the August Bank Holiday.

THE PINNER WALK

Start and finish Pinner Station.
Distance 2¼ miles (4.4 kilometres).

Come out of the station and turn left down the hill. At the bottom turn right onto the main road and then right again into the High Street. Bridge Street is really Pinner's main shopping street and has most of the big stores you would expect to find in any modern town centre. Fittingly, High Street is reserved for more individual shops, including Corbett's bookshop and one or two antique shops. It also has a couple of ancient pubs, the Queen's Head on the left and the Victory on the right. The latter is dated 1580, but while the building itself might be that old, the pub has only been here since the late 1950s. They have been pulling pints at the Queen's Head, on the other hand, since at least the days of Charles I (1625–49).

At the top of the street on the left – beyond the green donated to the village in 1924 – is the long, low Church Farm, one of the oldest buildings in Pinner. The fact that this was a farmhouse as late as 1906 shows just what a modern phenomenon the modern suburb of Pinner is. Opposite, the Hilltop Wine Bar was a butcher's shop from the 1600s until the 1930s. Animals were slaughtered in the building to the right with the louvred roof (now a chiropodist's surgery). Between Church Farm and the wine bar is a house with an unusually large window facing down the High Street. As the Harrow Heritage Trust plaque says, this was a Victorian temperance tavern and tea garden called Ye Cocoa Tree. Opened in 1878 by 45-year-old local resident and property lawyer William Barber, who must have been something of a temperance enthusiast, it was popular with day trippers from London (the Metropolitan Line railway arrived at Pinner in 1886) and lasted well into the 1920s, by which time much of the central area of the village had been developed.

PINNER

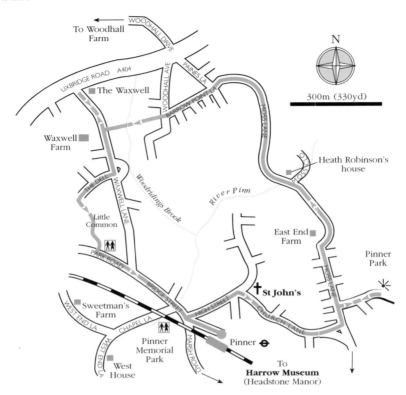

St John's Church

Continue to the right into Church Lane. Built in flint, the only building material available in any quantity locally, **St John's Church** was dedicated in 1321, though it did not become a parish church in its own right until 1766 when Pinner broke away from Harrow. St Johns' great tower, which dominates Pinner High Street, is a 15th-century addition. The entrance to the church is via the lychgate and the sunken path leading to the south door. To the right, the curious monument with the stone coffin sticking out either side commemorates John Claudius Loudon's parents and is no doubt another product of their son's fertile, if slightly eccentric, imagination. Inside the church there is a memorial to the poet laureate Henry Pye, of whom more later when we come to East End.

Pinner House

Carry on past the church. Round the corner you come across Pinner House, the grandest house in Pinner village proper. Dating from around 1700, it has a very gracious aspect and must at one time have enjoyed wonderful views southwards across the fields towards Harrow. Apart from Pinner Hill away to the north, it is the only one of Pinner's mansions to survive into the late 20th century. Since the late 1940s it has been an old people's home. Further on around another corner you come to a cluster of comfortable-looking old houses: on the right The Grange; on the left the grey-painted Bay House (timber-framed behind a deceptive Victorian façade); and then, on the right again, the substantial Elmdene facing Nower Hill Green. Here, in the 19th century, lived the natural daughter of Horatio Nelson and Lady Hamilton, Horatia Nelson Ward. Horatia died when she was 81 and is buried in the village cemetery in Paines Lane. More recent occupants of the house include the comedian Ronnie Barker and the actor David Suchet, star of the TV series *Poirot*.

Nower Hill Green is sometimes known as Tooke's Green because of the Victorian drinking fountain in the centre that commemorates village benefactor William Tooke. Tooke, who lived at Pinner Hill, was as near to a squire as Pinner could have in the 19th century. He paid for the rebuilding of the church in 1880. His clergyman grandfather − whose inheritance of a fortune in 1792 enabled him to devote himself to historical studies − was one of the first historians of Russia.

From deer park to farm

Walk past the memorial to the top of the green and turn left and then right into Wakehams Hill. At the top where the road bends right, bear left down the track. From the gate, where there is a thoughtfully provided seat, there is a splendid view north over Pinner Park towards the high ground beyond. Up in that high ground near the River Pinn's source are two of Pinner's three surviving farms: Pinnerwood Farm and Oxhey Lane Farm. The third is the one you can see in the middle of Pinner Park, just beyond the main road. Sometimes called Hall's Farm, it is named after the family that have tenanted it (from St Thomas's Hospital in central London) since the end of the last century. Before that the Halls were at Headstone Manor. In medieval times Pinner Park was a 250-acre (100-hectare) deer park used for hunting. Farming gradually took over in the 16th century.

East End

Re-trace your steps down Wakehams Hill. Facing you across Moss Lane at the bottom is The Fives Court, a notable Arts and Crafts house designed at the beginning of this century by Cecil Brewer for Ambrose Heal of Heal's furnishing store in Tottenham Court Road. Turn right into Moss Lane. A fairly long section now ensues until you come to the nucleus of the old outlying settlement of East End. You will know it when you see it, for the ancient houses are conspicuous among the newer buildings. Three houses remain out of the original half dozen or so. First, on the left behind a crazy wall, is Tudor Cottage, an old house tarted up with an assortment of architectural antiques. Beyond is East End Farm, the brick indicating a later date and greater prosperity. Here lived George III's poet laureate Henry Pye (1745–1813), whose memorial is in the church. Ridiculed even in his own day, he is only remembered now, if at all, because of fellow writer George Steevens' punning put-down of his first birthday ode to the king using the line 'When the PYE was opened' from the 'Sing a song of sixpence' nursery rhyme. At the end of the farmyard is the 15th-century East End Farm Cottage, the oldest house in Pinner, if not in the whole of Middlesex. Amazing enough from the outside, inside it has a superb, roughly contemporary, wall painting. Clearly the house must have been grander when it was built than the farm labourer's cottage it later became. The old farmyard on the right survives virtually intact and is still in semi-agricultural use (by a firm of fruit and potato merchants).

River Pinn

Carry on along Moss Lane, around the corner and down the hill. At the bottom you cross over the River Pinn: the name Pinner is thought to mean 'settlement on the banks of the Pinn'. The path on the left by the postbox leads through to Paines Lane. No. 75 on the right has a blue plaque to the illustrator William Heath Robinson, a resident of Pinner for some 13 years. He actually lived in this house for five years from 1913.

Another long section now ensues until you reach the junction of Moss Lane with Paines Lane (Moss Cottage is on the left). If you would like to catch a glimpse of Loudon's Woodhall Farm, turn right here, walk to the end of the road, cross the main road into Woodhall Drive and walk up the left-hand side for about 100 yards (90 metres). Otherwise, cross Paines Lane diagonally to the left into Barrow Point Lane and carry on to the bottom.

Waxwell Lane

Where the lane turns sharp left, bear right through the hedge and then immediately left into the footpath, signposted Waxwell Lane, though the name has been painted over. At the low point in the middle of the path you cross over Woodridings Brook, a tributary of the Pinn. Emerging in Waxwell Lane, Waxwell Farm is immediately opposite. No longer a farm, it still has a huge garden and is another reminder of Pinner's not too distant agricultural past. The house is now used by the Holy Grail, a Roman Catholic organization.

Waxwell Lane takes its name from a medieval spring or well, which until the arrival of piped water was a major source of fresh drinking water in the area. If you turn right in Waxwell Lane you will find the well, reached by a short flight of steps but now bricked up, just by the junction with the main road, on the right-hand side. The main route of the walk turns left along Waxwell Lane and then, opposite Waxwell Close, an elegant crescent of 'artisan' housing dating from the 1920s, right into the Dell. The great hollow of the Dell, now filled with modern houses, was man-made over the centuries by locals digging for lime and flint. Both were used for building, but lime, of course, was also applied as a dressing to farmland. Elsewhere in Pinner, people mined underground for these valuable materials. Some of the mines, which still exist but are not open to the public, are over 100 feet (30 metres) below ground level.

Pinner Common

As you approach the Dell, keep on the left-hand side and walk along the pavement as the ground drops away to the right. Just beyond White Cottage, turn left through the gate into Little Common, relic of a once much larger piece of common land

Plate 11: *The Flask in West Hill, Highgate, has been a popular drinking place for over 300 years (see page 55).*

Plate 12: *One of the five lakes that make up Highgate Ponds on Hampstead Heath: this one is used by model boat enthusiasts (see page 54).*

Plate 13: *The narrow stretch of the Thames between Isleworth and Isleworth Ait provides a sheltered location for a boatyard (see page 59).*

Plate 14: *Kensington Church Walk: a quiet corner close to the parish church in the heart of the village (see page 66).*

Plate 15: A profusion of flowers decorates the exterior of the Elephant and Castle in Holland Street, one of Kensington's most popular pubs (see page 66).

Plate 16: The Wax Well in Pinner is now disused but it was once an important source of drinking water (see page 72).

Plate 17: *The timber-framed East End Farm Cottage dates from the 15th century and is probably the oldest house in Pinner (see page 71).*

Plate 18: *Once the boyhood home of Arts and Crafts designer William Morris, this Georgian mansion in Walthamstow is now the William Morris Gallery (see page 78).*

(another area, called Pinner Green, survives to the north). Follow the path out of the park and turn left on Park Road. Ahead you can see the spire of Harrow church breaking out of the trees on top of Harrow Hill. Carry on down the hill to the Oddfellows Arms pub at the junction with Waxwell Lane. Here there is an old milestone giving the distance to London. Around the corner in Waxwell Lane there are two charming old timber-framed cottages, Orchard Cottage and Bee Cottage, which are well worth a look.

Carry on down Bridge Street. At the bottom you pass the entrance to Chapel Lane, leading to West End and West House whose grounds are now a public park. You then cross (although you are not really aware of it) the bridge over the Pinn, from which, of course, Bridge Street takes its name. The Pinn flows to the right here in a southwesterly direction and eventually joins the Colne (and thence the Thames) a few miles south of Uxbridge. Pinner Station, and the end of the walk, is 100 yards (90 metres) or so ahead, *this* side of the railway line.

Walthamstow

Location	7½ miles (12 kilometres) northwest of Charing Cross.
Transport	Walthamstow Central Station (Underground Victoria Line; overground trains from Liverpool Street), Walthamstow Queens Road Station (overground North London Line trains between Gospel Oak and Barking).
Features	**St Mary's Church**; Monoux and Squires Almshouses; **Vestry House Museum**; 15th-century Ancient House; **William Morris Gallery**.
Events	**Village Festival**.
Refreshments	*Orford Road in Walthamstow village* bakery, café/takeaway, Chinese takeaway/fish and chip shops, two pubs, two Italian restaurants, Indian takeaway; *High Street in town centre near station* cafés, restaurants, sandwich bars and fast-food outlets.

The village of Walthamstow – meaning 'a place where travellers are welcome' – grew up on high ground east of the River Lea, opposite Tottenham on the London bank. The village was well established by the time of the Domesday survey in 1086 and subsequently expanded to include several outlying settlements; for example, Kings End in the south and Chapel End (where there was a chapel-of-ease to the main parish church) in the north. Subsequently, the centre of the village, where the main parish church was situated, became known as Church End.

After the Norman Conquest, the manor of Walthamstow was granted to the de Toni family. They are credited with building the present church, which is certainly medieval in origin and appears to date from the 13th century. There is some doubt about the location of the de Toni manor house. Some sources say that it was at a place called High Hall between the village and the river; others that it stood opposite the church on the site of the present Ancient House, a half-timbered 15th-century house featured on the walk. Either way, the last de Toni died childless and his sister took the property into the Beauchamp family, earls of Warwick. From the 15th to the 17th centuries it passed through many, including royal, hands. The last squires were the Maynards, first baronets and then viscounts. Charles Maynard, auditor of the exchequer, acquired it in 1639 and a Maynard was still lord of the manor 300 years later.

Walthamstow benefactor

From the late Middle Ages rich City merchants built country houses in the beautiful wooded countryside around the village. One of these in the early 16th century was

Sir George Monoux, Lord Mayor of London in 1514. Although not lord of the manor, Monoux was one of Walthamstow's most generous benefactors, founding the Monoux Almshouses and Grammar School, and paying for the rebuilding of the church. He died in 1544 and was buried at St Mary's, where there is a commemorative brass to him. His house in the north of the parish near Chapel End survived until 1927 and is now covered by Monoux Grove.

Gentlemen's residences

By the middle of the 19th century, the still-rural parish was well sprinkled with fine gentlemen's seats. Several of these are still standing today, including Walthamstow House in Shernhall Street to the east of the village and The Chestnuts to the south in Hoe Street. These do not feature on the walk, but the 18th-century Water House and Brookscroft and the 19th-century Orford House do. Although some distance from the village centre, Water House, a fine Georgian mansion on a low-lying site to the north of the village, has been included on the walk because it was the boyhood home of the great designer and socialist William Morris and is now a gallery devoted to his life and work. The walk between the village and the house is not particularly attractive, but it cannot be avoided.

Following the arrival of the railways in the 1840s and the enclosure of all the old common land in the 1850s, the way was clear for the speculative builders to transform the old village into a modern suburb. Elsewhere in London this process usually involved the destruction of the old village. But at Walthamstow new village/town centres were built (first in Orford Road and then in Marsh – now High – Street). As a result the original Walthamstow village survives today, complete with medieval church, 15th-century Ancient House, 16th-century almshouses, 18th-century workhouse and vestry room, and 19th-century cottages and schools. It is a rare little oasis of history in the otherwise rather ugly sprawl of contemporary east London.

THE WALTHAMSTOW WALK

Start and finish Walthamstow Central Station.
Distance 2¼ miles (4.4 kilometres).

Turn right out of the station and walk up Selborne Road to the traffic lights. Cross the main road and go straight on into St Mary Road. At the end of the road continue on into Church Path. This takes you past some pretty Victorian cottages, and then a row of rather older ones built in 1825, before bringing you out in the centre of Church End, the original village centre of Walthamstow. On the right are the old school and workhouse, of which more later. On the left are the Squires almshouses, founded in 1795 by Mrs Squires for six tradesmen's widows. Mrs Squires lived at Newington and died the year after the almshouses were founded.

Ancient House

Carry on past the almshouses into Church Lane. On the left now is **St Mary's Church**, standing in its three-acre (1.2-hectare) churchyard. The many fine tombs reflect Walthamstow's former status as an up-market residential area. Opposite the church is the so-called Ancient House, a timber-framed structure dating from the 15th century. In the 19th century it was converted into four shops, hence the large windows on the ground floor. Now it is a private home again. The bare plot on the other side of the entrance to Orford Road was the site of the village inn, the Nag's Head, until it was rebuilt behind the Ancient House in Orford Road in 1859.

Walk on past the Ancient House. The small but elegant house on the far side (No. 10 Church Lane) was built in 1830 for a family of local builders called Reed. A little further on in Bishop's Close is the Chestnuts, built by the Rev. J. Roberts, headmaster of the Monoux School from 1820 to 1836. It was partly a residence for himself and partly a boarding house for the private pupils he taught at the school. Bishop's Close was later built in the grounds of the house.

Vinegar Alley

Continue on down Church Lane for some way. Just beyond the pillar box near the end, turn left into Vinegar Alley. This takes you back through the churchyard towards the east end of the church. To the right, opposite the church, are the Monoux Almshouses and Grammar School for boys, founded by Sir George Monoux in 1527 and completed before his death in 1544. The school was in the

WALTHAMSTOW

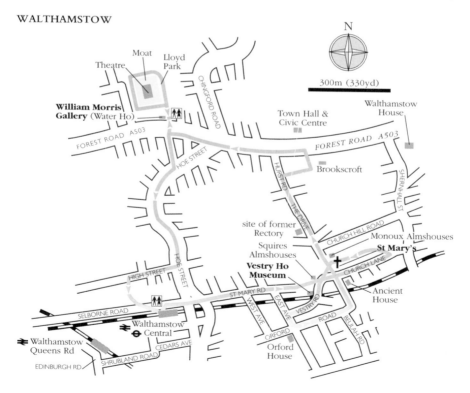

brick part at the far end (rebuilt in 1955 following bomb damage during World War II) and the master lived in the protruding section in the middle. The much-expanded school moved to a new site in Chingford Road in the last century and is still there today.

At the west (tower) end of the church, turn left and bear right at the fork. On the right now, on the far side of the churchyard, is the old St Mary's infants school, founded in a barn on the vicar's glebe in 1824 and then provided with this handsome building four years later. The vicar at the time, the Rev. William Wilson, was a pioneer of infant education and St Mary's was the first school of its kind established by the Church of England. The building was last used as a school in 1978 and is now the church's Welcome Centre.

Parish workhouse

Back in Church End, cross the road, turn right and follow it round to the left as it becomes Vestry Road. The road takes its name from the building on the right, built by the parish in 1730 as a combined workhouse and vestry office (the vestry was the local authority in those days). The parish poor were moved to a new workhouse in Stratford in 1840 and the building subsequently became, among other things, a police station and a private house before being turned into a local history museum in 1931, now the **Vestry House Museum**. A plaque on the wall by the barrel marks the site of the old parish watch-house and lockup. Nearby stands the top of a column from the old General Post Office in St Martin-le-Grand in the City. The building was demolished in 1912 and this relic brought here by a local resident. On the other side of the road is the National School. This was built in 1819 to take the overflow from the old Monoux School and was in use till 1906. Since 1924 the building has been used by the National Spiritualist Church.

Carry on along Vestry Road, crossing the deep railway cutting made in 1870, and following the road round to the right past the playground and the old (1903) postal sorting office on the left. As the plaque on the sorting office says, this area was once the Bury Field, or Church Common, one of three large areas of common land in the old rural Walthamstow. All the commons were enclosed in 1850 and subsequently built over with streets and houses.

New centre of Walthamstow

At the end of Vestry Road, turn left into East Avenue. The large house ahead is Orford House, built on the edge of Church Common in the early 19th century for Whitechapel merchant John Case. Now it is a social centre with a bowling green in the garden behind. Before you reach the house, turn left by the Queen's Arms pub into Orford Road and walk along past the shops. Orford Road was built from the 1860s onwards as the new centre of Walthamstow: further on you pass the new school (now the Asian centre) and the new town hall (now a nursery school), which were put up at that time. As Walthamstow continued to expand, the centre of the growing town moved to yet another new site, still further from the old village. Today Orford Road serves the Walthamstow Village conservation area and surrounding streets.

Follow the road when it bends round to the left and crosses back over the railway line, passing the rebuilt Victorian Nag's Head pub on the far side. Cross straight over Church Lane and walk past the west end of the church once more, but this time in the opposite direction. Carry on past the almshouses into Church Hill. Beyond the almshouses on the right is the new rectory; on the left is the old vicarage, absorbed into Walthamstow High School in 1974. The old rectory, owned all through the Middle Ages by the Priory of Holy Trinity, Aldgate, in London, stood across the road ahead to the left until its demolition at the end of the last century.

The Ching valley

Cross straight over the road ahead (Church Hill/Prospect Hill) and walk along The Drive. Although you cannot see it, the ground now drops away on all sides as you approach the top of the hill that once protected Walthamstow village from the worst of the north winds. At the end of The Drive the steepness of the descent into the Ching valley becomes apparent. Go straight over into Hurst Road, and halfway down turn right by the Hurst Road Health Centre sign into the path to the right of the railings. This brings you out in front of a block of flats. At the far end there is a car turning area and next to it more railings. Turn left here and follow the path downhill again to the junction with Forest Road. On the right now is Brookscroft, another of old Walthamstow's surviving 18th-century mansions. Once it looked out over woods and fields. Now, converted into a YMCA hostel, it surveys the borough of Waltham Forest's impressive civic centre, opened in 1941.

William Morris's home

Turn left along Forest Road. At the lights cross straight over and at the zebra cross the road and go through the gates into Lloyd Park surrounding the **William Morris Gallery**. Go through the gate to the right of the house and walk around the moat in the park behind in either a clockwise or an anti-clockwise direction. The original house stood on the island in the centre of the moat. The present house was built in the mid-18th century. William Morris was born at Elm House further along Forest Road in 1834 and moved here with his parents in 1848. Eight years later Morris senior lost a lot of money in the City and the family had to leave. The house was bought by newspaper publisher Edward Lloyd. In 1950 it was turned into a museum celebrating William Morris's achievements as a designer, craftsman, poet and socialist.

Walthamstow Market

Exit Lloyd Park by the same gate and cross straight over the main road into Gaywood Road. At the top, turn right on Hoe Street. Follow this winding road for some distance until you pass the cinema and reach the lights. Here turn into the modern High Street, the post-Orford Road town centre and the site of Walthamstow's mile-long (1.5-kilometre) street market. Originally called Marsh Lane, High Street connected the village with the marshes down by the Lea. As Walthamstow expanded, costermongers started setting up the stalls here from the 1880s and so the market, now one of the longest in Europe, grew up. When you reach the town square, turn left along the tree-lined avenue and make your way back to the station, where the walk ends.

Villages South of the River Thames

Barnes

Location	5½ miles (8.8 kilometres) west of Charing Cross.
Transport	Barnes and Barnes Bridge stations (overground trains from Waterloo).
Features	**St Mary's Church**; Barnes Terrace; site of Barn Elms manor house; Barnes green and common; Thames and Beverley Brook riverside walks; **Barn Elms Nature Reserve**.
Events	**Barnes Village Fair**.
Refreshments	*overlooking river* Café Uno, Bulls Head pub (start of walk) White Hart pub (end of walk); *High Street* fish and chip shop, pub, café/patisserie, bakery, vegetarian takeaway, brasserie; *Barnes Green* Sun Inn; *Church Road* Délice de France café (village end), cafés, Indian restaurant, Red Lion pub (Barn Elms end); *White Hart Lane* (junction with The Terrace near end of walk) Thai, Indian and Chinese restaurants.

Long before the Norman Conquest King Athelstan gave to the Dean and Chapter of St Paul's Cathedral in the City of London an estate to the west of the city on the south bank of the Thames. The estate consisted of a neck of land opposite Chiswick and Hammersmith bordered on three sides by the Thames. The whole of the peninsula was low-lying, between about 14 and 20 feet (4 and 6 metres) above sea level. The top end was marshy and subject to flooding. But the bottom, landward, end was firmer. Here a road ran between Putney and Mortlake. Barnes grew up at the west, Mortlake, end of the road, just at the point where it intersected with the river.

At the intersection point, where the Bulls Head pub now stands, the village had its own wharf. Shops and houses lined the road approaching the wharf, in time forming today's High Street. At the other end of the High Street was the common. The part of the common nearest the village, where there were several ponds, became the village green. Several large houses in spacious grounds were built overlooking it. Beside the green, a lane led off from the High Street past the church to the grounds of the manor house, called Barn Elms after the great elm trees that populated its large park.

Bridge and waterworks

North of the village and manor house, the bulk of the peninsula was a quiet, remote farming district traversed by no roads except a lane leading to Chiswick ferry (now represented by Ferry Road). Progress arrived in the early 19th century in the form of the Hammersmith Bridge Company which, in 1825, bought the Barn Elms estate in order to build an approach road to Hammersmith Bridge, opened in 1827. The bridge company was followed almost immediately by the West Middlesex Water Works Company. In 1828 it built the first of several massive reservoirs and filter beds, which in time came to occupy a substantial chunk of the peninsula. As the 19th century advanced, the rest of the peninsula was covered by roads and houses, especially after the opening of Barnes Station in 1846. The Barnes Bridge Station line was built three years later, but Barnes Bridge Station, where the walk starts and finishes, was not constructed until 1916.

Barnes today

Although it has lost its manor house and several of the fine houses that once surrounded the green, Barnes is still an exceedingly attractive London village. It has its terrace of elegant 18th- and 19th-century houses overlooking the river – a popular vantage point for the closing stages of the annual Oxford and Cambridge University Boat Race; its High Street with its individual shops; its green and church with some lovely old houses along Church Road; and finally its common and its open parkland, once the grounds of Barn Elms House. Barnes also has something that many other London villages lack – a strong community spirit, carefully nurtured by the local community association. This should be evident on the walk, along with all the physical features just listed.

THE BARNES WALK

Start and finish Barnes Bridge Station.
Distance 3¼ miles (5.2 kilometres).

Come out of Barnes Bridge Station and turn right along The Terrace, keeping to the raised riverside walkway on the left and walking in the direction of Chiswick, which you can just make out in the distance on the opposite side of the river. The Terrace dates from the 18th century when people began to move to Barnes from the city in increasing numbers. Several houses survive from that time, including No. 10, the red brick house on the corner of Cleveland Gardens, which has a plaque recording the residence of Gustav Holst. Best known for his suite *The Planets,* the composer lived here from 1908 to 1913 while teaching music at St Paul's girls' school in Hammersmith.

The Bulls Head pub stands opposite the site of the old village wharf. At the roundabout here turn right into the High Street. This has been largely redeveloped since Barnes became a railway suburb, but it still contains many small shops offering specialist products and personal service. At the far end you pass the 18th-century Rose House – once a pub and now the headquarters of the local community association – before arriving at the village green, part of the old village common. The pond is the only one of four to survive. It used to be fed by the Beverley Brook (which you will see later), but now it depends on a mixture of rainwater and mains top-up, rather like the ponds at Carshalton.

BARNES

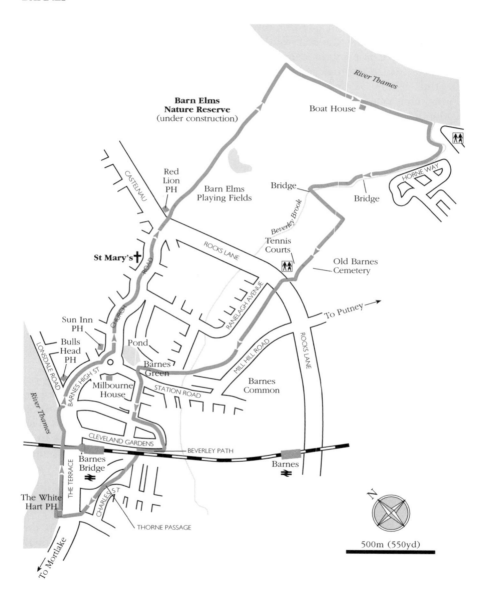

River Thames

Barn Elms
Nature Reserve
(under construction)

Boat House

CASTELNAU

Red
Lion
PH

Barn Elms
Playing Fields

Bridge

Beverley Brook

Bridge

HORNE WAY

ROCKS LANE

St Mary's

Tennis
Courts

Old Barnes
Cemetery

CHURCH ROAD

RANELAGH AVENUE

To Putney

Sun Inn
PH

Bulls
Head
PH

Pond

Barnes
Green

MILL HILL ROAD

ROCKS LANE

LONSDALE ROAD

BARNES HIGH ST

Milbourne
House

STATION ROAD

Barnes
Common

River Thames

CLEVELAND GARDENS

BEVERLEY PATH

Barnes
Bridge

THE TERRACE

Barnes

The White
Hart PH

CHARLES ST

THORNE PASSAGE

To Mortlake

N

500m (550yd)

Gothic novel

Turn left at the green into Church Road and walk past the Sun on your left and the green on your right. The building in the middle of the green is a Victorian girls' school, closed in the 1920s and now used as a senior citizens' day centre. At the end of the Victorian developments and just before the terrace of shops you come to a handful of 18th-century houses (one, pink Gothic) making a very pretty little group next to the little green with tree and bench underneath. The last house in the row is The Grange (now an old people's home run by the Julian Memorial Trust). Behind The Grange, in the appropriately named Hermitage Cottage, the author 'Monk' Lewis lived on and off from about 1801 to his death in 1818. Lewis earned his nickname and his reputation (though not his living which came from slave-ownership in Jamaica) from his 1795 publication, *The Monk,* an early and very successful Gothic novel. The site of his cottage is now covered by a modern development called The Hermitage.

Now follow the road round by the parade of shops. On the right the green, ringed by a low white post and rail fence, extends right up to Glebe Road. Glebe Road was built on the glebe land belonging to the rector; the rector himself lived in the large Georgian house on the far side of the junction of Kitson Road on the left (Kitson Road, laid out in 1907, is named after Canon Kitson, rector of the parish at that time).

St Mary's churchyard

Beyond the former rectory (now called Strawberry House) is the parish church of **St Mary's**. The original church was destroyed by a fire in 1978 but the 15th-century tower survived. In the attractive old churchyard most of the gravestones date from the 18th and 19th centuries, though on the south wall there is a 17th-century plaque to Edward Rose, citizen of London, who died in 1653. He obviously had a sense of humour because he left £5 a year to the parish for roses to be planted on his grave.

From the churchyard carry on along Church Road, passing on the left the handsome Homestead House, dating from about 1700 and one of the finest of Barnes's surviving historic houses. At the end of Church Road you come to the junction with Castelnau, left (the new road built in 1827 as an approach to Hammersmith Bridge), and Rocks Lane, right. Cross straight over by the Red Lion into Queen Elizabeth Walk and walk on down beside the Barn Elms Playing Fields. The Walk was the drive to the manor house: one of the entrance lodges survives on the right-hand side. On the left redundant reservoirs built by the West Middlesex Water Works company a century ago are currently being dismantled and converted into a housing development and the 100-acre (40-hectare) **Barn Elms Nature Reserve** to be created by the Wildfowl and Wetlands Trust. You may have noticed as you passed the old entrance lodge that the Trust has taken it over for its Barnes office.

Pepys picnicking

When you reach the entrance to the Wandsworth borough sports centre, keep to the left along the footpath. A small wood in the centre of the sports centre covers the site of Barn Elms House. The original manor house was home to several historical characters, including Elizabeth I's spymaster, Sir Francis Walsingham. In the 17th century the grounds appear to have been at least partly public, for they were often used for picnics (by Samuel Pepys among others) and for duels. In 1698 the Cartwright family built a new house, which was extended in the 1770s by the Hoare banking family. The last tenant (apart from the army during World War II) was the Ranelagh Club, an upper-class social and sporting club, founded in Fulham in 1878 and based at Barn Elms from 1884 until its demise in 1939. The much-abused house was finally demolished in 1954. Its ancient elms fell victim to Dutch elm disease 20 years later.

Along the towpath

When you reach the end of Queen Elizabeth Walk turn right along the towpath beside the Thames. On the towpath you pass a couple of boathouses. Across the river is Fulham Football Club. Ahead is Putney Bridge. After some distance you come to a little bridge crossing the mouth of the Beverley Brook. This little river is thought to be named after the beavers that once inhabited its banks. Turn right just before the bridge and follow the path as it winds along between the stream and the sports centre. The brook rises in the vicinity of Nonsuch Park in south London and flows for 8 miles (13 kilometres) before arriving here to join the Thames.

After a while you pass a modern bridge with green railings, wide enough to take a vehicle. Carry on past it along the path. Later, opposite a corner in the sports cen-tre fence, you come to a similar but much narrower bridge. Cross this bridge into Barnes Common and follow the path along the wire fence to the right. Keep to the path as it first goes to the right round the corner of the fence and then bears slightly left through a belt of trees. You emerge by some tennis courts. Keep going along the path between the courts and the Victorian cemetery – opened in 1854 when the old churchyard you passed in the village was full – until you come to a car park.

Sir William de Milbourne and Milbourne House

Cross the car park and turn right on the road. At Rocks Lane cross slightly to the left into the tarmac path across the common (there is a 'Toilets' sign at the entrance to the path). Follow this path for some distance until you meet another, obviously more important one, crossing diagonally. Turn right on this and follow it back to the Beverley Brook. Here cross the bridge into the village green and take the left-hand avenue. When you reach the pond at the far end look diagonally left to the long house with the pebble-dash front. This and Essex House on its far side are the only two survivors of the colony of large houses that used to surround the green. Of the two, Milbourne House is by far the older and more important. Whereas Essex House only dates from the middle of the last century, Milbourne House has a history going right back to the 1400s when it belonged to Sir William de Milbourne, MP for Surrey in the 1370s. Later tenants included the 18th-century novelist Henry Fielding, to whom there is a commemorative plaque on the front. He lived here in the early 1750s and probably wrote his last book (*Amelia*) here.

From the pond turn left onto Station Road and then immediately right into Cleveland Road. Take the second left into Cambridge Road and follow it round to the right. As it bends right again into Cleveland Gardens, turn off it to the left to join Beverley Path and then immediately right along the path past some 19th-century cottages. Go under the railway line into Archway Street and then almost immediately right into Thorne Passage. You are now in the Westfields district of Barnes, the site of the great west field of the medieval manor. In those days Thorne Passage and Beverley Path formed a short cut across the fields by-passing Barnes for people walking between Mortlake and Putney. In the 19th century Westfield House, lived in by local brewer Benjamin Thorne, stood here. At the far end of the passage you pass, first, the old brick wall of Mr Thorne's residence and then the old coach house – now, appropriately, part of a garage.

Emerging from Thorne Passage, turn right on White Hart Lane and go straight over at the road junction into the short alley to the left of the riverside White Hart pub. This alley represents the boundary between the parishes of Barnes to your right and Mortlake to your left. Turn right now along the towpath and follow it past the upper section of The Terrace to Barnes Bridge Station where the walk ends.

Bexley

Location	12½ miles (20 kilometres) southeast of Charing Cross.
Transport	Bexley Station (overground trains from Charing Cross).
Features	**St Mary's Church**; **Hall Place and Bexley Local History Museum**; River Cray and water meadows; winding High Street with many 18th-century houses; Styleman's almshouses; **Bexley Cricket Club**.
Refreshments	*High Street* 16th-century King's Head pub, Chinese, Italian, Greek and Indian restaurants, fish and chip shop, Bon Appetit tearooms and sandwich bar, wine bar and brasserie, Bexley bakery, Old Mill pub-restaurant; *Bourne Road* Dennis the Butcher for award-winning pies; *Hall Place* (see map page 88) café and pub-restaurant.

The Kentish village of Bexley – meaning 'clearing among the box trees' – grew up at the point where two roads converged to cross the River Cray. One road led from Eltham to Dartford and the other from Crayford to Orpington. Today, these are represented respectively by Parkhill Road, Bexley High Street and Vicarage Road, and by Bourne Road, the High Street and North Cray Road.

The village was well established by the time of the Domesday survey. During the Middle Ages the Church of St Mary and the little rectory estate belonged to the Priory of Holy Trinity in Aldgate in London. From the Priory came the village's vicars. They lived in the medieval vicarage south of the church, which survived until the 1770s.

The main manor of Bexley, which included not just the village but the outlying hamlets of Blendon, Danson, Hurst, Upton and Welling, belonged to the great estate of the Archbishops of Canterbury. The archbishops did not live in the village, but they had a manor house there from which the village was governed. The manor house, rebuilt in the 18th century, still survives and can be seen – or rather glimpsed – on the walk.

In the 1530s the Crown acquired the manor and almost immediately leased it to a rich London merchant and ex-Lord Mayor of London, Sir John Champneis. Using old stone salvaged from demolished monasteries, Champneis built himself a fine house about 1 mile (1.6 kilometres) northeast of the village, on the north bank of the Cray. In the early 1600s James I granted the manor and Champneis' house to the antiquary and herald William Camden, author of Camden's *Britannia*. When Camden died in 1623 he left the estate to Oxford University to fund a history professorship. The university remained Lord of Bexley Manor into modern times.

Local history museum

In the meantime, the house – known as Hall Place – was acquired by Sir Robert Austen in 1649, the year of Charles I's execution. Adding a brick section on the south side that faces the river, he more than doubled the house in size. Today, half silvery Tudor stone and half weathered 17th-century brick, the building is more or less as Austen left it at his death in 1666. Now owned by the council, it houses offices and the **Bexley Local History Museum**, and together with its immaculate gardens, forms one of the highlights of the walk.

Hall Place was the big house of Bexley village, but there were several more mansions in the parish, mostly to the north and west, for the village is in the southeast. The two most important were probably Blendon and Danson. In the early 15th century Blendon was home to the archbishop's park keeper, Henry Castilayn, to whom there is a brass memorial in the village church. Danson was acquired by East India Company director Sir John Boyd in the mid-18th century. The architect Sir Robert Taylor built him a Palladian house in the 1760s and Capability Brown landscaped the park. Both house and park survive, but are unfortunately too far from the village to be included in the walk. Blendon was demolished and built over in the 1930s.

Water meadows and woods

In the 1770s Bexley was described as having many handsome, modern-built houses, inhabited by genteel families of fortune. Many of these houses survive today and are seen on the walk. Also still in existence and seen on the walk are the old water meadows bordering the river and the woods crowning the high ground to the south. What Bexley has lost as a result of suburbanization – following the arrival of the railway in 1866 – are its farmland and the great heath on the high ground to the north, crossed by the main road from London to Dover.

Once the villagers' common grazing land, the heath was enclosed in 1819 and subsequently developed. Within a few decades the village of New Bexley – now Bexleyheath – was bigger than the old one. Its growth took the pressure off Old Bexley and helped ensure the latter's survival as a pretty little village literally right on the edge of London, with one side built up and the other meadow and woodland. Today, with the new Dover road cutting it off from Hall Place and a constant stream of cars thronging the narrow High Street, traffic is Bexley's main problem, but as a London village it is hardly unusual in that.

THE BEXLEY WALK

Start and finish Bexley Station.
Distance 3¼ miles (5.2 kilometres).

Turn right out of the station and follow Station Approach down the hill to the junction with the High Street. Turn right and then immediately right again into Tanyard Lane. This takes you through the former tanning yard and under the railway line into the riverside meadowland. Across the meadows you can see the backs of some of the houses in North Cray Road. Follow the path until you reach **Bexley Cricket Club**. Founded by 1746, the club is one of the oldest in Kent and has been based at this pitch since about 1840. Match scores survive from 1802. The most celebrated match in club history took place in 1805, the year of the Battle of Trafalgar, when Bexley dismissed Kent for only six runs.

Turn right at the car park and go back under the railway line into Manor Way. When you reach Hurst Road cross slightly to the left and go into a footpath (the entrance is marked by a 'No Cycling' sign). This brings you out on Parkhill Road, the old main road from Eltham to Dartford. The houses on the other side of Parkhill Road, built from 1869 onwards for middle-class commuters attracted to Bexley by the new railway, were the first signs that the old country village was changing into a London suburb. St John's Church was completed for the new inhabitants in 1881 and became a parish church in its own right in 1936.

Almshouses and workhouse
Turn right past the church, and playground, and walk down the hill into the winding village High Street, which begins at the junction with Hurst Road. On the left,

BEXLEY

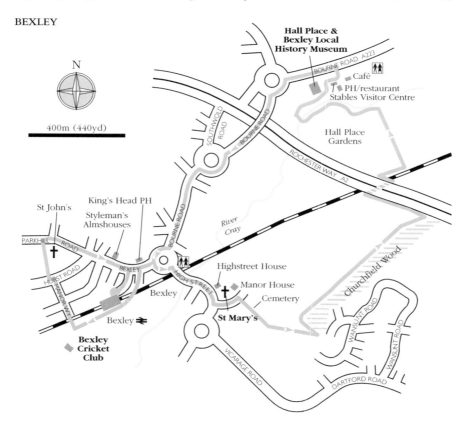

the long low building is Styleman's Almshouses. John Styleman made a fortune in India and owned Danson before Sir John Boyd. He died in 1734 and left money for the almshouses, but they were not built until several years after his widow's death in 1750. Ahead, the Georgian house with steeply pitched roof on the corner by the station entrance represents another 18th-century method of dealing with the poor: from the 1780s until 1834 this house served as the parish workhouse.

Beyond the old workhouse is the Railway Tavern, and then on the left is No. 57 High Street, otherwise known as Jackson House. Built in 1676 with a double-height porch, this is one of Bexley's finest houses and in the 18th century was lived in by the local builder. Still on the left, the building with the clock tower is the Freemantle Hall, built in 1894 as a public hall for the village. Just beyond is the 16th-century King's Head pub, probably the oldest building in the village centre apart from the church.

The mill

When you reach the little roundabout at the junction with Bourne Road, follow the High Street round to the right past the George pub (dating from at least 1717) and cross under the railway line once more. On the far side of the railway line you come to the river crossing. The Old Mill restaurant on the right is a modern replica of the 18th-century corn mill, built in 1775 and burned down in 1966. Beyond is Cray House, built at the same time as the mill, possibly for the mill owner. The cottages on the opposite side of the road are mainly early 19th century with the exception of No. 101 in the middle, which has a bit of style and which probably dates from the mid-18th century.

Following the High Street round to the right you come to the wisteria-clad Highstreet House, the finest house in the village with the exception of the Manor House. Built in 1761 over the foundations of an earlier house, it was, as the plaque on the front states, the home of the Kent historian and antiquary John Thorpe. Born in 1715, the son of a Rochester surgeon, he lived here until 1789, when his wife Catharina died. Thorpe died three years later. There is a plaque to his wife on the churchyard side of the garden wall.

Brasses and monuments

Walk beside the churchyard wall and turn left into Manor Road. **St Mary's**, with its unique cone and pyramid spire, dates from the early Middle Ages. Inside, besides the Castilayn brass, there are Champneis, Austen and Styleman monuments. Outside, the oldest tomb – belonging to the Payne family – dates from 1603. On the right you pass the entrance to Manor Farm House and then the footpath leading up the hill to an area that used to be called, for obvious reasons, Coldblow. Then go past the modern church hall, built on the site of the medieval tithe barn demolished about 1910, and the Victorian Manor Cottage.

Manor Road finishes at the entrance to the old manor farmyard, now the Bexley Sand and Ballast Company. The Manor House is to the left, but is hardly visible unless you go into the churchyard and peer over the fence. The walk turns right here into the lane leading to the churchyard extension, opened in 1857 and in 1990 turned into a protected ecological area. If you look back when you reach the corner of the wall, there is a good view of the upper part of the manor house across the old farm orchard.

Carry straight on along the now narrow path heading uphill through the cemetery. At the end, go through the gate and continue up the hill on the tarmac path leading through meadow land towards Churchfield Wood on top of the hill. Just before the path forks, turn left into Churchfield Wood (there is a Cray Riverway waymark here) and follow the lower of the two paths (the one on the edge of the wood next to the fence). From the path you can clearly see the sand and gravel workings beside the Cray.

When you reach the far side of the wood by the main road, exit via the stile and turn left down the tarmac path towards the railway line. Follow the path underneath the road and then round to the right, keeping tight to the embankment. When you reach the path leading up to the road level, take it and cross the bridge over the railway line, walking into the face of the oncoming traffic. On the far side, turn right down the steps back onto ground level and go through the gate into the grassy area beside the railway line, following the Cray Riverway waymark. Walk straight along here with the railway on your right and the hedge boundary of Hall Place gardens on your left. At the corner of the hedge turn left and follow the hedge all the way up to the river. Here turn left again and go straight on through the gate into the Hall Place grounds and walk along beside the river.

Hall Place and gardens

Beyond the first bridge – leading into the maintenance yard and marking the approximate site of the old watermill demolished in 1926 – **Hall Place** comes into view, presenting its 17th-century brick face. At the second bridge, cross the river and turn back towards the house, aiming for the gap in the hedge. You can then see the older stone part of the house and how the later section was simply added onto the south side. The Tudor part has two wings projecting to the north, but the 17th-century part is a quadrangle with a courtyard in the middle.

Once through the hedge look left and you will see the topiary garden started by the last private occupant of the house, the Countess of Limerick. She died in 1943. The figures at the front – looking like large teddy bears, but in fact intended to be heraldic beasts – were added by Bexley Council a decade after the countess's demise to mark the Queen's coronation. Follow the path round to the east side of the house where the public entrance is and then turn right past the granary (brought from Manor Farm in Bexley village in 1988) and the stables (now the Visitor Centre). Go out of the gate into the car park (café and toilets ahead) and turn left.

Victorian and Edwardian building

Turn left again out of the car park and walk along Bourne Road in front of the north front of the house, screened from the road by a fine pair of 18th-century gates. Continue on up to the roundabout and turn left. Follow the pavement over the motorway and River Shuttle back towards Bexley, which you re-enter at the second roundabout. As you approach the village centre once more, you pass on the right various institutions that reflect the growth of the village in the Victorian era and later: the National Schools, opened in 1834 and converted to industrial use 140 years afterwards; the Victoria Homes almshouses, built to mark Queen Victoria's Diamond Jubilee in 1897; the local library built at the junction of Albert Road in 1912; and the 1905 Baptist chapel across Albert Road from the library.

Across Bourne Road from the library is the old Refell's Brewery, in business from 1874 until 1956 and now converted into a business park. Further on, also on the left, you pass the entrance to a row of old workshops leading down to the railway viaduct, and then the original 1846 Baptist chapel with a louvre in the roof, converted into shops many years ago. At the roundabout you meet up with the High Street once more. Turn right here and make your way back to the station (the entrance is by the Costcutter Supermarket), where the walk ends.

Blackheath

Location	6½ miles (10.5 kilometres) southeast of Charing Cross.
Transport	Blackheath Station (overground trains from Charing Cross).
Features	Black Heath; some of the finest Georgian architecture in London (notably The Paragon); **All Saints Church**; Morden College; the Cator Estate.
Refreshments	*Tranquil Vale* pubs, tapas bar, bakery, patisserie, delicatessen and Indian restaurant;
	Montpelier Vale Café Rouge, Italian restaurants and wine bars, Indian/Nepalese restaurant;
	on the walk Hare and Billet pub (first half of walk – see map page 94), Princess of Wales pub (second half of walk – see map page 94).

Blackheath takes its name from the heath that divides it from Greenwich, its riverside neighbour to the north. Some say the name comes from the black, barren soil of the heath, but it is more probably a corruption of 'bleak'. Certainly the heath, a treeless plateau 125 feet (38 metres) above sea level, is empty and windswept enough today. In the days when it was covered with gorse and scrub and infested with highwaymen and footpads it must have been truly forbidding.

The heath was originally waste or common land for the inhabitants of the four neighbouring manors of Lewisham, Greenwich, Charlton and Kidbrooke. In those days Blackheath village did not exist in the way it does today. There were just a few large houses on high ground overlooking the valley of the Kid Brook and the heath beyond, and some cottages and a pub down in the dip where the roads from Lee and Lewisham met to cross the Kid Brook.

Having come together to cross the Kid, these two roads then divided again, one heading east to join the main road across the heath (now the A2 from London to Dover) and the other heading west to join the same road but going in the London direction. It was at this latter junction – on the west side of the heath – that the first developments in Blackheath took place when the new Lords of Lewisham manor, the Earls of Dartmouth, built Dartmouth Row and neighbouring streets in the 1690s.

Speculators move in

Later, in the 18th century, fine houses were built by speculators along the south side of the heath, first on the western side and then, right at the end of the century, on the eastern side. Tradesmen moved into the area to service these houses and so the village gradually came into existence – but at the low point where the Lee and

Lewisham roads crossed the river and not on the main road close to Lord Dartmouth's mansion and surrounding streets.

In the 19th century the river was covered over and the railway laid out along its length. Development proceeded apace after the opening of Blackheath Station in 1849. Much of this development took place on the largest single property in the area, the 293-acre (118.5-hectare) Cator Estate. The old name for the Cator Estate was Wricklemarsh and it was as such that the Blount family bought it in the late 16th century. In 1669 the estate was sold to Turkey merchant Sir John Morden and his wife. Having no children to leave their property to, the Mordens founded a large almshouse on the eastern edge of their estate for Turkey Company merchants who had been rather less successful than Sir John. Attributed to Wren, Morden College was built in spacious landscaped grounds on a knoll overlooking the Kid Brook in 1695. It survives, much expanded, to this day and features on the walk.

After Lady Morden's death in 1721, Wricklemarsh was bought by Sir Gregory Page. One of the few people to escape from the South Sea financial scandal in 1720 with his fortune intact, he demolished the old Tudor house and built a vast new one on the heights overlooking the Kid valley and the heath beyond. It was all in vain, however, for his nephew and heir found it far too large and promptly sold it to a self-made businessman from Beckenham, timber merchant John Cator. Cator auctioned off the fabric of the house and developed the northern fringe of the estate beside the heath into what is now Montpelier Row, South Row and The Paragon. Building on the interior of the estate started a little later − in about 1806 − and continued over a considerable period of time.

Starting and finishing at Blackheath Station, the walk takes in the Cator Estate and other Georgian and Victorian developments on the surrounding heights. It also, of course, includes the village centre and parts of the heath, but unfortunately not the Dartmouth streets of the 1690s, which are a little too far away.

THE BLACKHEATH WALK
Start and finish Blackheath Station.
Distance 3 miles (4.8 kilometres).

Turn left out of the station and walk through the centre of Blackheath village. This is the low point where originally the two roads from Lee and Lewisham joined to cross the Kid Brook. In early days it was known as Blount's Hole, after the residents of the nearby Wricklemarsh estate. During Lady Susannah Morden's long widowhood in the early 18th century it acquired the new, and somewhat less flattering, name of Dowager's Bottom!

When the road divides in front of the triangle, bear left into Tranquil Vale and walk up the hill. Before the village developed in the second half of the 18th century there were just a few cottages here, a public well called Queen Elizabeth's Well (its site is in Tranquil Passage which runs through the middle of the triangle) and the Crown pub, which you soon come to on the corner of Camden Row. Tranquil Vale was the beginning of the road that led off across the heath towards London; its sister, Montpelier Vale, headed off west in the Dover direction. Go past the entrance to Camden Row and the well-known Mary Evans Picture Library and you come out on the southern edge of the 275-acre (111-hectare) Black Heath. To the right is **All Saints**, the parish church, not built until the mid-19th century. Ahead is a cluster of buildings in the middle of the heath, hiding what is known as Blackheath Vale. The Vale is actually a huge pit dug in the days when Blackheath was an important source of sand and gravel. After World War II most of the pits were filled in with bomb rubble, but the Vale had long since been colonized, not just by cottages, but by a livery stable, a school and even a brewery. Today only the houses and the school survive.

City merchant

Walk on up the hill. At the top you come to a handsome semicircle of houses composed of Lloyd's Place, Grote's Buildings and Grote's Place. Lloyd's Place was built in the 1770s by John Lamb and takes its name from John Lloyd, a resident of No. 3 in the 1780s. Grote's Buildings and Place were a largely speculative development by City merchant Andrew Grote in the 1760s. The land belonged to Morden College, which wanted to create a fund for paying its chaplain. Grote built Lindsey House – the red-brick detached house behind the trees at the left end – for himself and then sold the other, terraced, houses to recoup his investment. All these houses enjoy fine views across the heath to All Saints Church and South Row and, beyond, to the houses along Shooters Hill Road and the spire of St John's Church.

Walk straight on across the green towards the clump of trees surrounding the Hare and Billet pond, probably an old gravel pit. As you pass between the pond and

BLACKHEATH

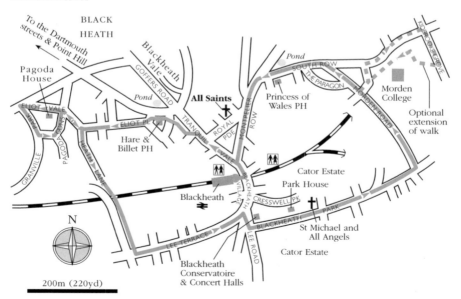

the pub you can see to the right the roofs of the houses in Blackheath Vale. Straight ahead in the distance are houses built on the west side of the heath close to Lord Dartmouth's original development of the 1690s. The most prominent house – white stucco with a pitched roof – is actually a pair and dates from 1776.

Turn left at the pub and cut across past Eliot Cottages to Eliot Place. The houses here were built between 1795 and 1802 on land belonging to the Eliot family, Earls of St Germans (hence St Germans House at No. 11). The central house, No. 6, is perhaps the most handsome. Built in 1797, it became the home and private observatory of merchant and amateur astronomer Stephen Groombridge five years later. Now Morden College almshouse uses it for out-pensioners. The last house in the terrace, No. 2, was the home of naval officer and polar explorer Sir James Clark Ross, after whom Ross Island and Ross Sea off Antarctica are named. Next door is the grand Heathfield House, built for Rotherhithe shipowner John Brent. The earliest and grandest house in Eliot Place, it has now been given a modern extension and divided up into flats.

Pagoda House

Go straight on down the hill into Eliot Vale and then up the far side, following the road round to the right. As you cross the entrance to Pagoda Gardens look left and you will see the house with the curly roof that gives the road its name. Standing by the pillar box, you can see away to the right on the other side of the heath a red-brick house called Ranger's House (see page 115). Next to it another mansion used to stand called Montagu House. Montagu House's grounds were mainly on this side of the heath, laid out on the south-facing slope of the hill, and the 18th-century Pagoda House was a kind of summer house. When George IV's wife Caroline was living at Montagu House in the early 19th century she was a regular user of Pagoda House and it was here that she was rumoured to have had her affairs and to have housed her illegitimate children. In reality she probably got up to nothing more suspicious than overseeing her little nursery school and tending her garden. The king had Montagu House knocked down in 1815 and divorced the unfortunate Caroline five years later.

Follow the road round to the left past Aberdeen Terrace, which consists of large 19th-century houses built on land once belonging to the Pagoda. When the Terrace turns left, keep going and on the far side of the green, behind the bushes, turn left down Granville Park. When you get to Pagoda Gardens turn left and then at the T-junction turn left again. Now you have a close-up view of Pagoda House.

Quaggy valley

Back on Eliot Vale, turn right and then a little further on right again into Heath Lane. Passing Eliot Vale House on the left and turning into a footpath, this goes down the hill into the former valley of the Kid Brook, crosses the railway line and the old course of the river and then climbs up the far side to meet Lee Terrace, the road connecting Blackheath (to your left) with Lewisham (to your right). Some distance ahead, down in the valley of the Quaggy river, lies Lee. The church here, St Margaret's, is Lee's new parish church, built in 1841. The ruins of the original one stand in the closed graveyard 100 yards (90 metres) or so to the right. The astronomer Edmond Halley, of Halley's Comet fame, is buried here.

Turn left on Lee Terrace and head back towards Blackheath, passing some fine 19th-century houses and some less impressive 20th-century infilling. As you pass Dacre Park there is a good view to the right over the Quaggy valley.

The Cator Estate

You arrive back in the village at the point where Lee Terrace meets Lee Road coming in from the right. Cross over to the partly ivy-covered Blackheath Conservatoire (founded 1881) and turn right. Immediately beyond the Concert Halls turn left through the gates into Blackheath Park and the Cator Estate. With the exception of Kidbrooke Grove near Morden College and the fine houses round the heath, the Cator Estate was, and indeed still is, the most select part of Blackheath village.

Laid out along the crest of the ridge dividing the valleys of the Kid and the Quaggy rivers, Blackheath Park is the main thoroughfare of the estate and the location of some of its earliest and finest houses. The row on the left starting at No. 7, for example, dates from about 1806. Just beyond it is a wooden fence atop a low brick wall. Behind here, set well back in a large garden, is the earliest and finest house on the estate, a silvery stone mansion constructed in 1788 with materials salvaged from Sir Gregory Page's house. Since the end of the last century it has belonged to the Catholic Church.

Now comes a row of three pretty detached villas and then St Michael and All Angels church, built in 1828. The junction of Blackheath Park with Pond Road next to the church marks the site of the great house built by Sir Gregory Page in the 1720s. From its hilltop site it had wonderful views north over the heath to Greenwich and south over the Quaggy valley.

Gounod's plaque

Carry on along Blackheath Park and then at the end turn left into Morden Road. No. 17 just beyond The Plantation on the right has a blue plaque on it recording the stay of French composer Charles Gounod in October 1857. At the end of Morden Road you leave the Cator Estate by another set of gates and return to the heath. To the right is Morden College, set in immaculate grounds. It is not very easy to see the actual College building from this point, but a better view can be obtained from the footpath (illustrated on the map) which starts to your right at the end of the green railings and runs all the way through the College grounds.

The Paragon

Walk straight on up the hill onto the heath. To your right is St German's Place. Ahead you can see Greenwich Park and the Canary Wharf Tower beyond. To your left is The Paragon, the first section of the line of houses built along the northern perimeter of the Cator estate from 1795 onwards. As its immodest name suggests, The Paragon is the finest Georgian set piece in Blackheath and one of the finest of its period anywhere in London. As you walk past you will see that it is composed of seven blocks linked by colonnades to form a crescent looking northeast across the heath towards St German's Place. They were designed, as were South Row and Montpelier Row which follow, by surveyor Michael Searles. Each block contained two houses so there was a total of 14 residences in all. Unfortunately they were very badly damaged during World War II, but afterwards they were acquired by a responsible developer to whom their restoration was something of a personal crusade. The original 14 houses are now split up into 100 flats.

Colonnade House

South Row continues the Cator Estate perimeter development. Cator Manor, the first house, is not an old manor house but a neo-Georgian house built on the site of outbuildings blitzed during World War II. Pond Road, named after the remnant of an ornamental lake that existed up until 1955, is the old drive up to Sir Gregory Page's Wricklemarsh. Beyond Pond Road more modern housing replaces another section of South Row destroyed during World War II. Then comes Colonnade House, built in 1804 for William Randall, shipbuilding partner of John Brent whom we encountered earlier at Heathfield House. Brent, Randall and a third partner made a fortune building warships at the time of the Revolutionary Wars with France.

At the end of South Row you come to the Princess of Wales pub (named after George IV's wife Caroline, who was never actually crowned). A plaque on the front records the fact that it was here in 1871 that the English team for the first-ever rugby international was selected. The team included four players from Blackheath Rugby Club, one of the oldest in the country.

Blackheath has always been used for sport. Golf was played here from early times, the old sand and gravel pits making excellent bunkers. James I (also James VI of Scotland, the 'home' of golf) is said to have introduced the sport to the area while staying at Greenwich Palace in the early 17th century. The local club, in existence by the 1780s, later developed into the Royal Blackheath Golf Club and is now generally regarded as the oldest in England. Since 1923 it has been based at Eltham.

Round the corner from the Princess of Wales pub, South Row turns into Montpelier Row. At the far end of the Row you return to the centre of the village. Follow Montpelier Vale down the hill to the junction with Tranquil Vale and make your way back to the station, where the walk ends.

Carshalton

Location	10 miles (16 kilometres) southwest of Charing Cross.
Transport	Carshalton Station (overground trains from Victoria).
Features	**All Saints Church**; the source of the River Wandle; **Carshalton House and Water Tower**; Carshalton Park and grotto; **Sutton Ecology Centre** and nature reserve; **Sutton Heritage Centre**; Grove Park, **Little Holland House** (not on walk – see map page 100).
Refreshments	*village centre (east of church)* pubs, Bon Appetit sandwich bar and deli, Village bakery and coffee house, fish and chip shop, burger bar, Indian restaurant/takeaway, Woodman's wine bar; *village centre (west of church)* Greyhound Hotel, tearoom in Heritage Centre.

Carshalton lies on the old road from Croydon to Sutton, about 1 mile (1.6 kilometres) east of Sutton. Behind are the chalk downs where the Epsom Derby is raced. North stretches a flat plain through which the Wandle river snakes its way towards the Thames. The larger of the two streams that join at Hackbridge to form the Wandle begins in the ponds at Carshalton. Originally these ponds were filled naturally by springs in the chalk. Now they have to be topped up from the mains because of a general lowering of the water table in the area. This general lowering has also caused all Carshalton's other streams and ponds – streams and ponds that once made the village famous for its trout and water cress – to dry up, as you will see on the walk.

The village High Street runs east–west along the foot of the downs. To the south, ascending the hill to the former common fields on the plateau, the old roads were Park Hill and Park Lane, embracing Carshalton Park between them. To the north, the main roads were West Street and North Street, converging after about three-quarters of a mile (1.2 kilometres) at Wrythe Green and then branching into three – one highway leading to Morden and Wimbledon, the middle one to Merton and Wandsworth, and the easterly one to Mitcham and thence to London, crossing the Wandle at Hackbridge. West Street Lane connected West Street and North Street and then continued east along the Wandle as Mill Lane, its name reflecting the presence of many water mills in this industrial part of the village.

Wandle mills

From at least the time of the Domesday Book there was a corn mill in the village. But from the late 17th century onwards, various entrepreneurs began to harness the

Wandle's power to drive other kinds of mills. Industrial milling reached its peak in the late 18th century and finally died out about a century after that. At various times the Carshalton mills produced – besides flour – paper, leather, snuff, drugs, linseed oil, sheet copper and gunpowder.

When it was just a small country village, Carshalton was dominated by three large houses whose estates intruded right into the centre of the village. To the west was Carshalton House, built in the time of Queen Anne (1702–14) by Edward Carleton and later added to by Sir John Fellowes. In the centre, between the High Street and the Wandle, was Stone Court, later The Grove. The original Stone Court – its name indicating the strangeness of the building material in an area where chalk and flint, and then brick, predominated – was built in the 15th century by Nicholas Gaynesford, at one time sheriff of Surrey. Then, south of the High Street, on the slope of the down, stood Mascalls, later Carshalton Place and later still Carshalton Park. Carshalton Park was bought in 1696 by merchant Sir William Scawen. The Scawens sold up in 1781 and were succeeded by the Taylors, a family of West Indian sugar planters and slave owners. Mascalls was the manor house of the village and the Scawens, followed by the Taylors, were the lords of the manor. Carshalton House and The Grove still stand and feature on the walk. All that remains of Mascalls is a large part of its park (also seen on the walk): the house itself was demolished in 1927.

Unlike its neighbour to the north, Mitcham, Carshalton never became a rural retreat for merchants and courtiers from London. The extra few miles needed to reach it seem to have made all the difference. Or maybe it was the paucity of good sites for houses. Whatever the reason, Carshalton's transition from rural village to London suburb had to wait until the arrival of the railway in 1868. Even then it was some decades before pressure for development really built up. As late as 1890 the three large estates strait-jacketing the expansion of the village were all still in private hands and undeveloped. The following year the first new roads were laid out in Carshalton Park and suburbanization then proceeded apace.

THE CARSHALTON WALK
Start and finish Carshalton Station.
Distance 2¾ miles (4.4 kilometres).

Come out of Carshalton Station and turn right down the hill. At the bottom turn left into West Street and walk in the direction of the village. Traditional weatherboarded houses, painted white, are a feature of this part of Carshalton. Beyond the Racehorse pub, the park wall and the Water Tower of Carshalton House come into view. Just beyond the Water Tower a gate in the wall allows you a view of the house.

Carshalton House
Having built **Carshalton House** around 1707, Edward Carleton went bankrupt in 1713. Two years later merchant Sir John Fellowes purchased it but, having become head of the South Sea Company, he encountered problems of his own in 1720 when the Company went bust. Carshalton House was confiscated to compensate

the victims of the crash and in 1724 Fellowes' brother had to buy it back for the family for twice the amount Sir John had paid for it less than ten years before. In possession once more, Sir John added the **Water Tower** to the amenities of the mansion. Its prime purpose, achieved through a rooftop reservoir, was to supply water to the house – even to the upper floors – but it also contained an orangery, a changing room and a Delft-tiled plunge bath, one of the earliest in the country.

In 1850 the last of Carshalton House's private occupants moved out and the Board of Ordnance moved in, using the house as a school for its military cadets. In 1892 the Daughters of the Cross arrived and opened St Philomena's girls' school. Over 100 years later the school is still here. Founded in Liège in 1833, the Daughters are a Roman Catholic organization and carry on the educational work of the convent of St Philomena.

CARSHALTON

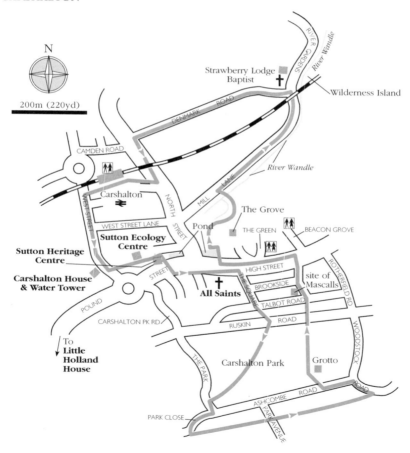

Ecology Centre

Cross West Street at the gate into Carshalton House and walk along Festival Walk by the side of the dried-up watercourse. Long ago a stream from the chalk downs used to flow into a lake in the grounds of Carshalton House and thence down this channel into the Wandle. The Old Rectory on the left, built about the time of Queen Anne, like Carshalton House, and raised well up to protect it from flooding was never the rectory as such, but the private home of a number of well-to-do rectors in the 18th century. The village's official rectory was in the High Street until it was pulled down for a shopping precinct in the 1960s. The present rectory is a modern house up the hill behind the church. Since the 1930s the Old Rectory has been public property and is now used, along with the grounds of a large 19th-century house called The Lodge, as the **Ecology Centre** of the Borough of Sutton. The Centre's nature reserve is well worth a visit. Just outside the main entrance stands the tallest London plane tree in Britain (see the plaque at its base).

Festival Walk takes you past the Ecology Centre and brings you out at Carshalton's famous ponds, one of two major sources of the Wandle (the other is at Whaddon ponds a few miles to the east, near Croydon). Originally there was only one pond here, but the building of a causeway across the middle into North Street during the Middle Ages divided it into two. Since that time the near pond has been public property and the far one part of the Stone Court/Grove estate.

Arts and Crafts

The Lodge to your left was built in 1866 on what had been the orchard and kitchen garden of Stone Court. Ahead right is a fine view of the church and the High Street. Immediately to the right is Honeywood, a house dating from the 17th century and once the home of the 19th-century author and civil servant Mark Rutherford, real name William Hale White. White lived in several houses in the neighbourhood and, being a friend of William Morris and John Ruskin, eventually built himself an Arts and Crafts-inspired house in Park Hill. Honeywood was later bought by the council and in 1990 converted into the **Sutton Heritage Centre** and local history museum. (Coincidentally, a few doors up from White's Park Hill house there is another Arts and Crafts house – **Little Holland House**, the home of the 20th-century designer and craftsman Frank Dickinson.)

Anne Boleyn's Well

Turn right past the entrance to Honeywood (note the dry watercourse running under the house) and walk up to the main road. This is the east end of Pound Street: the name comes from the village pound where stray animals were rounded up pending collection by their owners. Ahead is the elegant Greyhound Hotel, Carshalton's oldest and principal inn. Cross the road to the hotel and turn left. Opposite the entrance to North Street, the disused well surrounded by railings at the foot of Church Hill is known locally as Anne Boleyn's Well, Anne Boleyn being Henry VIII's second wife. A modern statue of the Queen is set into the corner of the new house in Church Hill. Legend has it that the Queen's horse kicked at a boulder here one day and in doing so brought a spring gushing forth. The truth is that in pre-Reformation days there was a little chapel here dedicated to Our Lady of Boulogne. Over time the name Boulogne simply became corrupted into Boleyn.

Monuments and stables

Pass to the right of the well and follow the raised path that leads past the entrance to the church. Medieval in origin, **All Saints** was enlarged to such an extent in the 1890s that the old nave was relegated to the status of a subsidiary chapel. Here is to be found the Purbeck marble tomb of Nicholas Gaynesford, the builder of the original Stone Court. Many other old monuments, including those of Sir William Scawen and Sir John Fellowes, are also in the church.

Just beyond the church is one of the oldest buildings in Carshalton, an ancient butcher's shop, now a wine bar. Carry on past the shop, turn right into The Square and walk up past the library. On the other side of the road is the remaining section of the Carshalton Park orangery, later used as stables. Before streets were built along the bottom side of Carshalton Park, The Square was a wide cul-de-sac, its top end closed off by the park wall and the stable entrance. Carry on up the road, cross Talbot Road into the path, cross Ruskin Road and enter Carshalton Park.

Squire of Carshalton

After he became squire of Carshalton in 1696, Sir William Scawen planned to replace the ancient Mascalls with a brand new house. Unfortunately, he died before he was ready to start building. His nephew and heir managed to complete the 2-mile (3-kilometre) park wall, the orangery and various other structures, but then the money ran out. So the great new house Thomas Scawen had commissioned from the Italian architect Giacomo Leonie was never built and Mascalls remained the mansion of the estate until the property was sold for development in 1895. Part of the park was developed and part – complete with some fine old trees – preserved as a public open space.

Ahead, the deep hole called the Hogpit started out before the Scawens' time as a chalk pit and was later excavated to form a deep pond, now dried up. Branch right up the hill, with the Hogpit on your left, and when the path stops continue straight on across the park. Exit opposite the hospital and turn left, occasionally glancing back for the views. At the top, before the road bends left, turn right into The Park cul-de-sac. Walk to the far end, continue on along the footpath and then turn left when you meet the track. This was formerly an old road that ran across the hill just outside the park wall: large sections of the latter survive on the left-hand side. Cross the first road you come to – Park Avenue – and continue on down into the low point. Then climb. At the end you will have to negotiate an overgrown section before finally emerging on Woodstock Road. Here turn left, and then left again, into Ashcombe Road and then right into the park once more.

The grotto

At this point you are right on top of the grotto, one of the park features built by Thomas Scawen in the 18th century. From the shell-covered grotto, which housed a source spring of the Wandle, water flowed down towards the High Street over a series of cascades, passing close by Mascalls near the bottom. Near where it joined the Wandle the stream powered a mill forming part of the Carshalton Park estate. Nowadays the grotto is derelict and the canal dry, but the whole structure is still a most impressive feature.

Mascalls

Walk down the left-hand side of the canal under the avenue of trees. Exit the park crossing Ruskin Road and continue. Talbot Road crosses the canal by means of a handsome little balustraded bridge, possibly a feature of the gardens around Mascalls, for the old house stood just here on the left until the 1920s.

When you reach the High Street, turn left, cross at the traffic lights and continue. Opposite the Coach and Horses turn right through the gates into the grounds of The Grove. In common with both Carshalton's other main estates, The Grove — named after a grove of trees with a temple in the middle cleared away during the 19th century — has passed through many hands since its early days as Stone Court, or Gainsford's Place, as it was later known. The present house, a Victorian-Edwardian hotchpotch, is largely the work of Sir Samuel Barrow, a wealthy tanner who owned the house between 1896 and 1923. The local authority bought it the following year and now uses it for offices.

Follow the path round to the left by the lake and then, before crossing the 18th-century bridge over the outflow, turn right, keeping the water on your left. Near the first bridge you come to stood what was called the Upper Mill, the original Carshalton corn mill, which finally went out of service in the 1880s after at least 800 years of operation. Barrow later used the mill's power source to drive electricity-generating turbines for his house. At the second bridge, cross the Wandle and turn right into Mill Lane. On the left the 19th-century mill workers' cottages still survive, but on the right the mills where so many of Carshalton's population once worked (nearly 60 per cent in the early 19th century) have recently been cleared away and replaced by housing.

Butter Hill

Continue along Mill Lane. Just before the railway bridge you pass one of the original bridges over the river leading into Butter Hill. The snuff mill driven by the grotto canal in Carshalton Park stood about halfway up the hill on the right. Carry on under the bridge to the entrance of Denmark Road. Ahead on the right you can see the signboard at the entrance to Wilderness Island, a 6-acre (2.5-hectare) nature reserve bordered by the Wandle and run by the Ecology Centre. Long before the railway arrived, the land covered by the reserve formed part of the rather larger Shepley estate, an industrial area first developed by gunpowder-maker Josias Dewye in 1692. Dewye lived across the road in a large house rebuilt in the 18th century as Strawberry Lodge. This still stands opposite the reserve entrance and is now owned by the Baptist Church, by whom it has recently been comprehensively restored.

Turn left now into Denmark Road. Follow this round to the end and then turn left into North Street. Go under the railway line and then right up the incline to the station entrance, where the walk ends.

Dulwich

Location	5 miles (8 kilometres) south of Charing Cross.
Transport	North Dulwich Station (overground trains from London Bridge), West Dulwich Station (overground trains from Victoria).
Features	Dulwich College (old and new versions); **Dulwich Picture Gallery**; Georgian houses in Dulwich Village; Dulwich Park and Dulwich Woods; last surviving tollgate in London; views of the City and West End from Sydenham Hill.
Refreshments	*Dulwich village* Greyhound pub, Le Piaf café-bar-brasserie, Bella Pasta restaurant; *Dulwich Park* café (see map page 106); *Sydenham Hill* Dulwich Wood House pub (see map page 106).

Although one is hardly aware of it today, Dulwich lies in the bottom of a shallow valley, bounded on the north by Denmark Hill and Dog Kennel Hill and on the south by Sydenham Hill and One Tree Hill, Honor Oak. The name is supposed to mean 'the meadow where dill grows'.

The village is one of the oldest in London. The earliest reference to it occurs in a Saxon charter dated 967. After the Norman Conquest the manor was granted by Henry I to the Priory of Bermondsey (see Rotherhithe and Bermondsey, page 136). The Priory continued to own it throughout the Middle Ages until the dissolution of the monasteries when it was seized by Henry VIII and granted to the Calton family (remembered today in Calton Avenue).

The most significant event in Dulwich's history occurred in the early 17th century, when the estate was bought by Edward Alleyn. Born in 1566, Alleyn (pronounced Allen) was one of the leading actors of the Elizabethan stage. He was also a successful businessman and impresario, with stakes in a theatre and in a bull- and bear-baiting arena. In 1604 he reached the summit of his career when he was appointed Joint Master of the Royal Bears, Bulls and Mastiff Dogs, a lucrative post which made him an extremely wealthy man.

College of God's Gift

Alleyn bought the Manor of Dulwich in 1605. At first he used the old moated manor house – known as Hall Place – as a summer residence, much as the prior of Bermondsey had done. But in 1613 he left his London home in Southwark and moved into Hall Place permanently. In the same year he began work on the College of God's Gift, a combined school and almshouse. The almspeople and schoolchildren came from the three London parishes with which Alleyn had connections, and from St Giles, Camberwell, of which Dulwich was part (it did not become a parish in its own right until late in the 19th century). Alleyn managed and paid for the College until his death in 1626 and then left the bulk of his estate to support it after he was gone.

Both almshouse and school still survive and feature on the walk. The almshouse is still in the original building, but the school, which has grown into one of Britain's leading public schools, moved into new premises on Dulwich Common to the south of the village in 1870.

With the improvement of roads in the 18th century, it became possible for merchants and stockbrokers in the City, and for civil servants in Whitehall, to live in Dulwich and commute daily to work. The College estate let off building plots to these commuters and they built fine Georgian houses down the eastern side of the long village street, set back from the road behind elm and chestnut trees and little green verges protected by white posts and chains. Opposite were the village shops and other business premises.

Dulwich Common

In 1805 the Common was enclosed and more fine houses were built along its northern fringe, along what is now the busy Dulwich Common road. The arrival of the railways in mid-century (West Dulwich, 1863, and North Dulwich, 1868) further increased pressure for development, and gradually all the land in the vicinity of Dulwich was built up, with the manor house and manor farm on the outskirts of the village disappearing in the process.

But the village itself was preserved, as was a green belt around it, composed of former farm, common and park land. Preservation of the historic village centre in its green oasis was due mainly to control exercised by the College estate and its resident architect and surveyor, first Sir Charles Barry, architect of the Houses of Parliament, and then his son, also called Charles. Today, even though leaseholders have the right to buy their freeholds, the College Estate retains control over the appearance of the village so it is likely to remain one of the most attractive and unspoilt in the capital for some time to come.

THE DULWICH WALK
Start and finish North Dulwich Station.
Distance 4¼ miles (6.8 kilometres).

Come out of North Dulwich's elegant station, designed by Dulwich College architect Charles Barry in 1868, and turn left down Red Post Hill (named after a red post that once stood at the summit of the hill pointing the way to Dulwich). At the crossroads go straight over and keep walking. Already you can tell you are on College property because of the old-fashioned finger posts and the post and chain fences around the grass verges.

After a while you come to a parade of shops called Commerce Row, built by the College in 1860 on the site of an old pond to cater for new Victorian housing

DULWICH

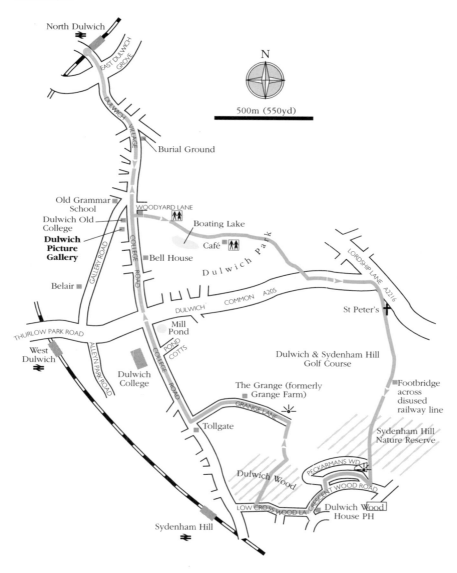

developments in the area. Opposite is another Victorian building housing the Dulwich Hamlet school and the Dulwich Society, one of the two local amenity societies. The building was originally constructed for the James Allen Girls School, an institution that grew out of a 'reading school' for poor girls and boys established over a century earlier by James Allen, Master of the College from 1721 to 1746.

The school became an all-girls' school in 1857 when it was taken under the wing of the College foundation, and moved to this new building in 1866. Twenty years later it moved out of Dulwich Village to East Dulwich Grove, where it still is.

Gypsy queen

At the end of Commerce Row, Calton Avenue leads left, past Ash Cottage and the entrance to Court Lane, to St Barnabas's Church, built in 1894 when Dulwich first became a parish in its own right. Until then it had been part of Camberwell parish. All through the Middle Ages villagers had to trek 2 miles (3 kilometres) north to Camberwell parish church to attend divine service on Sundays. Then, in 1616, they at last had their own place of worship when the chapel in Alleyn's almshouse was consecrated. At the same time Alleyn donated to the village the burial ground you can see straight ahead. Those laid to rest in the cemetery before it was closed in 1898 include Dulwich's 35 plague victims in 1665, Old Bridget, queen of the Norwood Gypsies, in 1768, Samuel Mathews, the Dulwich Hermit, murdered in 1802, and Richard Shawe, solicitor to Warren Hastings during his famous impeachment trial, in 1816. Shawe, whose tomb can be seen from Court Lane, lived at Casina, a country house built for him on the high ground north of Dulwich ten years earlier.

Cross Calton Avenue and walk along Dulwich Village beside the burial ground. Now you are entering the village proper. The fine Georgian town houses start immediately on the left, the eastern side of the village street. The first one still has its original coach house. Opposite is the original row of village shops, built at various times between 1765 and 1837. The one with the wrought-iron canopy over the front used to be a butcher's shop. Bella Pasta on the corner of Aysgarth Road is a 1930s' reproduction of the Georgian coaching inn that used to stand on the site.

Belair

Continue on down the left-hand side of the road, past the Crown and Greyhound and Le Piaf and then more shops and houses. At the junction ahead the road divides. Gallery Road on the right leads to Belair, one of several country houses built in the neighbourhood of Dulwich in the 18th century. Acquired by the local council after World War II, the grounds were turned into a public park, protecting Dulwich's western flank, and the house was expensively restored. Now it is in a sorry state, in stark contrast to properties belonging to the College.

The Tudor-style building on the right of the entrance to Gallery Road is the Sir Charles Barry-designed Old Grammar School, set up by the College in 1842 after complaints from local people that it was not doing enough to promote education for village boys. Like the girls' school, it was taken under the wing of the College foundation in 1857. Thirty years later, having grown from its original complement of 60 boys, Alleyn's School moved to Townley Road near St Barnabas's Church. It has been there ever since. In 1975 it became co-educational.

The old College

Across the road from the Old Grammar School is the original College of God's Gift. The building has inevitably been altered over the years, but it is essentially as it was when first constructed. Looking at it from the front gates surmounted by Alleyn's coat of arms, the central portion is the chapel, the left wing the almshouse, and the right wing the former school and now the estate office. The gardens in front were originally the village green. The layout is said to have been based on a similar institution in Amsterdam and there is talk of Inigo Jones having been the architect. He was certainly present at the foundation ceremonies on 21 June 1619, but there is no direct proof that he played any part in designing the college.

Dulwich Park

Carry on down College Road beside the College and turn left through the gate into Dulwich Park. When Dulwich Court, the manor farm and the closest farm to the centre of the village, was demolished and Court Lane laid out over the site, the College gave five of its former fields to the Metropolitan Board of Works. The Board then created this public park complete with boating lake and opened it to the public in 1895. When the road forks, bear left and then go straight on between the white bollards and over the riding track onto the tarmac path beside the boating lake. Go past the restaurant and carry straight on between the children's playground and the bowling green. At the crossroads in front of the rhododendrons, turn right and then fork left. Take the first right, join up with the outer, vehicle, road and exit from the park by the Rosebery Gate.

Across the main road is what was Dulwich Common, covering the northern slope of Sydenham Hill and now playing fields and golf links. On top of the hill (the southern boundary of the old manor of Dulwich), the slender Eiffel Tower-like TV mast is a landmark for miles around. Turn left on the busy road and walk for some way to the junction with Lordship Lane, the eastern boundary of the manor of Dulwich.

Dulwich Wells

The Harvester pub at the road junction was called the Green Man in 1704 when John Cox, the innkeeper, obtained permission to create a walk through the woods on the Common side of the road leading up to the local spa of Sydenham Wells. In 1739 Cox's son discovered a mineral spring in the grounds of the inn and developed the Green Man's own spa of Dulwich Wells, complete with bowling green and assembly room for breakfasts and dancing. Later a Dr Glennie opened a school here at which the poet Byron was a pupil for two years. Today's Grove Tavern opened in 1863, though the actual building dates from the 1920s.

Pissarro paints in Dulwich

Opposite the pub, turn right across the road and go through the gate into Cox's Walk, passing between Charles Barry's St Peter's Church and the Marlborough Cricket Club, founded in 1870. Follow the avenue up the hill and round the bend to the right. At the end, the footbridge crosses the railway line, now disused, that once carried passengers to Crystal Palace after it was re-erected on Sydenham Hill following the 1851 Great Exhibition. Art lovers might be interested to know that Camille Pissarro painted at least one picture from this bridge when he was living at Upper Norwood in 1870–71.

Instead of crossing the bridge go straight on through the gate into Dulwich Woods and keep to the high track on the left with the green posts (marking the boundary between the College's property and the London Wildlife Trust's Sydenham Hill Nature Reserve) on your right. After 50 yards (42 metres) or so, follow the path left down the embankment onto the old railway track (No. 6 marker post here) and turn right along the track. After a while you will come to the sealed entrance of the tunnel under Sydenham Hill. Take the path to the right and follow it up and over the tunnel entrance and out onto Crescent Wood Road. Turn immediately sharp right off the road into Peckarmans Wood and follow it round to the left in front of the houses in order to see the fine view, rather obscured by trees, of Canary Wharf, the East End and the City.

TV comes to Dulwich

At the end of Peckarmans Wood turn left, then right back onto the main road. The big houses up here were mostly built in the second half of the 19th century after the relocation of the Crystal Palace put the area on the map. An exception is the modern house on the left, an early (1933) work of the modernist architect Berthold Lubetkin. On the right the penultimate house has a blue plaque to the inventor of television, John Logie Baird. He lived here between 1934 and 1946 after moving his laboratories to Crystal Palace from Soho, where he had given the first public demonstration of his invention ten years earlier.

Dulwich Wood

Opposite the Dulwich Wood House pub, opened in 1858, turn right down Low Cross Wood Lane. It was somewhere near this lane that Samuel Mathews, the Dulwich Hermit buried in the village burial ground, was murdered in 1802. About 100 yards (90 metres) before the bottom of the lane, go right through the gate back into Dulwich Wood, a remnant of the ancient Great North Wood which once spread south from here to Croydon. Follow the path through the wood, bearing left at the central clearing where three paths branch off to the right. At the end of the path, exit through the gate and turn left on Grange Lane between the allotments and the golf club. Just beyond the golf club entrance there is a viewpoint cut in the hedge offering a fine panorama of the West End. The British Telecom Tower is the most conspicuous feature, but left of it the Houses of Parliament also stand out well in the right conditions.

The tollgate

Follow the lane down the hill. Where it bends left you pass what was Grange Farm, built in the early 19th century after the enclosure of the old common. The lane brings you out at one of Dulwich's most unusual features, the tollgate, the last one still operating in London. The gate was put up in 1787 when a neighbouring landowner built College Road as a short cut between his farm at Penge and fields he rented in Dulwich. He was not averse to other people using the road, but he was not going to let them use it for free. When his lease expired, the College kept both the road and the gate. A few years ago it was reported to be making about £17,000 a year.

Dulwich school

Turn right down College Road, passing between the tennis courts and buildings of Dulwich school, the modern incarnation of Alleyn's original foundation. Having made a lot of money out of selling land to the railway companies in the mid 19th century, the College commissioned Charles Barry to design these impressive new buildings in the 1860s. The school moved into them in 1870. The old manor house of Dulwich where Alleyn lived between 1613 and 1626 stood a few hundred yards behind the school buildings, roughly at the junction of Park Hall Road and Croxted Road. It was demolished in 1883.

Further on, on the right, you come to a pretty row of old cottages called Pond Cottages, with the Mill Pond, from which the cottages take their name, in front. In the 17th and 18th centuries this was a small industrial centre. The cottages belonged to a tile kiln where bricks and roof tiles were made. The pond was originally a clay pit from which the tile kiln obtained its main raw material until the pond naturally filled with water. The kiln seems to have ceased operating by the end of the 18th century and the pond subsequently acquired its name from the windmill that stood opposite on the other side of College Road. Following the enclosure of the Common, the mill was demolished in 1815.

When you reach the junction with Dulwich Common, cross straight over and continue along College Road. After some modern developments you come to Bell House, the finest Georgian house in the village. It dates from 1767 and was built for City stationer Thomas Wright. He later became Master of the Stationers' Company and then Lord Mayor of London before dying here in 1798. The house is now one of the School boarding houses.

Dulwich Picture Gallery

Beyond Bell House and its weatherboarded neighbour, you come, on the left, to Dulwich's main claim to fame apart from the school, the **Dulwich Picture Gallery**. This, the oldest public picture gallery in England, was designed by Sir John Soane in 1817 to house a superb collection of paintings bequeathed to the College by Sir Francis Bourgeois. Bourgeois, himself an artist, had in turn inherited the collection from the man who put it together, the dealer Noel Desenfans. Desenfans had originally intended to sell it to the King of Poland for a projected national gallery, but war prevented the deal from going through. Poland's loss was Dulwich's gain. Now a humble south London suburb is home to a collection of old masters that any national gallery would be proud to possess.

Now make your way back along Dulwich Village to North Dulwich Station, where the walk ends.

Greenwich

Location	5½ miles (8.8 kilometres) southeast of Charing Cross.
Transport	Greenwich Station (overground trains from Charing Cross and Cannon Street), Island Gardens Station (Docklands Light Railway and then Greenwich Foot Tunnel), Greenwich Pier (boats from **Charing Cross Pier**).
Features	**St Alfege's Church**; *Cutty Sark*; *Gypsy Moth IV*; **Royal Naval College**; **Trinity Hospital**; **National Maritime Museum**; **Queen's House**; **Old Royal Observatory**; **Ranger's House**; **Fan Museum**; Greenwich Park; Croom's Hill and elegant Georgian streets of West Greenwich; riverside walk; views of London; arts and crafts market (weekends).
Events	**Greenwich Festival**; **Tourist Information Centre**.
Refreshments	*in Greenwich centre* numerous cafés, bars, pubs and restaurants; *along the walk* various pubs plus café at Visitor Centre in Greenwich Park (near Circus Gate – see map page 113).

Greenwich was established as a little fishing port on the Thames long before the Norman Conquest. Its recorded history begins in the 9th century when King Alfred and his daughter granted it to the Abbey of St Peter in Ghent. Two hundred years later marauding Danes captured Archbishop Alfege at Canterbury and brought him hostage to their camp at Greenwich. In 1012 he was murdered following a drunken feast. The parish church, dedicated to his memory, was later built on the site of his martyrdom. In the early 1700s it was wrecked in a storm and replaced by the existing church, a monumental work by Nicholas Hawksmoor.

Greenwich's real history begins with its acquisition in 1427 by Henry VI's uncle, Humphrey, Duke of Gloucester. Humphrey transformed the old abbey buildings into a mansion called Bella Court, constructed a fortified tower on the hill behind and enclosed 200 acres (80 hectares) of wild Black Heath to form a deer park. Bella Court was subsequently enlarged by the Tudors into the great royal palace of Placentia, the birthplace and favourite residence of Henry VIII and Elizabeth I. Meanwhile, Greenwich village blossomed into an elegant court suburb and aristocratic playground.

England's first classical domestic building
In the 17th century Placentia was replaced by two new buildings: the early-17th-century Queen's House, the first classical domestic building in England, and the later 17th-century palace begun by Charles II after his restoration. The new palace, unfinished by Charles and lying in between the two royal dockyards of Woolwich

and Deptford, was completed by his successors as the Royal Hospital for old sailors. From the early 1800s, the Queen's House, an exquisite building designed by Inigo Jones, housed the Royal Hospital School. Since the 1930s, when the school moved out of London, it has been part of the National Maritime Museum. The old Hospital, later a naval college and most recently a joint defence college, is currently in the process of being taken over by the Museum and by Greenwich University.

The old village centre of Greenwich stretched back from the riverside along Greenwich Church Street, with the church on one side and the Royal Hospital and Queen's House on the other. After Charles II began his new palace, the village began to expand, mainly around the park, which Charles had commissioned André Le Nôtre to landscape. The earliest developments were along Croom's (i.e. Crooked) Hill, the road that runs up the hill along the west side of the park. Later came Park Vista along the south side, and Maze Hill along the east side. Croom's Hill, the finest street in modern Greenwich, and Park Vista both feature on the walk.

Regency rebuilding

In the late 18th and early 19th centuries elegant streets were added to the west of the village below Point Hill, and in the 1830s the old congested village centre was rebuilt in Regency style. Following the building of the pier for steamboats in 1836 and the opening of the railway station in 1838 (the Greenwich–London Bridge line is the oldest railway in London), the village rapidly developed into a suburb and tourist centre.

Today its main attractions are concerned with its maritime past and its role in the development of the world's time zones. (The two are not, in fact, unrelated since the Old Royal Observatory in Greenwich Park, through which runs the Greenwich meridian line, was originally set up by Charles II to solve the longitude problem for sailors.) In the near future people will also come to Greenwich to see the Millennium Exhibition. This is being built on the Blackwall peninsula about 1 mile (1.6 kilometres) downstream and will be ready in time for the first day of the year 2000.

THE GREENWICH WALK

Start and finish Greenwich Station.
Distance 3½ miles (5.6 kilometres).

Come out of Greenwich Station onto the forecourt. Directly opposite across the High Road is Queen Elizabeth's College, the almshouse founded by historian and local landowner William Lambarde in 1574 and rebuilt by the Drapers' Company, who now run it, in 1817. Turn right on the High Road, go past the garage and take the first right into Straightsmouth. Follow this road under the railway bridge and then round to the right. As you approach the village centre, you get a fine view of the parish church of **St Alfege's**.

Go straight on into Churchfields. At the end look left along Roan Street and you will see the early 19th-century headmaster's house of the Roan School, one of Greenwich's old charity schools founded in the 1670s by John Roan, a local man and Yeoman of Harriers to Charles I. The original school building lay just to the

GREENWICH

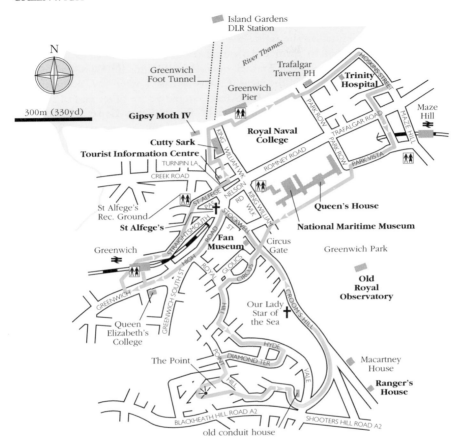

right of the schoolhouse and the site is marked by a plaque. Today the Roan School is situated in Maze Hill in East Greenwich.

Continue straight across Roan Street into St Alfege Passage. This takes you past the old burial ground on the left and the church and 1814 National School on the right, and brings you out in the centre of the village in Greenwich Church Street. Left is the river and right is the park. Crossing by the zebra (right), go straight over Church Street and through the arch into Turnpin Lane. This is one of the old lanes of medieval Greenwich, but the block it bisects was the part of Greenwich rebuilt around a new covered market between 1828 and 1831. Halfway along the lane, turn left into the market (originally for food, now arts and crafts at weekends) and walk straight through, noting the curious (and ungrammatical) traders' admonition above the arch as you pass out into College Approach (right are the gates of the old **Royal Naval College**).

Dockworkers' tunnel

Turn left into College Approach and then right, following Greenwich Church Street down onto the waterfront. Originally the street ran right down to the riverside past the Ship Hotel on the right. Having been bombed during World War II, the area was left open to form today's esplanade. In the middle is the domed entrance to the Greenwich Foot Tunnel, opened in 1902 to allow workers to reach the docks on the other side of the river (Canary Wharf Tower now dominates the newly redeveloped Docklands). From Island Gardens at the other end of the Foot Tunnel there is a famous view of Greenwich. To the left is *Gypsy Moth IV*, the first boat to be sailed round the world single-handed (by Sir Francis Chichester in 1966–67); and to the right is one of the great sights of maritime Greenwich, the *Cutty Sark*, a clipper ship that brought tea from China and wool from Australia in record times in the 1870s and '80s.

Walk down the side of the *Cutty Sark*, turn right under its bowsprit and continue past the pier entrance along the riverside walk. Ahead is a fine view of the Blackwall peninsula, the site of the Millennium exhibition and the new Port Greenwich. On the right you pass the pink granite monument put up in 1853 to the memory of Frenchman Joseph Bellot who lost his life attempting to discover the fate of Sir John Franklin's doomed Northwest Passage expedition.

Charles II's palace

Then you come to the old Greenwich Hospital, opened in 1705, closed in 1865 and replaced by the Royal Naval College and now set to become part of the National Maritime Museum and Greenwich University. The first block on the right was the one intended by Charles II to form part of a new palace. The other buildings were all completed later once the decision had been taken to build a seamen's home instead. From the centre there is a fine view of the Queen's House and behind it, up on the hill, the 17th-century **Royal Observatory**. The Observatory is both the home of GMT (Greenwich Mean Time) and the dividing point between the east and west hemispheres. The ball on top, originally installed in 1831, drops at 1pm precisely to signal the correct time for ships passing down the Thames.

Whitebait dinners

Beyond the College turn right by the Trafalgar Tavern (a favourite resort for dinners of Thames whitebait in the last century) and then immediately left into Crane Street behind it. Crane Street takes you into High Bridge and High Bridge brings you in turn to the Trinity Hospital almshouse. Courtier Lord Lumley had a house here in Tudor times. After the court left Greenwich in 1601, Lord Northampton acquired the house and in 1616 converted it into an almshouse for 21 local men. Rebuilt in Gothic style in 1812 and run by the Mercers' Company, it still fulfils that function today, though it looks somewhat incongruous in this rather industrial location.

Carry on under the power station gantry and turn right along Hoskins Street past the scrapyards. At Old Woolwich Road turn right behind the power station and then first left (the trees on the right belong to Trinity Hospital's garden) into

Greenwich Park Street. Cross Trafalgar Road (traffic lights on the left) and walk up to Park Vista and turn right. Here many of the houses – such as the Manor House at No. 13 – date from the expansion of the village in the late 1600s and 1700s.

Meridian

When you get to Feathers Place look left and you will see a plaque in the wall (and a metal strip in the pavement) marking the meridian, i.e. 0° longitude. The row of houses here – Nos. 36–33 incorporating The Chantry – was originally built for the Admiral Commissioner of the Naval Asylum (school). The westernmost section at the end of Park Vista now serves as St Alfege's vicarage.

The storming of Quebec

Beyond the vicarage, turn left into the park and then right along the walk beside the **Queen's House** and the **National Maritime Museum**. Up on the hill, where Duke Humphrey's Tower used to stand, is the Observatory and to the left of it the statue of General Wolfe. Wolfe's parents lived in Greenwich and Wolfe was buried in St Alfege's church after his death at the successful storming of Quebec in 1759.

Gloucester Circus

At the end of the tarmac walk, carry on past St Mary's Gate and then branch left past the Visitor Centre and the herb garden. Exit from the park at Circus Gate and go straight over Croom's Hill into Gloucester Circus, keeping to the left-hand side of the central garden. You are now in West Greenwich, the suburb adjacent to the old village developed from the late 18th century. The Circus was the work of Michael Searles (he also designed The Paragon in Blackheath) and dates from the 1790s. Unfortunately, only the south crescent was built. The north side was completed as a square over 30 years later and then patched up after World War II, following bomb damage.

Leave the Circus at the far end and turn left up Royal Hill, named after its main developer, Robert Royal. Opposite the Prince Albert pub, turn left into Hyde Vale and walk up the hill past rather exclusive houses, particularly the villas on the right which date from the 1830s. Opposite No. 67 turn right into Diamond Terrace. Follow this round the side of the hill and then, at the end, turn left up steep Point Hill. Opposite West Grove Lane, turn right onto the tarmac path. From here there are wonderful views of east London and the City and the Northern Heights beyond. When you reach the steps climb up to the summit of the hill where there is a panel identifying some of the landmarks.

Lord Chesterfield's letters

Cross straight over the open space on top of Point Hill and continue on into West Grove. The busy road on the right is the main road across Blackheath to Dover. Stick close to the left-hand side of West Grove. At the junction with Hyde Vale there is a small 18th-century brick conduit house, once part of the water supply system for the Royal Hospital. Go straight over Hyde Vale, up the steps and left onto Cade Road. Away to the right now you can see **Ranger's House**, built in 1699 on the edge of the park and between 1748 and 1773 the home of the fourth Earl of Chesterfield. Chesterfield's letters to his son, published in 1774, became a standard guide to good manners, and many were originally written from here.

Croom's Hill begins at the junction of Cade Road and General Wolfe Road. Macartney House, on the right, was Wolfe's home after his father bought it in 1751. The Manor House on the left, behind the copper beech hedge, was built about 1690 for Rear Admiral Sir Robert Robinson and is one of the oldest surviving houses in the road. Below the Manor House is a green with a Catholic church and a fine presbytery next door. Downhill from the church is the oldest house in Croom's Hill, Heathgate House, built about 1635. Just further on you come to the second oldest building in the road, the roadside gazebo built in 1672 overlooking the park. The gazebo belongs to The Grange, a large 18th-century house standing behind the gazebo wall in its own grounds.

The Fan Museum
There are some late 18th-century houses in and around King George Street, but from Gloucester Circus the houses are older as you approach the foot of the hill. On the left near the bottom is a particularly fine early 18th-century terrace, with No. 12 and its neighbour now forming the **Fan Museum**, the only one of its kind in the world. On the right the Spread Eagle on the corner of Nevada Street is an old coaching inn and a relic of the days before the building of Nelson Road and College Approach when Nevada Street (then called Silver Street) was the main road through Greenwich. The increase of traffic along this road and the need for a more direct route through the town was one reason for the improvement scheme of 1830.

Carry on past the Spread Eagle down Stockwell Street. At the bottom turn left onto Greenwich High Road. After about 250 yards (128 metres) you will reach the station, where the walk ends.

Ham and Petersham

Location	9 miles (14.5 kilometres) southwest of Charing Cross.
Transport	Richmond Station (Underground District Line; overground trains from Waterloo or on North London Line), then either walk (1½ miles (2.4 kilometres) – directions given below) or bus 65 or 371 from station forecourt to The Dysarts bus stop in Petersham.
Features	**St Peter's Church**; **Ham House**; numerous historic houses of the 17th, 18th and 19th centuries; Petersham Meadows and farm; Ham Common; riverside walk and views of Thames and Richmond; **Ham Polo Club** (not on walk – see map page 119).
Refreshments	*Petersham* The Dysarts and Fox and Duck pubs; *Ham* various pubs, Chinese takeaway/fish and chip shop/café; *Ham House* tea room (closed Fri); *Richmond* cafés, sandwich bars, patisseries, pubs, restaurants and fast-food outlets.

Ham and Petersham lie side by side on the south bank of the Thames between Richmond and Kingston. In the Middle Ages Ham was part of the royal demesne of Kingston, whereas Petersham was monastic property belonging to the Abbey of Chertsey. In the 15th century the Abbey transferred its Petersham property to the Crown, so from that time on both villages were in royal hands and generally treated as a single place when it came to grants of land and other royal favours.

In the early 1600s both places had their big houses. Ham's was **Ham House**, territorially in Petersham but geographically in Ham. It was constructed in 1610 for Sir Thomas Vavasour, an adviser to James I's son, Prince Henry, who had recently been given his own household in nearby Richmond Palace. Petersham's manor house stood opposite the present Dysarts pub and was occupied by London lawyer George Cole and his family.

When King Charles I established his huge new deer park at Richmond, great changes came to Petersham and Ham, both of which lost much land to the new park. The Coles left Petersham Lodge, which became an official residence of one of the two deputy keepers of the new park. Meanwhile, the manors of both Ham and Petersham were granted to the King's childhood companion and whipping boy, William Murray, created Earl of Dysart in 1643. Dysart established himself in Ham House. The house was completely transformed in the 1670s when Dysart's daughter married, as her second husband, the Duke of Lauderdale. He was one of Charles II's ministers and member of an unofficial cabinet group called the Cabal, which often met at Ham House in a room now known as the Cabal Room. Ham House today is very much the creation of the Duke and Duchess.

The Dysarts of Ham

The Duchess's first husband was Sir Lionel Tollemache. It was a son of this marriage who inherited the Dysart title and with it Ham House and the lordship of the manors of Ham and Petersham. The Dysarts of Ham House remained the dominant family in the neighbourhood right down to 1948, when they finally gave up the house to the National Trust and decamped to pastures new. It was only 15 years before that that the village of Ham had finally been absorbed into the Borough of Richmond (Petersham was included in the borough when it was created in 1890).

Ham House may have been the 'big house' of the two villages, but it was not by any means the only mansion in the area. Attracted by the political importance of Ham House and New Park, by the royal presence in the palace and park of Richmond, and by the idyllic setting between park and Thames, many other wealthy and titled people built themselves suburban retreats in Petersham and Ham in the late 17th and 18th centuries. Most of these houses remain and feature on the walk.

England's most elegant village

The impressive houses in Ham are grouped around the large triangular common and spaced out down the long Ham Street leading from the common to the river. But in Petersham they are concentrated in a much smaller area around the junction of Petersham Road and River Lane. This concentration has led to Petersham's description in the past as the most elegant village in England. Today much of that elegance remains, but it is difficult to appreciate it with heavy traffic thundering along the dangerously narrow Petersham Road. Step off the road, however – into the churchyard next to Petersham Meadows or into River Lane where the farm is – and you quickly recover that feeling of rural tranquillity, as you will discover on the walk.

Ham, too, has its quiet places, thanks, ironically, to this same heavily used road. After leaving Petersham it crosses Ham Common in a southwesterly direction towards Kingston, so cutting off the village cradled in its great bend of the Thames. Standing close to the river, Ham House is àt the farthest point from the road and it is here, surrounded by fields, parkland and the river, that you will probably feel yourself farthest away from the great city close by.

THE HAM AND PETERSHAM WALK

Start and finish Richmond Station or The Dysarts pub in Petersham (reached by buses 65 and 371 from Richmond Station).
Distance 2¾ miles (4.4 kilometres) starting and finishing at The Dysarts. (Richmond is another 1½ miles (2.4 kilometres) *each way*).

From Richmond Station to The Dysarts

Turn left out of Richmond Station and walk through the centre of the town, following the road round when it bends left. Go past the old town hall, now the library, on the right and at the roundabout (Richmond Bridge to the right) go

HAM AND PETERSHAM

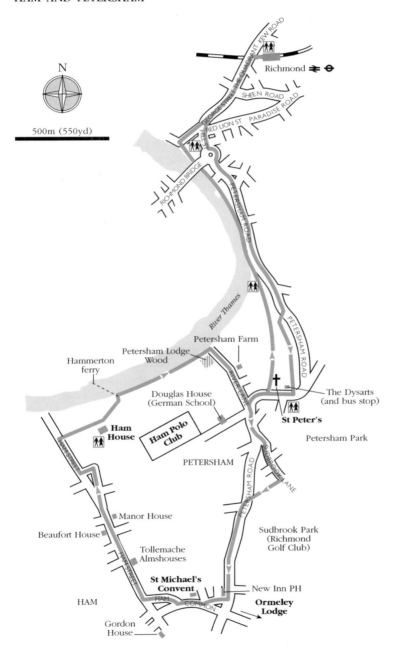

N

500m (550yd)

Richmond

THE QUADRANT
KEW ROAD
GEORGE STREET
SHEEN ROAD
PARADISE ROAD
RED LION ST
THE HILL

RICHMOND BRIDGE

PETERSHAM ROAD

River Thames

Hammerton ferry

Petersham Lodge Wood

Petersham Farm

PETERSHAM ROAD

RIVER LANE

Douglas House
(German School)

Ham House

Ham Polo Club

PETERSHAM

The Dysarts
(and bus stop)

St Peter's

Petersham Park

Manor House

Beaufort House

Tollemache Almshouses

St Michael's Convent

HAM

Gordon House

PETERSHAM ROAD

SUDBROOK LANE

HAM STREET

HAM COMMON

New Inn PH

Ormeley Lodge

Sudbrook Park
(Richmond Golf Club)

119

straight over, keeping right along the main road when a side road branches left up the hill. You are now on Petersham Road. Follow this for some way until, having reached relatively open country with Terrace Field on your left and Petersham Meadows on the right, you come to the Rose of York pub. Just beyond the pub, branch right along a woodland track. This takes you across what is actually part of Petersham Common, past the riding stables and brings you out on the main road once more at the entrance to the village. The Dysarts bus stop is just to the right.

The Dysarts and beyond

The section of Richmond Park opposite The Dysarts pub and accessed by Petersham Gate is the former Petersham Park where the Cole family lived in the early 1600s before Richmond Park was created. The house stood just off the road and the surrounding parkland covered both the flat ground around the house and the hillside to the east. When the Earl of Rochester was appointed Ranger of the new Richmond Park in 1687 he re-created Petersham Park, knocked down the Coles' old house and built himself a fine new mansion called New Park. This, in turn, was destroyed in 1721, when a fire broke out in the linen cupboard. William Stanhope then bought the estate and built a third house on the site, which – designed by the architect-Earl of Burlington – was one of the first Palladian houses in England. The Stanhopes, created Viscounts Petersham and then Earls of Harrington, lived on at Petersham Lodge until 1783. In 1834 when the property came into Crown hands, the house was knocked down and the grounds merged once more with Richmond Park.

From The Dysarts walk on into the village, taking care to keep well into the pavement, for the road is very narrow here and lorries sometimes have to mount the kerb in order to pass vehicles coming in the opposite direction. The fine houses start immediately with Parkgate and Church House on the right and then on the left, opposite the turning to the church, Reston Lodge. These houses date from the late 18th or early 19th century. The earliest houses come next, with Montrose House on the left, and Petersham House (with the round porch) and then Rutland Lodge on the right. These three houses all date from the late 17th century, when Petersham first became a fashionable suburb for the aristocracy. Montrose House takes its name from the Dowager Duchess of Montrose, who lived here between 1837 and 1847. Petersham House was built about 1674 for one of the keepers of the park. Rutland Lodge was built in the early 1660s for a Lord Mayor of London, subsequently disgraced for misappropriating funds intended for the rebuilding of the City following the Great Fire. It takes its name from a mid-18th-century resident, the Duchess of Rutland. In more recent times a serious fire destroyed the interior of the building and it was converted into flats.

Personal relationships

To some extent, personal relationships determined the occupancy, if not the building, of these houses in their early days. Montrose House, for example, was built for lawyer Sir Thomas Jenner. His daughter married another lawyer, Sir John Darnall, who lived in Rutland Lodge. Darnall's daughter married yet another lawyer,

Plate 19: *The Terrace in Barnes is an attractive collection of 18th- and 19th-century houses overlooking the Thames (see page 81).*

Plate 20: *Topiary is one of the features of the immaculate gardens at picturesque Hall Place in Bexley (see page 90).*

Plate 21: *These houses in The Paragon, Blackheath's finest Georgian development, were converted into flats following bomb damage in the Second World War (see page 96).*

Plate 22: *Pagoda House in Blackheath was built as an aristocratic summer house in the 18th century (see page 95).*

Plate 23: *Hare and Billet pond and All Saints Church on Black Heath (see page 94).*

Plate 24: *The centre of Carshalton village is graced by a large expanse of water (see page 101).*

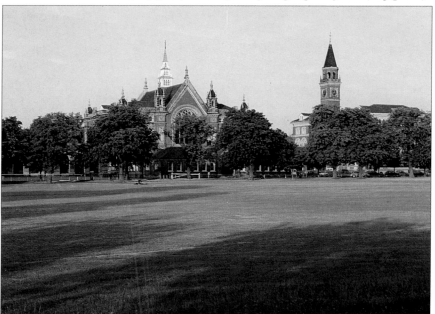

Plate 25: *In Victorian times Dulwich College was rebuilt on a new site on Dulwich Common and surrounded by well-kept playing fields (see page 110).*

Plate 26: The Dulwich Picture Gallery, the oldest public art gallery in the country (see page 110).

Plate 27: The old tollgate on College Road, Dulwich, is the only one still operating in London (see page 109).

Robert Ord, Chief Baron of the Exchequer in Scotland, who built new Petersham Lodge halfway down River Lane. We pass this house on the way back from Ham.

The two houses facing you on the bend, one of which is now called the Manor House, were both built later than the three houses just mentioned, probably in the second half of the 18th century. Follow the road round to the left here. Beyond the garden walls where the road begins to widen out, you come to the east lodge of Ham House. This is also the main entrance to the **Ham Polo Club** and to Douglas House, another of Petersham's fine late-17th-century houses. This one takes its name from the eccentric Kitty Douglas, Duchess of Queensberry in the 18th century. She was a great patron of artists and writers, particularly of John Gay. She looked after his money, built him a summerhouse down by the river so that he could write in peace and allowed him to have his *The Beggar's Opera* rehearsed in her house. The house was bought by the German government in the 1960s and incorporated into a German school.

All Saints Church

Opposite the Ham House lodge, built in 1900, is a pair of much older cottages. These houses are, in fact, the original lodge houses for Ham House, constructed about the same time as the mansion itself. In those days the road from Richmond to Kingston passed behind Montrose House, rather than in front of it as now, and then joined up with the existing road about where the Fox and Duck is. Looking between the old lodges and the Fox and Duck you can see the campanile of All Saints Church. This has a curious history. The 18th-century Bute House (former home of George III's prime minister the Earl of Bute) used to stand on the site. In 1894 Mrs Loetitia Warde of Petersham House bought the empty house, knocked it down and built this extraordinary red brick church, partly as a memorial to her parents and partly because she expected Petersham's population to expand like Richmond's when the village was built up. But Petersham never was built up, so the church was never even consecrated, let alone used. It is now a recording studio.

Dickens writes *Nicholas Nickleby*

Cross the road at the traffic lights. When Petersham Road bears right past Cecil House, go straight on into Sudbrook Lane, Sudbrook (i.e. Southbrook) being an old hamlet to the south of Petersham. There are more handsome old houses down here, but they are far more modest in size than those in the centre of the village. One of them is the now-unidentifiable Elm Lodge where, in the summer of 1839, the 27-year-old Charles Dickens wrote the greater part of *Nicholas Nickleby*. Bute Avenue on the left leads to All Saints. Dickens Close on the right commemorates the writer's stay in the village. At the end of the road is the grand entrance to Sudbrook Park, home of Richmond Golf Club. The clubhouse, designed by James Gibbs and completed in 1728, was built for John Campbell, 2nd Duke of Argyll and Greenwich. Being the grandson of the Countess of Dysart who married the Duke of Lauderdale, and having been born in Ham House himself, Argyll had natural connections with Petersham.

In front of the gate, turn right into Hazel Lane. As you walk along you can glimpse the Campbell house through the trees. They had given it up by 1842.

Subsequently it was used as hydropathic treatment centre and hotel before coming into the possession of the seven-year-old golf club in 1898. At the end of the lane, turn left, cross at the traffic lights and continue walking along the road. You have now left Petersham and are on the way to Ham.

Ham Common

Ham starts with a row of cottages and the Fox and Goose pub on the right. The New Inn further on, and Sudbrook Lodge opposite, mark the beginning of Ham Common. Much of the Common was lost when Richmond Park was created, but substantial chunks remain. The area of Common on the left, crossed by Ham Gate Avenue, the entrance to which you can see up ahead, is mostly scrub and wood-land. That on the right of the main road is mown grass and more like a large village green, with a cricket pitch in the middle and a pond over in the far right corner. One or two fine houses, notably **Ormeley Lodge**, were built in Ham Gate Avenue from the late 17th century, but the most popular sites for suburban retreats were around the triangular Common and down Ham Street, which we come to shortly.

St Michael's Convent

Turn right by the New Inn. Stafford Cottages here (now one house, but formerly a pair of cottages) is a comparatively rare survival from maybe the late 16th or possibly the early years of the 17th century when Ham House was built. Cross Bishops Close. South Lodge was built by Ham resident and wealthy philanthropist John Minter Morgan as a home for girls orphaned by the cholera epidemic of 1847–9. It has now been converted into flats. Morgan's own house on the other side of the Common has been a psychiatric hospital since 1948. More substantial houses follow – Hardwicke House and then Orford Hall, now **St Michael's Convent**. Beyond Avenue Lodge you come to another pair of lodges like the ones in Petersham. These flank the entrance to the southern drive of Ham House, which you can just make out at the far end. Across to your left, 18th-century Gordon House closes a fine view across the sunken pond in the corner of the Common.

Keep right, follow the road to the end and then turn right into Ham Street, the main thoroughfare of the old village. Well within living memory farms and cottages stood on the left side of the street, with a back lane behind (sections of which still survive) and farmland (and originally the common fields of the manor) beyond. Most of this land has now been filled up with housing estates. Unlike the farms, a few of Ham Street's big houses have survived. Beyond the 1892 Tollemache Almshouses and the Grey Court School is Grey Court, the boyhood home of Cardinal Newman, to whom there is a blue plaque on the front. Opposite the junction with Sandy Lane is Beaufort House and on the right another large house now called the Manor House.

Foot ferry

Carry on down Ham Street, past the allotments and games fields, until you come to the entrance to Ham House. Here turn right (if the gate is closed walk on down to the river and turn right along the towpath). Ahead is a fine view of the Star and Garter home for disabled soldiers on top of Richmond Hill. Just beyond the gates leading into the forecourt of the house, branch left along a track worn in the grass, aiming for the corner of the field. Go through the gate and out onto the towpath and turn right. Here Hammerton ferry, one of the last surviving foot ferries on the Thames, connects with Twickenham and its various attractions, including the Orleans House Gallery and Marble Hill. The latter, a beautiful white Palladian house, gradually comes into view as you walk back towards Petersham and Richmond.

When you reach the boats moored upstream of the island, you pass Petersham Lodge Wood on your right. Down the horse chestnut avenue in the middle is a vista of a bust on a pedestal in the grounds of Petersham Lodge. Once part of the Lodge's grounds, the wood is now owned by the local council and managed jointly with the London Wildlife Trust, assisted by local volunteers. Progress is slowly being made to turn the wood into a public nature reserve.

Eggs and honey

Beyond the wood turn right into River Lane. You re-enter the village between the council-owned farm on the left (where you can buy eggs and honey) and new Petersham Lodge on the right. This is the house built by Chief Baron Ord in 1740. Beyond you come to the Navigator's House and pink-painted Glen Cottage. Originally these two were one house and it was here that naval officer George Vancouver, the discoverer of the island that bears his name, lived from 1795 while writing up the official account of his 1791–94 Pacific voyage. Vancouver died in 1798 when he was only 40 and was buried in Petersham churchyard, the next stop on the walk.

At the top of River Lane turn left along Petersham Road once more and then left again into Church Lane, signposted to **St Peter's Church**. In most other London villages churches have been progressively enlarged over the years to accommodate increasing populations, but Petersham's, although a lot of work was done on it in 1840, has stayed more or less the same, reflecting the fact that as late as 1891 the population of the village was still only 629. Inside, the church still has its gallery and box pews, and there are memorials to many local people, including a fine effigy of George Cole (died 1624) of the original Petersham Lodge and a plaque to Sir Thomas Jenner (died 1707) of Montrose House. Outside, unusually for a London church, the churchyard is still being used for burials. One of the latest is that of Major-General Sir Humphrey Tollemache, sixth baronet, who died in 1990 aged 93. Vancouver's simple grave is halfway along the south wall, in between the wall and another Tollemache tomb.

From Church Lane a path leads off to the right along the north (Richmond) side of the churchyard. It comes out by The Dysarts bus stop, so go down it if you want to take the bus back to Richmond. If you would prefer to return on foot, go straight on down Church Lane and continue on into the path by the lampstand when the lane turns left to the nursery. Pass through the metal barrier and then go straight on (not right to the Rose of York) across the meadow, where from spring onwards cattle from the farm will probably be grazing. When you come to the riverside gardens carry straight on, go under the bridge across the river and then when you get to the White Cross Hotel turn right up Water Lane. Go straight on at the top and you will eventually reach the station and the end of the walk.

123

Kew

Location	7½ miles (12 kilometres) southwest of Charing Cross.
Transport	Kew Gardens Station (Underground District Line; overground North London Line trains), Kew Bridge Station (overground trains from Waterloo), Kew Gardens Pier (boats from **Westminster Pier**).
Features	**St Anne's Church**; **Royal Botanic Gardens and Kew Palace**; Kew Green and cricket ground; 18th-century houses, riverside walk and views of Strand on the Green; Maids of Honour tearooms (closed Sun).
Refreshments	*outside station* variety of cafés, bars, restaurants and takeaways; *between station and Kew Green* (see map page 126) Newens' Maids of Honour tearooms; *junction of Kew Road and Mortlake Road at entrance to Green* pubs, bars, restaurants; *north side of Green* pubs and Greek restaurant.

Kew is thought to derive its name from the old Anglo-Saxon word for quay or landing place. This is plausible since the village grew up at the south end of a ford across the River Thames. This ford – which gave its name to Brentford on the north bank – was the lowest on the Thames and therefore strategically significant in times of conflict. But commercially it was of little value and so Kew remained an unimportant place throughout its early existence. In the Middle Ages it was neither a manor nor a parish in its own right (it formed part of Richmond and Kingston respectively) and it was not even mentioned in any surviving documents until the early 14th century.

What really put Kew on the map was the development of Richmond as a royal residence by Henry VII and his Tudor successors in the late 15th and 16th centuries. With the court based at Richmond for extended periods, courtiers needed houses close by. Kew was a popular location because it was on the way to or from London, whether travelling by road or – as was more common in those days – by boat. Various royal children and more or less famous courtiers lived at Kew in the 16th century. One courtier was the unfortunate Henry Norris, executed for dallying with Henry VIII's second wife, Anne Boleyn.

Fishing village

In the early 1600s, Princess Elizabeth, sister of Prince Henry of Wales who resided at Richmond Palace, had her own little court at Kew. But despite this and other royal connections, the village remained little more than a tiny fishing and farming hamlet with – in 1664 – only 29 houses. Three of these were, however, large.

In those days, the Green – then an empty common – extended all the way through what is now Kew Gardens to the ferry landing at Brentford Ferry Gate. The three large houses – Kew Farm, Kew House and the Dutch House – were all clustered near the ferry landing. The Dutch House – so called because of its Dutch style of architecture – was built in 1631 by Samuel Fortrey, a City merchant of Flemish extraction whose family had fled to England to escape Catholic persecution in the Spanish Netherlands. Kew House, about 100 yards (90 metres) to the south, was effectively the manor house of Kew. The Capel family lived here for half a century from the 1670s, and made a famous garden, full of rare trees and plants.

Royalty arrives

In the 18th century the Kew we know today began to emerge, particularly after the new Hanoverian royal family discovered its attractions as a country retreat. Prince George – later George II – moved into Richmond Lodge at the south end of what is now Kew Gardens. His son, Prince Frederick, succeeded the Capels in Kew House. The Dutch House and the other houses by the ferry were also acquired for use by royal children and courtiers. More courtiers' houses were built around the common, henceforward known as Kew Green. Over time all the royal residences, with the exception of the Dutch House – which is now **Kew Palace** – were demolished and their grounds combined to form one large garden. When George IV blocked off the road leading across the Green to the ferry and diverted the road beside the river, the **Kew Gardens** we know today were complete.

Botanic gardens

The botanic gardens were developed out of the Capels' old garden by Prince Frederick and Princess Augusta and much expanded during the reign of George III (who died in 1820). George's successors were not interested in Kew, so in 1840 the royal gardens were transformed into a publicly owned, professionally managed botanical institute. By 1865 the gardens were attracting 500,000 visitors a year. Within 20 years that figure had risen to 1.25 million. In 1869 Kew Gardens Station opened and, more than anything, changed Kew from a village to a suburb. Pollution had already killed off the fishing industry by mid-century. Now house-builders bought up the farmland and market gardens for city commuters. The old village remained relatively unchanged, however, and still looks today much as it must have done in the 18th century.

THE KEW WALK

Start and finish Kew Gardens Station.
Distance 2 miles (3.2 kilometres).

Come out of the station and take the right fork ahead (Station Approach). When you reach Kew Gardens Road, turn right and follow it as it winds down to the junction with Kew Road. Kew Gardens is behind the wall on the far side of the road. Turn

KEW

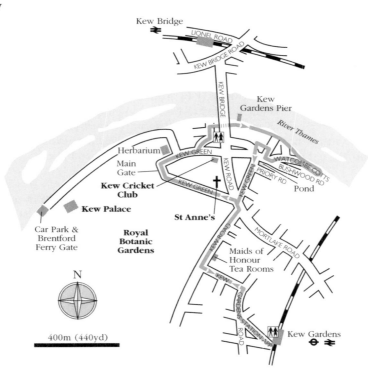

right on Kew Road and go past the famous Maids of Honour tea rooms run by the Newens family. The Newens make many kinds of delicious cakes and pies, but the star is the eponymous Maid of Honour, a little curd pastry that literally melts in the mouth. In 1887 Alfred Newens brought the recipe from Richmond – where the cakes had been made at least as far back as the early 18th century – and it remains a jealously guarded secret in the family to this day.

The old village of Kew starts just beyond the tea rooms with a row of early 19th-century houses and cottages facing the gardens. No. 300, for example, has a stone plaque on it saying 'Cumberland Place 1831'. Right at the end, the last two houses before the traffic lights (Nos 356 and 358) were originally one house and were the residence of Francis Bauer, Kew's chief botanical draughtsman and painter until his death in 1840.

Kew Green

At the traffic lights cross over to the left and follow the road round to the left into the main part of Kew Green. Not being a parish, Kew had no church of its own until a group of influential residents successfully petitioned Queen Anne for permission to build one on a disused gravel pit on the common. **St Anne's Church** on the right, completed in 1714, was the result. It was first extended in 1770 after

Kew had been made a parish in its own right, and thereafter several more times as the parish grew in population. Inside there are monuments to, among others, Lady Capel (died 1721), Francis Bauer and the 18th-century painter Thomas Gainsborough (1788). Gainsborough's grave is outside the church on the south side. Clearly visible nearby are the graves of several fellow artists: Jeremiah Meyer, miniature painter to George III; Joshua Kirby, Gainsborough's friend and the subject of the latter's *Joshua Kirby and His Wife* in the National Portrait Gallery; and Johann Zoffany. Zoffany did a painting for St Anne's, but it was rejected because he included one of the churchwardens as Judas! It can now be seen across the river in St Paul's Church in Brentford (see page 17).

Cambridge Cottage

The south side of the Green has perhaps the finest collection of period houses. No. 33, the one with the bow window over the garage, was owned in the 18th century by the Marquis of Bute, the man who helped Princess Augusta develop the botanical garden after Prince Frederick's death in 1751. Bute also owned the largest house on this side of the Green, No. 37 ahead with the porte-cochère protruding over the roadway. Later it became the residence of the royal Dukes of Cambridge and was renamed Cambridge Cottage. Edward VII donated it to the Gardens following the second duke's death in 1904. At this end of the Green many other buildings have been taken over by the Gardens, just as the court took them over in a previous phase in Kew's history. Note the plaque on the right of the gate into No. 47. This was the original main entrance to the gardens: at that time the road you are on went straight onto the ferry landing.

Follow the road round in front of the new main entrance (created after George IV blocked off the old road in 1824) and keep going past more of the Kew Gardens buildings, notably the Herbarium and the Library. Just beyond is the entrance to Ferry Lane, resited here when George IV blocked the original road. There is no ferry any more and the lane merely leads to a car park covering the lawn where Elizabeth I is said to have had secret assignations with her lover, Lord Leicester.

Beyond Ferry Lane is another row of exceedingly pretty houses, all different styles and sizes. In the 18th century, No. 77 (Beaconsfield) was the home of Mrs Papendiek, a minor court official whose memoirs are an important source for the history of court life at Kew during the time of George III. Over on the right is the **Kew Cricket Club**. Cricket has been played on Kew Green since at least Prince Frederick's time. He was a keen player himself and in 1737 captained a side against the Duke of Marlborough's eleven. The royal team won. Nowadays charity matches with show-business stars are a feature of the ground.

Kew's first bridge

Keep left when the road rises to join the bridge approach and turn left between Capel House (one of the finest houses on the Green) and the King's Arms. Walking down towards the river you see the modern developments in Old Brentford, and rising above them, the graceful campanile of the old waterworks, now the Kew Bridge Steam Museum. At the river turn right on the towpath and go under the bridge. Robert Tunstall, the owner of the ferry, built the first bridge across the Thames at Kew in 1759. A toll was charged until 1873, when the bridge was bought for the public and made free. The present bridge dates from 1903.

On the far side you pass Kew Gardens pier (boats to Hampton Court and central London) and the war memorial gardens. When you reach the steps leading down to Thetis Terrace/Willow Cottages, a good view of Strand on the Green, another former fishing hamlet, opens up on the far side of the river. As you walk along you are crossing what was the entrance to Kew dock, the main centre of the local fishing industry until it was wiped out by pollution around 1850. Looking across the river when you reach the modern flats you can see a large five-bay house to the right of the willow tree with a blue plaque on it. This is where the painter Johann Zoffany came to live in 1789 after making his fortune in India.

When you reach the end of the long low row of cottages, turn right into the passage next to the allotments, and then right again into the road (Watcombe Cottages). Go past the entrance to Old Dock Close and when you get to the pond turn right into Cambridge Cottages and then left again. When the creek leading to the pond and the old dock were filled in in the late 19th century, all the cottages here were built on the site. The area generally was known as the Westerly Ware, after the weir which the fishermen constructed across the river. There was an Easterly Ware further downstream. Take the first left, go past the entrance to Westerly Ware and Willow Cottages/Thetis Terrace on your right and pass through a narrow bottleneck to emerge on the Green by the pond again.

Painted by Gainsborough

Go straight on between the Green and the pond, passing the entrance to Priory Road (built on the site of a neo-Gothic house called Kew Priory). The biggest house on this side of the Green is No. 24, Haverfield House. John Haverfield managed the royal estates in Kew in the 18th century. His son was Robert Tunstall's partner in the building of the bridge. His granddaughter was the subject of the Gainsborough portrait *Miss Haverfield,* now in the Wallace Collection. (Gainsborough, incidentally, never lived in Kew. He generally stayed with his friends the Kirbys or with his daughter.)

Pissarro in Kew

On the far side of Haverfield House, No. 22 has a blue plaque to the Pre-Raphaelite painter Arthur Hughes, who came here in 1858 and stayed until his death in 1915. A little further on there is a blue plaque to the Impressionist Camille Pissarro in the entrance to Gloucester Road. In 1892 he stayed in a flat here for several months while trying to reassure the parents of a Jewish girl that it would be alright for their daughter to marry his son Lucien. He succeeded, and meanwhile painted several views in and around Kew.

From Gloucester Road carry on past the Coach and Horses (Kew's oldest inn) to the traffic lights. Go straight over and walk back along Kew Road, turning left at the Maids of Honour into Kew Gardens Road. From here make your way back to the station, where the walk ends.

Mitcham

Location	8½ miles (13.7 kilometres) south of Charing Cross.
Transport	Mitcham Station (overground trains from Waterloo – change at Wimbledon, and from Victoria – change at Mitcham Junction). On Sundays there is no service at Mitcham, so travel from Victoria, alight at Mitcham Junction and walk (approximately 1 mile or 1.6 kilometres).
Features	**St Peter and St Paul's Church**; Cricket Green and **Mitcham Cricket Club**; The Canons and **Merton Heritage Centre**; **Wandle Industrial Museum**; Ravensbury Park and River Wandle.
Events	**Mitcham Fair**.
Refreshments	*London Road* fish and chip shop, burger bar, Stagecoach café and Burn Bullock pub; *Ravensbury Park* Enzo's café (see map page 132); *Mitcham town centre in Upper Green area* variety of fast-food outlets.

Mitcham lies in the Wandle plain on the road connecting Tooting with Sutton. Spread out along the road over a considerable distance, it is centred on not one but two village greens, the Upper Green to the north and the Lower Green to the south. The Upper Green, which is not covered on the walk, is now the main shopping centre of the modern town of Mitcham. The Lower Green, which is covered by the walk, is the historic heart of the village and is a protected conservation area.

In the Middle Ages four separate manors emerged in Mitcham, all belonging originally to the church. The most important, lying to the east of the village centre, was Mitcham Canons, a property of the Priory of St Mary Overie in Southwark. The monastic estate was administered from the manor house just to the east of Lower Green. In its grounds it had a dovecote and a carp pond. Both these features survive and are seen on the walk. The manor house has disappeared, but a late-17th-century house called The Canons, now the home of the Merton Heritage Centre, stands on the site.

After the dissolution of the monasteries, the main secular owners of the manor of Mitcham were the Cranmer family. Robert Cranmer, descendant of the 16th-century Archbishop Cranmer and a wealthy East India merchant, bought the estate in 1656. It remained in his descendants' hands until shortly before World War II. The family lived not in The Canons, but in another large house called The Cranmers a few hundred yards to the south. This was demolished and a hospital built on the site when the estate was broken up and developed.

John Donne

Even before the dissolution of the monasteries, many merchants, lawyers, courtiers and government officials from London had discovered Mitcham as a pleasant and healthy rural retreat. The Ravensbury Manor on the River Wandle to the south of the village was acquired by a City vintner as early as the 14th century. Later, many country houses were built in and around the village, their amenities attracting Queen Elizabeth I here no fewer than five times in the 1590s. The poet and Dean of St Paul's, John Donne, lived in the village from 1605 to 1611. At about the same time, Sir Walter Raleigh acquired land in the village through his marriage into the Throgmorton family. Unfortunately, he had to sell it in 1616 to finance his disastrous expedition to the Orinoco. About a century later court physician Fernando Mendez built the magnificent Eagle House on the former Raleigh property. This and The Canons are the only two of Mitcham's historic mansions to survive. Unfortunately, Eagle House, recently restored as offices, is too far to the north of the village to be included in the walk.

Just at the time Eagle House was built, Mitcham was developing – for reasons that are not now clear – as one of the great early centres of cricket. The game was played on the Lower Green East, now renamed Cricket Green, from at least 1685, and in 1707 the villagers challenged an All-London team to a match on Lamb's Conduit Fields in Holborn which the rustics unfortunately lost. The first recorded match in Mitcham was played in 1711, and the game has thrived here ever since, making the village a shrine for devotees.

Mitcham 'shag'

Apart from cricket, Mitcham was also known in the 18th and 19th centuries for its industries on the Wandle and for its herbs. The Wandle mills turned out flour, paper, colourful printed calico cloth and tobacco products, particularly snuff and Mitcham 'shag'. The herb fields and distilleries produced lavender, camomile, wormwood, aniseed, liquorice and damask rose, and associated essential oils and waters. In 1805, the firm of Potter and Moore, pioneers of lavender water distillation on an industrial scale in 1749, had at least 500 acres (200 hectares) of medicinal and aromatic herbs under cultivation. No trace of the herb industry remains in Mitcham today, but the Ravensbury snuff mill and the Mitcham flour and paper mill still stand on the Wandle.

Public railway

Industrial development in the early 19th century in the Wandle area south of the village was helped by the arrival of the Surrey Iron Railway. Opened between Wandsworth and Croydon in 1803, this was the first public railway in the world. Horses pulled waggons along the tracks and users paid tolls at various gates as on a turnpike road. The steam railways killed it off quickly, but the Mitcham section of the track was incorporated into the Wimbledon–Croydon line, opened through Mitcham Station in 1855. When the main line from Victoria arrived at Mitcham Junction a few years later, Mitcham's transition from country village to urban suburb was set in full motion.

THE MITCHAM WALK
Start and finish Mitcham Station.
Distance 3 miles (4.8 kilometres).

Come out of Mitcham Station onto the London Road and turn right past the old station house with the arch in the middle. Built in the early 1800s as a private house, this was taken over by the railways in the 1850s and used until the 1980s. It has now been converted into offices.

Cricket Green
Carry on up London Road towards the village centre. After a while you come to Cricket Green, formerly Lower Green East and the larger of the two open spaces that together make up the Lower Green. All the historical landmarks in Mitcham are illustrated and described on the information panel across the road at the corner of the green. The green itself, of course, is the Mitcham cricket pitch and one of the oldest such pitches in the country. To the left is the White Hart, a former coaching inn dating from at least 1603 and given a handsome Georgian facelift around 1750. The Burn Bullock to the right is similarly a Georgian coaching inn with earlier origins (the fact that both were modernized and enlarged about the same time is clear evidence of the growth of road traffic). Originally it was called the King's Head, but it was renamed in 1975. Burn Bullock was a famous Mitcham cricketer, a member of the local club from the age of 17 and landlord of the pub from 1941 until his death in 1954. His wife Lil ran it until her retirement in 1975. Inside, the walls are covered with cricketing photographs.

Turn right by the pub. Behind the Georgian section you can clearly see the inn's original half-timbered part, certainly more than 300 and possibly as much as 400 years old. Beyond the pub is the pavilion of the **Mitcham Cricket Club**, with its verandah for watching play. Crossing the road to the pitch was a relatively easy matter when the pavilion was built in 1904. Now, with the great increase of traffic, it is infinitely more hazardous. Maybe it is just as well that there is a clause in the lease forbidding the club to have its own bar!

Miraculous appearance of water
Carry on along Cricket Green and past Mary Tate's almshouses, put up in 1829 on the site of the Tates' Mitcham house. The Tates were a wealthy family and had other property elsewhere. Miss Tate was the last surviving member of the Mitcham Tates and lived out in Northamptonshire at a large place called Burleigh Park, so she could afford to be generous. Just beyond the Queen's Head pub, cross the road to the obelisk on the north side. Mitcham went through a few years of drought in the early 1820s. When an artesian spring suddenly appeared here, locals took it for a miracle and the lord of the manor's son, the Reverend Richard Cranmer, decided to commemorate it with this monument, erected in September 1822. The Cranmer family lived in a large house to the right off what is now Cranmer Road.

Continue past the obelisk into Madeira Road and then after a short time turn left into the gates of The Canons. This is the house built in 1680 on the site of the

MITCHAM

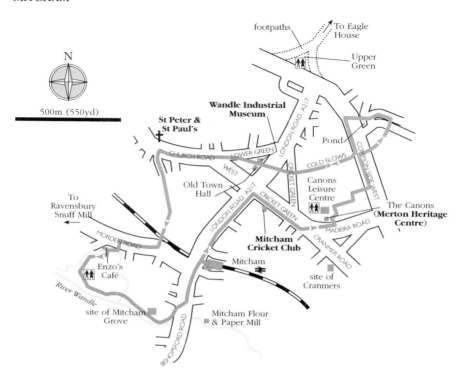

original monastic manor house. Now it is owned by the local council and used as the **Merton Heritage Centre** and local history museum. Turn right down the side of the house to the back garden. Here you can see the monks' carp pond and beside it the stone dovecote, dated 1511. Turn left along the back of the house, and then right, along the garden wall. When you reach the car park you can see dead ahead of you a stone let into the wall in 1816 by Mrs E. M. Cranmer to mark the eastern boundary of her property. Turn left along this wall and then right when you reach the playing fields.

The handsome Georgian mansion on the right now is Park House, built in 1780 for City lawyer Francis Gregg. Gregg was also manager of the Earl of Carlisle's extensive estates in the north, and served a s MP for one of the Earl's pocket boroughs in the 1790s. When you reach Mitcham Common, turn left along Commonside West and walk past the Windmill pub, which dates from about 1870 and recalls a former windmill. When you reach the lights, cross the road and walk along the path across the Common. This section of the Common is known as Three Kings Piece (after the pub of that name which you pass in a minute) and it is here that the annual **Mitcham Fair** is held every August.

Five generations of Charts

At Commonside East, turn left past the row of cottages and the Three Kings pub. In front is a duck pond, at least 300 years old, fed by a covered-in stream running alongside Commonside. At the junction with the main road, the weatherboarded Clarendon House was at one time the home of the Chart family, noted local builders and administrators. John Chart built the parish church in 1821. Five generations of Charts served in the local vestry and its successors. William Chart was appointed vestry clerk in 1761. His descendant, Colonel Stephen Chart, retired as town clerk in 1946.

At the traffic lights just beyond Clarendon House, cross the main road and turn left back along Commonside West. When you get to the lights where you turned onto the Common, turn right along Cold Blows, an aptly named footpath that once connected the village with the common fields on the far side of Commonside East. The path brings you back to Cricket Green and to some of the elegant houses overlooking it from the northeast side. Carry straight on across the Green towards the Victorian vestry hall, Mitcham's first town hall, designed by a Chart and built in 1887 on the site of the village lockup.

Cross London Road and pass between the vestry hall and the **Wandle Industrial Museum** on the right. Go straight across Lower Green West, passing on your left the old village school topped with a cupola and clock tower. Built as a Sunday school for 150 children in 1788, it became a National day school in 1812 and then one of the new elementary schools in 1870. From 1897 until 1987, when the church sold it, it served as the parish rooms. It has now been converted into flats and artists' studios.

14th-century chapel

As you continue into Church Road you pass a newer school on the left. At the entrance behind the fence you might just be able to make out a ruined arch. This is the only surviving portion of Hall Place, the manor house of Vauxhall, one of medieval Mitcham's three other manors besides Mitcham Canons. The now lonely arch was the entrance to the house's private chapel, constructed in 1349. Further along noisy Church Road you come to the vicarage on the left and then the parish church of **St Peter and St Paul** on the right. Mitcham once had its traditional medieval parish church, but in 1821 it was demolished and a larger one built in its place.

Cross the road by the church into Church Path (to be on the safe side use the zebra crossing round the corner ahead). At the end of the row of cottages, continue on along the footpath, called Baron Path because it once led to Baron House, named after an 18th-century barrister occupant, Oliver Baron. Two centuries before Baron lived here Queen Elizabeth I stayed in the house on two of her five visits to Mitcham.

Ravensbury Park

Having crossed the railway line and reached the end of the path, turn right onto Morden Road and then, just beyond Morden Gardens, left into Ravensbury Park. Follow the path round to the right past Enzo's café and across one of the channels of the Wandle. At the toilets the path forks. The right one leads to the Ravensbury snuff mill, in production until 1925 but now converted into flats. The walk takes the left fork, passing on the right the site of the old manor house of Ravensbury Manor acquired by a City wine merchant in the 1300s. At the bridge an information panel recounts the history of the area and tells how the last owners of the estate before it was developed and part preserved as a public park were the Bidder family, descendants of an engineering associate of George Stephenson of Stephenson's Rocket fame.

Private bank

Carry on along the path beside the Wandle. Having crossed two small bridges you pass houses on your left. Here, until 1846, stood Mitcham Grove, generally reckoned to have been the most beautiful of Mitcham's many secluded and gracious country houses. Between 1786 and his death in 1828, it was the home of Henry Hoare, senior partner of the private bank still flourishing in Fleet Street in the City and one of Mitcham's most public-spirited and generous residents. Hoare bought the house from Alexander Wedderburn, the lawyer and later Lord Chancellor, who in turn had been presented with it by Clive of India after successfully defending him against charges of corruption in the early 1770s.

The path brings you out on the London Road again. From the bridge on the right, the white Mitcham mill can be glimpsed a short distance upstream. The route of the walk, however, is to the left and Mitcham Station, where the walk ends, is up ahead by the traffic lights.

Rotherhithe and Bermondsey

Location	3¾ miles (6 kilometres) east of Charing Cross.
Transport	*Rotherhithe* Rotherhithe Underground Station (East London Line);
	Bermondsey London Bridge Station (Northern Underground Line and overground lines to the southeast).
Features	**St Mary's Church, Rotherhithe**; **St Mary Magdalen Church, Bermondsey**; **Bermondsey Street, New Caledonian Antiques Market**, remains of Bermondsey Abbey; Thames-side walk with views upriver to City and downstream to Canary Wharf; Rotherhithe wharves and warehouses; **Brunel's Engine House**.
Refreshments	*London Bridge Station and Tooley Street* numerous bars, cafés, takeaways and fast-food outlets;
	Bermondsey Street cafés and pubs;
	on the riverside between Bermondsey and Rotherhithe Angel pub; *Rotherhithe* Mayflower pub in village centre, Chinese restaurant near station, fish and chips/kebab/burger bar in Albion Street.

If its name is anything to go by, the little Docklands village of Rotherhithe on the south side of the River Thames started out as a landing place (hithe) for cattle (rother). No doubt the beasts were brought here by boat from south Essex and north Kent, were grazed in the fertile meadows behind the village and were then herded up to market at Smithfield on the northeastern flank of the City of London.

The village and its hinterland were low-lying and subject to frequent inundations by the Thames, so as more people settled in the area a great river wall (which may originally have been begun by the Romans) was built extending west to Bermondsey and east all the way around the peninsula opposite the Isle of Dogs to Deptford. Rotherhithe Street then emerged on top of the embankment, with houses, wharves and shipyards strung out along its 2-mile (3-kilometre) length. Here were built, repaired and berthed many of the ships that made London from very early times the busiest port in the world. Here also lived many of the seamen and ships' captains who sailed those ships to the four corners of the earth in search of maritime trade.

Greenland dock

As the number of ships using the port of London increased, more and more vessels were forced to anchor downriver in less sheltered reaches. To counter this problem the Howland family of Rotherhithe built on their property in the east of the parish

London's first major wet dock, surrounded by a windbreak of trees and capable of accommodating 120 sailing ships. Completed in 1700 and known originally as the Howland Wet Dock, it was later leased by the South Sea Company for their Greenland whaling fleet and re-christened the Greenland Dock.

Throughout the 18th century the Greenland Dock was surrounded by the meadows and market gardens of rural Rotherhithe, by this time criss-crossed with a complex, Dutch-style network of drainage ditches and dykes. In the 19th century, as the British trading empire got into full swing, these meadows were gobbled up by more and more docks on the Greenland model until virtually the whole Rotherhithe peninsula was one vast sheet of water. The four companies that built the docks amalgamated in 1864 to form the Surrey Commercial Dock Company. The Surrey docks subsequently became the main centre of London's imported timber trade.

The growth of the great docks on the peninsula mirrored Rotherhithe's decline as a shipbuilding centre. In place of the old shipyards, wharves, warehouses and mills came to dominate the waterfront. These in turn became redundant in the 1960s and 1970s when London's historic docks were closed. Eight out of the 11 Surrey docks were subsequently filled in and many of the warehouses demolished. But the Greenland Dock, not seen on the walk because it is too far away from the village centre, survives at the heart of a modern housing and leisure development and a number of warehouses have been converted into homes or workshops. The empty warehouses that remain in the heart of Rotherhithe serve as an evocative reminder of the village's maritime past and add a kind of Gothic atmosphere to the walk, which passes right by them.

Bermondsey Abbey

The connection between Rotherhithe and Bermondsey is based on more than geography: in the Middle Ages a large part of the manor of Rotherhithe was owned by Bermondsey Abbey. Founded in 1082 by Aylwin Child of London and endowed with the manor of Bermondsey by King William Rufus, the Cluniac priory of St Saviour's was built in open countryside between Southwark and Rotherhithe about 1 mile (1.5 kilometres) inland from the river. Servants and tenants of the priory (which converted into a Benedictine abbey in the 1390s) lived in houses around it and formed the nucleus of the village, worshipping in St Mary Magdalen Church just outside the abbey's north gate. The lane connecting the north gate with London Bridge gradually became Bermondsey Street and the high street of the village. In the vicinity of modern Tanner Street, Bermondsey Street crossed the River Neckinger. Where the Neckinger joined the Thames the abbey built a mill and a dock. The latter still survives as St Saviour's Dock.

The leather industry

In the Middle Ages, drawn by the water supply and the availability of oak bark for tanning, leatherworkers settled at Bermondsey and made it the centre not only of London's, but the country's, leather industry. Skins came from the Smithfield slaughterhouses to be processed at Bermondsey before being marketed at Leadenhall Market in the City. When Leadenhall became too small in the 19th century, the

Plate 28: *The main entrance of the Trinity Hospital almshouse in Greenwich (see page 114).*

Plate 29: *A pretty cottage tucked away in Diamond Terrace, Greenwich (see page 115).*

Plate 30: *Cows from Petersham Farm graze contentedly in the lush meadows between the village and the Thames (see page 123).*

Plate 31: *One of the finest 17th-century houses in England and now the property of the National Trust, Ham House was formerly the ancestral home of the Earls of Dysart (see page 117).*

Plate 32: *The pond on the east side of Kew Green originated in Tudor times as a riverside dock for the royal barge (see page 128).*

Plate 33: Mitcham's immaculately maintained Cricket Green has witnessed matches ever since the game began 300-odd years ago (see page 131).

Plate 34: Ducks and swans cohabit peacefully on a quiet backwater of the Wandle in Ravensbury Park, Mitcham (see page 133).

Plate 35: *The hollow-post windmill on Wimbledon Common dates from 1817 and now houses a fascinating windmill museum (see page 146).*

leather market was brought to Bermondsey, so making the area the centre of the leather trade as well as the leather industry. Both have departed now and been replaced by the New Caledonian Antiques Market.

After the closure of Bermondsey Abbey, the first and greatest secular owner of the manor was the courtier and administrator Sir Thomas Pope, the builder of Bermondsey House on the site of the abbey, and founder of Trinity College in Oxford. Rotherhithe, meanwhile, passed through various hands until the early 19th century when it came into the possession of Court governess Jane Gomm and then her brother, Field Marshal Sir William Gomm. The Gomms married into the Carrs, becoming the Carr-Gomms. The Carr-Gomms were the last lords of the manor of Rotherhithe and their name lives on in the area in various local charitable institutions.

THE ROTHERHITHE AND BERMONDSEY WALK
Start London Bridge Station.
Finish Rotherhithe Station.
Distance 3½ miles (5.6 kilometres)

Turn right out of London Bridge Station onto Tooley Street. Opposite the entrance to Hay's Galleria, turn right into Weston Street and walk underneath the station overhead. Turn left onto St Thomas Street and then right into Bermondsey Street. Apart from some warehouses and factories at this top end, Bermondsey Street retains – unusually for this part of London – much of its original character as a community high street, and also many of its original houses, particularly the little row on the right, of which No. 78, with its oriel window and weatherboarded attic workroom, is the highlight. Restoration will no doubt reach these houses before long, for Bermondsey Street is now a conservation area and much refurbishment work has already been done in the lower half of the street.

St Mary Magdalen
Further on, the street names of Tanner Street and Morocco Street, where Bermondsey Street crossed the River Neckinger, flag the site of the former leather market. The market building, now converted into offices, stands on the far side of the market area at the end of Morocco Street. The parish church of **St Mary Magdalen**, built around 1680 on the site of an earlier church which had become unsafe, is at the bottom of the street, with the old Georgian rectory on one side and the modern rectory on the other. All around are warehouses full of antiques, spilling over from the Friday morning **New Caledonian Antiques Market** which moved here from north London after World War II. It is mainly a market for dealers, but collectors come here too. You have to be here early to get the best bargains though: like most wholesale markets, most of the day's business is done while ordinary folk are still tucked up in bed.

Resurrection men
Carry on the past the church and the disused graveyard. The building on the corner is the old parish watch-house where the parish constables reported for duty and

ROTHERHITHE AND BERMONDSEY

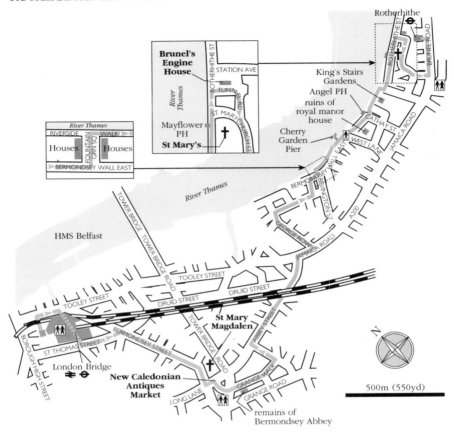

where a watch was kept on the graveyard to prevent resurrection men stealing fresh corpses to sell to nearby hospitals for dissection. At this point you are standing on the site of the north gate of Bermondsey Abbey. Bermondsey Square ahead represents the main quadrangle of the abbey. The abbey church lay along Abbey Road to your left. After acquiring the dissolved abbey in the 1540s, Sir Thomas Pope knocked the church down and used the stone to build Bermondsey House on the eastern side of the old abbey quadrangle. As you can see, nothing substantial is left of the abbey now, or indeed of Pope's house. Even Georgian Bermondsey Square has almost entirely disappeared: only a rather forlorn group of houses from the southwestern corner is left. On Friday mornings the open space in the middle of the square is filled with antiques stalls.

Cross the square diagonally to its southeastern corner and turn into Grange Walk. Grange Walk ran from the abbey's eastern gatehouse to the abbey grange or farm. Several very old houses survive on the right-hand side of the street. No. 7, one of the oldest, must have been part of the gatehouse, for the gate hinges still protrude from its pink-coloured façade. Having passed the disused 1830 girls' charity school building on the right, you come to No. 67 on the left, the most handsome house in the street, currently being restored with the assistance of English Heritage.

Now you are at the eastern extremity of the Bermondsey village area. Open fields originally stretched from this point to Rotherhithe. Today housing estates, industrial buildings and main roads are more in evidence. We now have to make our way through all these developments until we reach the docklands strip beside the Thames.

London's first railway line

Turn left into The Grange and then right into Abbey Street. Ahead Canary Wharf Tower rises above the bridge carrying the railway line to London Bridge Station. Opened in 1836 and extending as far as Greenwich, this was the first railway line in the capital. As you pass beneath the bridge, note the handsome fluted columns and fine brickwork of the original structure and the way it has been widened over the years to accommodate more tracks.

At Jamaica Road turn right and then first left into George Row. Jacob Street at the far end marks both the beginning of the riverside warehouse area and the site of Jacob's Island, a notorious Victorian slum surrounded by polluted mill streams. This is where Dickens set the death of Bill Sikes in *Oliver Twist*. Turn right into Chambers Street, where there are still many vacant warehouses and mills, and then left into Loftie Street. Here film studios and scenery makers have put some of the empty spaces to productive use. At the end of Loftie Street turn right into Bermondsey Wall East and then left through modern Fountain Green Square to reach the riverside directly opposite Wapping Pier Head, the former entrance to the London Docks. Turning right along the riverside there are fine views of the great terraces of warehouses on both sides of the river. On the left, the modern building painted white and blue is the base of the river police. On the right, in front of Canary Wharf Tower, are the warehouses and church spire of Rotherhithe, your ultimate destination.

Turner's *Téméraire*

At Cherry Garden Pier, named after a 17th-century resort visited by Samuel Pepys and the spot where Turner stood to paint his National Gallery picture of the warship *Téméraire* on its way to the Rotherhithe breaker's yard, you have to leave the riverside walk and return to the road. As you pass the entrance to West Lane on your right you cross from the ancient parish of Bermondsey into Rotherhithe. The first feature you come to is an open area with the Angel pub on the riverside and, in the centre, the partially excavated remains of Edward III's 14th-century moated manor house. Three panels around the site tell the story of the house, which was probably the manor house for that part of Rotherhithe not granted to Bermondsey Abbey. Originally in the hands of the noble Clare family, the house and land seem to have passed into royal control in or shortly before Edward III's time. A successor, Henry IV, is said to have lived here in 1412 while recovering from leprosy.

Royal landing stage

Carrying on, you come to the solitary office of Braithwaite and Dean, one of the few surviving firms of Thames lightermen. For centuries, lightermen have conveyed cargoes from ships out in the middle of the river to the warehouses ion the riverside quays. Beyond Braithwaite and Dean are the King's Stairs Gardens, the King's Stairs being the landing stage for the royal manor house. In the gardens you rejoin the riverside and walk through an arcade under a modern apartment block before coming back onto the road at the start of Rotherhithe Street. At this point it is hemmed in by tall warehouses and so narrow that it seems amazing that it should go on for almost 2 miles (3 kilometres) and be one of London's longest streets.

From this narrow section of the street you emerge in the centre of the old village of Rotherhithe. On the left beyond the Thames Tunnel Mills, one of the first industrial buildings in docklands to be converted into residential use, the Mayflower pub provides a clue to Rotherhithe's main claim to fame: the *Mayflower,* the ship that carried the Pilgrim Fathers over to America in 1620, was berthed here. Its master and part-owner, Captain Christopher Jones, moved to Rotherhithe from Harwich in 1611. He is buried in the churchyard, as are his three co-owners of the ship.

Continue on under the gantry. The late 18th-century warehouses left and right were formerly a granary belonging to the Grice family. Now they are home to Sands Studios, where the film *Little Dorrit* was made, and the Rotherhithe picture library. Behind the granary you come to **Brunel's Engine House**. This is the original pump house used during construction of the Wapping–Rotherhithe tunnel between 1824 and 1843. Inside, an exhibition tells the story of the tunnel – the first ever built under water – and the heroic struggle needed to complete it. Engineered by the Brunels, father and son, it is now used by the East London Underground line.

Prince Lee Boo

Turn right into Tunnel Road between the Engine House and the granary and then right again into St Marychurch Street. **St Mary's Church** was built by local people in 1715 and deliberately raised up high on a plinth to protect it from flooding. Inside there are many memorials to local ships' captains and some pieces of furniture made by wood salvaged from the *Téméraire*. The pillars look like stone, but are in fact tree trunks encased in plaster. The roof, resembling an upturned boat, must have been a doddle for the local boatbuilders who fashioned it. Outside the west end of the church are two interesting memorials: a modern one to the captain of the *Mayflower* and an original commemorating two people linked together by a fascinating story. In 1783 Captain Henry Wilson's ship was wrecked and he and his crew were cast away on the Pacific island of Cooroora, east of the Philippines. They got on so well with the islanders that, when they had built themselves a new ship and were about to return to England, the king of the island asked them to take his son with them to be educated in an English school. Wilson gladly brought Prince Lee Boo to his home in Rotherhithe and sent him to the local school. Although much older than the other pupils he was a great favourite, but unfortunately had no defences against western diseases. After only six months he succumbed to smallpox.

You come out of the churchyard directly opposite the rectory and the former village school with its little figures of a boy and a girl above the door. The charity school was founded in 1612 by Robert Bell and Peter Hills, a seaman, to whom there is a brass memorial in the church. In Prince Lee Boo's day the school house was at the east end of the church, but in 1797 it moved to this house, where the master also lived. It still survives today as a modern primary school in Beatson Walk.

Sufferance Wharf

Turn right past the school. On the left now are the village watch-house and fire-engine house, both built in 1821, and on the right Hope Sufferance Wharf. From Tudor times onwards goods could only be unloaded in the port of London at 'legal' quays. When these became congested, other quays were licensed or 'suffered' to admit goods bearing low customs duties. Hope Wharf at Rotherhithe, stretching back from the riverside to this point, was one of these sufferance wharves. Follow the road round to the left, and at the end turn left into Brunel Road. Rotherhithe Underground Station, where the walk ends, is about 100 yards (90 metres) ahead on the left.

Wimbledon

Location	7½ miles (12 kilometres) southwest of Charing Cross.
Transport	Wimbledon Station (Underground District Line; overground trains from Waterloo and London Bridge stations).
Features	**St Mary's Church**; High Street and Eagle House; Wimbledon Common and Georgian mansions; **Southside House**; **Wimbledon Society Museum**; views of London; **Wimbledon Windmill Museum** and **Wimbledon Lawn Tennis Museum** (not on walk – see map page 144).
Refreshments	*Station and adjoining streets and shopping centre* variety of fast-food outlets, pubs, takeaways and cafés; *High Street* pubs, restaurants and coffee houses; *Crooked Billet and Camp Road* (halfway through walk) pubs; *Wimbledon Windmill Museum* (not on walk) café (and toilets).

Wimbledon has been one of London's most select suburbs for over two centurie snow, but its history goes right back to prehistoric times. Ridgway is presumed to be a relic of an ancient track leading to a ford over the Thames at Kingston, and the so-called Caesar's Camp on the Common – a circular space surrounded by a nearly levelled ditch and rampart – is actually an Iron Age hill fort. The village grew up to the east of the Common, on the edge of the high ground overlooking the valley of the River Wandle. The church and rectory stood, as they still do, on the lip of the plateau, enjoying fine views to the north and east now obscured by trees and buildings. The manor house joined them later. The two main roads of the village, Church Road and High Street, lay further back between the church and the common land where the villagers grazed their animals and gathered turf and firewood.

The manor of Mortlake

In the Middle Ages, Wimbledon was merely an outlying part of the Archbishops of Canterbury's great manor of Mortlake, which also included Putney, Roehampton and East Sheen. But whereas the manor house of the archbishops was at Mortlake, the parish church of the district was at Wimbledon. **St Mary's Church**, therefore, has been an important religious centre for the best part of a thousand years. This perhaps accounts for the substantial size of the new rectory built beside the church around 1500. Though much altered, the house still survives and is, by a margin of a century or so, the oldest building in Wimbledon – older even than the church which, having been rebuilt to provide more space in 1789, was again rebuilt for much the same reason in 1841.

Forced to surrender

In 1536 the then Archbishop of Canterbury was forced to surrender his Wimbledon property to Henry VIII and, shortly after, the virtually new rectory was leased out as a country retreat to politician and courtier Sir Thomas Cecil. The Cecils took to Wimbledon and, having risen to become one of the most powerful dynasties in Tudor England, moved out of the old rectory into a huge new country house completed in 1588 a few hundred yards/metres to the east. Sir Edward Cecil, third son of the builder of the house and a professional soldier, inherited the estate and was created Viscount Wimbledon in 1625.

The Cecils' house was pretty much in ruins by 1700, so when Huguenot merchant and financier Sir Theodore Janssen bought the estate, he demolished the old house and used the bricks to build a brand new one on the opposite side of the church. He did not enjoy his new property for long, however, for the South Sea Bubble ruined him and he had to sell up to the Duchess of Marlborough in 1724. The Duchess then built yet another house, but her descendant, Earl Spencer, had to replace it in 1799 after it had been destroyed by fire. This century has seen the destruction of both Lord Spencer's and Sir Theodore Janssen's houses, so although Wimbledon has had no fewer than four great manor houses over the centuries, not one has survived the vicissitudes of time to grace the village today.

The Spencer family finally left Wimbledon in 1846. After their departure the park, landscaped by Capability Brown, was mostly sold off for development. Later the local council was able to acquire one part, including the lake, and open it to the public. Another part was bought in 1920 by the All England Lawn Tennis Club and subsequently developed as the home of the Wimbledon tennis championships.

Healthy position

Wimbledon's healthy position at 150 feet (45 metres) above sea level and its proximity to London combined to make it a desirable retreat for wealthy merchants and professional men from the time of the Cecils onwards. In the beginning, the big houses these successful individuals built for themselves were, like the manor house, close to the centre of the village. Eagle House, built in 1613 by a founder of the East India Company, survives at the north end of the High Street and is seen on the walk. Later houses tended to be built outside the village, facing the common around Rushmere Pond. Those in Parkside on the east side have all disappeared, but several on the south and particularly the west sides have survived and are also seen on the walk.

Since the village was not on a main road and lacked any industry except for a few mills down on the river, Wimbledon's shopkeepers and tradesmen relied on the custom from these big houses for their living until well into the 19th century. Then came the railway and with it the tide of building that eventually filled in all the open land between the once-isolated village and central London. Luckily, however, the railway had to be built in the valley bottom, about half a mile from the centre of the village, so, as the following walk shows, Wimbledon was able to preserve much of its individual identity in a way that many of the other old village centres in and around London were not.

THE WIMBLEDON WALK

Start and finish Wimbledon Station.
Distance 3¼ miles (6 kilometres).

From the station forecourt turn right along the main road. Cross at the traffic lights and go straight on, passing the library on your right. At the end of the shops and just before the main road starts to climb the hill, turn right into Woodside. Walk along here and then take the first left into St Mary's Road. Follow this road – once called Hothouse Lane because it connected Lord Spencer's house at the top of the hill with his kitchen garden at the bottom – as it winds its way uphill to the top of the plateau on which the old village of Wimbledon and its Common sit.

Eventually you reach the junction with Arthur Road in front of the church. The edge of the plateau is to your right. Here stood three of the four manor houses: the Cecils', the Duchess of Marlborough's and Lord Spencer's. The last, Lord Spencer's, was demolished in 1948 and replaced in the 1970s with a school. All that is left of it is a well house across the road from the school entrance, built in 1798 to cover the earl's private artesian well and converted into a private house about the time the school was built. The fourth manor house – the one built by Sir Theodore Janssen about 1720 and demolished in 1900 – lay to your left in the vicinity of Alan Road. Nothing remains of this except a length of kitchen garden wall in one of the roads built over the site.

WIMBLEDON

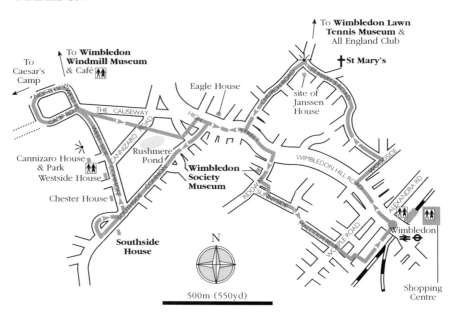

Memorials in the church

In the days of Wimbledon Park, Arthur Road did not exist. But when the estate was sold to John Beaumont for development in 1846, he built the lodge house in front of you to provide an entrance to the grounds. In 1872, when Arthur Road was constructed, Stag Lodge, as it is called, became redundant and was subsequently converted into a private house. Behind the lodge, the church, though relatively modern, contains many old memorials, particularly the large black marble tomb of Lord Wimbledon in the 17th-century Cecil Chapel and the fine memorial to James Perry in the entrance lobby. Perry, a Wimbledon resident, owned and edited the *Morning Chronicle* newspaper in the early years of the 19th century and had a large flour mill down on the Wandle. Round the back of the church you can see the tomb of Sir Joseph Bazalgette, one of the greatest British engineers of the 19th century and the builder of London's remarkable sewer system. Looking over the churchyard wall, the upper parts of Wimbledon's historic Old Rectory are also visible. The present rectory is a more modern house close by.

Fine view of London

Turn left at the junction with Arthur Road and continue along St Mary's Road. From the roundabout junction with Church Road there is a fine view to the north towards central London: if you cross over to the entrance to Burghley Road the British Telecom Tower in the West End stands out prominently. Turn left now into Church Road. Large houses line both sides of the road, those on the left being built on the site of Janssen's house, originally called Wimbledon House to distinguish it from Wimbledon Park and later renamed Belvedere House, not because of its hilltop site but because that was the name of the road in Lambeth where the then owner of the house – a wealthy timber merchant – had his yard.

Beyond Belvedere Avenue you come to Old House Close, a modern development laid out on the site of a late-17th-century merchant's house pulled down in the 1960s. Beyond the close the little houses and shops of the village start. This next section of Church Road, together with the short High Street, was really – apart from the large mansions – all there was to Wimbledon for centuries until the railway brought commuters, particularly from the 1860s onwards. At the junction with the High Street, the nucleus of the village, turn right along the oldest section of the street and cross to the other side at the lights. Continue and then turn left when you get to Southside Common. This soon brings you to the beginning of the Common behind the village.

What you see here is only the southeastern tip of Wimbledon Common, perhaps one-twentieth of it at most. People started building houses here during the late 17th century after all the best plots in the village had been taken. By the end of the 18th century the south, west and east sides of this little section of the Common – more a large village green really – had been almost completely built up. On the west side (opposite you now) most of the mansions remain. Here on the south side, survivors are less frequent. Claremont House on the left is one of the originals; it was built in 1650 by Thomas Hilliard, a retired merchant from the City of London. Beyond it, the crescent at the entrance to Murray Road is the old entrance drive of

Wimbledon Lodge, home of the Murray family from 1812 to 1905 when the house was pulled down. On the corner of Lauriston Road the former coach house of Lauriston House still stands, bearing a plaque to William Wilberforce. He inherited the house from his uncle in 1777 and lived here until he started his anti-slavery campaign nine years later.

King's College School

At the junction with West Side Common you come to King's College School, founded in 1829 under the auspices of King's College, part of London University. The school moved here from central London in 1897 – taking over an existing house and its 8-acre (3-hectare) grounds – and is now a well-known and highly successful boys' public school with associated junior school. On the far side of the school you pass the entrance to Wright's Alley, an ancient right of way between the common and the village fields below the Ridgway. Next is the late 17th-century **Southside House**, one of Wimbledon's finest houses and the ancestral home of the Pennington-Mellor family who still occupy it.

The Crooked Billet

A little further down the hill, turn right by the green-painted Gothic House (1763) and cross over into Crooked Billet, a collection of workmen's houses carved out of the Common when the big houses were being built. A 'billet' is a piece of wood cut to the right length for fuel, but the curious name presumably comes from the eponymous pub. Go past the rebuilt Cinque Cottages (originally built in 1872 for poor men over the age of 55) and turn right, passing in front of the Crooked Billet pub and the Hand in Hand. At the end of Crooked Billet turn left along the west side of the Common.

The first mansion is Chester House, dating from the 1690s and a century later the home for 20 years of the radical John Horne Tooke, one-time rector of Brentford. Next, where the tarmac gives way to the unsurfaced path, is Westside House, built in the time of Queen Anne by London merchant William Bourne. Continuing on, the pink and white house set well back from the road is Cannizaro House, also built by Bourne and in the 19th century the home of an impoverished Sicilian nobleman called the Duke of Cannizaro. Though the house is now a hotel and restaurant, its magnificent grounds – reached by a gate just beyond the hotel entrance – are public property and are well worth a look, both for themselves and for the views to the west across the valley of the Beverley Brook.

Wimbledon Windmill Museum

At the end of West Side, cross straight over into West Place, like Crooked Billet another collection of mainly workmen's cottages built on a patch of common in the 18th century. When you reach the corner, paths lead on into the main part of Wimbledon Common. The one marked as a cycle track and going straight on from the road is the way to the **Wimbledon Windmill Museum** in the centre of the Common. It takes about ten minutes to reach it, and it is well worth visiting as there is a café (and a public toilet) there too.

Caesar's Camp

Meanwhile the walk turns left, following the road round the houses to the junction with Camp Road. The Iron Age hill fort known as Caesar's Camp is about ten minutes' walk down the road to the right, in the middle of a golf course. On the left just here is the old village school, established in 1758 and used as such up until after World War II. It is now a private girls' school, but the original school building with its central octagon is still standing. Turn left past the school and then past the village's modern almshouses, former site of the old parish workhouse. When you get to the Common again, take the path between the roads heading back across the Common towards the village and passing the Rushmere Pond on the way.

Instead of re-entering the village by means of Southside Common, take the unsurfaced road called The Green to the left of it. This brings you back to the High Street opposite the entrance to Marryat Road, the site of Wimbledon House Parkside, one-time home of the novelist Captain Frederick Marryat's parents. Turn right along the High Street, passing first the Rose and Crown pub and then Eagle House, Wimbledon's oldest house apart from the Old Rectory. Built by an East India merchant, it became a school at the end of the 18th century and was extended forward to the High Street at that time in order to create extra space. It was fortunately saved from demolition at the end of the 19th century when the school moved out, and is now the office of the Islamic Heritage Foundation.

Prehistoric track

Keep going along the High Street and carry on when you get to the Church Road junction. This next section of the High Street was only created from the mid-19th century onwards when the village started to expand – the shops on the left where the Belvedere House garden had been were not built until 1924. Just before the road sets off down the hill, turn right into Ridgway, the former prehistoric track running along the southern edge of the plateau to the ford over the Thames at Kingston. On the corner of Lingfield Road is the **Wimbledon Society Museum**, a local history museum housed in the premises of the original village club and hall which were opened in 1859.

Cross over Ridgway here and turn left down Oldfield Road, a row of labourers' cottages built about 1820. Near the bottom go right into the passageway. This brings you out on Sunnyside Place. Here turn left and then, when the road comes to an end, carry on downhill via Sunnyside Passage. Both this and the previous passageway represent former footpaths leading from Wimbledon to the neighbouring village of Merton down in the valley. Sunnyside Passage brings you into Malcolm Road and Malcolm Road brings you to Worple Road. In a field a few hundred yards to the right of this point the original Wimbledon croquet and tennis club was founded in 1868 and the first croquet championship was held at the club two years later. Tennis was added in 1877, when the club was renamed the All England Croquet and Lawn Tennis Club. Cross straight over Worple Road and continue on into the next passage (lampstand at entrance). At the end, turn left, then right into Alt Grove. At the end of Alt Grove turn left along the path by the railway line and carry on until you reach the main road and station opposite, where the walk ends.

Further Information

Opening times

Opening times are constantly changing, so telephone before a visit to avoid disappointment. Churches are open at service times as well as at times indicated. Church phone numbers are for the vicarage/rectory unless otherwise indicated. Brief descriptions are given for places that are not otherwise described in the text.

National Gardens Scheme
Various private houses throughout London open their gardens on selected summer days to raise money for this national charity. Those featuring on the walks appear on the maps and in the listings below. For opening times see the Scheme's yellow booklet distributed to public libraries, or call the Hon. County Organizer, Mrs Maurice Snell, on 01932 864532.

BARNES
Barn Elms Nature Reserve Tel: 0181 876 8995 (Wildfowl and Wetlands Trust) for update on progress of nature reserve and details of public access.
Barnes Village Fair Takes place second Sat in July. Tel: 0181 878 2359 (Barnes Community Association) for details.
St Mary's Church Church Road. Tel: 0181 741 5422 (parish office); 0181 878 6982 (rectory). *Open* daily 10.30–12.30.

BEXLEY
Bexley Cricket Club Manor Way. Tel: 01322 524159 for fixture list.
Hall Place and Bexley Local History Museum Bourne Road. Tel: 01322 526574. *Open* Apr–Oct: Mon–Sat 10.00–17.00, Sun 14.00–18.00; Nov–Mar: Mon–Sat 10.00–16.00. *Grounds open* daily through the year. *Admission:* free.
St Mary's Church High Street. Tel: 01322 523457. *Open* by appointment.

BLACKHEATH
All Saints Church All Saints Drive. Tel: 0181 852 4280 (parish office, *open* Mon–Fri 10.00–12.00); 0181 293 0023 (vicarage). *Open* by appointment.

BRENTFORD
Boston Manor House Boston Manor Road. Tel: 0181 570 0622. *Open* last Sun in May to last Sun in Sep 14.30–17.00. *Admission:* free. *What to see:* ground and first-floor rooms with fine fireplaces and notable plaster ceilings.
St Paul's Church St Paul's Road. Tel: 0181 568 7442. *Open* daily. *What to see:* award-winning modern church plus Zoffany's 18th-century painting, *The Last Supper,* which was originally intended for Kew church and supposedly incorporates portraits of local people and the artist (Zoffany was living in Strand on the Green when he painted the picture).

CARSHALTON
All Saints Church High Street. Tel: 0181 647 2366. *Open* May–Sep daily 14.00–16.00.
Carshalton House and Water Tower St Philomena's School, Pound Street. Tel: 0181 773 4555 (Sutton Heritage Centre). *Open* **House:** selected dates from Easter, telephone

for details. **Water Tower:** Easter Mon, Easter–Sep: Sun 14.30–17.00 (**Hermitage** also *open* first Sun every month). *Admission:* charge. *What to see:* Blue Room, Painted Room, other principal rooms in the house; and plunge bath and orangery in the Water Tower.
Little Holland House 40 Beeches Avenue. Tel: 0181 770 4781. *Open* first Sun every month plus Bank Hol Sun and Mon 13.30–17.30 *(closed* Jan). *Admission:* free. *What to see:* Arts and Crafts house and interior, designed and made by craftsman Frank Dickinson, whose home it was until his death in 1961.
Sutton Ecology Centre The Old Rectory, Festival Walk. Tel: 0181 773 4018. *Open* reception and shop: Mon–Fri 10.00–16.00; nature reserve: daily 09.00–dusk; information sessions: Tue and Thu 16.00–18.00. *Admission:* free.
Sutton Heritage Centre Honeywood, Honeywood Walk. Tel: 0181 773 4555. *Open* Wed–Fri 10.00–17.00; Sat, Sun and Bank Hol Mon 10.00–17.30; tearoom: Tue–Sun 10.00–17.00. *Admission:* charge.

CHIPPING BARNET and MONKEN HADLEY
Barnet Museum 31 Wood Street, Chipping Barnet. Tel: 0181 440 8066. *Open* Tue–Thu 14.30–16.30; Sat 10.00–12.00, 14.30–16.30. *Admission:* free.
St John's Church High Street, Chipping Barnet. Tel: 0181 449 3894. *Open* Sat mornings and occasional afternoons.
St Mary's Church Hadley Green Road, Monken Hadley. Tel: 0181 449 2414. *Open* Second Sun every month 14.00–16.00.

CHISWICK
Chiswick House Burlington Lane. Tel: 0181 995 0508. *Open* Apr–Sep: daily 10.00–13.00 and 14.00–18.00; Oct–Mar: Wed–Sun 10.00–13.00, 14.00–16.00. *Admission:* charge.
Hogarth's House Hogarth Lane, Great West Road. Tel: 0181 994 6757. *Open* Apr–Oct: Tue–Fri 13.00–17.00, Sat and Sun 13.00–18.00; Oct–Dec and Feb–Mar: Tue–Fri 13.00–16.00, Sat and Sun 13.00–17.00. *Admission:* free.
St Mary's Convent Burlington Lane. See note on National Gardens Scheme on page 148.
St Nicholas's Church Church Street. Tel: 0181 995 4717. *Open* Sun 14.30–17.00.
Walpole House Chiswick Mall. See note on National Gardens Scheme on page 148.

DULWICH
Dulwich Picture Gallery College Road. Tel: 0181 693 5254. *Open* Tue–Fri 10.00–17.00, Sat 11.00–17.00, Sun 14.00–17.00. *Admission:* charge. *What to see:* works by Claude, Poussin, Rembrandt, Rubens, Van Dyck, Gainsborough, Reynolds, Velázquez, Murillo, Canaletto and Tiepolo, plus collection of 18th-century furniture, and tombs of the Desenfans and Sir Francis Bourgeois in purpose-built mausoleum.

ENFIELD
Forty Hall Forty Hill. Tel: 0181 363 4046. *Open* Thu–Sun 11.00–17.00. *Admission:* free. *What to see:* the mansion and local history collections, plus early packaging and advertising material, and the designs, tools and products of Aesthetic Movement furniture-maker Ada Jacquin. *Access from Enfield on foot:* along Silver Street, continues as Baker Street, right at roundabout into Forty Hill, follow signs – about 1½ miles (2.5 kilometres).
St Andrew's Church Church Street. Tel: 0181 363 8676 (parish office). *Open* Mon–Fri 09.00–15.00, Sat 09.00–13.00.

GREENWICH
Charing Cross Pier Tel: 0171 987 1185 for sailing times.

Cutty Sark and Gypsy Moth IV King William Walk. Tel: 0181 858 3445. *Open Cutty Sark:* Mon–Sat 10.00–18.00 (10.00–17.00 Oct–Mar), Sun and Good Fri 12.00–18.00 (12.00–17.00 Oct–Mar). *Gypsy Moth IV:* Apr–Oct as for Cutty Sark; Nov–Mar closed. *Admission:* charge. *What to see:* built in 1869, the *Cutty Sark* is the only surviving 19th-century tea clipper; lower hold contains large collection of ships' figureheads. The *Gypsy Moth IV* is the yacht in which Sir Francis Chichester made the first single-handed navigation of the world in 1966–7.
Fan Museum 12 Croom's Hill. Tel: 0181 858 7879. *Open* Tue–Fri 11.00–17.00 (16.30 in winter), Sat and Sun 12.00–17.00 (16.30 in winter). *Admission:* charge.
Greenwich Festival Summer arts and cultural festival. Tel: 0181 305 1818 for dates and programme.
National Maritime Museum, Queen's House and Old Royal Observatory Romney Road. Tel: 0181 858 4422. *Open* daily 10.00–17.00. *Admission:* charge. *What to see:* the National Maritime Museum is one of the leading museums of its kind in the world; the Queen's House is a former royal palace with royal apartments furnished in the style of the 17th century – the Great Hall on the ground floor contains the Maritime Museum's collection of marine paintings; the Old Royal Observatory consists of Flamsteed House, containing the Astronomer Royal's 17th-century apartments and observatory, and the Meridian Building housing the historic telescope collection.
Ranger's House Chesterfield Walk. Tel: 0181 853 0035. *Open* Apr–Oct: daily 10.00–13.00, 14.00–18.00 (dusk in Oct); Nov–Mar: Wed–Sun 10.00–13.00, 14.00–16.00. *Admission:* charge. *What to see:* the mansion plus important collections of Jacobean portraits and historical musical instruments.
Royal Naval College King William Walk. Tel: 0181 858 2154. *Open* daily 14.30–16.30. *Admission:* charge. *What to see:* decorated chapel designed by 'Athenian' Stuart and painted hall completely covered in magnificent murals by Sir James Thornhill between 1708 and 1723.
St Alfege's Church Greenwich Church Street. Tel: 0181 853 0687. *Open* by appointment.
Tourist Information Centre 46 Greenwich Church Street. Tel: 0181 858 6376. *Open* daily 10.15–16.45.
Trinity Hospital High Bridge. Tel: 0181 858 1310. *Open* by appointment with the Warden. *Admission:* free. *What to see:* courtyard, chapel and courtroom of the 17th-century almshouse rebuilt in 1812.

HAM and PETERSHAM

Ham House Ham Street, Ham. Tel: 0181 940 1950. *Open* Apr–Oct: Mon–Wed 13.00–17.00, Sat 13.00–17.30, Sun 11.30–17.30; Nov–mid Dec: Sat and Sun 13.00–16.00. Gardens open throughout year daily (except Fri) 10.30–18.00 or dusk if earlier. *Admission:* charge to house. *What to see:* outstanding 17th-century mansion with contemporary interior and furnishings largely intact.
Ham Polo Club Between Petersham and Ham, near the River Thames. Tel: 0181 334 0000. Afternoon matches every Sun May–Sep, spectators welcome.
Ormeley Lodge Ham Gate Avenue, Ham. See note on National Gardens Scheme page 148.
St Michael's Convent 56 Ham Common. See note on National Gardens Scheme page 148.
St Peter's Church Church Lane, Petersham. Tel: 0181 549 8296. *Open* by appointment.

HAMPSTEAD

Burgh House and Hampstead Museum New End Square. Tel: 0171 431 0144. *Open* Wed–Sun 12.00–17.00, Bank Hols 14.00–17.00. *Admission:* free.
Fenton House Windmill Hill. Tel: 0171 435 3471. *Open* Mar: Sat and Sun 14.00–17.00; Apr–Oct: Sat, Sun and Bank Hol Mon 11.00–17.30, Wed, Thu and Fri 14.00–17.30. *Admission:* charge (free to National Trust members). *What to see:* the mansion, plus

outstanding collections of porcelain and early keyboard instruments, and large walled garden.
Antiques and Crafts Market Entrances in Perrin's Court and Heath Street. *Open* Tue–Fri 10.30–17.00, Sat 10.00–18.00, Sun 11.30–16.30.
Hampstead Scientific Society Lower Terrace. Tel: 0181 346 1056 (roster secretary). *Open* mid-Sep–mid-Apr if sky is clear: Fri and Sat 20.00–22.00, Sun (for sun spots) 11.00–13.00. *Admission:* free, but donations welcome.
Keats House Keats Grove. Tel: 0171 435 2062. *Open* Mon–Fri 14.00–18.00 (13.00–17.00 Nov–Mar), Sat 10.00–13.00 and 14.00–17.00, Sun 14.00–17.00. *Admission:* free.
St John's Church Church Row. Tel: 0171 794 5808 (parish office); 0171 435 0553 (rectory). *Open* all day Mon–Fri, Sun and most Sats.

HARROW–ON–THE–HILL
Cat Museum The Other Shop, 49 High Street. No phone. *Open* Thu–Sat 10.30–17.00. *Admission:* free.
Harrow Old Speech Room Gallery Old Schools, Church Hill. Tel: 0181 869 1205 or 0181 422 2196. *Open* daily except Wed 14.30–17.00 (other closures during school exeats and at half term – call before visiting). *Admission:* free. *What to see:* school treasures (mostly donated by Old Harrovians) include collections of watercolours (with works by Cotman and Turner), butterflies and Greek, Roman and Etruscan pottery.
Harrow School Guided Tours One 'turn up-and-go' tour a term; others are prearranged, any time in term or holidays. Details from Mrs. Jean Leaf, Harrow School, 15 London Road, Harrow-on-the-Hill, Middlesex HA1 3JJ. Tel: 0181 422 2303. *Admission:* charge. *What to see:* a selection or all of the following – Fourth Form Room (the original school room with carved names), Old Speech Room Art Gallery, Speech Room, Chapel, Shepherd Churchill Dining Room, Fitch Room and, by special arrangement, the Vaughan Library.
Harrow Museum and Heritage Centre See page 153 under Pinner.
St Mary's Church Church Hill. Tel: 0181 422 2652. *Open* daily except Fri.

HIGHGATE
The Grove Several houses in this road participate in the National Gardens Scheme. See note on page 148.
Highgate Cemetery Swains Lane. Tel: 0181 340 1834. *Open* **Eastern Cemetery:** Apr–Oct: Mon–Fri 10.00–17.00, Sat and Sun 11.00–17.00; Nov–Mar: Mon–Fri 10.00–16.00, Sat and Sun 11.00–16.00. **Western Cemetery:** guided tours only, Apr–Oct: Mon–Fri 12.00, 14.00 and 16.00, Sat and Sun on the hour every hour 11.00–16.00; Nov and Mar: same as for Apr–Oct except last tour is at 15.00; Dec–Feb: Sat and Sun on the hour every hour 11.00–15.00. Both cemeteries closed during funerals. *Admission:* charge.
Kenwood Hampstead Lane. Tel: 0181 348 1286. *Open* Good Fri/1 Apr (whichever is earlier)–Sep: Mon–Sun 10.00–18.00; Oct–Maundy Thursday/31 Mar (whichever is earlier) Mon–Sun 10.00–16.00. *Admission:* free. *What to see:* 18th-century mansion with superb Adam interiors and major collection of paintings, including works by Reynolds, Gainsborough, Romney, Snyders, Van Dyck, Vermeer, Rembrandt and Boucher.
Southwood Lodge 33 Kingsley Place, off Southwood Lane. See note on National Gardens Scheme page 148.
St Michael's Church South Grove. Tel: 0181 340 7279. *Open* Sat 10.00–12.00.

ISLEWORTH
All Saints Church Church Street. Tel: 0181 568 4645. *Open* ruins of old church visible through door.
Syon House Syon Park. Tel: 0181 560 0881. *Open* Apr–Sep: Wed–Sun 11.00–17.00; Oct–mid-Dec: Sun 11.00–17.00 or dusk if earlier. *Admission:* charge. *What to see:* Tudor

house remodelled and, inside, completely redesigned with magnificent neoclassical interiors by Robert Adam in the 18th century; grounds landscaped by Capability Brown.

KENSINGTON

Commonwealth Institute Kensington High Street. Tel: 0171 603 4535. *Open* Mon–Sat 10.00–17.00, Sun 14.00–17.00. *Admission:* free (but sometimes charge for special exhibitions). *What to see:* three levels of galleries illustrating the art, history and culture of the 50 nations that make up the British Commonwealth.

Kensington Palace Kensington Palace. Tel: 0171 937 9561. *Open* Mon–Sat 09.00–17.00, Sun 11.00–17.00. *Admission:* charge. *What to see:* King William's and Queen Mary's private apartments, the magnificently decorated early Georgian state rooms, the suite of rooms where Queen Victoria lived until she was 18, and the court dress collection with men's and women's costumes dating from 1750.

Kensington Roof Gardens 99 Kensington High Street (entrance in Derry Street). Tel: 0171 937 7994. *Open* daily 09.00–17.00 (unless booked for a function – telephone before visiting). *Admission:* free. *What to see:* Europe's largest roof garden, built in the 1930s as an attraction for the Derry and Toms department store (closed 1973) and divided into three different areas: English Woodland, Tudor and Spanish.

Leighton House Museum and Art Gallery 12 Holland Park Road. Tel: 0171 602 3316. *Open* Mon–Sat 11.00–17.30. *Admission:* free. *What to see:* former home and studio of the painter Lord Leighton (1830–96); interior is one of the finest examples of aesthetic styling in the country; good collection of High Victorian aesthetic art, plus changing exhibitions.

Linley Sambourne House 18 Stafford Terrace. Tel: 0181 742 3438. *Open* Mar 1–Oct 31: Wed 10.00–16.00, Sun 14.00–17.00. *Admission:* charge. *What to see:* former home of *Punch* cartoonist Edward Linley Sambourne (1844–1910); decorated and furnished by him in classic Victorian 'artistic' style and perfectly preserved by his descendants.

St Mary Abbots Church Kensington High Street. Tel: 0171 937 5136. *Open* daily.

KEW

Kew Cricket Club Kew Green. Matches most Sat and Sun afternoons May–Sept.

Royal Botanic Gardens and Kew Palace Kew Green. Tel: 0181 332 5000. *Open* **Gardens:** daily Apr–Sept 09.30–18.00 (approx); Oct–Mar: 09.30–16.00 (approx). **Palace:** daily Apr–Sep 11.00–17.30. *Admission:* charge. *What to see:* world-famous botanical gardens covering some 300 acres (120 hectares) with huge glass houses, picture gallery and various garden buildings such as pagoda, orangery and thatched cottage; Kew Palace was last used by King George III (reigned 1760–1820) and Queen Charlotte, and contains much of their furniture and personal possessions.

St Anne's Church Kew Green. Tel: 0181 940 4616. *Open* Easter–Sep: Sat 10.00–12.00 and most Sat afternoons, Sun afternoons (with afternoon tea); Oct–Easter: Sat 10.00–12.00.

Westminster Pier Tel: 0171 930 2062 for sailing times.

MITCHAM

Merton Heritage Centre The Canons, Madeira Road. Tel: 0181 640 9387. *Open* Fri and Sat 10.00–17.00. *Admission:* free.

Mitcham Cricket Club Cricket Green. Matches take place virtually every Sat and Sun afternoon late Apr–Sept.

Mitcham Fair Funfair on Three Kings Piece. Takes place 12–14 August (if one of these days is a Sun, fair is closed and held over till following day).

Wandle Industrial Museum Vestry Hall Annexe, London Road. Tel: 0181 648 0127. *Open* Wed 13.00–16.00, first Sun every month 14.00–17.00. *Admission:* charge. *What to see:* exhibitions on the snuff, tobacco and textile industries and special features on William

Morris and Arthur Liberty (of Liberty's in Regent Street).
St Peter and St Paul's Church Church Road. Tel: 0181 648 1566. *Open* by appointment.

PINNER
Harrow Museum and Heritage Centre Headstone Manor, Pinner View, Harrow. Tel:
0181 861 2626. *Open* Wed–Fri 12.30–17.00 (dusk in winter); Sat, Sun and Bank Hols
10.30–17.00 (dusk in winter). *Admission:* free. *Access on foot from Pinner:* from Nower Hill or
Marsh Road, straight on into Pinner Road, cross George V Avenue into Headstone Lane –
about 1¾ miles (2.8 kilometres). *Access on foot from Harrow-on-the-Hill Station:* take north exit
from station, left on College Road, right into Headstone Road, straight on into Harrow View,
left into Headstone Gardens, right into Pinner View – about 1½ miles (2.8 kilometres).
Pinner Fair Takes place Wed after the Spring Bank Hol.
St John's Church High Street. Tel: 0181 886 3869. *Open* daily.

ROTHERHITHE and BERMONDSEY
New Caledonian Antiques Market Bermondsey Square. *Open* Fri mornings (early).
Brunel's Engine House Railway Avenue. Tel: 0181 318 2489 or 0181 748 3545. *Open*
first Sun every month 12.00–16.00. *Admission:* charge.
St Mary's Church, Rotherhithe St Marychurch Street. Tel: 0171 231 2465. *Open*
vestibule daily; nave visible through locked glass doors.
St Mary Magdalen Church, Bermondsey Bermondsey Street. Tel: 0171 407 5273.
Open by appointment.

WALTHAMSTOW
St Mary's Church Church End. Tel: 0181 521 0290 (church administrator); 0181 520
4281 (rectory). *Open* by appointment.
Vestry House Museum Vestry Road. Tel: 0181 509 1917. *Open* Mon–Fri 10.00–13.00,
14.00–17.30; Sat 10.00–13.00, 14.00–17.00. *Admission:* free. *What to see:* star exhibit is the
Bremer car, built in Walthamstow and a candidate for the title of first car built in Britain.
Walthamstow Village Festival Takes place in July. Tel: 0181 521 3864 or 0181 521
7111 for exact date and other details.
William Morris Gallery Lloyd Park, Forest Road. Tel: 0181 527 3782. *Open* Tue–Sat
10.00–13.00, 14.00–17.00; first Sun every month 10.00–13.00, 14.00–17.00. *Admission:* free.

WIMBLEDON
Southside House 3 Woodhayes Road. Tel: 0181 946 7643 or 0181 947 2491. *Open*
guided tours, 1 Oct–31 May: Tue, Thu, Sat and Bank Hol Mon 14.00, 15.00, 16.00 and
17.00. *Admission:* charge. *What to see:* house is mainly noted for its eclectic collection of historical memorabilia, including Anne Boleyn's vanity case and Marie Antoinette's necklace.
St Mary's Church St Mary's Road. Tel: 0181 946 2605. *Open* church is usually open; if
closed, enquire at adjacent Fellowship Office Tue, Wed and Fri mornings, and Thu all day
(closed Mon, Wed and weekends).
Wimbledon Lawn Tennis Museum All England Club, Church Road. Tel: 0181 946
6131. *Open* Tue–Sat 10.30–17.00, Sun 14.00–17.00 (times change during championships).
Admission: charge.
Wimbledon Society Museum Ridgway SW19. No phone. *Open* Sat 14.30–17.00.
Admission: free.
Wimbledon Windmill Museum Windmill Road, Wimbledon Common. Tel: 0181 947
2825. *Open* Apr–Oct: Sat, Sun and Bank Hols 14.00–17.00. *Admission:* charge. *What to see:*
early 19th-century hollow-post windmill plus pictures, models, machinery and tools, and
the story of windmills and windmilling.

Libraries

For readers who wish to delve deeper into the history of the 25 London villages described in this book, I have compiled a list of relevant libraries, both general community libraries and libraries specializing in local history. The community libraries are usually in the villages themselves and are a good place to start because they often have a handful of local history books. For more comprehensive local history coverage – and to be sure of seeing the books cited in the Bibliography on page 156 – a visit to the local history library covering the village in question will probably be necessary. (These generally cover whole boroughs rather than just one district.) Sometimes this will be in the same building as the community library. Sometimes, however, it may be in a completely different part of London. If the latter, I recommend making an appointment before your visit. Where all available local history information on a village is to be found in the community library, one address only is given below.

BARNES
Castelnau Library, 75 Castelnau. Tel: 0181 748 3837.
Local History See below under **Ham and Petersham.**

BEXLEY
Bexley Village Library, Bourne Road. Tel: 01322 522168.
Local History Hall Place, Bourne Road, Bexley. Tel: 01311 526574.

BLACKHEATH
Blackheath Village Library, 3–4 Blackheath Grove. Tel: 0181 852 5309.
Local History See below under **Greenwich.**

BRENTFORD
Brentford Library, Boston Manor Road. Tel: 0181 560 8801.
Local History See below under **Chiswick.**

CARSHALTON
Carshalton Library, The Square. Tel: 0181 647 1151.
Local History Central Library, St Nicholas Way, Sutton. Tel: 0181 770 4700.

CHIPPING BARNET and MONKEN HADLEY
Chipping Barnet Library, 3 Stapylton Road, Barnet. Tel: 0181 449 0321.
Local History Hendon Library, The Burroughs, Hendon. Tel: 0181 202 5625.

CHISWICK
Chiswick Library, Duke's Avenue. Tel: 0181 994 1008.

DULWICH
Dulwich Library, 368 Lordship Lane. Tel: 0181 693 5171.
Local History Southwark Local Studies Library, 211 Borough High Street, Southwark. Tel: 0171 403 3507.

ENFIELD
Central Library, Cecil Road. Tel: 0181 366 2244.
Local History Local History Unit, Southgate Town Hall, Green Lanes, Palmers Green. Tel: 0181 982 7453.

GREENWICH
West Greenwich Library, Greenwich High Road. Tel: 0181 858 4289.
Local History Woodlands, 90 Mycenae Road, Blackheath. Tel: 0181 858 4631.

HAM and PETERSHAM.
Ham Library, Ham Street, Ham. Tel: 0181 940 8703.
Local History Central Reference Library, Old Town Hall, Whittaker Avenue, Richmond. Tel: 0181 940 5529.

HAMPSTEAD
Heath Library, Keats Grove. Tel: 0171 435 8002.
Local History Holborn Library, 32–38 Theobalds Road, Holborn. Tel: 0171 413 6342.

HARROW-ON-THE-HILL
Gayton Library, Gayton Road. Tel: 0181 427 8986.
Local History Civic Centre Library, Civic Centre, Station Road, Harrow. Tel: 0181 424 1055.

HIGHGATE
Highgate Library, Chester Road. Tel: 0171 272 3112.
Local History See above under **Hampstead.**

ISLEWORTH
Isleworth Library, Twickenham Road. Tel: 0181 560 2934.
Local History Hounslow Library, Treaty Centre, High Street, Hounslow. Tel: 0181 570 0622.

KENSINGTON
Central Library, Hornton Street. Tel: 0171 937 2542.

KEW
Kew Library, 106 North Road. Tel: 0181 876 8654.
Local History See above under **Ham and Petersham.**

MITCHAM
Mitcham Library, London Road. Tel: 0181 648 4070.

PINNER
Pinner Library, Marsh Road. Tel: 0181 866 7827.
Local History See above under **Harrow-on-the-Hill.**

ROTHERHITHE and BERMONDSEY
Rotherhithe Library, Albion Street, Rotherhithe. Tel: 0171 237 2010.
Local History See above under **Dulwich.**

WALTHAMSTOW
Central Library, High Street. Tel: 0181 520 3031.
Local History Vestry House Museum, Vestry Road. Tel: 0181 509 1917.

WIMBLEDON
Central Reference Library, Wimbledon Hill Road. Tel: 0181 946 1136.

Bibliography

Place of publication is London unless otherwise stated.

Arthure, Humphrey, *Life and Work in Old Chiswick* (Old Chiswick Protection Society, 1982)
Barker, Felix, *Greenwich and Blackheath Past* (Historical Publications, 1993)
Bate, G E, *And So Make a City Here* (Hounslow, Thomasons, 1948)
Batey, Mavis, et al, *Arcadian Thames* (Barn Elms, 1994)
Blomfield, David, *The Story of Kew* (Richmond, Leyborne, 1992)
Blomfield, David, *Kew Past* (Historical Publications, 1994)
Boast, Mary, *The Story of Dulwich* (London Borough of Southwark Neighbourhood Histories 2, 1990)
Boast, Mary, *The Story of Rotherhithe* (London Borough of Southwark Neighbourhood Histories 6, 1980)
Boast, Mary, *A Trail Walk Around Old Rotherhithe* (Time & Talents Association, 1994)
Cameron, A, *Hounslow, Isleworth, Heston and Cranford. A Pictorial History* (Chichester, Phillimore, 1995)
Canham, Roy, *2000 Years of Brentford* (HMSO, 1978)
Clegg, Gillian, *Chiswick Past* (Historical Publications, 1995)
Cloake, John, *Richmond Past* (Historical Publications, 1991)
Cluett, Douglas, *Discovering Sutton's Heritage: the Story of Five Parishes* (Sutton Heritage Service, 1995)
Courlander, Kathleen, *Richmond* (Batsford, 1953)
Druett, Walter, *Pinner through the Ages* (Uxbridge, King and Hutchings, 1965)
Druett, Walter, *Harrow through the Ages* (Wakefield, S. R. Publishers, 1971)
Faulkner, T, *The History and Antiquities of Brentford, Ealing and Chiswick* (Simpkin, Marshall & Co, 1845)
Gelder, W H, *Monken Hadley Church and Village* (The Author, 1986)
Green, Brian, *Dulwich Village* (Dulwich, Village Books, 1983)
Green Brian, *Around Dulwich* (Dulwich, Village Books, 1982)
Grimwade, Mary, & Hailstone, Charles, *Highways and Byways of Barnes* (Barnes, Barnes and Mortlake History Society, 1992)
Higgs, Tom, *300 Years of Mitcham Cricket* (The Author, 1985)
Hounslow, London Borough of, Department of Arts and Recreation, Libraries Division, *Isleworth As It Was* (Hendon, Nelson, 1982)
Jones, A E, *An Illustrated Directory of Old Carshalton* (Carshalton, The Author, 1973)
Law, A, *Walthamstow Village* (Walthamstow Antiquarian Society, 1984)
McEwan, Kate, *Ealing Walkabout* (Warrington, Pulse Publications, 1983)
Mercer, John, *Bexley, Bexleyheath and Welling. A Pictorial History* (Chichester, Phillimore, 1995)
Milward, Richard, *Historic Wimbledon* (Wimbledon, Windrush and Fielders, 1989)
Milward, Richard, *Wimbledon. A Pictorial History* (Chichester, Phillimore, 1994)
Montague, Eric, *Mitcham. A Pictorial History* (Chichester, Phillimore, 1991)
Norrie, Ian, *Hampstead, Highgate Village and Kenwood* (High Hill Press, 1983)
Pevsner, N, & Cherry, B, *The Buildings of England. London: South* (Harmondsworth, Penguin, 1983)
Rhind, Neil, *Blackheath Village and Environs* (Bookshop Blackheath, 2 vols, 1976 and 1983)
Rhind, Neil, *The Heath* (Bookshop Blackheath, 1987)
Richardson, John, *Highgate Past* (Historical Publications, 1989)
Spurgeon, Darrell, *Discover Bexley and Sidcup* (Greenwich Guidebooks, 1993)
Spurgeon, Darrell, *Discover Greenwich and Charlton* (Greenwich Guidebooks, 1991)
Taylor, Pamela, & Corden, Joanna, *Barnet, Edgware, Hadley and Totteridge. A Pictorial History* (Chichester, Phillimore, 1994)
Tester, P, *Bexley Village* (Bexley Libraries and Museums Department, 1987)
Verden, Joanne, *Ten Walks Around Pinner* (Pinner Association, 1991)
Victoria County History: volumes for *Essex, Hertfordshire, Middlesex* and *Surrey* (Oxford University Press, various dates)
Wade, Christopher, *Hampstead Past* (Historical Publications, 1989)
Wade, Christopher, *The Streets of Hampstead* (High Hill Press, 1984)
Weinreb, Ben & Hibbert, Christopher, eds, *The London Encyclopaedia* (Papermac, 1993)

Index